JACK'S JOURNEY

I0893902

JACK'S JOURNEY

An Anzac's descent into death, disaster and controversy at Gallipoli

KIT CULLEN

ALLEN&UNWIN
SYDNEY • MELBOURNE • AUCKLAND • LONDON

All attempts have been made to locate the owners of copyright material. If you have any information in that regard please contact the publisher at the address below.

First published in 2013

Australian Government

Australia Council for the Arts

This project has been assisted by the Australian Government through the Australia Council for the Arts, its arts funding and advisory body.

Allen & Unwin
83 Alexander Street
Crows Nest NSW 2065
Australia
Phone: (61 2) 8425 0100

Email: info@allenandunwin.com
Web: www.allenandunwin.com

Cataloguing-in-Publication details are available from the National Library of Australia
www.trove.nla.gov.au

ISBN 978 1 74331 770 9

Maps and sketch drawn by Darian Causby
Design by Stephen Smedley, Tonto Design
Set in 10.5/14 pt Granjon by Post Pre-press Group, Australia
Printed and bound in Australia by Griffin Press

10 9 8 7 6 5 4 3 2 1

MIX
Paper from responsible sources
FSC® C009448
FSC www.fsc.org

The paper in this book is FSC® certified. FSC® promotes environmentally responsible, socially beneficial and economically viable management of the world's forests.

Contents

List of maps and illustrations

Author's note

You will see fearsome sights that will shake you to the roots of your being; you will see war not as a beautiful, orderly and gleaming formation, with music and beaten drums, streaming banners and generals on prancing horses, but war in its authentic expression—as blood, suffering and death.

Leo Tolstoy, 'Sevastopol in December', 1854[1]

This is the story of an unheralded and virtually unknown ANZAC action that occurred in Death Trap Valley on 1 and 2 May during the period of the Landing at Gallipoli. The protagonist, Jack Collyer, was an unassuming soldier who landed on 25 April as a member of No. 12 Section, No. 15 Platoon, D Company, 4th Battalion. Jack, christened John, was a country boy from Mudgee, New South Wales, and was aged 23 when he joined the battalion in Sydney on 21 September 1914. According to his nephew, Ray Warry, Jack wanted to serve King and Country, being very much a child of the British Empire.

Jack's story and that of his mates in the 4th Battalion in Death Trap Valley over the first weekend in May has remained hidden, largely because of C.E.W. Bean's unscrupulous treatment of it in his published works, notably in the revised second edition of *Volume 1, The Story of Anzac, The Official History of Australia in the War of 1914–1918.* Other historians, taking their cue from Bean's encyclopaedic tomes, have remained ignorant of the 4th's involvement, its significance at the time and its place in the annals of Australian military history. British accounts of the same action barely mention the Anzacs, let alone any decisive involvement by them. Consequently, there is a dearth of documentation about their feats in the valley. What the men of No. 15 Platoon and No. 3 Platoon, 4th Battalion, did nearly one hundred years ago deserves to be told and acknowledged.

My discovery of those events and Bean's surprising but deliberate strategy began, unwittingly, about ten years ago. I asked my close friend David 'Mac' McClymont if I could do something with his Great-Uncle Jack's three Gallipoli diaries for the centenary of the Landing at Anzac in 2015. At the time I was unsure just what I would do with the diaries, but Mac readily agreed, the only proviso being that at the end of that period the diaries would be donated to the Australian War Memorial.

My request was based on my memory of the diaries from an earlier time. Rewind to the late 1960s when, as an eleven-year-old, I was first shown these diaries by Mac. I was into all things military and leapt at the chance to read actual Gallipoli diaries, having just finished reading *The Anzac Book*. It was thrilling to handle and read the small faded volumes, with their copperplate writing, that had been at Gallipoli in 1915.

Fast-forward to 2005 and I read Jack's diaries again. The thrill had not diminished, but I had no idea where they would lead me. Unfortunately, there are no surviving letters from Jack, apart from his Christmas letter from Mena in 1914 which was published in *The Mudgee Guardian*. I didn't find it until a few years after I began my quest, so all I had to start with were his diaries and personnel dossier, including his service record.

The diaries traced Jack's journey from boarding the transport, *Euripides*, in Sydney Harbour on 17 October 1914, as part of the Australian contingent sent overseas to serve the British Empire during World War I, to training in Egypt, then to landing at Anzac Cove; in effect invading Turkey. Unfortunately, the third tiny diary ended abruptly as Jack took charge of No. 12 Section, No. 15 Platoon, 4th Battalion, when they entered the firing line at dusk on 25 April on Bolton's Hill. Thanks to the casualty form in his personnel dossier I knew Jack was wounded a week later on Saturday, 1 May 1915. However, where Jack was and what he was doing when he was hit was a mystery.

Collyer family legend held that Jack was wounded while helping another soldier. What I subsequently discovered was extraordinary. Jack and his mates were ordered to undertake what amounted to a suicide mission. While such missions were common enough for both sides at Anzac, nearly all of these are well known. In this case, their orders did not involve attacking a Turkish position; rather it was a rescue mission of a detachment of Royal Marines during the third Turkish counterattack on 1 May 1915. The other remarkable aspect of the 4th Battalion in this action was the corruption of the historical record in regard to their experiences and participation by Charles Bean, Australia's Official War Historian.

As my research unfolded I realised I needed to examine the personnel dossiers of the original 4th Battalion and the first three reinforcements for the 4th from which the men who landed in the battalion on Sunday, 25 April 1915, at Anzac were drawn. Consequently, over a year I examined 1377 personnel dossiers, compiling a statistical picture of the men's military experience, country of birth, height, misdemeanours, disease and injury in Egypt, casualty figures and bravery awards for Gallipoli from 25 April to 2 May 1915. At various points in the narrative I refer to these statistics and the scenarios they portray. Throughout the story I have used the word ANZAC to refer to situations involving the Australian and New Zealand Army Corps. I have described the men fighting in that unit as Anzacs. The place where they fought at Gallipoli was known as Anzac.

While this is Jack's journey, it is also the story of the men in the 4th Battalion. In many ways Jack was a universal figure. His story was both common and unique. Many of his experiences were shared by all Anzacs of the First Contingent who landed at Gallipoli or, as Jack wrote, 'Gollipoli'. However, some of his journey was atypical and personal. I have let the men and women—nurses—who were there tell the story as much as possible; after all, they witnessed what happened. I make no apologies for long quotes. Paraphrasing the recollections of those who were there seemed self-defeating. Like Bean, I have tried to avoid second- and thirdhand accounts. Their diaries, letters and formal documents form the basis of the story. These are all quoted verbatim. I have deliberately left the wording, punctuation and spelling of the original documents intact. This means I have not used '[sic]' in the text to indicate the veracity of what is written. It also means that the spelling of a particular word or even a name may differ within the same document. As well, some of the views expressed are archaic. However, language, like history, is not static, and terms that are offensive or obsolete today reflect the society of one hundred years ago.

What those sources reveal is a validation of Tolstoy's poignant comments about war. It is, in its authentic expression, about 'blood, suffering and death'. This is their story.

Introduction

Mr John Collyer, son of Mr. George Collyer, sen., has joined the Expeditionary Force. This young fellow is a fine stamp of a man, and will make a splendid type of soldier. We wish him luck at the front. Such fine representatives of Australia will do more to impress the old countries with the virility of the race in the southern seas than thousands of pounds spent in advertising.

The Mudgee Guardian, 1 October 1914

When war was declared on 4 August 1914, Australia dutifully and legally followed the mother country, Great Britain. It was eager to play a role in international affairs, even if it was in the constitutional and political petticoats of its parent. On the eve of war, on 3 August, the Australian government made the following generous offer to the British government by telegram:

> In the event of war the Government [of Australia] is prepared to place the vessels of the Australian Navy under the control of the British Admiralty when desired. It is further prepared to despatch an expeditionary force of 20,000 men of any suggested composition to any destination desired by the Home Government, the force to be at the complete disposal of the Home Government. The cost of despatch and maintenance will be borne by this (i.e., the Australian) Government.[1]

In 1914 Australia was a dominion of the British Empire, a self-governing colonial federation whose foreign policy was dominated legally and, for reasons of obsequiousness, loyalty or realpolitik, by the British monarchy and parliament.[2] In effect it was a vassal state, happily beholden to Great Britain and its powerful navy and army. When King George V declared war on 4 August 1914, the Empire followed, constitutionally tied to his whims. On 6 August, Australia's largesse was readily accepted by the British government. Recruitment of the force began in earnest across Australia.

By the time Jack's farewell notice appeared in the Local Brevities section of Mudgee's paper on 1 October, he had already enlisted in the army in Sydney. His was a jubilant send-off, repeated in newspapers around the country as a steady stream of recruits fronted places of enlistment. Nationalism and imperialism were rampant in the press once war broke out. Australia was part of the Empire and would fully support the mother country in this time of crisis. Newspapers were the most popular social media of the day, publishing international, state, regional and local news, information and gossip. Every settlement, regardless of its size, boasted at least one paper. The announcement in the local newspaper of Jack's departure to serve his country and the Empire was very adulatory. He was held in high esteem in his home town. Hopefully, he would live up to the hype.

Jack was born on 18 October 1890 to George and Jessie Collyer. He was their first child and was followed by nine siblings. He also had three older sisters and an older brother who were from his father's first marriage, George's first wife having died. The Collyer family lived in a beautiful Victorian house known as Redbank, set on their farm in South Mudgee, where Jack grew up. He was the product of a Christian upbringing, having been born into a family with very strong Salvation Army convictions and, being her first-born, was especially close to his deeply religious mother, Jessie. Not surprisingly, Jack saw himself as a faithful servant of the British Empire and felt it was his duty to volunteer for overseas service.

Before enlisting, Jack worked as a labourer for his father, who was a prominent and prosperous local builder. The Collyers had two building contracting firms in Mudgee: Collyer & Carmichael Builders and Contractors, and Collyer Bros, Bricklayers. When war broke out Jack was living in town at 'the Zoo', a local boarding house. As a result of his bush upbringing, Jack could shoot, ride and live off the land. He had previously served in the militia in the Mudgee district, 'F' Company, 41st Australian Infantry Regiment. Jack was almost 24, single, teetotal, 5 foot 8 inches (1.72 metres), of fair complexion, with strawberry blond hair and blue eyes, and weighed 11 stone 5 pounds (72 kilograms) when he enlisted—prime cannon fodder.[3] He smoked, but so did virtually everyone else in the AIF.

While Jack was single he did have the following name and address in the back of his first diary: *'Miss M. Wilson, "Newlyn", Cnr. Church + Patrick Sts, Hobart, Tas.'* Who was Miss M. Wilson? How did they meet? Did they write to one another while he was on active service? Were Jack and Miss Wilson an item? Jack wrote many letters to his family during his military service but only one has survived. Due to this disappointing paucity of Jack's correspondence, except for his Christmas missive—as well as the lack of relevant oral family history about any possible liaison—Miss Wilson remains a mystery.

Above all else, Jack was a British subject, answering 'Yes' to Question 3 on his Enlistment Form, which asked if he was a natural-born British subject or a naturalised British subject. There was no mention of Australia in any of 14 questions on the form. Questions 10, 11 and 13 were concerned with the applicant's previous military service in His Majesty's Forces. This was a different time with different thinking. Having been founded, colonised and developed almost exclusively by English-speaking migrants from England, Ireland, Scotland and Wales, Australia naturally regarded Great Britain as the mother country. To serve that entity was one of the great aspirations of ordinary citizens.

Today, Australia has a similar military relationship with a different world power, the United States of America. Australia is, in military terms, a sheriff in an outpost of the global western interests of the United States. We are strategically positioned in regard to Asia, near enough to be a base, far enough away to be beyond simple reach. Occasionally we act on our own, but generally we support the American line, politically and by the deployment of military assets.

In mid-September Jack farewelled his parents, George and Jessie, and nine younger siblings, at Mudgee Railway Station and headed east over the Great Dividing Range to the big smoke, Sydney, to join up. He joined the 4th Battalion on 21 September 1914 at Kensington in Sydney. His actual enlistment date was 29 September 1914, when he swore an oath attesting fealty to the king. The oath was as follows:

> I, John Collyer, swear that I will well and truly serve our Sovereign Lord the King in the Australian Imperial Force from today until the end of the War, and a further period of four months thereafter unless sooner lawfully discharged, dismissed, or removed therefrom; and that I will resist His Majesty's enemies and cause His Majesty's peace to be kept and maintained; and that I will in all matters appertaining to my service, faithfully discharge my duty according to law.
> SO HELP ME, GOD.

Jack was given the regimental number 1241 and became a member of H Company.[4] Like all new recruits, he had signed on for the duration of the war plus four months. At this stage, the general community didn't contemplate the idea of the war lasting more than four years.

The 4th Battalion was one of four New South Wales battalions that constituted the 1st Brigade, itself part of the three brigade strong 1st Australian Division. At this point each of the Australian battalions, totalling just under 1000 men, consisted of eight companies. In Egypt, from 1 January 1915, this structure was abolished and a new four (double) company battalion organisation instituted. The 4th Battalion was formed by Major Astley John Onslow Thompson from 15 August 1914 at the behest of Colonel Henry Norman MacLaurin, who was the commanding officer of the 1st Brigade.[5] Onslow Thompson was promoted to lieutenant-colonel on 17 September, a rank befitting the commanding officer of a battalion. He was a Welshman, born in Glamorgan on 3 January 1865 and educated at one of the Old Dart's most famous public schools, Rugby. Onslow Thompson had served in the NSW Mounted Rifles and the Australian Light Horse for 22 years. Prior to enlisting he was a grazier, managing one of the new dominion's most famous properties, Camden Park.[6] Even though he was 49, Onslow Thompson, according to Charles Bean, 'conspicuously possessed the energy and dash which would make him fit for hard fighting, and the fine principles which would make him a sure leader of men'.[7] In turn, Onslow Thompson selected Major Charles Melville Macnaghten, a 38-year-old Englishman, as his second in command. Macnaghten was described by Bean as 'distinguished by a vigorous impetuosity'.[8] This trait was to have significant repercussions at Gallipoli the day after the battalion landed.

The 4th Battalion, like its sister battalions of the newly minted Australian Imperial Force (AIF), was a fascinating microcosm of adult, almost exclusively white, male Australia. The men who sailed in the first contingent from this battalion came from all over Australia and the British Empire. Every state was represented. Within NSW the recruits were drawn from city and country. Jack wasn't the only Mudgee boy in the 4th. Other Mudgee recruits included Mordyke Barton and George Plows.

The country of birth of the men in the battalion indicates Australia's demographic at the time. The following information was derived from a sample of 959 personnel dossiers of enlisted men in the 4th Battalion who embarked as part of the First Contingent. Five hundred and thirty of the men were born in Australia, 408 were born in Great Britain and only 21 were born in other places, most of them being parts of the British Empire. An amazing 266 men listed their place of birth as England. This meant that over a quarter of the original battalion was English and nearly half of its members were born in Great Britain. Interestingly, there was a German-born recruit, Private James Gough; and a member of the battalion who gave his place of birth as Egypt, Private Elton Patrick, was to return to his birthplace sooner than he imagined.[9]

The military experience of the battalion was typical of the 1st Division. Apart from a sprinkling of 39 Boer War veterans, including four officers, very few of the men had been under fire. However, 59 per cent of enlisted men had served or were still serving in pre-war military units. This was virtually the same as the percentage for the 1st Division overall at 58.5 per cent.[10] An impressive

69 per cent of overseas recruits had previously served, some of them in prestigious units from the British Army and Navy such as the Gordon Highlanders, the Royal Irish Rifles, the Royal Marines and the Scots Guards.

Thanks to compulsory military training, which began after Federation in 1909, 51 per cent of native-born Australians who enlisted, including Jack, had some form of military service.[11] However, none of these figures included cadets. Question 11 on the first page of the enlistment form concerned the applicant's prior military service and, even though cadets did not appear in the wording, it was recorded regularly. One 4th Battalion recruit, Private Ralph Arnold, an Englishman, wrote 'Eton College Cadet Corps' for his response to Question 11.[12] Occasionally a rifle club was recorded as constituting previous military experience, rifle clubs having an affiliation with the militia. Almost to a man the officers of the battalion—29 out of 32—had undergone previous military training. Although most of the 4th Battalion lacked actual combat experience, it did have large numbers of men in every platoon who had undergone military training prior to enlistment. Some of the recruits from Great Britain had considerable military service under their belts.[13]

The average height of this first intake, taken from 949 personnel dossiers (not 959—10 dossiers did not record the applicant's height) of enlisted men in the 4th Battalion, was 5 foot 7.8 inches.[14] Jack came in at 5 foot 8 inches—the average height. The tallest man was 6 foot 5 inches, while the shortest was 5 foot. Well may you choke slightly at the last figure. According to Charles Bean, the minimum height for the First Contingent of the AIF was 5 foot 6 inches,[15] yet in the 4th Battalion there were a surprising 181 recruits who were under five-six. In fact, the records indicate 234 men were 5 foot 6 inches or less.[16] When introducing the AIF in his first volume of the *Official History*, Bean had an agenda. This force was the cream of Australia's manhood and he saw them as a unique, virile expression of life Down Under. The height of the recruits was a key component of Bean's vision of the AIF. Australians, especially men from the bush, were big and bold in Bean's Anzac legend. Drawing on the 4th's statistics as a sample, there were possibly thousands of men under the minimum height requirement across the 12 infantry battalions of the 1st Division. This did not suit the image Bean wanted to project, so he omitted any reference to this obvious anomaly. Rather than qualify or comment on it, Bean simply ignored it. Every day during the voyage to the Middle East, training in Egypt, and the Landing and occupation of Gallipoli, Charles Bean, in his capacity as Official War Correspondent, dealt with enlisted men and officers who were below the minimum height. Bean was described as tall and gangly. He would have towered over some of them. By not acknowledging the men below the minimum height, Bean gave the distinct impression that the entire First Contingent was 5 foot 6 inches or more, in keeping with the image he wanted to convey about the original Anzacs. Therein lies a cautionary tale, certainly in regard to Jack's story. This was a quirk of Bean's writing style. What Bean left out of his narrative was significant; at times, very significant.

The minimum height requirement was only lowered in June 1915. *The Tamworth Daily Observer* reported on Monday, 7 June 1915, that 'the height standard for recruits for the Australian Imperial Expeditionary Forces has been reduced to 5 feet 3 inches'. Regardless, this stipulation was flouted from the first influx of recruits. The initial intake of officers in the 4th Battalion was almost exemplary in regard to their height. Their average height was 5 foot 10 inches, with the tallest being 6 foot 4 inches, but the shortest came in at 5 foot 5 inches.

Another aspect was the marital status of the force. According to Bean, 'Nearly 90 per cent were single men, although of the officers a quarter were married.'[17]

The average age of the other ranks in the 4th Battalion was 26.01 years,[18] which was quite close to Jack's age on enlistment. He was 23 years and 11 months old. The majority of the battalion was aged between 20 and 30 years. At just 19 years of age on enlistment, Ern Robson, who was a mate of Jack's, was one of the younger members of the battalion. The officers were slightly older than their charges, their average age being 29.03 years. Fittingly, the sergeants and warrant officers were the group with the oldest average age, coming in at 32.2 years.[19] On the outbreak of war NCOs in the AIF battalions were generally appointed on the basis of their considerable previous military experience, hence their older age on enlistment.

Jack spent nearly a month training with the battalion before its embarkation. When he joined in September, the battalion was housed in tents in Kensington in Sydney. Prior to this the battalion moved regularly between camps.[20] Jack, in a passing comment, referred to the Kensington ration as being inferior to the tucker aboard the transport, *Euripides*. Considering comments made about the food aboard ship by some of Jack's travelling companions, the Kensington ration must have been a culinary catastrophe.

After being accepted into the ranks, Jack received his uniform and equipment. The recruits' uniforms consisted of:

> khaki woollen Norfolk jackets, with four large pockets and brass buttons oxidised black, brown boots, leather belt and ammunition pouches, and webbing packs. In addition, each had received a slouch hat bearing the rising sun emblem of the newly created Australian Imperial Force.[21]

The other all-important piece of equipment was the rifle. The men of the 1st AIF were issued with bolt-action magazine-fed Lee-Enfield .303 calibre rifles,[22] commonly known by the acronym 'smellie' from the initials of its informal designation—Short Magazine Lee-Enfield. In fact, the Mark III version used by the Anzacs, which came into service during 1907, did not have a short magazine, rather the rifle's overall length had been shortened from previous 19th-century models. Its magazine held ten rounds and it had an effective range of 500 to 1000 metres, although it was capable of indirect fire to more than 3 kilometres. Well-trained infantrymen could fire at least 15 to 30 aimed shots per minute, and, when fired collectively in volleys, gave the impression of the volume of fire from a machine gun.[23] In World War I it proved to be an effective killing device, much prized by the men wielding it.

Training pre-embarkation consisted of parades, drill, route marches, guard duty and live firing on rifle ranges. The recruits received training from experienced drill instructors, some of whom were recently retired from the ranks of famous British regiments. Men such as Colour Sergeant Coxhead worked them hard and unsparingly, impressing the boys with their regular army demeanour. Jack later fondly remembered Coxhead and his blunt but effective bearing while a gaggle of junior officers and NCOs blundered about attempting to establish camp at Mena soon after the battalion's arrival in Egypt. Their ineptitude was exasperating and Jack bemoaned the absence of Coxhead, who he believed would have sorted out the mess in no time.[24]

By the middle of October 1914, the 4th Battalion, as part of the 1st Brigade, was ready to start the great adventure. The 1st Brigade was one of the units in the First Contingent of 20,000 Australian troops to leave for overseas service in, it was assumed, the war in Europe. The ultimate destination of the force was at the discretion of the British government. Many of the untried troops privately hoped to disembark in England, which was home for many, but at this stage they were in the dark as to their final port of call. Australian-born Lance Corporal Harry Smith of the 3rd Battalion began his diary aboard the *Euripides* on 20 October by optimistically declaring, 'Weighed anchor and set sail for England.'[25] Jack was another who anticipated reaching England. He wrote the names and addresses of a couple of English relatives, Chas Collyer and Joseph Collyer, at the back of his first diary. He was going to look them up when the convoy reached England.

The contingent was known as the Australian Imperial Force. Its name was selected by Major-General William Bridges, the commanding officer of the 1st Australian Division. This came to be known simply as the AIF. The name was chosen ostensibly to differentiate between it and a smaller contingent of Australian troops who sailed into action and history on 19 August 1914 to take possession of German colonies and interests in the Pacific, notably German New Guinea. It was known as the Australian Naval and Military Expeditionary Force and its troops were among the first Australians to go into battle in World War I. However, the larger contingent was also initially described as an expeditionary force. Some of its members and some government institutions referred to it as the Australian Imperial Expeditionary Force or AIEF. Jack was one who adhered to this name, as did the Public Trust Office in its dealings with the families of veterans. The New Zealand contingent was known as the New Zealand Expeditionary Force. The invasion force being assembled in the Middle East in early 1915, bound for the Hellespont in Turkey, was the Mediterranean Expeditionary Force or the MEF. The British and their French allies provided the units for it, including troops from their respective empires. The word ANZAC was not yet part of the Australasians' identity and history.

PART I
Journey

1 The voyage

The scenery is getting more beautiful daily, or perhaps we are learning to appreciate the beauty of the scene to the full. A most glorious sunset, the grand positions of the fleet, steaming majestically, in perfect order, over a smooth sea. The effect of the setting sun on the water is truly magnificent. A battleship is plainly visible on the skyline ahead, another on either flank, + one following up in the rear. The whole scene is perfect, + it is impossible to draw the slightest imagination of its grandeur.

JACK'S DIARY, TUESDAY, 10 NOVEMBER 1914

Before the four battalions of the 1st Brigade embarked for overseas service, they paraded through the streets of Sydney on 6 October to huge public acclamation. Crowds in the thousands, up to twenty deep, lined the footpaths, cheering, singing, waving Union Jacks and shedding tears as the men strode past. *The Sydney Morning Herald* captured the moment, its correspondent impressed by the emotion of the crowd and the formidable demeanour of the troops:

> The people, judging by the way they lined the thoroughfares at such short notice, had evidently expected a great deal, and, if it had not been a really splendid spectacle, they would have been disappointed. But they had their enthusiasm raised to such a degree that many of them appeared to vie with each other, in their frequent outbursts of patriotic emotion. They were not satisfied with cheering and waving miniature Union Jacks and handkerchiefs, but they joined with the music of the bands in singing the popular airs, such as 'Sons of the Seas,' 'Soldiers of the King,' and 'Advance Australia Fair' . . .
>
> The fine physique of the men and their soldierly bearing deserved all praise, more especially when it is remembered that but a few weeks ago many of them were performing their ordinary duties as citizens, and never, perhaps, ever contemplated being soldiers. The movement was magnificent

in its precise swing. Each man looked hard and wiry and capable of undergoing all the rough treatment that active service might demand.[1]

Jack Collyer left Sydney on Tuesday, 20 October 1914, aboard His Majesty's Australian Transport A14 *Euripides* and arrived in Alexandria, Egypt, on Thursday, 3 December 1914. His first diary describes the voyage and the first two weeks training in Egypt:

With the Australian Imperial Expeditionary Force. (Infantry)
1914.
H. Coy. 4th Battalion. A.I.E.F.
Officer Commanding Battn.
Colonel Onslow Thompson.
(Senior) Major McNaughton. 2nd.
Major Storey. 3rd.
Capt. Coltman. 4th.
Adjutant Lieut. Massey.
Regt Serg.-Major Pearce.
O.C.H.Coy Capt. Coltman.
Sub. 1st Lieut. Seldon.
2nd Lieut. Fanning.
Col. Serg. Nicholls
Sen. " Dooling No. 1 Section.
2nd " " Rice No. 3 "
3rd " " Wright No. 4 "
4th " " Pitt No. 2 "

The Voyage
Saturday Oct. 14th (17th) 1914. [Date error by Jack]
We left Kensington camp at 5.45 A.M. on 17th, through heavy rain, the left half of H. Coy. 3 + 4 sections forming advance guard for the Battalion. Marched as far as R. Agricultural grounds, where we entrained to Circular Quay, then marched to Fort Macquarie, drenched to the skin. We then formed a guard + fatigue, to unload kit bags + stores, re-loaded them on launches, + escorted them to transport No. A. 14. S.S. Euripides. By 12.30 all was safely alongside + we went aboard, where a good meal awaited us. After lunch, we unloaded the launches, + stowed the baggage in the hold. Had tea at 5.30 P.M. drew hammocks at 6, retired 9 P.M.

Oct. 18th Sunday.

Reveille. 6 A.M. breakfast 7. Were not detailed for any duties for to-day, but each man was told off as a guide, to get the battalion comfortably settled down when they came aboard to-morrow. Our duties are to get each mess together as they arrive, + show them to their quarters. Each of us must get an officers or N.C.O.s signature to our list to signify that they have received eating utensils, hammocks etc. in good condition, before our duties are complete. Dinner 12 noon, tea 6 P.M. Retired 9 P.M. [Jack's 24th birthday.]

Monday Oct. 19th 1914.

At 8 a.m. we could see the troops gathering on the wharf from our position a short distance out. At 11.30, a launch loaded with troops came alongside. They embarked with practically no confusion. After lunch, ferry steamers + motor launches hovered around us, loaded with crowds of cheering passengers. The garrison brass band, in a small boat, hung round in the vicinity, playing popular airs, "the girl I left behind me," "it's a long way to Tipparary" "Rule Britannia" "Advance Australia" etc. Towards evening we began to move, but only went a short distance towards the heads, where we moored for the night. The boys are all in excellent spirits.

Impressions when all are on board. Very crowded. Beside the 4th Batt., we have 3rd Batt. About 200 A.M. Corps [Army Medical Corps] + several horses, making the boat very crowded. Wash basins + baths not nearly sufficient. Very little room for exercise. Dry canteen arrangements very poor. One small store-room to supply the whole lot. It only remains open for five hours a day, + to-night I have spent more than an hour in trying to make a purchase. We have to go along a passage, + long before the time of opening, the passage is lined from either end with men waiting their turn to be served. The wet canteen is opened for one hour a day. 11 to 12. Beer only is served, + each man is allowed 1 pint. They have to fall in single file with their pannikins + 3d [3 pence], march past several policemen + officers, + as they pass a window, are handed a pint of Toohey's or Tooths beer. Our exercise decks when off duty are:- fore + aft well decks, bridge + poop decks.

As Jack described, the *Euripides* was packed with all sorts of passengers, including the 1st Brigade Headquarters staff, both the 3rd and 4th battalions and the 1st Field Ambulance—in total nearly 2300 troops. Of these, about 78 were officers.[2]

There was also a crew of 300 sailors on the 15,000-ton ship[3] and 15 horses below decks. Another passenger was the celebrated writer, bushman and poet A.B. 'Banjo' Paterson, a frustrated aspirant for the Official War Correspondent position. Banjo described the ship's passengers as:

> A topsy-turvy force this, for the Brigadier, General MacLaurin, has never seen active service, while the ranks are full of English ex-service men, wearing as many ribbons as prize bulls. These English ex-service men, by the way, volunteered to a man when the war broke out, and the Australian ranks were full of Yorkshiremen, Cockneys, and Cousin Jacks. Every one of them had the fixed idea of getting a transfer or clearing out and rejoining his old regiment as soon as he got to England. Who can blame them? It is the English way. Any one of them would sooner be shot as a private in the Coldstream Guards than get a decoration in a nameless Australian force. By the end of the war, we ourselves had a tradition.[4]

Despite eventually missing out on the Australian job, Banjo was hoping to cover the hostilities in Europe as a war correspondent. He had successfully covered the Boer War, writing about people and places on both sides, as well as the ebb and flow of the military actions across the veldt. He failed to get the necessary accreditation to report from France, instead serving there as an ambulance driver. This was short-lived; Banjo returned to Australia and in October 1915 enlisted as an officer in a newly formed remount unit where he found his wartime home. Banjo spent the next few years in Egypt and Palestine with his beloved 'Horsedung Hussars', breaking in and training horses for Light Horse units campaigning in the Middle East.[5]

Private Arthur Belling of the 3rd Battalion was far from impressed by the conditions aboard the *Euripides*. He later recalled:

> Conditions on board were appalling. We were packed in like sardines, head to tail in hammocks. No porthole open until everyone in his hammock, then lights out and portholes open. The bit of air that came in the portholes was used up by the ones lucky enough to get close. The stench and heat was awful and quite a number sickened. The cooking was atrocious.[6]

Equally outraged was another 3rd Battalion member, Private Geoff Leslie, who had this to say in a memoir:

> Life on the ship could have been pleasant enough had we not been forced to sleep in hammocks slung from the ceiling of a deck well below water line and so close together that the hammocks touched each other and any movement of one man was felt by others on each side. Also the food was dreadful and outbreaks of Ptomaine poisoning were frequent and widespread. I had two attacks, one of which was fairly bad.[7]

This last comment by Private Leslie concerned a nasty ship-wide phenomenon on the eve of reaching terra firma in Egypt.

Another passenger was Chaplain Bill McKenzie, a Salvation Army officer, who was appointed to the 1st Brigade as its 'Other Protestant Denominations Chaplain' on 25 September, although he largely served the 4th Battalion in that capacity.[8] Bill, who would become well known to Jack, had no such reservations about his accommodation, which was unlike the troops' overcrowding:

> Never before have so many troops left Australia in one single ship. We lay all afternoon and night in the Harbour and set out at 6.30 a.m. The sea was fairly rough outside so many were sick within a short time. I was OK. I was given a cabin to myself a large roomy state-room, with a porthole, so I am very comfortably fixed up and have heaps of room and plenty of quiet.[9]

~

20.10.14 Tuesday.

At reveille, several transports passed us, + shortly afterwards, we began to move, but where we are bound for, none of us know. Cleared the heads at about 7, + the sea was fairly rough. Breakfast was out of the question with a good many of us. I was too busy feeding the fishes to give it a thought. I was present for dinner, + felt A1 afterwards. Parade at 2.30 P.M. for those well enough to attend. After parade, some heavy gambling was noticeable. A good many play a game called "house", + the stakes in some cases reach 10/- [10 shillings] each player. After tea, a short service + prayers were conducted by 3rd Batt. chaplain, Colonel Talbot, Dean of Sydney.

21.10.14 Wednesday.

Weather beautifully calm. Parade for 2 hours, + after parade, the wet canteen was opened for 1 hour. It is interesting to watch the line, pushing + scrambling in their eagerness to get their "pot." Many tried to come the "double", but few succeeded, as there were military police posted at short intervals along the line, + a q.master [quartermaster] + several other officers watching closely. Dinner was served at 12 noon, + was very tasty, after the Kensington ration. Consisted of pork sausages, potatoes, peas, soup + bread, butter + jam was also issued. Parade for two hours after dinner, tea at 5, after which the 3rd Battn. brass band + 4th Battn. pipers gave an hours performance.

22.10.14 Thursday.
Grand smooth sea, + one would be apt to forget that our boat was moving but for the throb of her engines. Whales are very plentiful, + we spent our leisure hours sighting them. After tea, a service was conducted by Capt. McKenzie, 4th Batt. Chaplain, + a member of Salvation Army naval + military league.

This was the first reference in Jack's diary to Chaplain Bill McKenzie. At this point of the war, McKenzie was relatively unknown, but he was to become a legendary character in not just the 4th Battalion, but also the AIF generally. His nickname, 'Fighting Mac', distinguished him as a revered figure who spent the war giving his heart and soul to the troops. Nothing was too hard, everything was possible. Stories about this larger-than-life clergyman abound, some of them apocryphal, but there's no doubt Bill McKenzie was a most formidable character, physically and spiritually:

> He was a big man [6 foot 2 inches and 17 stone, or 187 centimetres and 109 kilograms] with a big voice to match. Unlike many chaplains he joined in the men's recreations, taking particular delight in the boxing contests. His long reach, jarring uppercuts and dangerous half-hooks left some of the AIF's best fighters dazed.[10]

Bill was also an aficionado of concerts, leading the singing with his booming voice.

~

23.10.14 Friday.
Another beautiful day. Usual duties. A very enjoyable concert rendered by members of A.A.M.C. [Australian Army Medical Corps] at night.

24.10.14 Saturday.
Weather a trifle cold + hazy. Duties as usual, with an interesting lecture by Major McNaughton on fire tactics and control.

Sunday 25.10.14

Reveille 7 A.M. Weather a little rougher than usual. Compulsory church parade at 11 A.M. for all denominations. Both chaplains taking part. The ships orchestra, which consists of two violins, piano, cornet + cello, + all splendidly manipulated, played accompaniment to hymns. After dinner, we had a re-hearsal of the procedure to be adopted when we approach Albany, where we expect to reach to-morrow.

Monday 26.10.14.

Sea again rough, atmosphere heavy, + occasional showers. Morning parade of two hours. At 12 o'clock, mess orderlies had drawn dinner, + served it, when the bugle sounded attention, + all hands were ordered on deck, so there was nought left but to leave our dinner to spoil, + double on deck to carry out the general salute, while approaching Albany. We stood to attention while the bugles sounded the general salute, + the band played "Rule Brittannia," + "God save the King." The bugles then sounded the "stand at ease,"+ there we stood for half an hour or so. The attention again sounded, + we stood in that position while we passed the transports already moored outside the harbour. As we passed, a dozen or so hearty cheers went up from the troops of Victorian + other contingents, but, as much as we would have liked to return the compliment, not a murmur was heard, nor a body moved, which brought forth the inquiry from the other troops if we were all dead, + they also counted us out. When we had anchored, we were allowed to go to our mess deck to eat our spoilt meal, which was well punctuated with fluent growling. Our usual 2 hours parade was carried out in the afternoon. [Growling was a euphemism for whingeing characterised by liberal swearing. It was part and parcel of army life. See the map of the First Contingent's voyage on page 15.]

Tuesday 27.10.14

We are still anchored in the same place as yesterday. The transports lying around us present a grand picture. It is raining heavily. A warship is discernable in the distance. About dinner time, another troop ship steamed in, + anchored amongst those already here. They are now about 20 in number. We were informed that letters will be taken ashore this morning, + as there are no stamps on board, have to mark our letters On active service. No stamps available, so that the ordinary rate of postage only will be charged on delivery. General Bridges inspected the troops on board in the afternoon.

The fleet carrying the AIF First Contingent was assembled in King George Sound, Albany, on the coast of south-west Western Australia. Ships carrying troops and supplies as well as a protective escort gathered in its vast waters. Even though the *Euripides* spent a week at anchor the men weren't allowed to disembark.

Wednesday 28.10.14.

The weather has cleared. Morning parade as usual. In the afternoon, we were told off into boat crews, + instructed in boat drill. 28 men were put into each boat, + we went for a row. We were informed that our letters in future must be left unsealed for censorship. We do not know what has become of the letters we posted yesterday, + posted 6.

Thursday 29.10.14.

Light rain is falling, + it is very cold. It was stated in Battalion orders that no more letters were to be written except on plain post cards, to be provided for us by O.C. [Officer Commanding]. These must contain only brief information regarding ourselves, + our probable movements not be mentioned. Letters were delivered on board, + I received two.

Friday 30.10.14.

A glorious morning. We were given an opportunity to purchase any article we required from Albany, an officer + a few men being despatched to get the goods. We had a lecture on transport organisation, delivered by a transport officer.

Saturday 31.10.14.

H Coy. is the duty coy., forming all guards, fatigues, sweepers, Regt. Orderly corporal + Serg. The guard tour of duty is for four hours, with eight hours off. The duties are to keep order, prevent spitting on decks, while the gang way is lowered to prevent anyone going off or coming aboard without a pass, give the alarm in case of fire or man over board etc.

Sunday Nov. 1st 1914.

At 7 A.M several transports left their moorings, + moved slowly out to sea, the fleet's flagship "Orvieto" leading. At 8 o'clock, we were relieved from guard, + at the same time our ship put out. We formed up in three lines, Orvieto leading the centre line, Euripides leading the right hand line. We were followed by 6 or 7 other boats, the names of which I do not know, but hope to find out. The fleet presents a magnificent spectacle, the like of which has probably never been seen before on the Australian coast, unless the visit of the American fleet equalled it. (I think it impossible that it surpassed it.) A beautiful calm sea, the escort of 4 battleships just discernable on the horizon, the three lines of ships steaming majestically along the smooth surface, all go to make a beautiful picture. Church parade at 11 A.M. to 12.

The American fleet Jack referred to was the Great White Fleet, which visited Australia in 1908 during its circumnavigation of the globe. It had also lain at anchor in King George Sound and consisted of 16 battleships and five auxiliary vessels.[11]

Bill McKenzie was also very impressed by the unique spectacle presented by the ships carrying the First Contingent:

> We lay at anchor until Sunday morning November 1st when we set sail at 6.45 a.m. A good crowd of people lined the hills at the mouth of the harbour to see the awe-inspiring sight, as the convoy of cruisers with the transports left the harbour under sealed orders. The New Zealand Fleet had come in on Wednesday morning, 10 transport and 2 cruisers. The morning we left was ideal, the atmosphere clear, the sea calm and the sun fairly warm. What a magnificent sight.[12]

When the fleet weighed anchor at Albany it was made up of 36 transports and three escort warships—the *Minotaur*, the *Sydney* and the *Melbourne*. A couple of days later, two more transports and the Japanese warship, the *Ibuki*, joined the convoy on the open ocean.[13] With the fleet complete, 30,000 troops, including about 10,000 of the New Zealand Expeditionary Force, were on board.

Monday 2.11.14.

Parades as usual. Concert at night by members of 4th Battn. Enjoying beautiful weather.

Tuesday 3.11.14.

Weather getting warm. Afternoon parade consisted of fire alarm. The bugles sounded a series of "Gs", + those on the lower decks had to get a life-belt, fasten it on, + rush on the bridge deck, sit down, take off boots, + wait for orders. Perfect silence to be maintained. The boys did the movement in good time, + were complimented by Major McNaughton.

Wednesday 4.11.14

Sky overcast. Sea a trifle rough. From the upper decks, we feast our eyes on the grand sight the fleet presents. It is a sight that never gets less beautiful.

Thursday 5.11.14.

A nice warm day. Sea smooth. The day passed uneventfully, until about 7 P.M. when a large vessel hove in sight, + when she came close to us, we saw that she was the "Osterley." She passed us on the starboard side, quite close, + as she passed, the passengers sang + cheered, + the boys returned the cheers vigorously. She was advised not to proceed further than the H.M.A.S. Sydney, but kept on her voyage.

On this day, 5 November, a momentous decision was made in the British corridors of power, one that would affect every man in the convoy—Great Britain declared war on Turkey. German courting of the Ottoman Empire was successful and the Turks entered the realm of the Triple Alliance, basically replacing the Italians, who had an uneasy relationship with Germany and the Austro-Hungarians prior to the outbreak of war. Italy regarded the treaty as a defensive one and was reluctant to act offensively against members of the Triple Entente—Britain, France and Russia, the other players in the European pre-war manoeuvring.

In Egypt, as part of this aligning of forces, the final vestige of Ottoman influence, the last khedive, Abbas Hilmi Pasha, was deposed on 11 November, thus ending the Ottoman suzerainty over Egypt. For many years the British had been in de facto control of Egypt and, most importantly, the Suez Canal. After the opening of the canal in 1869 the British stepped up their influence in Egypt, purchasing a significant share in the operation of the waterway and flexing their considerable military muscle by defeating an Egyptian revolt in a series of battles during July, August and September of 1882. The final and most significant one was at Tel-el-Kebir on 13 September, when 17,000 British troops under Lord Wolseley defeated 22,000 Egyptians under Colonel Arabi Pasha. The victory resulted in the British triumphantly parading through Cairo on 15 September 1882 as the undisputed, albeit unofficial, political and economic masters of Egypt.[14]

Friday 6.11.14.

Many exciting rumours are drifting round, concerning our destination, war news that is merely manufactured by some good "liar." Of course, the further the yarn goes, the larger it grows. One tale has been going round that 12 British ships were sunk by 3 German cruisers, + the teller solemnly swears that he overheard the wireless operator telling the head steward.

Saturday 7.11.14.
Fine day. Usual parade for the 4th Bn. 3rd Battn. sports were held in the afternoon. We had a mock fire alarm at 8 P.M. everyone knowing exactly the time the alarm was to take place, + when the bugles sounded, few were unprepared.

Sunday 8.11.14.
Weather very hot, with a calm sea. H. Coy for duty. The sad news was circulated this morning that one of our comrades had died during the night. He was a signaller, attached to the 3rd Battn., an ex trooper, recently stationed at Bathurst + married only a few weeks before sailing. The remains were buried at sea at about 10 A.M. In the afternoon, the dead comrade's kit was sold by auction, + realized something like 50 pounds, which is to be sent to the widow.

Private Varley Kendal, 3rd Battalion, died from pneumonia. Lance Corporal Harry Smith wrote in his diary on 8 November 1914: 'During the night one of the men in "A" Coy died . . . Pte Kendall buried at 10.30 am cast gloom over all ship.'[15]

Monday 9.11.14.
We were dismissed from guard at 8 A.M. Everything was going along smoothly, when it was officially stated that a wireless message had been received from H.M.A.S. Sydney. "Sydney engaging enemy." Excitement ran high. This was at 10 A.M. A few minutes later the Japanese cruiser, which formed part of our convoy, passed our bows at a tremendous speed. She skimmed over the water like an arrow, + was out of sight in a very short time. Another message was then announced:— "Emden beached to avoid capture. Sydney chasing enemy's collier. Our casualties 3 killed. 13 wounded." The excitement was splendid. The troops are fairly carried away, + cheering excitedly. Even the beer line was broken, + nothing else but a cannonball would move that.

Even the Brigadier feels the strain, + granted an extra hour's serving in the canteen. The band was mustered, + played the national anthem, while everyone stood motionless. While the band was playing, another comrade passed away, also from 3rd Batt. signallers. He had been in hospital for some time, suffering from pneumonia.

We were granted half holiday, in honour of Australia's first naval battle + victory. At 1 P.M. the Jap. Cruiser returned, passing close enough for us to see the sailors on board quite plainly, + took up her original position. Our comrade was buried at 3.30., the ship having stopped while the buglers sounded the "Last post," + the remains were committed to the deep.

The comrade Jack referred to was Private John 'Jock' Lowe, 3rd Battalion. Chaplain McKenzie conducted his funeral service. McKenzie's diary recorded the occasion:

> The band was paraded to play the national anthem and while the strains of this were floating over the water the immortal spirit of Private Loe of B Company 3rd Battalion was called to the presence of his Maker. Another victim of 'pneumonia'. He was a fine sweet-spirited young man of 21 years formerly resident in Surrey England . . . the body was buried at 3.30 p.m. It was a solemn procedure. We marched with slow stately tread from the hospital at the poop deck to the forward well deck, the Dean and I alternately reciting the 90 Psalm. I read the lesson, he the committal and prayer and 30 buglers sounded the last post. It was a solemn undertaking; the ship's captain was greatly moved.[16]

Jack's diary of Monday, 9 November, continues:

> It is estimated that our position is 60 miles from the scene of battle. Few lights were allowed to-night, + none could be seen outside, as other enemy's ships may be in the vicinity. We are warned to sleep with our life-belts alongside us, in case we should get an alarm. Also informed that no sham alarms will be carried out to-night. Later received orders to sleep at our boat stations on deck. I was innoculated this afternoon, + my arm is very painful.

The battle involving the German *Emden* was the first action involving the contingent and it made a significant impression on Jack and the rest of the convoy. The sailors killed on the *Sydney* were Ordinary Seaman Robert Bell, Able Seaman Albert Hoy and Petty Officer Tom Lynch. One of the wounded, Able Seaman Reginald Sharpe, later died of his wounds. (See the map of the First Contingent's voyage on page 15.)

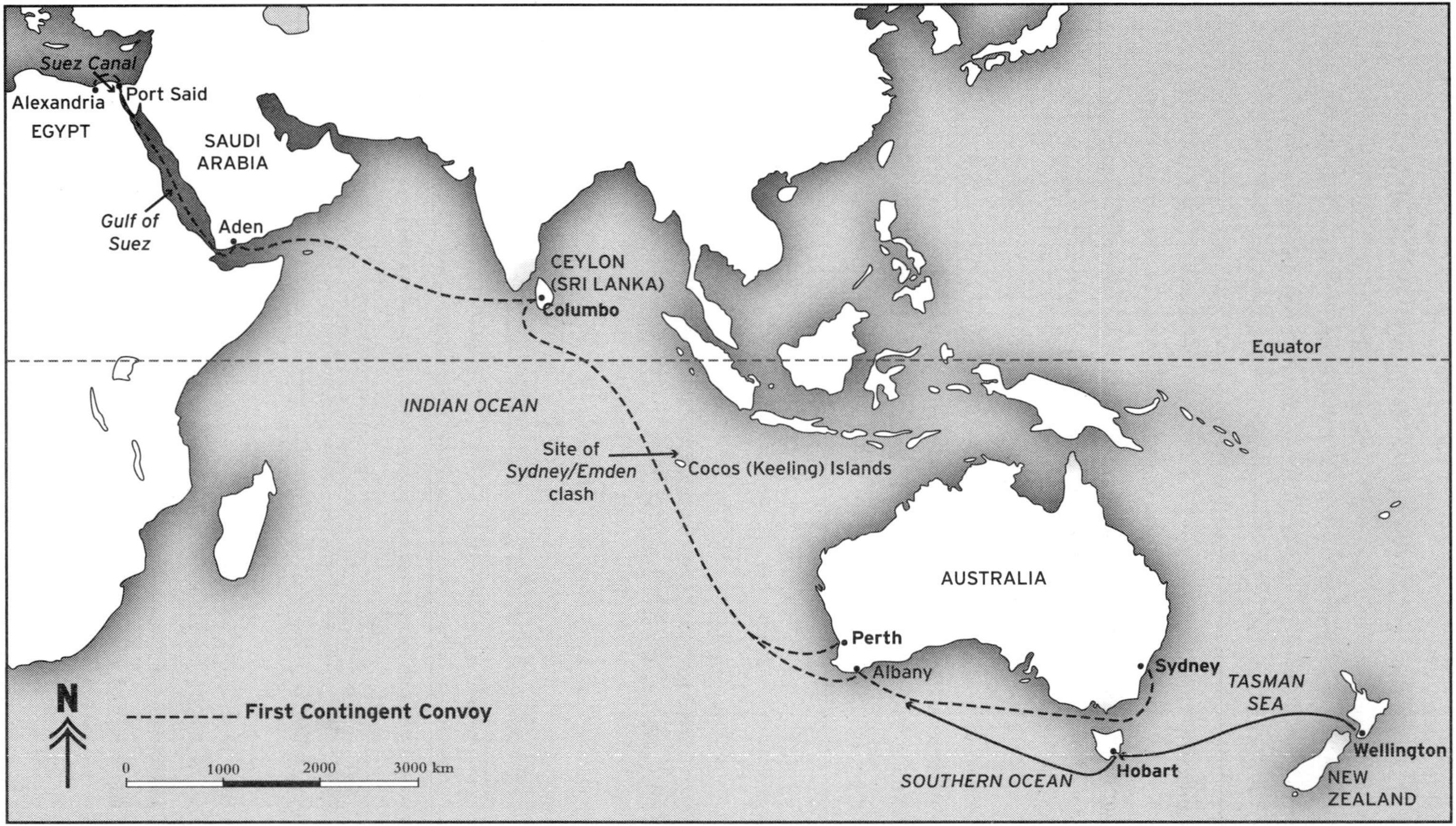

Route of the First Contingent Convoy

The 4th Battalion, part of the First Contingent, departed Sydney on 19 October 1914 and arrived at Alexandria on 3 December.

Banjo Paterson, aboard the *Euripides*, wrote the following graphic account about the battle between HMAS *Sydney* and the *Emden* in his book, *Happy Dispatches*, which was first published in 1934. It is based on an interview he had with Captain John Glossop, the commanding officer of HMAS *Sydney*, aboard the *Sydney* in Colombo Harbour on 15 or 16 November, following the destruction of the *Emden* on 9 November. After the battle Glossop famously signalled the convoy, '*Emden* beached and done for'.[17] Paterson initially used the interview as the basis of a press report he sent to *The Sydney Morning Herald*, published on 30 December 1914. This was his shorter account in *Happy Dispatches*:

> The gigantic Massie [Jack Massie, the 4th Battalion's adjutant, was an impressive 6 foot 4 inches and 15 stone, or 192 centimetres and 95 kilograms] offers to take me off to interview Glossop, the hero of the *Sydney–Emden* fight. Massie's people are of considerable importance in Sydney and he has entertained Glossop at his house; so he says that if I go with him and listen to what Glossop says I may get some stuff that the other correspondents wouldn't get [Unfortunately for Banjo, Charles Bean and Peter Schuler were also privy to the good captain's private thoughts, having had a similar opportunity on 11 November in Colombo Harbour—'Hearing the recital of that chapter by Captain Glossop in the cabin of the *Sydney*, two days after the engagement, I (Peter Schuler) consider myself amongst the most fortunate.'—[18]] . . . We find Glossop in mufti having a drink by himself, a typical English sailor-man, not a bit excited by the fact that he has 'woke up to find himself famous': to him the whole affair is a matter of range of guns, weight of metal, speed of ship, and of course a good deal of luck.
>
> 'Well Massie, I had a lot of luck, didn't I?' he says. 'Fancy her coming to Cocos just when we were right on the spot, and fancy just having the luck to be on that side of the convoy. If I'd been on the other side, then I wouldn't have got the job. Of course I had the speed of her and the guns of her, but if our people hadn't served the guns properly or if she'd dropped a shell into our engine-room, we might have been sent to the bottom instead of her. You can work out a fight on paper, and one shell will upset the whole calculation.
>
> 'She had no idea that there was any vessel of her own power in that part of the Pacific [actually the Indian Ocean], and she came out looking for a fight—and she got it. She must have got a surprise when she found out she had to fight the *Sydney*; and I got a surprise, too, I can tell you. When we were about ten thousand five hundred yards apart I turned nearly due north so as to run parallel with her, and I said to the gunnery

lieutenant that we had better get a thousand yards closer before we fired. I knew the *Emden*'s four-point-one guns would be at their extreme limit at ten thousand yards, and I got a shock when she fired a salvo at ten thousand five hundred and two of the shells came aboard us. That's modern gunnery for you. Fancy one ship, rolling about in the sea, hitting another ship six miles away! She must have elevated her guns and fired in the air, for we were technically out of range; but it was great gunnery.

'Her first salvo was five guns, of which two shells came aboard us. One shell burst and took away the after-control, wounding all the men, including Lieutenant Hampden, but no one was killed. The other shell passed within six inches of the gunnery lieutenant and killed a man working a range-finder, but it never burst. There was luck again for me—I was in that control and if the shell had burst I suppose I would have been a goner.

'There was a boy about sixteen in the control working a telescope. When the shell landed he was stunned by the concussion and was lying under the body of the man that was killed. As soon as he came to himself he threw the man's body off him and started looking for his telescope. "Where's my bloody telescope?" was all he said. That's the Australian Navy for you.

'The whole thing didn't last forty minutes, but it was a busy forty minutes. She tried to get near enough to torpedo us, but she could only do seventeen knots and we could do twenty-seven, so we scuttled out of range. The *Emden* had a captured collier called the *Buresk* hanging about, trying to get near enough to ram us, and I had to keep a couple of guns trained on this collier all the time. We hit the *Emden* about a hundred times in forty minutes, and fourteen of her shells struck us but most of them were fired beyond her range and the shells hit the side and dropped into the water without exploding.

'When the *Emden* made for the beach we went after the collier, but we found the Germans had taken the sea-cocks out of her so we had to let her sink. They were game men, I'll say that for them.

'Then we went back to the *Emden* lying in the shallow water and signalled her "do you surrender." She answered by flag-waving in Morse "we have no signal book and do not understand your signal." I asked several times but could get no answer and her flag was still flying, so I fired two salvos into her and then they hauled their flag down. I was sorry afterwards that I gave her those two salvos, but what was I to do? If they were able to flag-wave in Morse, they were surely able to haul a flag down. We understood there was another German warship about and I couldn't have the *Emden* firing at me from the beach while I was fighting her mate.

'We waited off all night with lights out for this other vessel, but she never showed up, and then we sent boats ashore to the *Emden*. My God, what a sight! Her captain had been out of action ten minutes after the fight started from lyddite fumes, and everybody on board was demented—that's all you could call it, just fairly demented—by shock, and fumes, and the roar of shells bursting among them. She was a shambles. Blood, guts, flesh and uniforms were all scattered about. One of our shells had landed behind a gun shield, and had blown the whole gun-crew into one pulp. You couldn't even tell how many men there had been. They must have had forty minutes of hell on that ship, for out of four hundred men a hundred and forty were killed and eighty wounded and the survivors were practically madmen. They crawled up to the beach and they had one doctor fit for action; but he had nothing to treat them with—they hadn't even got any water. A lot of them drank salt water and killed themselves. They were not ashore twenty-four hours, but their wounds were flyblown and the stench was awful—it's hanging about the *Sydney* yet. I took them on board and got four doctors to work on them and brought them up here.

'I've seen my first naval engagement, Massie; and all I can say is, thank God we didn't start the war.'

We left Captain Glossop to handle his very turbulent lot of prisoners and went back to our ships. The next night a message came that the *Sydney*, with the German prisoners on board, would pass us at sea about two o'clock in the morning. The Brigadier ordered that all ranks should parade and stand at attention as she went past: an order that started a lot of grumbling among the recruits until a Yorkshire ex-sergeant-major said:

'Tha'll be proud, laad, some day to say tha' did it. Yesterday ye were nowt but a handful o' blacks; but the world's talkin' about ye today.'

Under the tropic night the ghost of a warship glided by and all ranks on our transport fell in and stood at attention until she passed out of sight. A formality, perhaps; but it might have satisfied even Mr Kipling that we were growing up.[19]

In contrast to Glossop's interview with Banjo Paterson was the following after-action report written by an officer of the *Emden*:

We sighted Cocos Island 6 p.m. 9/11/14 and the lookouts reported the harbour free of enemy warships.

The landing party left at 7 a.m. and consisted of 3 officers, 5 N.C.Os. and 45 men with a machine gun and 1200 rounds, 47 rifles and 60 rounds per rifle. Only on our landing did the inhabitants learn that we were Germans and they were not too pleased. The Wireless Station now sent out calls for help which our people spoiled by jamming.

In a short time we heard the roar of shells and saw the Wireless Installation fall to the ground. About 9 o'clock the lookout reported 'Smoke on the horizon' and at first mistaken for our collier '*Burisk*', she was later recognised as a warship. She steamed with tremendous speed and we had to leave our landing party to its fate. At 8,700 metres the Commander gave the order to open fire. Our shooting was good, but after a time the enemy opened fire tho' his range was faulty. Salvo followed salvo but our guns could not effect much damage owing to the great distance. At about the 12th round our enemy had got his range and smashed our wireless installation with his first hit, killing all its personnel. The enemy kept the fight at 8,000 metres and by her heavier guns and superior speed turned the fight which way she wanted. Right at the commencement our range finder was short [shot] away.

We now lost our first funnel, foretopmast, and other two funnels and the ammunition chambers having been hit were flooded to prevent explosion. We answered the fire of the enemy already feebler. The ship was on fire in several places. Blood was flowing in streams on the deck and terribly mutilated corpses were laying about.

We only fired now and again and soon these few men were dead also, only the Artillery Officer and a few unskilled chaps were still firing. These also were soon put out of action.

The Commander decided to run the ship ashore and ten minutes later the proud "*Emden*" had finished her last work. We had already learnt that our adversary was the "*Sydney*" and she now took leave. The battle had lasted from 9 a.m. to 11 a.m. and at about four in the afternoon the "*Sydney*" reappeared and then they fired on a defenceless ship. We knew the reason very soon. On our one and only mast which was already very shaky was our War flag. A sailor tried to climb the shaky mast and the "*Sydney*" ceased firing at once and sent a boat along with the order that we would be taken off in the morning. Towards midday she appeared and carried out very cleverly and carefully the job of transhipping us.[20]

After the euphoria of the *Sydney*'s victory abated, life on board the *Euripides* resumed its normal rhythm, although the weather was becoming increasingly hot and uncomfortable.

Tuesday 10.11.14.

Weather hot + stifling. Sea smooth. A few minutes past 6, the Japanese cruiser passed quite close to us, giving us a good opportunity to see the sailors and guns quite plainly. She steamed a short distance ahead, + it is said that she is trawling for mines. The remaining escort come in quite close, + are steaming right from front to rear of the fleet. There is no parade this afternoon, owing to the excessive heat. There was a large amount of clothing, including socks, gloves, knitted caps, mufflers, canvas slippers, pyjamas etc, given for the comfort of the troops, by our Australian relatives + friends, +, it was generally understood, to be issued free to us. A day or two ago, our Capt. informed us that these articles would be sold:- socks 1/- pair, caps 2/6 [2 shillings and sixpence] each. This, in my opinion, is not fair to the donors, although we are assured that the proceeds will be devoted to a good cause:- ⅓ to go to troops sports fund while on board ship, + ⅔ to go to distressed seaman's fund. The scenery is getting more beautiful daily, or perhaps we are learning to appreciate the beauty of the scene to the full. A most glorious sunset, the grand positions of the fleet, steaming majestically, in perfect order, over a smooth sea. The effect of the setting sun on the water is truly magnificent. A battle-ship is plainly visible on the skyline ahead, another on either flank, + one following up in rear. The whole scene is perfect, + it is impossible to draw the slightest imagination of its grandeur.

Troops are dressed in all kinds of attire, the majority following the teachings of Chidley, clad only in a flannel shirt, others in pyjamas, bathing costumes etc. All are in high spirits, not having recovered from the effect of the glorious excitement of yesterday.

Jack's reference to the men's fashion adhering to 'the teachings of Chidley' was about the informality and lack of clothing the troops wore in the tropics, a climate foreign to the predominantly New South Welshman of the 3rd and 4th battalions. The substantial numbers of the British-born contingent in the two battalions would have also sweltered in the hot, humid conditions, hence the shedding of their apparel.

William James Chidley was an eccentric philosopher who came to prominence in the years immediately before the outbreak of the war. Chidley advocated, among other controversial views, the wearing of loose clothing, a vegan diet and the abstinence of sexual intercourse, believing coition should 'take place only in Spring . . . and between true lovers only'.[21] With the publication of *The Answer:*

A Philosophical Essay in 1911, his treatise on sexual ethics and his way of life, Chidley entered public life in Melbourne and Sydney in particular, and embarked on a crusade to enlighten society.[22] He might have been regarded as harmless and unusual but for his unfortunate penchant for self-aggrandisement to publicise his cause. Chidley's choice of the Domain as the venue for his public pronouncements in Sydney certainly ensured an audience, but inevitably meant the constabulary took a dim view of his radical philosophy. A tall, striking, sunburnt figure dressed in a loose violet or white shift that left his arms, legs and feet exposed, Chidley spoke and sold copies of his book on the street in spite of being arrested regularly for such transgressions as offensive behaviour, obstructing the footway and 'not dressing in accordance with the rules governing social decorum'.[23] Despite the largely God-fearing society, he had many prominent supporters; equally there were Establishment figures, in the police and judiciary, who regarded him as insane and had him locked up. But neither convictions nor spells in mental institutions dissuaded him from his mission. Tragically, Chidley died suddenly, a broken man, from natural causes in Callan Park Hospital for the Insane on Thursday, 21 December 1916, having survived an earlier suicide attempt on 12 October.[24]

Jack had, no doubt, read with interest about this divisive proponent of unusual sexual practices parading publicly in Melbourne and Sydney in what to some was regarded as 'a bathing costume' prior to the war.[25] Chidley would have approved of the fashion on board the transports in the tropics and in the hotter months at Anzac, as well as the men's sexual abstinence, albeit enforced, at both places. However, he would have been horrified by some of the men's sexual proclivity in the back streets of Cairo in between.

Wednesday 11.11.14.
Sky overcast, sea smooth, atmosphere very heavy. Two large canvas baths, erected a day or two ago, well patronised, + it is unwise to venture too close, unless one wants to get unceremoniously dumped in, clothes + all.

Thursday 12.11.14.
Still cloudy, atmosphere a trifle cooler, with a refreshing breeze. At 6 A.M. the "Orvieto" [flagship of the fleet] had left her original position, + was quite close to us, on the starboard side, to collect mails for censorship. At 7 A.M. mail bags were taken by her boat, + she returned to her old position. A strong wind—6.30 A.M.—is rising, the sky is heavily clouded, + every indication of a storm is apparent. At 8.30 P.M.

a large vessel passed us, travelling in opposite direction. She carried only two lights.

Friday 13.11.14.
Sea fairly calm. A light breeze is blowing, + light rain is falling. There is no parade to-day, as we are to cross the line. The officers had taken charge of the 3rd Bn. brass instruments + were marching around the decks making the most unearthly blast, + bulging their cheeks to the utmost capacity. Many of the boys got a free bath before dinner, but the real fun did not start until 2 o'clock. Some got their free bath in the morning, but as it looked a riot, the Colonel warned the boys not to go too far, + ordered that no more baths were to be indulged in until 2 P.M. but the strain was too great, + long before 2, buckets of water began to fly around, + before the appointed hour, not a dry uniform could be seen. Sergeants + Corporals held a special fascination for the boys, but this may have been a way of settling differences, which don't come very often to a private. The serg. were taken from their mess, hauled up the stairs,+ straight head first into the bath, where half a dozen pairs of strong arms waited to finish the ducking by holding them under. The more they struggled, the worse they got it. At 3.30 a sergeant drew his bayonet on the boys when they came to collar him, + the C. O. stopped the fun, A pte. hit the sgt. in the chest with his fist + was awarded a district Court Martial.

The *Euripides* crossed the Equator about 700 kilometres south of Ceylon (now called Sri Lanka) and the traditional crossing of the line festivities ensued. Howard McKern also recorded the equatorial frivolities on the *Euripides* in his diary:

> Crossed the line early this morning . . . We were all initiated and made freemen of the Northern Seas. A number of men were put through the ceremony by Father Neptune. Father Neptune came on board at 2 pm and announced through trumpet 'I am the ruler of the seas. Whomsoever on board this ship has not passed into these seas before shall be made to taste of the water thereof and shall henceforth be a freeman of all the seas under my dominion'. The first man to be initiated was the Sgt. Cook who was thrown bodily into the bath with a millstone of plum duff hung round his neck. Each man in turn was made to pass before Neptune and his Court and was then seated on a barrel and lathered with a whitewash brush and then shaved with a huge wooden razor. The doctor then

examined him and prescribed a pepper pill. As soon as the patient had taken the pill he was thrown over backwards into the bath where he was instantly pounced on by the bears and vigorously dunked four times.[26]

Saturday 14.11.14.

Weather sultry. Sea calm. Parade 8.40 to 11 A.M. I was vaccinated this afternoon.

Sunday 15.11.14.

Roused out of hammocks at 4 30 A.M. to see H.M.A.S. Sydney pass the fleet. Just arrived on deck on time to see her, but it was quite dark. We had orders not to cheer, on account of the wounded sailors on board. Immediately following the Sydney, was the "Empress of Russia," carrying German prisoners + wounded. We can see a light-house in the distance, + as dawn opened on us, we could see the coast of Ceylon, a very pleasing sight. Church parade was held at 10.30. Letters can be posted until 12 noon to-day. At 12.30 the boats drew close together, + hundreds of small craft are to be seen stationary on the water, presumably, native fisherman. At 1 P.M. we could plainly see the break-water of the harbour, + beyond it, in the harbour, several cruisers + transports, mostly of the latter carrying N.Z. troops. At 1.30 we were called on deck to carry out the general salute, + half an hour later, fastened to a buoy just outside Colombo harbour. Colombo seems a very interesting place, + I should like to spend a day or two ashore. The harbour is very beautiful, but not a natural formation like Sydney can boast of. Large buildings are to be seen on the edge of the water, + green trees are plentiful. At 4 P.M. a Russian cruiser steamed out of the harbour, + the bugles sounded attention as she passed. [See the map of the First Contingent's voyage on page 15.]

Monday 16.11.14.

Small canoes all around us containing, 2 + 3 natives, termed by the boys, "bum boats." Coins are thrown into the water, a native dives from the boat, + returns a second later triumphantly holding the coin in his hand. They would not dive for pennies, + towards the end of the day, they would dive for nothing less than 6d. When they had satisfied the donor that they had secured the coin, they put it in their mouth, + some left the side of the ship with mouths so full, that it would not hold another 3d. I have been detailed as mess orderly for the week, a thankless job. I have often heard it said that it's a soldiers privilege to growl, + there is no place that this privilege is taken advantage of more than at the mess tables, + the addition of adjectives (Australian) is not forgotten. Our coy. is on duty, but few are well enough to go on guard, as they were innoculated yesterday, + their arms are swollen a treat. My vaccinated arm is very painful at times. As we anchored near Colombo, the guard has been issued with ball ammunition with orders to keep all launches, canoes, etc. at a distance. Several Ceylon newspapers have just come aboard, + the price charged is 1/- a copy. The only news I can find in them is the announcement of the death of Lord Roberts. For the past fortnight, there has been a famine of both matches + cigarettes, + a few of our "comrades," (if such we may call them) who scented the scarcity, monopolised the remaining boxes before the canteen had sold out, + when the famine was on, commenced selling cigarettes (capstan) at 9d + 1/ a pkt. + matches as high as 6d a box of safety's. I saw two boxes raffled a few nights ago, 1d a member, + they secured 100 members. However, we are hoping that the drought will break to-morrow, as several boats have gone ashore for provisions.

Tuesday 17.11.14.

We moved from our mooring at 7 A.M. + steamed into the harbour. On the ship dropping anchor again, we were immediately surrounded by natives, selling cigarettes (scissors) + charge 1/- a packet of 10. The British, Russian +Japanese cruisers went out during the afternoon, also several transports. All was quiet on our boat, all standing to Attention as the boats went past, until the Omrah came past, when a series of tumultuous cheers went up from our boys, returned vigorously by Omrah troops. The Officers seemed disgusted, + threatened all sorts of agonising tortures, such as 2 hours pack drill etc., but it had no effect. Eventually, at 7.30 P.M. we left our moorings, + steamed out of the harbour.

Since leaving Sydney, we have not set foot on land, + it seems very unfair to us, when we see other boats putting their troops ashore for exercise, + moreover, I believe our boat is carrying the largest number of troops. A list headed, "What we would like to know," was posted up in the letter rack for the officers to get a look at. It was signed. A patriotic Australian, + among a number of other queries, asked: "What has become of the gifts, presented to the troops, for our personal comfort by our relatives + friends in N.S.W.? What has become of the free beer, presented by the proprietors of Sydney breweries, for the use of the troops on the voyage? Why were "fiver" + "Oceanic" cigarettes substituted for "capstan" also given by our kind friends, + served out to us in place of the real gifts (capstan)? + a score of other questions that strike one as shady. There was also a newspaper printed by one of my coy. named Haney, a real artist, + put up in the letter rack for perusal. It contains very laughable pars. concerning different men in the coy, + has a special page for the doings of the N.C.O.s. The "Euripides Herald" is the name of it.

The *Euripides Herald* was one of the first of a long line of troopship publications that appeared during the war. Nearly every ship transporting Australian troops to and from the northern hemisphere had one. They helped to pass the interminable days on board the men and women from Down Under faced when travelling to the Front on the other side of the world or when returning home. These papers offered a unique insight into the attitudes of the enlisted men and allowed them to vent frustrations, pass on important news and anecdotes, light-heartedly send up their superiors and chew the fat about the latest gossip. Most had a literary bent, including poems and short stories. Cartoons and caricatures were also a staple. Private John Haney, the creator of the *Euripides Herald*, was a tramway conductor before enlisting. Haney was obviously a talented, creative bloke with a critical eye for life on the transport.

Wednesday 18.11.14.

Atmosphere almost stifling. Sea calm + smooth. Parade in morning, afternoon to ourselves. We witnessed the most beautiful sunset it has ever been my lot to see. Concert at night.

Thursday 19.11.14.

We have again come up with the other transports, + taken up a position in front. We have a supply of cigarettes, matches, tobacco + eatables in the canteen at last, for which we are genuinely thankful. The prices charged are disgracefully high on some articles, someone is making a profit of anything up to 150%. For example, a few articles I have purched myself, after waiting an hour for my turn to be served at the canteen Safety matches 8d a dozen. Tooth powder (small tin) 9d, + inferior stuff at that. Salmon 1/2 a tin. Cigarettes, three castles in tins of 50. 2/1. I could mention a score of other items, but as the profit may be going towards some "charitable" institution or some other good cause, its well to let it drop, but in the meantime, the troops must be content to be swindled. Even at these prices, the ships Quartermaster + staff are not too particular whether they serve us or not. The canteen is supposed to be open for 5 hours a day, little enough if it were strictly adhered to, but it is very often a quarter to the following hour when the serving men condescend to put in an appearance, + never punctual, but they invariably close at the time laid down, + to the minute. Another beautiful sunset. The Dean of Sydney, Col. Talbot, conducted a service after tea, after which, the 3rd Batt. band rendered some fine music. At 9 P.M. a nice refreshing breeze sprang up, + we were thankful for a grand nights sleep.

Friday 20.11.14.
A glorious morning, with just a faint show of clouds in the sky. Sea smooth as glass, + but for the throbbing of the engines, one would be apt to forget that we were moving, the boat is so steady. At 2 P.M. a parade was called to hear the result of a district court martial. The accused was one John Robinson [John Robertson, regimental number 994], an old soldier, who had over 6 years service to his credit, + an excellent discharge, + his present charge was for striking a sergeant in the chest with his clenched fist on the day we crossed the line. He was sentenced to 21 days detention. In civil life his was a very trifling offence, + two more good hits would have settled the matter. We had another very enjoyable concert at night, some jolly fine comedians taking part with Capt. McKenzie as stage manager.

Saturday 21.11.14.
Rose at 5.30 A.M. to find all boats stationary. We hear all kinds of tales as to the cause, but I think the most reliable is what a serg. told me, that a man fell over-board, another jumped over to save him, the boat steadied down to pick them up, + the following boat ran into her, + they were examining the damage. I have since heard that this was correct, + that both men were saved, + the damage caused by the collision is only slight. At night, we secured the use of the ships piano, + had a real good rough + ready singsong for an hour. A concert was given by members of 3rd Batt. afterwards, which was very much appreciated by all hands.

Sunday 22.11.14.

Finished my week's term as Mess orderly, for which I am very thankful. I would not go over another week in the same position for five sovereigns. For the first three days, it seemed like one long sentence of growling, but as I gave no "change," they gradually settled down, + let me have my own way.

Church parade from 11 till 12. Weather very sultry. I attended sick parade this afternoon with my arm, the pain of which is excruciating, + discharging horribly. No matter which position I try to rest, I get no ease. Dr told me I should have gone to him days ago, + put me off all duties.

Monday 23.11.14.

Spent a very restless night, although there was a splendid breeze blowing. Dr parade again this morning, + was marked "unfit" for duty. Land is in sight, although a long distance off.

Tuesday 24.11.14.

We have been informed that letters may now be written + posted without being censored, so the boys are all busy writing letters.

Wednesday 25.11.14.

When we came on deck, we found our boat moving very slowly, + eventually anchored just outside Aden. The coast is very rugged, + looks a barren, desolate place. Rumour has it, that we are landing in Egypt, but we have become so accustomed to these wild-cat stories, that its hard to make us swallow them, although this one is likely to prove correct. [See the map of the First Contingent's voyage on page 15.]

The fleet's anchoring point at Aden on the southern tip of the Arabian Peninsula didn't impress the troops. Other diarists were very scathing. Lance Corporal Harry Smith of the 3rd Battalion, who was on the *Euripides*, wrote:

> 25th/11 Dropped anchor Aden Harbour 6.45 am—very desolate looking place—surrounded by high peaks guiltless of a blade of grass or a tree even.[27]

Private Oliver Giddings, also from the 3rd Battalion, was equally unimpressed:

> Wed 25 We arrived at Aden . . . It is a god forsaken looking place . . . Thursday 26th Leaving Aden at 6 o'clock and can see all along the coast.

> It is all one vast sandy plain. *Sydney* blew up a Turkish Fort on the coast . . . Just before dark we passed the destroyed fort. The ground was all torn around it.[28]

Soon after leaving Aden the First Contingent of the Australian Imperial Force was directed to disembark and train in Egypt. A telegram from Sir George Reid, Australia's High Commissioner in Britain, to Major-General Bridges gave the new orders without offering any explanation:

> Unforeseen circumstances, decide that the force shall train in Egypt and go to the front from there. The Australians and New Zealanders are to form a corps under General Birdwood. The locality of the camp is near Cairo.[29]

A combination of the poor winter weather in Britain, insufficient accommodation for the Australian and New Zealand troops, and the spectre of a disgruntled Ottoman Empire attempting to regain its latest lost province in the Middle East resulted in a hurried but pragmatic decision. The weather in Egypt in winter was conducive for military training; the lack of rain meant that tents could be used to house the troops and the mild to hot daytime temperatures were ideal for whipping the Antipodean contingents into a viable force. Importantly, the Western Front and the Dardanelles were only across the Mediterranean Sea from Egypt.

Thursday 26.11.14.
We left Aden at 6 A.M. but have got no definite information as to where we are bound. Still on sick list, + my arm is very painful. Got very little sleep last night, although the weather was cool. Concert at night by members of 3rd + 4th Battalion.

Friday 27.11.14.
Weather calm, + we are travelling very slowly. I was sent to Dr for my second innoculation, but he said I have enough to put up with my vaccination, + would not do me.

Saturday 28.11.14.
We are enjoying glorious weather, + have not had one rough day so far, the worst being when we left the heads at Sydney, but perhaps that was only imagination, for most of us were sick. The whole fleet are to-gether, + form a pretty picture.

Sunday 29.11.14.
Weather very chilly, + the old "Chidley" style of dress has been replaced with full uniform, + in some cases, overcoats. Church parade in the morning for an hour, + many sly games of poker + banker were noticable all the afternoon.

Monday 30.11.14.
In sight of land again to-day. The boats are opening out from one another, + seem to be getting into a different formation.

Tuesday 1st Dec. 1914.
Still in sight of land. The coast scene is one of barren, desolation, void of any kind of vegetation, + not a sign of life is to be seen. Great jagged rocks are projecting from the water near the edge, + further back, another great reef of rock sets the picture off. About 1.30 P.M. we came up with a number of boats which left the fleet this morning, lying outside the entrance to the canal, + our boat fastened to a buoy. It was a grand sight to watch the remaining boats coming up into their positions, + manouvreing about as skilfully as if they were mere rowing boats. About 11 P.M. we moved into the canal, though few knew that we were in there until reveille to-day (2nd).

Originially the Suez Canal was over 160 kilometres long, 8 metres deep, 22 metres wide on the bottom and 58 metres across on its surface. It began at Port Suez, at its mouth to the Red Sea, and carried on north to Port Said on the coast of the Mediterranean.[30] In 1914 British troops garrisoned posts along its length as an early warning system and defence against any Turkish incursions. That year 5000 ships negotiated the canal; 3000 of these were British.[31]

Wednesday 2.12.14.
At reveille, we found ourselves well into the Suez, with walls of sand on either side. In front, another boat is clearly visible, + another at the rear, ploughing their way majestically through the canal. It would appear as if a man could stand on deck + hurl a stone on to either bank of the canal, it is so narrow. Indian troops are posted in parties along either bank, +sent several semaphore signals as we passed. We then came on to a batch of British Tommies, who sent us several signals. At 8 A.M. we came to where gangs of native workmen were engaged, moving sand. They shout strangely, + cut all sorts of capers as we pass.

Finally, the end of their voyage was approaching. The presence of Indian and British troops along the Canal alerted the men that the war was getting closer. After much speculation regarding their port of disembarkation, it became clear that Egypt was to host the Australasian contingents.

2 Egypt

We have been marooned in this wretched hole too long . . .

MAJOR JAMES HEANE, COMMANDING OFFICER D COMPANY, 4TH BATTALION, IN A LETTER TO HIS BROTHER TED[1]

The following entry at the end of Jack's first diary was not in sequence and did not include a date. Jack offered no further explanation.

> On Wednesday, 800 of the 4th Batt., including myself, were poisoned.

The Wednesday in question was 2 December 1914. Other firsthand accounts confirm this dramatic statement. There was indeed a mass outbreak of food poisoning on the *Euripides* just as the ship reached Port Said, Egypt. (See the map of the First Contingent's voyage on page 15.) What happened was both cruel and very nearly disastrous. After six and a half weeks cooped up on the *Euripides* with dry land finally beckoning, hundreds of men from the 3rd Battalion, 4th Battalion and the 1st Field Ambulance suffered severe food poisoning and could be seen writhing with abdominal pain throughout the ship. Many were hospitalised on the *Euripides* and some underwent further treatment at Mena Camp. Charles Bean described it as:

> The only misfortune of importance that occurred during the whole voyage—for on the very last night of it, between Port Said and Alexandria, some 500 of the men on board of her [the *Euripides*], mostly belonging to the Fourth Infantry Battalion, fell in with something suspiciously like ptomaine poisoning. They were unable to land that day and some of them had eventually to be brought on to Mena House Hotel at the Pyramids, which has been turned into a hospital for the Australian troops.[2]

At the time food poisoning was often erroneously called 'ptomaine poisoning'. Bacteria—not ptomaines—were responsible for the outbreak.

The following accounts of this most unfortunate incident showed the difficulty of finding out what actually happened in a given situation. In this case the cause of the outbreak was subject to much speculation. Also the number of men affected by it varied wildly in the witnesses' accounts from 100 to 'practically every man on board', keeping in mind there were about 2300 troops on the transport. This was a foretaste of the men's different individual perspectives on recalling and explaining the same event, such as an action or incident at Gallipoli. Like the men's Anzac experiences, these accounts dovetailed or agreed on some important aspects, but each was unique with points of difference.

In a letter to his family, Private Vern Smythe, 3rd Battalion wrote:

> The cooks very nearly disposed of some of our men the other night. They had not kept their cooking boilers over clean, & the result was that about 400 of the men had an attack of ptomaine poisoning. Luckily it was not severe enough to be fatal, but it was pretty bad. The poor beggars were lying all over the deck and were fearfully sick. Nearly every man had to be carried to the hospital. By great good luck Bert and I escaped it. It was so bad that at 2 am the Master of the ship, & all his officers, as well as all our head officers, got up & had an inspection of the cook-house, & gave the cooks the soundest shaking up ever they are likely to get. Our Brigadier [Colonel MacLaurin] told them that if any man died over it, he would hand them over to the civil power to be tried for manslaughter. I guess that after this we will get our food cooked in clean boilers.[3]

Vern's brother, Private Bert Smythe, 3rd Battalion, also wrote to his family about the disconcerting incident:

> At present there are a large number of the 4th men down with severe internal pains. A few days before 100 odd men were taken suddenly ill during the night & there was a great to-do about it. The cooks were all roused out of bed about 1 pm & an inquiry held. The A.M.C. & all the officers were up all night trying to ease the men's sufferings.[4]

Private Richard Roberts, 3rd Battalion, was another to record the suffering:

> Thursday 3rd December. Last night almost the whole of the 3rd Battalion were half poisoned. Some of the men started to get bad an hour or so after

dinner and there was a run on the AMC all night and even this morning. The writer took bad about 10 o'clock and was vomiting until about 3 in the morning. He was also pretty crook until dinner time when he had a cup of tea and some of that doubtful creation known on board as 'Duff'. Had no breakfast at all. The sickness was accompanied by more or less violent pains in the higher abdominal regions. We got to Alexandria this morning but I was too crook to take much notice.[5]

Private Oliver Giddings, 3rd Battalion was very concise in his recollection:

Thursday 3 Dec Over 400 men sick this morning from ptomaine poison caused by the rabbit they had for dinner yesterday. I am down myself.[6]

In his diary, Lieutenant William McDonald, 4th Battalion, recorded:

Wednesday Dec 2nd . . . arrived Port Said at 2.30 pm harbour litterely jambed with shipping just crawling through nearly touching ships on each side. Town very large and dirty looking . . . proceed by train to Cairo + thence don't know how we will manage march, boiled rabbit issued to troops yesterday + over 700 down with Ptomaine poisoning. All very bad this morning so that as far as this ship concerned, disembarkation will be delayed.[7]

Private Tom Barr, 4th Battalion, was fortunate to be spared the worst of the outbreak:

Alexandria was reached this morning (3/12/14) . . . We were aware that our Batt would not disembark today as most of our boys are still suffering from some poison which was put in our food to cool our blood. One did not fail to observe that all who were laid out were mainly composed of Aus. I felt the effects just a little. The officers pretended to take the business serious but the fact of the matter was, these were not troubling as they knew only too well that it was all in the game. We were 48 hours in port before disembarking . . . [8]

However, Lance Corporal Howard McKern, 4th Battalion, suffered badly. He wrote in his diary:

2nd December 1914 We arrived at Port Said 3 pm + passed transport after transport which we had to give ship's salute to . . . Practically every man on board was down that night with ptomaine poisoning from eating some frozen rabbits. I never want to get another touch of that. Everyone was rolling about with agony.[9]

In a letter to his family, dated 11 February 1915 and published in the *Windsor and Richmond Gazette* on 26 March 1915, Private Oscar Ward 141, 1st Field Ambulance, described his experience tending to the poisoned troops before falling victim himself:

> We stayed a few hours at Port Said leaving at night, about 8.30, and arriving at Alexandria next morning. That was the most eventful night we had, at least so far as we on the *Euripides* were concerned. It was the worst night I remember putting in, for more than half the troops, who numbered 2500 odd, were down with ptomaine poisoning. Oh, it was a night of horror. All round the deck the poor chaps were moaning and groaning. It was terrible to hear them, and I will never forget it. You people in Australia can't possibly realise what an outbreak of ptomaine poisoning on a closely-packed troopship means. I worked under great difficulty, for I was very queer, and kept dosing myself from the dispensary to keep going. After going from 8 p.m. till midnight, I went to bed, but not to sleep, for I was in too great pain, and at 1.30 I was doubled up and in trying to reach the hospital for treatment collapsed on the floor, and remained there till carried into the hospital, where a hypodermic injection of morphia sent me to sleep about 3 for a couple of hours. Next day I resumed work for we were busy packing hospital stores etc., for disembarking; but I was far from well, and that feeling remained with me for about a week, but I kept going. Some of the poor chaps went straight into the hospital from the ship. I might in passing, pay a tribute to the officers both military and A.M.C., from the colonel down. They worked like Trojans. The night of the poisoning outbreak it was no uncommon sight to see an officer of high rank with his coat off almost carrying a writhing private into the hospital for treatment, and there help to administer treatment, for understand there was no poisoning in the officers' mess.[10]

Fortuitously, the officers were spared this ordeal and were able to tend to their men. Captain Jack Bean was the 3rd Battalion's medical officer and Charles Bean's brother. He initially enlisted in the 4th Battalion as its Regimental Medical Officer on 20 August 1914. He signed off on the medical examinations of two of Jack's H Company mates, privates Clyde Bock and Syd Bartle, on 27 and 29

August, respectively. Captain Bean knew senior officers in the 4th Battalion, courtesy of his pre-war service of three years as medical officer in the 24th Infantry, East Sydney Regiment, a militia unit. His other military experience was more exotic, having spent three years in the Cambridge University Volunteer Rifles while studying at the university during the family's extended stay in England. However, soon after enlisting, Jack Bean transferred from the 4th Battalion to become the medical officer of the 3rd.[11] He wrote an account of the poisoning episode in the 3rd Battalion history, *Randwick to Hargicourt*:

> Regarding the health of the troops, in those early days an interesting statement is contributed by the battalion medical officer, Captain J.W.B. Bean:
>
> 'We had a great deal of sickness on board [*Euripides*]. The men were very crowded, and the heat of the tropics was stifling. We had quite a lot of pneumonia, and two of our poor chaps died of it. Just as we got to Egypt there was a tremendous epidemic of colic, hundreds suffering, many were brought to the hospital in a state of collapse. We made them very sick with soda, gave injections of morphia and atropine, lots of hot water bottles and abdominal massage and nobody died though some looked rather near it. It was a mystery. The steam cooker was found in a very dirty state, much food refuse having silted between the inner and outer jackets. This may have had something to do with it. One of the horses, too, had strangles, and sprayed his nasal discharges over the lines of mess orderlies as they waited by the kitchens with their dixies. This was looked on as a possible cause and the third idea was arsenical poisoning by a spy but we never knew for certain. I shall never forget the hospital deck, strewn thick with writhing, groaning men—for all the world like a battlefield.'[12]

It was odd that Jack Bean didn't mention the cooked rabbits harbouring the infection, considering three of the other accounts did blame them. He seemed to air possible causes without determining the real culprit. As the 3rd Battalion's medical officer, Jack Bean answered the call for help that night and later conducted a thorough investigation, hence his detailed report. The rabbits were the catalyst; the filthy steam cooker the likely cause. Vern Smythe's account pointed to the probable cause being the dirty steam cooker, judging by the agitated response after the officers' inspection of the cook house and the brigadier's threat to the cooks.

The list of possible contaminants was quite entertaining—the rabbits themselves, dirty cooking facilities, infected nasal discharges from horses spraying onto the dixies used to carry food, arsenic administered by a spy, poison to cool the men's blood—the ship was rife with theories. Another explanation was offered by Corporal George Mitchell of the 10th Battalion on the *Ascanius* who claimed in his diary that 500 men on the *Euripides* were struck down by infected products bought from local boats circling the transports as they manoeuvred in the harbour.[13]

However, the sad case of Percy Parker showed how serious the outbreak really was. Parker was one of the 4th Battalion's signallers, an English-born veteran of the Royal Navy and Australian militia. A victim of the food poisoning on the *Euripides*, he was initially hospitalised on the transport and cared for by the 1st Field Ambulance. After further hospital treatment in Egypt over the next two months, Parker appeared before a medical board convened at Mena House on 9 February 1915. The proceedings of the board were recorded. The response to the query, 'Date and place of origin of disability', was 'Had Ptomaine Poisoning on board transport *Euripides*. Never felt well since. Weak and sick ever since.' Another question sealed his fate, 'What is his present condition?' The response was 'Weak + ill looking. Heart Weak'. Consequently, the board recommended Parker be 'Discharged as permanently unfit'. Parker was sent home, returning to Australia on the *Ulysses* on 15 April 1915 as a 'Non Venereal'. (At least he was spared the stigma of being sent home as a 'Venereal'.) He was ruled 'Permanently Unfit' and discharged after a second medical examination on 25 June 1915 in Sydney.[14] Other men, such as Private James Brown and Private Stan Randall, were hospitalised at Mena as a result of the poisoning but were released to the 4th Battalion after receiving further treatment.

~

Thursday, 3 December 1914, was the day the 4th Battalion finally reached their point of disembarkation—Alexandria in Egypt—to what must have seemed like the fabled Promised Land after spending six and a half weeks on board a very crowded vessel.

Egypt in December 1914 was changing its political status from a self-governing province of the Ottoman Empire to a protectorate of the British Empire, effectively changing one colonial master for another. By 1914 Egypt was very much under the economic and political control of Britain. The change in status was a formality, a realpolitik recognition of the de facto situation. Under the new arrangement, while the government and leader were Egyptian, the British were 'responsible for the protection of her interests'.[15] This change was enacted on 18 December when Sultan Hussein Kamel was declared the ruler of the protectorate.[16] So it was to a welcoming Egypt that Jack and the battalion arrived.

Thursday 3.12.14.

We arrived at Alexandria at 11 o'clock. Several other transports were in before us, + we got a cheer as our vessel passed them, on her way to the wharf. In the afternoon several men came on board, selling newspapers, but they contain very little news of interest. We were ordered to prepare to leave the boat, + after waiting for some time, were alowed to take our gear back to the mess deck, as there was no train to take us to our destination [Cairo]. Light rain was falling during afternoon.

Friday 4.12.14.

After breakfast, we were set to roll our blankets, + get everything squared up on our mess deck, + prepare to leave. At about 10 A.M. we were taken off the boat, (the first time we have touched land since leaving Sydney.), + commenced loading our kits + stores in 3rd class railway carriages. At 12 o'clock, all was safely on the train, + we started on our journey, a distance of something like 100 miles. A + H Coy's forming advance guard for the 4th Batt. The engines + carriages are comical concerns, + managed by natives. Before we left the wharf, we had orders not to buy goods from natives along the route, but this rule was severely broken before we went far, + to the sorrow of the culprits. Many were trying to sell whisky, bearing the label of well-known brands, as Dewars, black + white, + others, + I saw one chap hand 2/- out of the window to purchase a bottle. The nigger at once took to his heels, while the victim stood by, giving vent to his feelings to an unsympathetic crowd of listeners. The scenery is very interesting. After about ½ hour in the train we passed a native village, the whole concern being made of mud, + looks like one large building, with many doors, + a few windows. Part of the roof is dome shaped, + the rest is covered with corn stalks. The whole thing is built of mud, roof + all. A little further on, we passed a few palm trees, presumably date-palms, as the fruit on them is covered with canvas. Here + there, is a vegetable garden, being tended by natives + the vegetables look very healthy. A small canal of water runs on one side of the line, + the whole field is well irrigated therefrom. Cotton is also grown along the route, + corn is abundant, bearing splendid large cobs. The stations all bear peculiar names, written in Arabic + also French, + native porters + police were the only ones on the platforms, except for an occasional hawker. At about 4.30 P.M. I got my glimpse of the pyramids, a great distance to

> the west of us. At 5.45 we arrived at Cairo. It was quite dark, + after staying at the station for a few minutes, we were taken a little further in the train to a siding, where we detrained. After a fatigue party had been detailed to unload train, the remainder of us were taken a few yards away piled arms, + after a short wait, were marched in single file, past a table, where each man was handed a pannikin of steaming chocolate, a French roll, + a piece of Dutch cheese, all of which I thoroughly enjoyed, as we had only a few hard biscuits + a little tinned beef for lunch, + the atmosphere was very chilly. After about an hour + a half wait, we were marched to the tram terminus, where we were lined up to wait for trams to take us to Mena, the site of our camp. Eventually, we got on trams, + were whisked off at a great pace. The journey took a little more than an hour, + at last we found ourselves almost at the foot of the two great pyramids.

The site selected for the 1st Australian Division camp was at Giza, just below the plateau with its imposing pyramids and Sphinx, and was, according to Bean:

> . . . ten miles from the centre of the city. Mena Camp stretched for nearly a mile up the desert valley. The headquarters offices of the division were in the manager's house behind the hotel; the hotel itself was taken over as an Australian hospital. The ramshackle grandstand of the old racecourse on the desert became the ordnance store. Close to it, at the end of the extended tramway, gradually rose stacks of fodder and supplies.[17]

The New Zealand Expeditionary Force quarters were across town on Cairo's northern outskirts at Zeitoun. The 1st Australian Light Horse Brigade settled into Ma'adi Camp, south of Cairo.[18] (See the map of Egypt on page 47.)

Jack described the arrival of the 1st Division at the camp:

> The natives who could speak English, did not lose any time in testing our mental faculties, for, they crowded round the tram, wanting to tell our fortunes, sell us "ancient" coins etc. but they got no patronage. Donkey carts + camels were lined up on the road, to carry our kit + stores to the camp, about ½ a mile away. We unloaded the baggage, + put it on the new transport. Two men were put in charge of each load, to see it safely brought to camp. I was put in charge of a camel, laden with A.M.C. stores. No sooner were we outside the avenue, + out of the officers sight, than my guide suddenly stopped. I made signs for him to

keep going, but he insisted on an explanation. At last, I understood. He wanted a piastre, (2½d) to make the camel lie down + let me ride to camp. The only money I had was Australian silver, so I handed him a 3d piece. He refused it at first, did not like the look of the Kangaroo, probably, but eventually took it, + I climbed on. Up got the camel, + away we went, but never again. It was the roughest ride I have ever had, or want. Arrived at camp at 11.30 P. M. unloaded my charges, + went on helping the boy to get things a bit straight. At 1.30 A.M. the whole of our baggage had arrived, + we got one blanket each, stretched out on the sand, + had a few hour's well deserved sleep. It was frightfully cold, though, + the blankets were saturated with dew when we rose.

Winter in the desert in the northern hemisphere meant freezing nights and days that varied in temperature from hot to occasionally cold. That first morning must have seemed slightly surreal for the goggle-eyed first AIF arrivals camped next to the Giza plateau, with the pyramids of the Old Kingdom's 4th Dynasty rulers Khufu, Khephren and Menkaure towering over them and below, facing the Nile, the inscrutable Great Sphinx,[19] impassively watching their antics as it had a myriad of previous invaders—Hyksos, Macedonian, Roman, Crusader, Ottoman, French and British. The Great Pyramid of Giza, Khufu's burial place, was the only remaining wonder of the Seven Wonders of the Ancient World that was largely intact. Built in about 2560–2540 BCE,[20] the tomb's dimensions were quite staggering—it was originally 146 metres in height, 230 metres square and contained 2,300,000 stone blocks, each weighing 2.5 tons or 2.26 tonnes.[21]

Many Australian accounts mention the pyramids, especially Khufu's, which is also known as Cheops' Pyramid. In a letter to his family, Lieutenant Owen Howell-Price, a 3rd Battalion subaltern, described it as 'a wonderful piece of work, there is no doubt'.[22]

Naturally enough it soon became an Australian rite of passage to climb the pyramids. One who did was Private Ted Meggy of the 3rd Battalion, who wrote in a letter to his sister:

> We are camped about 10mls from Cairo right below the three famous Pyrimids and the Spinks. The Pyrimids I have climbed to the top and been all through and I had my photo taken in front of the Spinks and Pyrimids.[23]

A holiday snap in front of these wonders became *de rigueur* for the Australians. Jack and his mates had their photograph taken in front of the Sphinx, with Khufu's enormous edifice looming faintly in the distance.

Saturday 5.12.14.
Reveille 6.30. A bitterly cold wind is blowing, but it is a gloriously fine morning. For breakfast, we scored a very small piece of tinned meat, a pot of tea, + a couple of biscuits, which were very hard, + tested our masticating organs. I was detailed for guard, + spent an uninteresting day. The pyramids tempt one sorely, to be explored, as we can see many of our coy, who are off duty, climbing to the top. Some territorials are camped a short distance off. The natives are continually asking us for cigarettes, + their language gets on one's nerves. We had biscuits for dinner, + for tea, a small allowance of stew. When the sun went down, it was again very cold.

Sunday 6.12.14.
Breakfast consisted of two or three biscuits, + a dixie of tea. Our 24 hour's guard should have ended at 8.30, but we were not relieved until after 10. We hoped for a few hours rest for the remainder of the day, but were disappointed. After dinner, which consisted of a small Dixie of stew, we were fallen into line up kits etc, + mark out positions for the tents when they come, which job took 4 hours, (only) 3 officers + 5 sergeants being in charge. Talk about muddling: they know nothing about the job, + Color-serg. Coxhead, I'll wager, would supervise the lot, + have it finished in half an hour. It was quite dark when we finished, + were given a piece of bread + pot of tea for our evening meal. Of course, we must make an allowance for the scarcity of food, as I believe the people here only had 3 days notice of our landing. We have no tents, but every man has two heavy blankets, + with the greatcoats, we manage to keep fairly warm at night.

Monday 7.12.14.
A gloriously fine morning, a bit on the cold side. We formed a fatigue, straightening the lines again, or at least, trying to, + when we had finished that job, I could see no improvement on yesterdays work.
In the afternoon we were marched to the top of the hill near the pyramids, + formed a long line to the camp. The men on top gathered stones + passed them down along the line, the idea (a slow one) being

to make a road. Some of the boys worked well, but towards evening, they began to disappear, + visit the pyramids, so that made it much harder for those left in the line.

Tuesday 8.12.14.

We had a short march this morning, along the avenue leading to town. It is a most glorious avenue, with beautiful large trees on either side of a splendidly kept level road. After marching about two miles to a place called Chareh el Haram, we halted for a short spell. On looking round, I got a glimpse of the sphinx. On one side of the road, large fields of well cultivated land can be seen corn, lucerne, + green herbage is abundant. On the other side, is a vast stretch of desert, + in the far distance, a native village is clearly discernible. Eventually, we marched back to camp at a fast pace. Bread + butter for dinner, + a very small allowance of it. In the afternoon, more fatigue, passing stones, etc. + another go at the lines, which, by the way, are not yet anything like straight. The water is now laid on to the camp. Many men have broken camp, + gone in to Cairo, + as a consequence, all good conduct men have to suffer. In Battalion orders to-day, it is laid down that no leave whatever is to be granted, until the others return. The Colonel, however, expressed his satisfaction of the way the willing workers stuck to their work, + got the camp ship-shape, + promised to see the Brigadier personally, + do his best to get leave for us. He succeeded in getting permission to grant leave to 25% of the battalion from 2 to 10 P.M.

Wednesday 9.12.14.

Our coy again for fatigue. We were marched a short distance from our lines with picks + shovels. A movable tram line had been laid down for a distance of ¼ of a mile, + there are several small trucks mounted on it. We were handed baskets, which the natives use for carrying stones, + instructed to fill them with stones, carry them to the trucks, + bring them along the tramline to finish our road. I don't know what the natives thought, but they sat a short distance from us, + jabbered incessantly. We worked hard till dinner time, when we returned to camp. Had dinner, which was a slight improvement on what we've been having. A streak of luck for me in the afternoon. I was granted leave. After being inspected by officers, color-sergeants etc, for an hour or so, we at last got beyond the camp boundary. We got into town in the tram at 4.30., + as soon as we stepped on the road; were surrounded by a crowd of youngsters, wanting the job to clean our boots. ½ piaster was the price they charged. The first place we made for, was a tuck-shop. We found one, + went in. We ordered eggs + bacon, which turned up after half an hours wait, but it was a job to find the bacon. No tea was served with the meal, so we made a separate order for that. When we had actually had an apology for a feed, we asked for the bill, which amounted to 12 piastres (about 2/6) each. By the time we walked up + down the street a few times, it was time to think of returning, so we saw very little of the town.

Thursday 10.12.14.

This morning was a very heavy one, the Coy formed upon Batt parade ground after breakfast, + after a couple of hours hard drill were taken for a march across the sand returning quite close to the pyramids, + were given 10 minutes rest when we got near the Sphynx, giving us a splendid opportunity of viewing it closely. It is a large concern, but not nearly so large as I expected it to be. We were given a whole afternoon to ourselves, without being called out even to line the tents! We are told by officers, that, instead of receiving full rations, as laid down by British Army regulations, we are to receive 6d a day, in addition to the present ration of meat, bread, potatoes, tea + sugar. They stipulate also, that the 6d Must be spent at Dickesons (who have a large marquee on the ground), we not being allowed to handle money, nor, by what I can see, examine the receipts. We have had 1/4 lb of butter per man, per day so far, which, they tell us, cuts out the money. Butter is 1/8 Per lb. In town now, so, if Dickerson is making the extra 4d per lb, why should we be compelled to spend with him, + why can we not buy what we wish? Of course, we know very well that a certain crowd would buy beer with it, but there is a way of beating them—by appointing a head of each mess, as we used at Liverpool, + giving the boss power to buy what he likes. If he goes beyond the mark, pitch him out, + get another. We must, however, give two of our officers, lieutenants Fanning + Seldon their due, for they are doing all in their power to make matters better, but older, +, it seems, more experienced hands have got in first, + the swindle will take some ferreting to expose.

In 1914 a significant part of the Sphinx was covered by sand. The creature's lower half, including its impressive 15-metre long front paws, was largely buried by the desert. Consequently, the full majesty of the monolithic statue was hidden.

Friday 11.12.14.

A gloriously fine day. Battalion drill all day. The food question is still being heatedly debated. A proposal has been put before us, that each man put in 1 Piastre a day, to bring up the amount of tucker a soldier needs, but we fail to fall in any further. With skilful management, I'm certain the 6d would be ample. Then it was decided to send a man from our coy to town, find out the prices of commodities, +, if he could purchase goods in town any cheaper than at the Army Contractor (Dickerson), to give the piastre business a trial for a week.

Saturday 12.12.14.

Parade on batt parade ground this morning, + half holiday this afternoon from 2 P.M. So far, we have 6 tents to accommodate the coy., one being reserved for officers, one for sergeants, + one for each section, so the majority of us are undergoing the good old open air treatment. Complaints about the shortage of food still roll in.

Sunday 13.12.14.

Church parade at 9.30. Went to the Methodist portion, the sermon being delivered by Capt. McKenzie + Chaplain of 1st Battalion. I spent the afternoon looking at the dead city, which is now being excavated near the Pyramids.

Monday 14.12.14.

A new, + heavy part of our training commences to-day. Reveille 6.15 breakfast + parade 8 A.M. Then we start out about 3 miles over the desert, to a parade ground, + after two hours drill + half an hours rest, set out on the return march at 12.45 P.M., being dismissed at 2. I fancy the Major, [Macnaghten] whom everyone has perfect confidence in, must have been testing our lasting powers, for he led the way at break-neck speed over the sand, never once stopping until he had gained the top of a rather steep sand hill, with the result that several hundred men got knocked up, + lagged behind, frightened to face the hill. Tucker still very scant, + complaints still poured into the seemingly deaf ears of the orderly officers.

During the first two weeks in Egypt the 4th Battalion suffered its first deaths since leaving Sydney. Somewhat remarkably, the two casualties were brothers, Privates Edward and Myles Cox, who died from pneumonia—Edward on

13 December and Myles three days later. Their mother, Alice, and father, Edward, were informed about Edward's death by the local Anglican minister, Reverend William Hereford, as the family belonged to the Church of England. This was arranged by the military authorities and became a common practice during the war in an attempt to ease the anguish of families and to give the terrible news some dignity and authority. The telegram from the AIF instructed:

> OFFICIALLY REPORTED THAT NUMBER 164 PRIVATE EDWARD KING STANDISH COX FOURTH BATTALION DIED AT ALEXANDRIA THIRTEENTH INSTANT FROM PNEUMONIA. PLEASE ARRANGE ANGLICAN CLERGYMAN CONVEY INTELLIGENCE TO FATHER E.S.COX WOY WOY AND CONVEY MINISTER'S SINCERE AND DEEP REGRET.

On 16 December, after visiting the family, Reverend Hereford replied to the relevant authorities, also in a telegram: 'Family appreciate sympathetic message further news acceptable.'

He returned to the family home in Woy Woy, New South Wales, a couple of days later with further, albeit tragic, news; this time to inform the Cox family that their other son in the AIF, Myles, had also died from pneumonia only days after his older brother.[24] There was no account of this visit in Myles's personnel dossier. His family would have been devastated. The boys were on active service, but they certainly weren't involved in any fighting. To lose one son to sickness was hard enough, but to lose two within days of one another to the same condition was heartbreaking.

The premature deaths of Edward and Myles Cox in Egypt from pneumonia might have been related to the effects of the food poisoning on the *Euripides* about a fortnight earlier. Private Oscar Ward, who gave an engrossing account of the mass poisoning, nursed one of the Cox boys at the newly established Mena House Base Hospital:

> First on arrival here I worked at our Base Hospital as night orderly in a medical ward, and it was my unpopular duty to nurse one of the Cox brothers who died of pneumonia, and whose photo appeared in one of the Sydney papers. Poor chap, he was delirious for several nights before he died, and kept one going, for as soon as I left his side to attend to another patient he would jump out of bed.[25]

Oscar was present when his patient, probably Edward, died. There was no cure for pneumonia in 1914 so doctors could only treat the symptoms.

A memorial service, conducted by Reverend Bill Hereford, was held in Woy Woy on Sunday, 20 December 1914. Originally planned to remember and to mourn Edward Cox, the service was dedicated to the inexplicable loss of both brothers. *The Nepean Times* offered a eulogy for the Cox boys the following Saturday, 26 December 1914:

> The two deceased scions of the great old Australian family enlisted among the first batch of volunteers . . . and were two fine strapping typical Australian youths, possessed of the gallantry and high spiritedness of their stock—a family which has contributed 'some of the best' to Australian Expeditionary Forces; as their forebears contributed to the roll-call of the British Armies in days of old.

The Cox brothers were buried in Egypt—Edward in the Alexandria (Chatby) Military and War Memorial Cemetery, and Myles in the Cairo War Memorial Cemetery.[26] Photographs of their graves were sent to Alice and Edward, their grieving parents, and the boys' siblings. It was odd that the brothers weren't buried next to each other.

The AIF settled into its new digs at Mena, 'home sweet home' as Jack called it in his Egypt diary, and commenced training in the desert. After nearly two months confined on transports, Cairo represented a huge temptation for the men, who were armed with money, appetites and a curiosity that needed satisfying. Initially, entertainment for the troops in the camp was limited. They climbed the pyramids, had their photographs taken in front of the Sphinx, went to the zoological gardens at nearby Giza and frequented Cairo, sightseeing, eating, drinking, carousing and, for some, indulging in its attractions of the flesh. Christmas celebrations were cause for more of these activities.

Although Jack kept a low profile, he thoroughly enjoyed himself, too. Jack was a 'good conduct' man during his time in the military. He took his soldiering seriously yet he retained his sense of humour. His diaries reveal a dry appreciation of his brothers in arms. They also show that Jack acted as a banker within No. 15 Platoon in Egypt—a position of trust. Jack didn't drink alcohol, didn't frequent brothels and only went on authorised leave. He certainly wasn't a wowser, as his Christmas letter showed. He had his own approach to the situation, based on his personal choices and his enlistment in the army. Most of his fellow soldiers had a similar commitment to their duties.

Jack's Christmas letter was published in *The Mudgee Guardian* on 4 February 1915. It is the only surviving piece of correspondence from Jack, even though he wrote regularly to his family.

XMAS IN EGYPT

Some Interesting News

Following is a letter written by Mr. Jack Collyer (who is with the Australian Expeditionary Force in Egypt) to his parents, Mr. and Mrs. G.T. Collyer, of South Mudgee:–

'We spent a fairly merry Xmas, but, of course, thought of home could not be dismissed. I woke at 5 a.m. to hear splendid music, a brass band playing Xmas carols, a hundred yards away from my tent. Talk about thrill—it was glorious. I lay awake listening to the grand strains of 'Hark, the Herald Angels Sing' and others, and my mind wandered to Mudgee. Our time is several hours behind Australian time. Reveille sounded at 6.15 a.m., and we had to turn out. Breakfast was in the tent, we prepared a stock of tinned fruit, biscuits, etc., the previous night, and, with our ration of bread and tea we had a meal. Then we had a roll-call, only about ten men being absent from camp without leave. At 9.30 the battalion was formed up for church. Dismissed at 11 a.m. and at 12 we had another roll-call. This time 36 men were found to be missing without leave. We had arranged messing tables and stools outside the tents and at 1 p.m. our food was brought. Our usual of meat, made into stew, which we got every day, and the table decorated with that we could get out of our kit bags to make it look a trifle homely. Fruit was in abundance, also nuts, and biscuits, raisens on a branch, a bottle of ale or a bottle of mineral water. These extras were purchased with money given for the purpose in Sydney, I hear. All were happy and we set to it. When we were fairly at our meal our good old Colonel (Thompson) came and wished us a merry Xmas and hoped we would be back with our loved ones for next Xmas dinner (I heard yesterday that Thompson was a brother to W Thompson, who used to live at Dewhurst). Then Major McNaughton came to greet us, and by the time the beer was gone the boys were a jolly party. I secured a pass for town after dinner. The natives at camp will never forget this Xmas. Not one was allowed to even look hungry, and they could not voice their thanks sufficiently. They do not recognise our Xmas and were working all day. I took my leave, arriving at Cairo at 3, per motor. The ten mile fare is 2/-. The town was crowded. Soldiers (Australians, New Zealanders and Territorials) were swarming everywhere. I was invited to the barracks where the Dragoons were quartered. Arrived there, I was shown round the various places and was informed that no Australian was going to leave there without getting gloriously drunk.

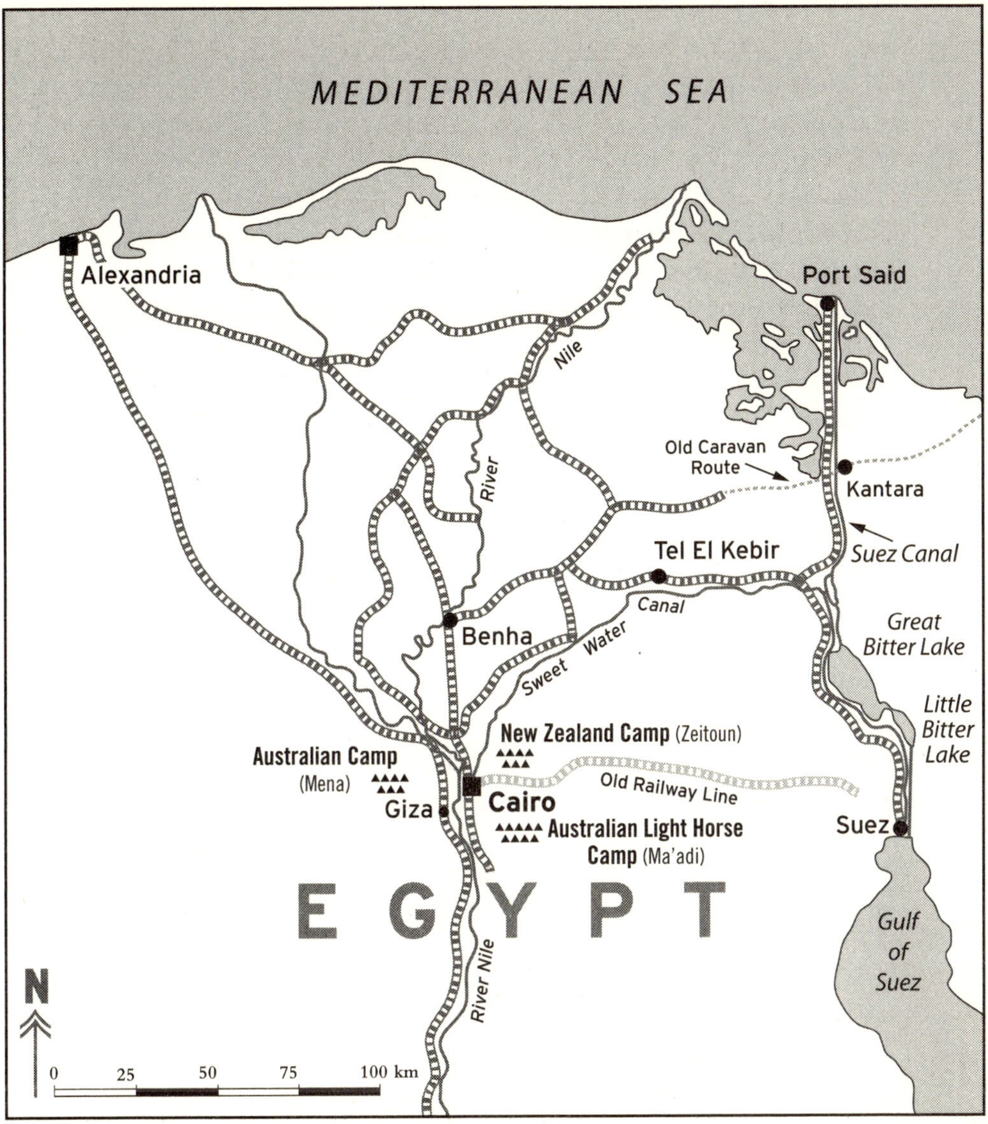

Australasian training camps in Egypt

The 4th Battalion trained at Mena, outside Cairo, from 3 December 1914 to 4 April 1915.

I gave them a bit of straight talk about Australia life, and the free and easy customs, and then finally succeeded in escaping—sober. After this war I believe we will get a run of splendid immigrants. They were a grand lot and one could not help feeling at home in their company. The think [sic] that tickled me was the proud way they told that their Colonel gave them all 5 piastres (10s 1/2d) and a box of five woodbines. I fancied our Colonel offering our boys the same amount. We were paid 8 pounds /4 on Xmas Eve, so were able to bless ourselves rather liberally. There is no one like the Australians in the eyes of the 'Terriers' and, in fact the whole of the Cairo populace and Australia is being advertised as it never was before. At 10 P.M. after several futile attempts to board a tram, a party of six of us secured a motor car, and were whisked at break-neck pace to camp, doing the journey in 20 minutes. If any man wants adventure and hair-breadth escapes he only needs to visit Cairo and engage a motor car. They have no speed limit, and seldom slacken speed to turn corners. The roads are always crowded with traffic, especially the pyramid road, when the boys are returning from leave. At roll-call this morning 20 men of our company were missing and at noon the number had swelled to 40, so you see they are going the pace. The penalty for this is 7 days' C. B. (confined to barracks) for each day's absence, and they have to answer every half hour until Tattoo, so we will have a list of defaulters next week. I visited the ruins near the pyramids this afternoon. They are still excavating and coming to fresh wonders daily. To go through one pyramid and see all that is to be seen in it takes a whole day, and, so far, I have not had one at my disposal. It is rumoured here, on good authority, that we are leaving for the front at the end of January. I sincerely hope it is so, for this sand marching is monotonous.'

By the end of December it was plain that not everyone in the AIF was totally committed to the arduous desert training program. As Jack's diary entries and Christmas letter showed, some men came and went, following their own agenda. However, Jack was upbeat about the favourable impression the contingent was presenting in Egypt. He also referred to 'the free and easy customs' of his homeland, his interpretation of the high-spiritedness of his mates on leave in what was a new world to them. Dubbed 'six bob a day tourists', according to Professor Bill Gammage—a prominent historian and author of *The Broken Years*, the acclaimed study of the Anzacs—the Australians:

With and without leave crowded into Cairo, first to a good meal at a 'posh' hotel, then, often, to the drinking and vice dens about the Haret el Wasser. They hired donkeys from the natives and ran wild, laughing races down the streets and along the footpaths and through the hotels. They upset fruit and lolly trays, they gambled, fought and played pranks, they brawled and rioted, they assaulted military police. When they were ready to return to camp, they would crowd onto a tram, toss off the driver, and career wildly at full speed through the darkened streets, some of them clinging boisterously to the sides and roof of the vehicle until at last it halted outside the camp. Or they commandeered gharries or bikes or donkeys to make the return journey . . . [27]

Snowy Robson, from Jack's section, recalled such a lark:

The funniest thing I saw was a party of about 50 soldiers waiting in Cairo for a tram. It was the last tram to the camp that night, and they could see from a distance it was packed; so they hired a donkey, put the most intoxicated man on it, and started running about saying the Sultan was coming. Everybody got out of the tram to see the Sultan and the soldiers got in—donkey and all. The donkey was put off at the next stop.[28]

New Year's Eve was another occasion that featured much revelry on the part of the troops. Howard McKern of the 4th Battalion enjoyed the evening's entertainment, writing in his diary:

Great Scotchman's evening tonight. All the bagpipes etc in the camp were massed for the occasion. We had a great Scotch concert too.[29]

Oliver Giddings of the 3rd Battalion had an even more memorable night:

I had the best New Year's Eve of my life . . . After we finished our feast and drank all the toasts imaginable we carried our Sergeant to his tent shoulder high. Then we started out through the lines after the drum and bugle and every tin dish available and we marched through the lines of the third, fourth and fifth batts then we held a meeting on the road . . . Then we made for the first and second and finally finished up by giving the Colonel three hearty cheers and he came out and made a speech and shook hands with us. It was two o'clock and then we made for the tent and met McGarlane at the tent with a bottle so we had a

> song and a toast and broke up. It was three o'clock when we finished and I went to bed just as I stood.[30]

Christmas spirit and New Year's Eve hijinks were one thing, but drunkenness, unauthorised leave and venereal disease began to appear in the ranks of the AIF. This became a problem across the contingent; so much so that by the end of December the hierarchy of the AIF decided on a simple but effective punishment—persistent transgressors and troublemakers would be sent home to Australia in disgrace. Some of the men who had contracted venereal disease were treated in Egypt, but the more severe cases were sent home. Each battalion removed from its strength those men whose actions had brought disrepute on the troops. On 3 February 1915 the hospital ship *Kyarra* departed Suez for Australia, carrying 304 returnees. Of these, 173 men were deemed medically unfit, including 24 men with venereal diseases. The rest, 131 men, were to be discharged for disciplinary reasons, their services no longer required.[31]

As well, Major-General Bridges asked Charles Bean, the Official Correspondent, to send a despatch to Australian newspapers, explaining why so many men were returning in order to prepare the ground for the reaction to the disciplinary measures at home. The following is a transcript of Bean's notorious communiqué, written on 29 December 1914, about undesirable elements in the AIF acting in a way that brought shame on it. He praised the bulk of the Australians for their creditable demeanour, but was scathing in regard to those few who were running amok. It was published in *The Argus,* a leading Melbourne newspaper, on Thursday, 21 January 1915. Unfortunately for Bean it ruined his relationship with many of the men, including officers, for a considerable time. It didn't seem to matter that Bean qualified his comments and only referred to a small minority. In the eyes of the troops the reputation of the contingent was damaged and they reacted accordingly. The overwhelming majority of the AIF were 'good conduct' men like Jack. They felt Bean had sullied the good name of the Australians. The backlash against him didn't surface until late February, when word from Australia about their apparently aberrant behaviour reached the troops in Mena Camp in letters from concerned relatives and friends. This is what Bean wrote:

> **WEEDING OUT PROCESS**
>
> **A candid statement**
>
> C.E.W. Bean, official reporter with the First Australian Expeditionary Force in Egypt, in a despatch dated from Mena Camp, Cairo, December 29, said:—It is idle to contend that the Australian is at present making

quite the impression which Australians hope he will make either on civilians or upon the great soldiers under whose eyes they come. I was speaking the other day to one of the most distinguished men in the British army. 'They are as fine a body of men physically as I have ever seen,' he said, 'but do all Australians drink so much?' The truth is that there are a number of men in those who were accepted for service abroad who are not fit to be sent abroad to represent Australia. They may, some of them, have been men who had seen service in South Africa or the regular army, or they may have appeared hard bitten, and used to hardship, but in recruiting an army, just as picking a cricket or football team to represent Australia, the inclusion of a man who has not got the necessary moral qualities, however splendid his physical qualifications may be, is apt to do more harm than good. There is only a small percentage—possibly 1 or 2 per cent—in the force, which is really responsible for the occurrences about which Cairo is beginning to talk: the great majority of the men are keen, intelligent, well-restrained young Australians, who you will meet enjoying their hours of leave in front of the cafes, or in the museum, or the zoological gardens, or the postcard shops, dressed as neatly as any of the other soldiers on a holiday would behave. They have the material in them not merely for as good a force as the New Zealanders, or the Territorials, but to one's own thinking, of a better force, because the Australians here, besides having the best physique, are, man for man, more highly strung, and if anything quicker-witted. But there is in the Australian ranks a proportion of men who are uncontrolled, slovenly, and in some cases, what few Australians can be accused of being—dirty. In a certain number of cases it is noticeable that these men are wearing the South African ribbon. Possibly they are the men who, since returning from that war, have never had any settled occupation, and who were therefore the first to enlist when recruiting for the present force was begun, or it may be that the discipline in the South African campaign was very much slacker than that required of troops before they will be permitted to go to the front in the present class of warfare. Or it may be merely that a certain class of old soldier is given to the very childish habit of showing off before the young soldier, and giving him examples of the sort of thing he thinks may with impunity be done by any one that knows the ropes. Whatever the reason, it has been noticed by too many people to admit of doubt that, whilst many of the most capable and splendid members of the force are men with South African experience, there is a class of old soldier who, so far from being the most suitable member of the force, is the least suitable of any. Many young soldiers take these men at their true worth.

Losing good name

'It's the likes of them that are going to spoil the game for the rest of us, and lose us our leave,' I heard one youngster say a few days since. 'The fellows are getting a bit fed up with them down amongst our lot.' But they are really doing a very much more serious thing than losing other soldiers their leave. They are losing Australia her good name in the outside world, and those Australians who happen to live in Cairo, or are in touch with the world outside the camps, have the mortification of looking on whilst day by day the reputation of Australia slowly vanishes before the actions of a handful of rowdies, who do not really represent the country. The Territorials have not the physique, and some of the Lancashire regiments seem to be composed largely of mere children, but by dint of hard work they have become thoroughly smart soldiers, and, although both amongst them and the New Zealanders there has been a certain amount of the hard living, which will always be found where great numbers of men are collected, none who is not deaf can hide from himself the fact that the talk at present current in Cairo attaches to the Australian force rather than to the Territorials, or, as far as I can judge, to the New Zealanders.

One does not wish to give the impression that things have reached the stage of a scandal or anything approaching it. Steps will doubtless be taken to correct it, as they have been taken before, and the Australian force will be doing itself credit before it has finished its training, and will be worthy of the majority of the men comprised in it. The New Zealanders have just taken steps to get rid of a certain number of men who were doing little good in their force, and the same, or some similar step, will no doubt be taken with the Australians. But it is just as well that the Australian public should be aware of the reason for the return of the majority of the men who are returning or have returned since the expedition sailed. It is easy for a man to return to his native village and reap a certain amount of heroworship on the ground that he was invalided, or to pitch a story before an admiring crowd at the local hotel of how he showed them that he was not going to stand any nonsense, and finally pitched in his resignation. The facts are that a certain number of men have been invalided through serious sickness or accident, neither of which were their own fault. A certain number also were sent back some time ago from Albany and

> Colombo because some of them, no doubt, on conscientious grounds, and others for reasons best known to themselves, refused to be vaccinated. A few others have been and will be sent back because they have contracted certain diseases by which after all the trouble of months of training and of the sea voyage they have unfitted themselves to do the work for which they enlisted. And a percentage will probably find their way back from here, the reason for those whose return has been that they have damaged their country's reputation, and a few of them have been got rid of as the best means of preserving it.

In his diary entries for 25 February and 13 March, Walter Dexter, the Anglican chaplain of the 5th Battalion, expressed the common outrage generated throughout the AIF by Bean's article. Dexter was no greenhorn when it came to military matters. He was a decorated Boer War veteran, a wearer of the South African ribbon and the holder of a Distinguished Conduct Medal, awarded to him during his South African service in Lumsden's Horse.[32] On 25 February he wrote:

> Great indignation in camp over Mr Bean's articles in the Australian papers about the behaviour of the troops in Cairo. It is a bit over the fence and altogether gives a false impression of the actual circumstances. Bean is foolish and has never had anything to do with Garrison towns. Our crime sheet will compare very favourably with the crime sheet of regular troops of equal numbers. Bean has made a mistake and the anger against him is great. Nothing else is talked about in camp . . . In the early days all the follies of the New Zealanders were put down to the Australians, for the people did not realise the difference. The Australian soldiers naturally predominate and hence everything gets blamed on them.[33]

Again on 13 March, Dexter was moved to remark:

> Mr Bean's letter has stirred up the whole Australian force as nothing else in the world could. They feel it was unjust, uncalled for and that anxiety has been raised in Australia amongst our loved ones . . . On account of the feeling in camp Mr Bean felt compelled to issue an explanation and also quoted two of his later telegrams in which he praised up the Australians to the skies.[34]

In a letter dated 17 and 19 March to Captain Ley of Dubbo, Major James Heane, the commanding officer of Jack's company, also commented on Bean's diatribe:

> The men are very wrath at the reports that have been put in the Australian papers about their misbehaviour and comparing them badly with the New Zealanders. Our men were no worse than either the New Zealanders or the 'Terriers,' and probably not as bad as either of them. The whole of the trouble arose at Christmas time after the men had no leave or no cash; and, of course, when they got both they got a bit merry, and I think a few of the 'Angels' would have done the same thing if they had been tied up on board ship for seven weeks.[35]

Poor old Charles Bean was unpopular at home as well, particularly once the men wrote to their families expressing anger over his despatch. Bean's newfound notoriety was shown in an article in one of Dubbo's newspapers, *The Dubbo Liberal and Macquarie Advocate*, on 23 April 1915 under the headline, 'A Sorry Man':

> A sorry man is Captain Bean, the Commonwealth correspondent with the Expeditionary Forces in Egypt. He wrote some most disparaging statements about the conduct of the Australian forces, and thereby brought a hornets nest about his ears. Now he is trying to hedge and retract his remarks with as much dignity as possible. Letters to hand in Dubbo this week—one from Major James Heane and another of Mr. W.H. Christie—assert that Bean's remarks were quite unwarranted. All who know Major Heane know that he of all men would be intolerant of loose conduct, and when he says there was none his word may be accepted as truth. Apparently Bean is out of his element among the rough and ready sons of Australia.

Bean's defence of his earlier article was in response to the vitriol at home and in camp. It was sent to the Australian press via cable near the end of March:

> An article in which I stated that the Australian troops were not responsible for certain rowdiness in CAIRO some months ago, but that it was due solely to a small percentage of unsuitable men, seems to have been so twisted and misquoted by a certain newspaper or newspapers as to appear to be an attack on the Australian troops in EGYPT—that is to say exactly the opposite of what was written by me or intended. Readers of my articles and cables know that the condition of the Australian Force in EGYPT, the way in which it has carried through its strenuous and tiring training and the condition in which it is emerging from it are such as would make Australians, if they could only see it, very proud indeed.

The article alluded to also contains sweeping criticisms on the whole of the officers who were never mentioned in my article and which are quite unjustified. Such offences as took place were military offences. Nothing else occurred which does not happen in Australian and other cities every day.

The article referred to omits the fact which I was careful to state, and which it is immensely important not to omit, that all the men returned to AUSTRALIA are not unsuitable; but that a large proportion consists of men whose health has broken down through hard work and exposure and who are bitterly disappointed at being unable to go on.[36]

Sadly for Charles Bean his attempts to quell the outrage at home and in Egypt were largely unsuccessful.

Despite Major Heane's denial, during the first few months of 1915, 79 men from the 4th Battalion's original enlistment, who had disembarked in Egypt, were sent home. Of these, 39 were deemed medically unfit, 20 men were banished for misconduct and 20 men suffering venereal diseases were forced to leave; the last two categories each being about 2 per cent of the original enlistment. The misconduct percentage of 2 per cent of the battalion was the very figure Bean estimated in his communiqué. A further 16 men afflicted with sexual infections were treated in Egypt and not ignominiously despatched. By 4 May another 14 men from the first three reinforcements allotted to the 4th Battalion were returning to Australia; five of these troops were deemed medically unfit for non-venereal reasons, five were 'venereals' and four were sent home for disciplinary breaches.[37]

The actual causes for the disciplinary discharges were quite diverse. John Robertson, the old soldier who faced a court martial on the *Euripides* for assaulting an NCO, was one who continued to transgress in Egypt. On enlistment, Robertson was a 38-year-old Scotsman who had served eight years in the Gordon Highlanders. His 'crime sheet' for Egypt had the following entries:

21.12.14 Awarded 1 day's C.B. for A.W.L. from defaulters roll call.
19.12.14 Awarded 4 days C.B. for drunkenness.
12.1.15 Awarded 21 days detention for breaking out of camp.
Report by O.C. Company:—'I strongly recommend the above mentioned man for discharge, as although he has had only four months service he has a bad record; further he is addicted to drink; he is also insubordinate.'

Major Storey was the officer in charge of A Company. Needless to say, Robertson was sent home.[38]

The most notable transgressor in the 4th Battalion was another old Scottish soldier, Private Ronald Murray. Murray stood 6 feet 5 inches, making him the tallest man in the battalion and one of the tallest men in the AIF. He was 42 years old and had spent six years in the Scots Guards prior to enlistment. He was a law unto himself in Egypt, successfully racking up multiple breaches of military discipline, contracting gonorrhoea and bullying his fellow soldiers, regardless of their rank. A report written by Captain Magee, his company commander, and his extensive 'crime sheet' clearly detail Murray's lawlessness:

> **Report by O.C. Company**
> An old soldier, unscrupulous, lazy, shirks all fatigues on all sorts of excuses, allows comrades to do all the work, greedy and a bully, uses his stature and strength to overawe his comrades, and secures more than his share of food, blankets and tent space, Endeavours to incite the worst and weaker characters to something almost amounting to mutiny, His attitude to all NCOs is always insubordinate. This man cannot be trusted in the field.

Murray's crime sheet included entries for refusing to obey orders, drunkenness, being absent without leave, and drinking while being treated for gonorrhoea. The only reason he stopped committing offences was because he was confined to the Venereal Isolation Tent near the end of January.[39]

Other men were discharged simply for being a waste of time and space. Private Bill Lawrence was one who was regarded, according to Lieutenant-Colonel Onslow Thompson, as 'worthless' and 'utterly useless'. Captain Magee's report on Lawrence was very negative:

> Absolutely hopeless as a soldier, or any thing else, has never done one whole days work, falls out on every march and is believed to be a malingerer, slovenly and unclean in his habits causing complaint among his tent mates, is constantly losing equipment, and is an obstacle in the way of obtaining company discipline.[40]

Lawrence was also an older, experienced soldier who was born in England. His discharge was recorded as disciplinary; incompetence might have been more appropriate. Murray, Robertson and some of their fellow transgressors from the 1st Brigade were sent home on the *Kyarra* on 3 February and discharged as disciplinary cases in early March 1915, soon after reaching Australia.

As Bean stated in his despatches from Egypt, just over half of the returnees on the *Kyarra* were men who were unable to continue training for a plethora of medical reasons. Their service records were clearly marked 'non venereal', thus avoiding the stigma venereal and discipline cases attracted.

~

At the end of December the 4th Battalion received its regimental colours of white and green. For the men these were in the form of colour patches showing a white rectangle over a green rectangle. These were worn on the upper sleeve of the uniform.[41]

On 1 January 1915 the AIF was reorganised. Within each battalion, the eight-company system was replaced by four companies, in line with the British Army. According to Bean:

> Under the new system a company consisted of 228 men, divided into four platoons of about 50 each. The company was commanded by a major or captain, with a captain as second in command, while each of the platoons was under a subaltern. The platoon really became the fighting unit in the army, when once battle was properly closed.[42]

Every platoon consisted of four sections, each of about 12 men, commanded by an NCO, usually a corporal. Jack was part of No. 12 Section, No. 15 Platoon, D Company under the new arrangements. Major James Heane was D Company's formidable commanding officer and 2nd Lieutenant Fred Fanning was in charge of No. 15 Platoon from 1 January.

At a farewell in his home town of Dubbo on Friday, 11 September 1914, James Heane was feted by his peers. A prominent and respected member of the local community, he was a farmer and militia area officer in the Dubbo district. Mr F. McManamey waxed lyrical about a man who:

> If a poll of the district were taken for a man to represent us at the front, he believed that poll would be unanimous in favour of their guest . . . a man who never sought prominence, but always fulfilled his duty in his many spheres in a way that had won the admiration of all of us. Captain Heane was a man of action rather than of words. His methods were quiet but effective, and he was an enthusiast in whatever he undertook. Strange it was that for years Captain Heane should have devoted his spare time to military service; strange it was that just at the time when he had attained to prominence as an officer, the call should have come to him; but it was not strange that such a man should promptly respond to that call.[43]

Another speaker, Lieutenant Ley, had spent three years in the militia training under Heane's guidance:

> Heane had helped him in every way, and the Captain had taken a deep interest in the training scheme, as well as in the welfare of the boys . . . there had not been a moment's unpleasantness . . . in the words of Lieutenant Nicholas, who said: 'If I were going to the front I would wish to be in Captain Heane's Company, and I wouldn't be afraid of going wrong.'[44]

Heane spent more than 15 years as an officer in various pre-war units, mainly the Light Horse. He was 41 when he took command of D Company.

His subordinate, Fred Fanning, was only 24 when he was appointed to lead No. 15 Platoon. Fanning spent nine years in the Great Public Schools Battalion of Sydney, the last two as an officer. Fanning's nickname, 'Maud', derived from the name of one of Australasia's most prominent vaudeville artists, Coon (blackface) singer Maud Fanning. It isn't known when his sobriquet entered the AIF's idiom. It's clear that in France, later in the war, Fanning was endearingly called Maud by the men. James Heane and Fanning were similar in their military bearing—driving the men hard under their command, but never asking anything of them that they wouldn't do themselves. A later description of newly promoted Captain Fanning, training his company in the Egyptian desert in early 1916, harked back to the training he put D Company and No. 15 Platoon through a year earlier:

> None of us ever forgot the education he imparted to us and the manner of it. He had a picturesque vocabulary; he knew the sort of training the 4th Battalion had gone through when the 1st Division was being made ready for Gallipoli; and he meant his company in the 56th Battalion to learn in the same style with the same thoroughness.[45]

Willie Wright, a tattooed 36-year-old Yorkshireman who had served in the 2nd West Riding Regiment in England, was appointed sergeant of No. 15 Platoon on 1 January 1915.[46] At this stage No. 12 Section's membership was still evolving, although 27-year-old Corporal Charles Macquarie was in charge of it. Macquarie had spent time in the NSW Scottish Rifles before the war. By the time the battalion left for the front, reinforcements formed part of the section's ranks. This was replicated across the AIF's battalions as miscreants and medically unfit men returned to Australia.

Measures to counter the disciplinary problems were enacted to keep the men busy and under control. Training was stepped up with longer desert marches.

Pickets were posted on the road near the camp to dissuade unauthorised leave. For his part, Charles Bean wrote a pamphlet, 'What To Know In Egypt: A Guide For Australasian Soldiers', in early 1915 in an attempt to breach the cultural divide between Antipodean and Egyptian and to direct the off-duty troops towards pastimes that involved fewer bars and brothels and more aesthetic pursuits. All manner of topics were covered, including Egypt's history, the Nile, the Mohamedan (Islam) religion, historical places of interest, the types of people living in Cairo, transport and Arabic phrases, and there was also a map of Cairo. However, at the heart of the publication were warnings about sex, women and alcohol.

One of the chapters, 'Health in Egypt (What is unsafe and the reasons why)', pulled no punches in warning the troops about the unsanitary nature of daily life in Egypt. Bean's analysis of sexual diseases was particularly grim:

> **A hot bed of disease.**
> Lastly Cairo has made itself a name in the world as a hotbed of both gonorrhea and syphilis. There is a reason for this. Egypt is not a country under the full control of its government. The Egyptian officials even though they had able British administrators to help them have possessed little control over the foreigners who live here. Egypt has been one of those countries which European nations have only admitted to their circle as probationers, as it were. Egyptian courts may not deal fully with European subjects. Europeans have been controlled by mixed tribunals of Egyptians and foreigners. The consequence is that although Cairo has long been a resort of foreign women riddled with disease it has been almost impossible to check this disease. Egypt has been an ancient home of syphilis—it was certainly here in Roman times; and there is found in the skull bones of mummies a disease which is almost certainly syphilis. Modern Cairo with its mixture of women from all nations, East and West has long been noted for particularly virulent forms of disease. Almost every village contains syphilis. And if a man will not steer altogether clear of the risk by exercising a little restraint, his only sane course is to provide himself with certain prophylactics beforehand to lessen the chance of disastrous results.[47]

Another of Bean's cautionary tales was in regard to local women:

> Women—Men must be careful to avoid any attempts at familiarity with native women; because if they are respectable they will get into trouble, and if they are not, venereal disease will probably be contracted.[48]

He also warned the men against certain alcoholic drinks:

> Alcoholic drinks sold under the name of Cognac, Absinthe and other aperitifs are liable, except at good restaurants, to be native imitations made from doubtful raw spirit and coloured. They may contain any percentage of alcohol and be practically pure poison; and in some cases the colour is obtained in ways too disgusting to be described. Some inhabitants have no conscience whatever in this matter—their only object is to sell.[49]

Bean's final plea was for the Australians to uphold the unparalleled reputation of the British in the Orient:

> Amongst all these people we have a great reputation for high principle and manliness, and even the humblest Britisher here in the East carries that reputation in his keeping . . . Throughout this country the phrase for truth or good faith is word of an Englishman. Is not that something for our whole race to be proud of?[50]

There was only one problem with Bean's logic—Australians weren't Englishmen, however proud they were of belonging to the British Empire and serving its interests. It was in the cultural cauldron of Cairo that the Australians began to assert their own identity, realising that they were physically more robust and of a different mindset to their British cousins. The Australians were more independent, more assertive and less cowed by authority than the British soldiers present in the Egyptian capital. Jack's Christmas Day chat with the Dragoons about Australia and its relaxed lifestyle was an example of this, although he did say that he felt at home in their company.

The Australians referred to Egypt as the 'land of sin, sand, shit and syphilis'.[51] Other derogatory terms were also applied, such as 'Sun, shame and sore eyes'.[52] By the time the AIF battalions were reorganised on 1 January 1915, the romantic allure of the Orient had well and truly passed. Cultural and religious differences, the language impasse, decidedly noxious sights and smells, inflated prices and the perception of Anglo-Celtic superiority over the local Arab population, coupled with the military nature of the AIF presence, all combined to produce an almost universal Australian disdain for Egypt and Egyptians. Private James Hagan of the 3rd Battalion was baffled by the locals, describing them in his diary as 'all kinds of peculiar people' who 'have the most peculiar Customs imaginable'.[53] One such custom, which particularly riled Major James Heane, was backsheesh or tipping:

The great bugbear in Egypt is backsheesh, or tips. Everyone who sees you wants a tip, whether he has done anything for you or not. All the kiddies have the same cry, and whatever amount you arrange for any service to be carried out you always have to pay extra.[54]

A poem by Trooper W. H. Johnstone of the Light Horse summed up the feelings of many of the men, swagger sticks in hand, towards the ancient world that confronted them:

Heliopolis : Egypt : Land of Sand.
Oh! Egypt, land of dreams and visions
Of dirty towns and street collisions,
Where Arabs sell their greasy wares
And cabbies charge you double fares,
Where sin and wickedness, dirt and smells
Make this a disease-stricken hell,
A land of sand and desert plain
Where no such thing is known as rain,
A drink of water is a treasure
And tucker's issued in half measure,
Where donks and camels bear huge loads
Across loose sand in place of roads,
Where donkeys, goats, fowls, dogs and natives
All live together, like relatives:
Such sights are common over here
Where soldiers drink cheap, doped-up beer
Then fall, drunk, helpless in the sand;
It makes your hair on end to stand
Two drinks will make a man dead tight
And make him argue all the night
Until his sleepy mates rebel
And wish him and his beer in hell;
'Tis here, midst sweltering sun and skies,
Tormented by insects and flies
The soldier trudges, sick and sore,
Cursing the Kaiser, and the war,
Which brought him from his home to dwell
In this dreary dried up land of hell.[55]

Private Thomas Bann of A Company, 4th Battalion, was also quite blunt in his assessment of the Land of the Pharaohs. In a letter to his aunt, Cicely Blamires, Tom was very disparaging in his description of Cairo:

> 2nd Jany, 1915
>
> Dear Auntie,
> I received your very welcome letter yesterday. It is the first letter I have received since I left Australia so you can guess how glad I was to get it . . . Will send you some postcard views of Cairo next time I get leave and can get some. I have been in Cairo a couple of times. It is a very lively place but we do not get much time to look round as the camp is ten miles from Cairo. To put it in plain language Cairo is very dirty and nothing more or less than a big brothel. The native parts especially fairly stink. Of course there is an Aristocratic quarter, but there are no amusements there, only one or two big shops. After being so long on the ship the troops nearly went wild the first time leave was given but have quietened down now.[56]

Egypt represented an enormous challenge for the chaplains accompanying the troops. In many cases they became de facto father figures in their designated battalions; Bill McKenzie certainly did so in the 4th. McKenzie turned 45 on 20 December, quite amazed to be celebrating his birthday in Egypt near the pyramids.[57] He deplored the men's weaknesses in regard to grog and prostitutes, and ranted and raved at them and the military authorities. To keep the troops occupied he organised activities at Mena, including boxing bouts—some of them featuring the good padre himself—and concerts involving sing-alongs, which he boisterously led. McKenzie went further by going into the back streets of Cairo and physically hauling young soldiers out of places of ill repute. His diary recorded such an occasion:

> I spent the afternoon in Cairo. I had a drive around the native quarter. There was much to interest, but the filth and smells were awful . . . and finally went into some dark lanes on foot and there found some awful hell holes out of which I dragged and ordered well on 100 men, some in a deplorable state. I had them taken into the well lit street and sent off to camp.[58]

A profile of Chaplain McKenzie written after the war described his brazen rescue technique:

> Well into those vile places strode Chaplain 'Mac' scattering confusion and pulling out the boys. 'What would your mother say to see you in such a place?' 'Boy how will you look your sister in the eyes again?' And not only this. He went to the Authority. What! Is this the reception prepared for pure and healthy boys going to face death for the Mother Country?—is this the glory of the British Empire?—is this the best that England can do for her sons?[59]

Only such a larger-than-life figure like Bill McKenzie could get away with being so confrontational. In the ensuing years McKenzie displayed these very qualities many times in or near the firing line, his overriding motivation being the spiritual, psychological and physical wellbeing of the men. Further diary entries by the chaplain were scathing about the twin evils of venereal disease and alcohol in Egypt:

> There are now 400 venereal cases in our battalion [surely McKenzie meant the 1st Division] and the number is increasing. Some are bad cases too. I have little sympathy with them after all the warnings and information entreaties that they have received from all sources. I strongly advocate a 'leper camp' and stop all pay while they are there, just giving the food and careful medical treatment. They are deliberately and wilfully bad and should be made to suffer for their sin and feel the situation . . . Had a very successful concert with the new reinforcements and also another on St Pat's night [17 March]. Much drunkenness this night. The wet canteen is an unmitigated curse and is ruining many bright boys. It should be stopped. I am afraid the 'profits' have too great an attraction for some folk to close it down . . . It should be able to prevent any man from getting more than two pints—a wise system would do this with strict supervision. It is dastardly to stoop to the making of money out of the weaknesses of the soldiers.[60]

The obligatory church parades, held in the open air in the desert, were particularly challenging for the padres attempting to guide and enlighten their somewhat errant flock. Walter Dexter was quite pragmatic in his approach. This was before microphones and public address systems, so the message of the gospel was dependent on the power of the messenger's voice:

> . . . and at 9 am church Parade with 5th and 8th. Frightful sand storm, or what should have been a sand-storm, but was in reality dust. About 2,000

> men with the wind behind the preacher, and the sand blowing in the faces of the men. However the parade was good. One can always tell by the faces of the men. In most of the church parades the men go to sleep and in the Dean's Parade they stand throughout and while the Dean preaches the men curse because they cannot hear him and have to stand in the sun. At my parades I always make the men stand at ease, and then immediately after prayers, sit during the lesson and address. On a day like this one cannot gauge one's voice and though I hardly thought it possible ¼ of a mile away every word was heard. That of course was the wind, but it was a terrible strain and result a headache immediately afterwards.[61]

Howard McKern of the 4th Battalion touched on the difficulties of a massed church parade in his Christmas Day diary entry, claiming that yet again the bulk of the congregation was unable to hear or see the service.

The camp at Mena evolved and became a second home to the 1st Australian Division over the months of its colourful tenancy. On 19 January, Private Ted Meggy of the 3rd Battalion wrote to his family, describing the changed nature of Mena Camp from its humble beginnings:

> By the way things are going ahead here. It looks as if we were here for life. There are four Y.M.C.A. Buildings, three picture shows, two stadiums, and shops of all descriptions, every second one being a barber shop where they tear one's beard off with a razor that's as blunt as a saw.[62]

In early January 1915 the weeding out of 'the wastrels of the city',[63]—Colonel MacLaurin's description of some of the 1st Brigade's recruits from Sydney—resulted in a more cohesive contingent. However, balancing the maintenance of discipline in the ranks against the seedy attractions of Cairo remained a problem throughout the AIF's training in January, February and March 1915. Unfortunately, the details of the battalion's daily desert forays, recorded in the 4th Battalion war diary, are extremely brief. For the whole of January the diary reported: 'Company training carried out daily during the Month.' The next available entry in the 4th's war diary came on 24 April 1915 as the battalion prepared to go into action.[64] In his Christmas letter Jack moaned about the monotony of sand marching, yet the AIF was to endure another three months of training in the Egyptian desert.

In the 4th Battalion and across the contingent, the first few months of the new year were spent undergoing company, battalion, brigade and, eventually, division exercises. They consisted of extended marches across the desert (occasionally at night), rifle range practice and competitions, trench constructions, sham fights—some involving rearguard actions and some the defence of fixed positions—and overnight desert bivouacs that also included battle scenarios. The men were literally becoming fighting fit.

In his letter to his aunt Cicely, dated 22 January, Tom Bann wrote about the men's daily routine:

> We are camped in tents on the Desert of Sahara quite close to the Pyramids and Sphinx. We are getting plenty of Drill and Marching and being all heavy sand here it is very tiring work. We have to get up when the bugle sounds reveille at 6 a.m. and be on parade at 8 a.m. and I can tell you that by the time we have folded our blankets, cleaned up the tent, had a shave, breakfast, and got all our gear ready there is no time to spare. Then we generally go for a march on the Desert and drill and return to camp by 5 p.m. I used to be dog tired at first but am getting in good trim and do not feel it so much now.[65]

Although Jack did not record the battalion's training during this period, unless it was in the Egypt diary he lost, Les De Vine of A Company did. His entries showed the gradual refining of the fitness and tactics of the men individually and on an organised unit level:

> 11/1/15 Went on the march today half way to Second Pyramids rather a severe test; nearly broke down, returned to camp vy tired, marched from 8 am until 3 p.m. = 7 hours.
>
> 15/1/15 Marched across desert to same hills, had sham fight, weather vy windy, covered with fine sand. Got another letter from mother night parade—vy tired.
>
> 21/1/15 Long march to rifle range at the 'Valley of Despair' passed all shooting tests. A and B Coys only on range heel of left foot very sore nearly fell out of march on return.
>
> 22/1/15 Marched to the 'Valley of Despair' for company training. C & D Coys on rifle range, very cold day wore overcoat all day night parade on returning to camp, shortage of food, general complaints about same.
>
> 27/1/15 Long march into the desert, very windy and cold all day, got into a heavy sand storm, eyes mouth and ears full of sand, rotten day for a

skirmish, we all arrived back at camp covered with sand, both inside and out.

29/1/15 Left camp at 8 o/c for a long march in the desert, the whole of the Bn marched ¾ of the way to the Sakarah Pyramids, fought a rear guard action all the morning, at mid day dug some very long trenches, and held the position we formed part of the 'Brown Army', the White Army attacked us about 3 pm, had an exciting fight, ball cartridge used by mistake, nobody hurt heat midday very great, the trench digging was stopped for 1½ hours for a long rest and lunch which we all carried, absolutely no shade in the desert you have to remain in the sun all the time. After the sham fight we reformed and marched to our bivouac for some hot tea, water is now very scarce. All water in our bottles used up during the heat of the day, we are absolutely parched with thirst, after our tea had a short rest, then took up our positions for the night, and dug a long trench, we struck rock about 18" down, very hard digging could not get down far enough before the whole white army attacked, ball cartridge again accidentally used, heard the bullets whistle quite close to me, attack stopped at 12 o/c midnight we are all very tired out with the long day, after posting sentrys and reliefs for the night, we settle down for the night in our overcoats, we could not get a wink of sleep, feet to cold, no blankets, this is our first bivouac.

30/1/15 Reveille at 5 o/c to man the trenches, had a fight before breakfast, back to our bivouac about 8.30 had breakfast, bread and butter only and lucky to get a little tea, absolutely no water for our bottles, fought a rearguard action all the way back to camp. Arriving in camp about 10.30 am pretty tired, another very hot day no further duties today, rest until Monday.

7/2/15 Sunday Attended Church Parade, visited Cairo during afternoon—1st reinforcements arrived today.

8/2/15 Holiday all day, visited Cairo from 10 am till 11 pm. Visited the Citadel, and the tombs of the Caliphs, also the 'City of the dead' & Napoleons fort.[66]

In a letter to his family, Private Oscar Ward of the 1st Field Ambulance described the state of the Australian Imperial Force in early February:

> The infantry have had very severe training, and those who have stood it look splendidly fit. A finer army of men will not be found in the present war than the Australians at present in Egypt, for they are splendid, and work like machinery. Of course we only see the pick of the men now for the severe training has sent a great many to the hosp, and at present there are well over 1000 in the hosp here, not all from hard drill, but a good many of them.[67]

In his diary Les De Vine concurred that training was stepped up in mid-February as the troops prepared for the front line:

> 14/2/15 Sunday No parades today, not even a church parade, all very tired, went to sleep all day warned to be ready for an all night march at 9.30 pm hot tea served out at 9 pm, started on our march punctually at 9.30, marched all through the night in absolute silence, ready for a night attack if the alarm should come.
>
> 15/2/15 Marched all through the night by a long circular route, and found ourselves at day break by the ruins of one of the Sakarah Pyramids, where we had a fight with the 3rd Bn and drove them off then settled down to some hot tea and bread & butter only for breakfast, after we took up positions at 9 o/c for another fight the 'enemy' retreated toward the North, so we chased them up and routed them out of their positions by 12 o/c. Returned to our bivouac and rest for the remainder of the day, march back to Mena Camp tomorrow morning.
>
> 16/2/15 Broke bivouac today. The whole of the 1st Brigade before moving off were drawn up in mass formation before the Brigadier. Brigadier MacLaurin who complimented us on our work; and said we were now fit for active service, and ready to leave for the front.
>
> 5/3/15 Parade at 2 pm for bivouac all night, carried water proof & 1 blanket, all section photographed in front of the Sphynx before march. The whole division is on bivouac tonight, skirmished & fought advance guard action until 12 o/c midnight then camped for the night no blankets issued which are being carried in the regimental transports, terribly cold, men walk about all night to keep their feet warm, absolutely no sleep for anybody, our worst and coldest night in Egypt. Stood to arms as reserves at daybreak.[68]

About this time Jack began to write the second version of his Egypt diary. Regrettably, Jack's initial second diary was lost and he began this replacement in early March. Jack wrote most of it while on the *Lake Michigan* during the weeks of training on Lemnos. He lost his original Egypt diary in the haste to leave Mena. In the replacement diary he described all manner of things Egyptian—very much the view of a 'six bob a day' Aussie tourist. Jack hardly mentioned the war and he didn't refer to their training in the desert.

March 2nd 1915.

I had leave today, my pass being from 10 A.M. to 9.30 P.M. but it was well after 1 before I got to Cairo. After a run round town for half an hour, I went to a restaurant + had dinner. I decided to take a run to Helliopolis, a suburb of Cairo, of which I had heard a great deal, but up to to-day, I had never been able to take the trip. Both trams + trains run out, + I selected the tram, as it was closer to where I was in town. I shall never forget the beauty of the place. The first place of interest that I saw was the Heliopolis hotel, a fine building of tremendous dimensions. It has now been turned into a military hospital, the patients from all the field hospitals have just been moved there in Motor ambulances. It is said to accommodate more visitors than any hotel in the world. Then I got to the terminus, got out of the tram, + strolled out towards the site of the 2nd contingent camp. I noticed a large church, a splendid dome shaped building, built of stone. The streets are wide + well kept, + on either side, are great white business houses, all spotlessly clean, quite a contrast to Cairo.

A few of my impressions + experiences in Cairo.

My first visit was not extra interesting, as my leave was very short, + time only permitted my strolling round the streets a few times, the remainder being taken up in looking for the tram to take me back to "home sweet home;" (Mena.) The remaining trips have not been so bad, but Cairo is the place to empty your pockets, + 2/- a day, which we are being paid now, takes husbanding to make it spin out. I will start right from camp, + try to detail some of the sights. The general run of leave has been from 12 Noon, some, of course, who get in the extra good graces of the "heads," + learn the run of the ropes, get it earlier, but the majority of those who "play the game" fairly, are generally kept until an hour or even two after 12, but that does not count here. After leaving camp, about 500 yds from the last line of tents, we come to the tram terminus, where several trams are waiting for their scheduled time to leave. A score or so of motor cars are lined up on one side of the road, soliciting patronage. At first it was difficult to get a seat in a motor, but now it is very different, only those alleged to have a "remittance from father" + officers using them, the fare, a days wages 10 piastres, being too high for the rest of us. Several carriages are also lined up, numerous donkeys are there offered for hire needless to relate, each one is the best, so the owners say. I went in per motor several times, after the first (+ last) big pay, but the pace was too hot for my liking. The drivers fairly fly. The road is a beauty, not a rut in it for the whole ten miles, but the way the drivers dart in + out through the traffic requires great nerve + skill, + makes the "fare" resolve to stick to the old electric tram in future, + it relieves the tension on the nerves when the car pulls up in the centre of the town, Opera square. There is not much noticed in these rides, all your attention is taken up in judging how close the driver will go to another car travelling in opposite direction. The journey is often done in 15 minutes, + the driver is cool + collected all the time. The tram is, as a rule, very slow, the journey very often taking 1½ hours. The fare for us is 1 piastre (2½d) At the beginning of the journey nothing can be seen beyond the road boundary but desert. The whole distance of the road is lined on either side by trees, forming the prettiest avenue I have ever seen. On looking out a few hundred yards along the line, a real Australian river flat scene is presented on one side. Beautiful green lucerne, barley etc is flourishing in abundance. No fences are to be seen, the boundaries being just marked out by stones at intervals. A bullock donkey + horse are staked to pegs + allowed to eat down a patch of the lucerne, but they are compelled to eat it down level with the ground, before they are moved further on. Then a flock of 20 or 30 sheep are being shepherded on a patch that has been cut. The soil looks of the richest possible, black colour. On the other side is still desert, with a native village half a mile or so away. Further on, we come to a fresh water canal, used for irrigation. It is said that without irrigation, the land is unfertile. Pumping stations are seen at intervals along the canal. The smaller land-owners have quite a novel scheme for irrigating their land. An upright forked pole is set in the ground. A lever of suitable length is placed in the fork. A bolt put through both, to act as a swivel a large stone plastered on one end with mud, about the weight of a full bucket of water, the bucket suspended by a rope on the other. The native stands on the edge of the canal, +

works the bucket. Its surprising the amount of land that is irrigated in this way. A little further on, both sides of the road is cultivated, vegetable gardens + young date palms + orange groves are seen. A native farmer is often seen, with his team of (two) bullocks, + his old fashioned wooden plough, tilling the soil. I have not had an opportunity of examining a plough closely, but they do not appear to move the soil, simply go through + loosen it. The team goes along at a very slow speed, so slow that you must take the second look to make sure they are not stationary. A week or so ago, I saw a farm being changed, or rather the soil being moved from one farm to another. I do not know what it is called in technical talk. A gang of natives were engaged in digging with pronged hoes, taking about 1 foot of the surface soil, another crowd with baskets, loading the soil on to drays, drawn by mules. It was then taken a mile or so along the road, + tipped near another cultivation plot. We next cross over a railway line, running out towards the pyramids of Sukkurah a little further on is "Girzah" where the the Zooligical gardens are. Here the tram is surrounded by dirty youngsters, selling oranges, lemonade, pea-nuts wanting to clean your boots etc, + a sly looking chap here + there, concealing something under his wraps. If you give him an inquiring glance, he comes towards you cautiously, + almost whispers "bottle o' biere sir" (beer) + for proof that he has it, he pulls it out from among his clothes to show it. He always has oranges or some other goods, to hide suspicion. We then come into the higher class part of the town, large well built + well kept houses where the wealthy Egyptian + European people have made their homes. We then pass a public school of large proportions + several public buildings, when we find ourselves passing through the native quarter, a butcher's shop, with about 10lbs of beef or mutton hanging in it, + a boy keeping the flies off it with a horse hair brush, while the owner sits by, smoking his pipe. Here + there, a youngster jumps on the moving tram with an armful of papers, + run some great risks, in the hope of making a paltry half piastre. I think they beat the Sydney boys in jumping on + off trams. We cross (Kasr El Nil) two grand bridges spanning the Nile, the names of which I do not know. We now find ourselves in the European business Centre of Cairo, + eventually alight at "Opera Square," to be immediately surrounded by a score of "Street Arabs" worrying the very life out of you, until you make them believe you have lost your temper, + swing a swagger stick at a few of them, but its almost impossible to get quite angry with them, for they are so pleading, so unhealthy looking + neglected. You succeed in leaving them behind, + walk in the direction of the Post Office, only to be molested by natives with menu cards, + directing you to the "best restaurant in town," where "Inglis biere" is served for 5 piastres a bottle. They are easily got rid of, + you get to the post office, where several dozen boys have congregated to wait on us, with lottery tickets at 1 piastre each. There is a different lottery drawn here every day, + a little bugler in our Coy. was fortunate enough to win 1st prize of 38 pounds a few days ago. The P.O. officials are, as a rule, very obliging and courteous, but sometimes are a trifle hard to make understand. A walk around the shops is full of interest. Hotels are rather numerous. Shepheards + the Grand Continental are about the largest, + both these have been placed "out of bounds," for the troops. They are the meeting places of officers. In each of the shop windows is a card, bearing the words "Special prices for military," but, we have found out that "special" part is well in their favour. An article which cost 1/- before we landed, costs 2/- or even more now. Of course, like in Australia, they blame the war. There are several large stores in town, the largest + most reliable general stores I have found is Steins Oriental stores, but even here, everything is very dear. The streets are well kept, but the sanitary conveniences are not nearly sufficient for the smallest town, let alone a city. Right in the centre of the town, is a statue of a man on a fine horse. To deal with a native hawker, was at first very difficult, but now it has come quite easy. An Arab puts a price on an article, the probable customer mentally divides the price by two, + makes an offer accordingly. Nine times out of ten, his offer is accepted, + the native goes off, chuckling to himself. Greeks are very numerous, hotels stores of all descriptions, money lenders being among their professions. Frenchmen are also well represented, + I have found them by far the best + squarest of the populace. Italians, +, in fact, few races are not represented here. There are a few English tradesmen, but they are not all fair in their prices. They employ native labor, just as the other shops, but have a "get rich quick" motto. For example, I went into an English Chemist shop + asked the price of a certain brand of tooth paste. I was told 10 piastres 2/- a tube. This was too hot for me, so I went a little further on to a Frenchman's place. The price there was 7 piastres (1/5½) so you see the difference. The native women wear a veil, covering the face as far as the eyes. Most of the natives are Mahomedans. No matter where one is about 4.30 or 5 oclock, he will see a native offering his prayer, which takes quite a time to perform. They invariably remove their shoes before praying, + I have also seen them make an attempt at washing the feet. No matter where they are, or what they are doing, at the appointed time for prayer, they obey their teaching on the spot. Friday is recognised as Sunday in most cases here, + I have seen the Arabs entering the mosques, with the greatest ceremony, always leaving their shoes outside the door. The first time I was passing a mosque, I saw a native removing his boots at the door, + walk inside very slowly. I grew inquisitive, + looked in the door, still standing on the foot-path, of course, but a native from a distance along the street, soon made his way towards me, + very politely made signs that the inmates were praying, + that it was not right for me to look at them. I took the hint, + went off, with him bowing his head off after me. He seemed very pleased.

I spent one of my leave days at the Citedal, where several battalions of Territorials are in barracks, + a great number of Indian troops are under-going repairs, having been wounded in the engagements on the Canal + elsewhere. A party of four of us were together, W.A.Bound, C. Buckland, T.J.Thomson + myself formed the party. We employed a guide, who could speak excellent English, + who told us he had been employed at the same game for 20 years. On getting to the door of the Mosque we were requested to either take our boots off, or slip a pair of soft sandals over them. The cost of these for an hours hire is 1 P.T. We enter into the fine large court yard, + the guide gets busy. The first thing he pointed out was a large tower, on which is a clock, which he explained was a present from the King of France. A well, the depth of which I have forgotten, was next shown us. I had everything put down in a separate diary of everything I saw, but in our hurry + scarcity of room at camp, I have lost it, so must try to remember as much as possible. We then entered the door of the Mosque, built by Mahomed Aly Pasha. The sight that meets the eye on entering is one of marvellous splendour. The floor is covered with thick costly matting. On the right hand side is a tomb, with several compartments, + barred by iron bar doors. (The body of the builder, Mahomed Aly Pasha, + his family are entombed there.) The cost of this tomb ran into over 7000 pounds, the guide told us. A little further on, is a pulpit, + on the opposite end to the door, is a semi-circle in the wall. I enquired its meaning, + was told that it was for the convenience of blind men, entering the mosque unaccompanied, following the wall round until they come to the hollow, where they can pray, facing the

> East, which is in their belief. On looking up at the roof, the coloured glass forms a pretty scene. All the colours of the rain-bow are represented. Lower down, is a platform, leading all round the whole building with hand-rails of brass, the whole, very prettily painted. From the centre of the building is suspended a great cluster of lamp globes, all of different shades + colours. The guide told us there were 1000 lamps in all, + these were lighted once a day, when the Sultan visited the mosque for worship. The walls are of alabasta, + are very pretty. Some of the alabasta is almost transparent, which was proved by the guide holding a lighted candle against a 6 inch block. The reflection showed through quite plainly. The mosque is little more than 100 years old. We then went out into another court-yard, + got a splendid view of Cairo. This is the highest point of the city, + can be plainly seen from any quarter. We were told that 49 of the men who worked on the building, were caught + imprisoned in this yard, + slaughtered like oxen at the command of

The diary ended there.

The Citadel—or 'Citedal', one of Jack's few spelling errors—which the party visited, dominated Cairo's skyline in 1915. It was a large fortified area built on Muqattan hill, the highest point in the city, encompassing the traditional Islamic seat of power in Egypt. Originally, the legendary Saladin built the Citadel between 1176 and 1183 as protection against the marauding Crusaders.[69] In 1915 there was a British military hospital housed in the Palace of Mahomed Aly, one of the Citadel's impressive buildings. Mahomed Aly, dubbed 'The Father Of Modern Egypt', ruled the country from 1805 until 1848 after massacring the rival Mamluk leadership. However, it was to Aly's mosque that Jack and his mates were drawn. Its twin minarets reached for the sky, higher than anything else in Cairo at the time.

The mosque was built from 1828 to 1848 on the summit of the Citadel, hence the amazing view Jack commented on. It was described as having 'a classical Ottoman design consisting of a large central domed area flanked by semi-domes and a large open courtyard surrounded by arcades covered by shallow domes'. Just as Jack described, on the west wall of the courtyard was a clock tower including a clock presented by King Louis Phillipe of France in 1846.[70] Many Australians reported visiting the Citadel in their letters and diaries. It certainly was very impressive—a non-pharaonic wonder.

In his account Jack briefly referred to Indian troops 'undergoing repairs' in the Citadel's military hospital after suffering casualties during the fighting on the Suez Canal. The Turks sent an expeditionary force of their own across the Sinai Desert from bases in Palestine in January 1915 to conduct a *jihad* or holy war against the British in Egypt; in effect to invade Egypt and disrupt the enemy's preparations for war. At the back of their thinking was their loss of face due to the British taking political control of their former province. To regain Egypt was something of a pipedream. To counter Turkish designs a series of posts manned by British troops, mainly Indians, dotted the western and, in a few places, eastern sides of the canal. A series of engagements occurred in late January and, in particular, early February, in and around the canal in which the New Zealanders distinguished themselves. The bulk of the fighting was borne by Indian troops who quickly repulsed the Turkish attacks, especially those attempted on 3 February. British casualties were about 160 men, while the Turk's losses were at least 1600 men.[71]

By March, despite signs they were leaving, Major James Heane, Jack's company commanding officer, was moved to exasperation. In his letter to Captain Ley, his old Dubbo militia mate, he wrote:

> We have been marooned in this wretched hole too long. I have already been warned two weeks ago to be ready at 24 hours' notice, but we are still here. We have heard to-night that we will go next week.[72]

The monotony of Egypt was about to end, but not before General Sir Ian Hamilton's inspection of the troops on Monday, 29 March. This was the second last entry in Jack's Egypt diary. It was a huge occasion for the troops of the Australian Imperial Force and the New Zealand Expeditionary Force. After their demanding desert training in all its permutations, the men were in fine fettle; however, whether they were ready for the rigours of war was another matter. Hamilton was the commanding officer of the Mediterranean Expeditionary Force, in charge of all British troops. Sergeant Tallisker McLeod of the 3rd Battalion described Hamilton's review of the troops in a letter home:

> Last Monday we were inspected by Sir Ian Hamilton, all the Infantry and the 1st Field Ambulance were formed up on the lovely sand and saluted him. We then marched past in double column (8 abreast), the marching and turn out of the troops was very good, we are now anxiously waiting his report.[73]

McLeod needn't have worried. The general was very impressed by the Australians and the New Zealanders. Hamilton's diary revealed his thoughts:

> 29th March, 1915. 9.30 p.m. Palace Hotel, Alexandria. Early start to the Mena Camp to see the Australians. A devil of a blinding storm gave a foretaste of dust to dust. That was when they were marching past, but afterwards I inspected the Infantry at close quarters, taking a good look at each man and speaking to hundreds . . . The troops then marched back to Camp in mass of quarter columns—or rather swept by like a huge yellow cloud at the heart of which sparkled thousands of bayonets . . . This took time, and I had to make the motor travel getting across twelve miles or so to inspect a mixed Division of Australians and New Zealanders at Heliopolis . . . These fellows made a real good show; superb physique . . . Tiring day if I had it in my mind to be tired, but this 30,000 crowd of Birdwood's would straighten up the back of a pacifist. There is a bravery in the air—a keenness on their clean cut features—they are spoiling for a scrap! . . . The spirit of War has breathed fire into their hearts; the drill sergeant has taken thought and has added one cubit* to their stature. [*A cubit was a traditional measurement used throughout the ages, particularly in ancient Egypt. It was the length of a man's forearm.][74]

British military authorities felt that the Australian and New Zealand Army Corps was ready to go to war, and plans were afoot for the men to go into action. The 3rd Brigade of the 1st Australian Division left Mena rather mysteriously some weeks before. Now it was time for the remaining Australasians to depart for places unknown.

Finally, the next part of the ANZAC odyssey was about to commence.

> Got orders to leave Mena on Easter Saturday April 3rd, entraining in Cairo at about 1.30 on Sunday morning.

This was the last entry in Jack's Egypt diary.

On 3 April Jack wrote the following entry at the end of his Voyage diary:

> I have shamefully neglected my diary, but will make another attempt later. The contents of this may be of a little interest. We are leaving to-day, but have no idea where we are bound for.

3 'Gollipoli Peninsular', 25 April 1915

Directly we halted, a shell burst among us, + our sergeant of no.12 section was hit by the case, + went over, + I as second in command of the section, took charge.

JACK'S DIARY, LANDING ENTRY

Jack was somewhat circumscribed in his description of leaving Mena Camp, embarking on the *Lake Michigan* from Alexandria, Egypt, and the training the battalion underwent at Lemnos after arriving there on 6 March. His tiny third diary, written in pencil in an immaculate script, briefly recorded the long-awaited move.

> **Easter Saturday. 3.4.15.**
> We got orders to prepare to leave Mena on 3.4.15 + left for Cairo at 9.30 p.m. Arrived at Cairo railway station at about 12 mid-night. Entrained for Alexandria at 1.30 a.m., + got a move on. Arrived at Alex, + embarked immediately on A.8. transport, Lake Michigan, one of the Canadian-Pacifics boats. We were not at all crowded, only having one battalion on board, + a fair number of transport horses. A few days after we came aboard, the canteen ran out of tobacco + cigarettes. Our voyage lasted two days, arriving at the island of Lemnos on 6th, where we cast anchor. A number of our transports arrived later, + a few battleships were already in the bay when we arrived. After 18 days aboard ship with an occasional landing in small rowing boats, we got orders to prepare for disembarkation, + a promise of getting into action on Sunday 25th (Am not sure of the date, for I have lost count).

Other diarists were more forthcoming, recording the minutiae of the move, although the 4th Battalion war diary was not among them and only began recording April's events the day before the Landing. Private Les De Vine's diary entry for 3 April 1915 was more expansive:

> Great excitement in the camp the 1st Brigade are packing up all day, orders probably due to the behaviour of yesterday evening. ('Wasser' riot) At 4.30 p.m. we march out of camp full marching order leaving Mena Camp for good. We march through Cairo to the railway siding; over the Masr-el-nil bridge & past the barracks filled with English troops confined to barracks as punishment for their part of yesterdays riots, they gave us a very wild reception with much abuse, we march to attention & make no reply. The route is about 10 miles, after loading the train with our baggage, cookers, etc we leave at 10.30 p.m. for Alexandria, arriving 3 a.m. next morning.[1]

The 'riots' Les mentioned was the infamous disturbance that occurred late afternoon on Good Friday, 2 April, in part of the Haret el Wassa, in Cairo's red-light district known as 'The Wozzer' to the troops. A small number of Anzacs were intent on payback for problems they perceived were caused by pimps and their prostitutes in Red Blind Street. The latter were manhandled out of their places of ill-repute, and their tools of trade—beds, mattresses and clothing—followed them onto the street, and were burnt in bonfires. A tense stand-off ensued between a large crowd, numbering in the thousands, and the Mounted Military Police, who responded to the uproar. In the early evening the police were reinforced by a mounted Yeomanry squadron. In attempting to control the crowd they wounded a few men, some of their rounds ricocheting off the ground. Eventually the situation calmed down and the aggrieved men and the onlookers departed, the fires and the ardour of the men extinguished.[2]

Private Les Lott wrote about leaving Mena Camp in his diary on Saturday:

> 3/4/15—The day we leave Mena to go to the front, after a busy day, cleaning up the grounds and lowering tents and packing kits. at 8.30 pm we started our march to Mena station, a distance of 12 miles. arrived there 1 am. entrained 1.30 am. midnight 4/4 transport sets sail.[3]

The transport, *Lake Michigan*, was derided as 'a cattle boat' by one wag.[4] Les De Vine was also critical of the conditions aboard ship:

> 5/4/15 At Sea. Parade at 9.30, we are told by Major McNaughton that we are bound for the island of Lemnos outside the Dardanelles, the accommodation on the ship is very rough, we have to sleep on the deck or in the hold in fact anywhere we can fit. Heavy gale blowing all night ship rolling a good deal.[5]

Staff Sergeant-Major John Sloan saw matters differently. In a letter home after the Landing he described the move from Mena to Mudros:

> We received a few hours notice to pack up and entrain at Cairo and soon were being rushed towards Alexandria where we arrived at daylight and soon found ourselves snugly aboard S.S. *Lake Michigan*, up-to-date trooper. The following morning we found ourselves in a nice harbour (and were told it was Lemnos) with a pretty shore clustered with villages . . . Every day brought fresh boats till one could count over 100 in the bay. It was estimated that the harbour ships contained over 100,000 men.[6]

Allied naval attempts to force a passage through the heavily guarded Hellespont and threaten Turkey's capital, Constantinople, had failed, notably on 18 March 1915, when the catastrophic loss of the *Bouvet*, the *Ocean* and the *Irresistible* to Turkish mines, and the near crippling of the *Inflexible,* the *Gaulois* and the *Suffren*, left the Allies seeking alternatives. March 18 has become the Turkish equivalent of the Antipodean Anzac Day, except the Turks celebrate a great victory. In order to achieve the Allied aims of knocking Turkey out of the war, thereby threatening their German masters in the Balkans and relieving the pressure on the Russians, a ground campaign to seize control of the western side of the Narrows via its southern end was adopted. In a secret order from the MEF General Headquarters dated 13 April, the objective was spelt out: 'The object of the expedition is to assist the fleet to force the DARDANELLES by capturing the KILID BAHR plateau, and dominating the forts at the NARROWS.'[7] Once this was achieved the combined navy, army and fledgling airforce could advance on Constantinople.

Lemnos, lying about 90 kilometres west of the Allied objectives, was an excellent staging post for the invaders. A generous Greek government, the current owners, offered it to the Allies as a base in February 1915.[8] The ANZAC covering force, the 3rd Brigade, had been ensconced on Lemnos since 4 March, practising for their all-important role as the first ashore at Z Beach to establish a beachhead.[9] From 6 March until their departure, the 3rd Brigade conducted disembarkations and landing exercises—including disembarkations with opposed landings, route marches and attack practice—almost on a daily basis, weather permitting.[10] Lemnos's only drawback was a shortage of water to service the huge demands of the Allied ships and men.[11] Consequently, most of the troops were kept on board for the duration of the interlude at Lemnos. The Gallipoli beaches to be attacked were only hours away. The anchorage was a huge natural harbour at Mudros on the island's southern shore, ideal for accommodating the massive invasion armada the Allies were assembling to attack the Gallipoli Peninsula.

More than 200 warships and countless other vessels assembled in Mudros Harbour, many of them brimming with troops.[12]

Private Bill Hutchison of the 4th Battalion described the scene:

> Arrived at Lemnos and entered big natural harbour crowded with warships. French, Russian, and British. The country reminds me of New Zealand especially the snow capped peaks of several mountains. There are a number of camps to be seen on the shore.[13]

During their incarceration on the *Lake Michigan*, Major James Heane wrote a letter home which one of the local papers, the *Dubbo Dispatch*, paraphrased, describing the conditions on board for the major:

> The boat, the name of which the censor forbids mention, was not so palatial as the old *Euripedes*, but Major Heane had a cabin to himself, small as it was. There was no room for drilling aboard, but there was room to do inspection work, clean arms, give physical drill, lectures . . . there was a great number of ships about, but he was precluded from saying anything about them . . . The major mentioned that all the handkerchiefs he took from Australia were left behind in his trunks at Cairo. An order had been given that no white handkerchiefs were to be taken on service. So coloured handkerchiefs had to be procured.[14]

In another letter home Heane commented on their training 'somewhere in the Levant':

> We have left Egypt and have been on board for about 12 days. We have been practising disembarking, and expect to go into action within a couple of days.[15]

According to Les Lott, to pass the time on the *Lake Michigan:*

> We used to swim about the Harbour from one boat to another, and having a good time. Cards was a general thing at night.[16]

Once the 4th Battalion reached Mudros Harbour, Chaplain McKenzie was at the forefront of entertaining its ranks on the transport. He reported:

> Thursday 8/4/15 . . . Each day brought fresh Transports into the harbour and also a number of fresh Warships until the sight was the most imposing

I have ever seen in wartime. I got ashore frequently to purchase food for the boys on the ship.

While in the harbour we held several concerts. Also a couple of consecration meetings for the Troops in addition to the usual Church Parades which were very successful on the Sunday mornings. At night we had a fine meeting on the aft main deck, the singing at which was a noteworthy feature. The boys calling for their favourites—we sang for fully half an hour after the service until 'lights out' was sounded on the bugle. Many of the boys said 'thanks it has been a great night'. During the days of waiting the troops practise landing in boats and pontoons etc. although they had a good deal of time on their hands when they practised gambling with cards.[17]

After an initial period of relative inactivity, training for the 4th Battalion was stepped up. The big day for not just the 4th Battalion, but for the 1st Brigade generally, was 14 April, when the troops of the brigade disembarked and were towed to the shore in 'small rowing boats', preparing them for an amphibious landing at Z Beach. Then they attacked local hills, again replicating their anticipated landing site. A number of diarists recorded the day's events.

Private Bill Hutchison remembered the training on 14 April in particular:

> Disembarked and landed on the Island for manoeuvres. Officers and crew from HMS *London* towed our boats ashore with their Steam Pinnace. We landed wading up to our knees, and carried out an attack on the island.[18]

Likewise, Les De Vine recalled the 1st Brigade's exercises:

> The whole Brigade landed today, the arrangements were very faulty, but this is our first attempt at being taken ashore by the naval authorities, the naval pinnaces tow our long string of boats to the shore, where we hop out & wade to the remaining distance, then a march through a few villages to the open country to attack some hills on the sky line. We meet the Dublin Fusiliers ashore, who were doing the same thing from their transports, in fact the whole fleet of transports are practising landing on an open beach from transports far out to sea, we are all very tired today & landed with full packs & ammunition which is very heavy.[19]

Corporal Howard McKern also recollected the training of 14 April:

> A large number of A.I.F. Batts and Dul. Fus. [Dublin Fusiliers] went ashore today in lines of open boats towed by pinnaces from HMS *London* and *Prince of Wales*. Had to wade ashore out of boats. Had landing attack on some hills.[20]

While according to Les Lott:

> We put in nearly three weeks on the Isl doing some severe training. In the morning we went ashore practising landing, jumping into the water and rushing different hills. It made us fit and well . . . in the afternoons we had lectures on what we were going to do when we landed on Turkish soil.[21]

Signaller Tom Barr of B Company, 4th Battalion, recalled the same disembarkations:

> Skirmishes took place on Lemnos Island; landing was made from small boats we plunged into the water, then raced for the beach, just a repetation of what really took place later.[22]

Private Richard Edwards had this to say about training on Lemnos on 15 April:

> We had orders this morn that we were to go ashore. We were towed by a motor launch. It was too shallow to take us right in, so we had to jump in about 2 ft. of water and wade ashore for about 200 yards and afterwards take a position (hill) about ½ mile away. It was a lovely day & we soon got dry again. Returned aboard again about 2.30 pm dinner at 4.30 pm.[23]

The plan for the amphibious operation involved British landings at five beaches around Cape Helles at the foot of the Gallipoli Peninsula, with the untried Anzacs landing at Z Beach some 20 kilometres further north on the Aegean coast near Gaba Tepe; hence the need at Lemnos to repeatedly practise disembarkations in small boats, ending in the troops rushing objectives onshore. In order to confuse the Turks as to the real focus of the Allied landings, French forces were to effect a temporary landing at Kum Kale on the Asiatic side of the Dardanelles while the Royal Marines were to enact landing at Bulair in a feint more than 50 kilometres to the north of the Anzacs' destination where the peninsula narrowed invitingly to an isthmus. Twelve hundred Royal Marines, using the same tow-in tactics as the Anzacs, were to remain in their boats north of Xeros Island from late afternoon to 9.30 p.m. on 25 April. These troops were from the Portsmouth, Chatham and

Deal battalions. The intention of the Allies was to use the British 29th Division to capture the high ground, Achi Baba, behind the beaches at Cape Helles. Once this was accomplished, the Kilitbahir Plateau, the massif dominating the central part of the peninsula, could be attacked.

In order to keep the Turks guessing and to draw valuable reserves away from the British operations at the foot of the peninsula, the ANZAC landing was, according to General Sir Ian Hamilton, the commanding officer of the Mediterranean Expeditionary Force:

> . . . of the nature of a strong feint which may, and we hope will, develop into the real thing. My general staff has marked out on the maps a good circular holding position, starting from Fisherman's Hut . . . round along the upper spurs of the high ridges and following them down to where they reach the sea, a little way above Gaba Tepe. If only Birdwood can seize this line and fix himself there for a bit, he should in due course be able to push on forward to Kojah Dere.[24]

He reiterated these objectives in a letter to Field Marshal Lord Herbert Horatio Kitchener, the British Secretary of State for War, written on the same day, 10 April, as his diary entry:

> I am convinced the very essence of success must lie in upsetting the equilibrium of the Turk by the most rapid deployment of force possible over a fairly wide extent of country combined with feints where troops and launches cannot be spared for an actual serious landing. My main reliance will be on the 29th Division . . . The Australians meanwhile will make a strong feint which will, I hope, develop into a serious landing operation north of Gaba Tepe, and if they can maintain themselves there, I should hope later on they may be able to make a push forward for Kojah Dere. Whatever this does, it will tend to raise anxieties in the minds of the men opposed to the 29th Division, and will prevent the plateau being reinforced.[25]

Hamilton was proposing the Anzacs probe the peninsula's core, with a view to further operations, depending on their initial success. Koja Dere was a village about 5 kilometres inland from Z Beach. In a despatch written after the event by General Sir Ian Hamilton to Lord Kitchener, in London, Hamilton again outlined the Anzacs' proposed part in the proceedings:

> I must begin by explaining that their role at this stage of the operations was—first, to keep open a door leading to the vitals of the Turkish position, secondly, to hold up as large a body as possible of the enemy in front of them, so as to lessen the strain at Cape Helles. Anzac, in fact, was cast to play second fiddle to Cape Helles . . . [26]

Lieutenant-General Sir William Birdwood, the Australian and New Zealand Army Corps' commanding officer, revealed his concerns regarding his force's objectives in a private letter written on 19 April:

> I hope my advance may not be checked, and that we may be able to shove through and gain the first ridge [what became known as Second Ridge], which is about three-quarters of a mile from the shore . . . I shall hope to secure the whole of the hill and entrench myself, when I shall feel pretty secure of holding my own against anything that can come against me and, if possible, I shall hope to shove on in the direction of Mal Tepe [a prominent feature, a few kilometres beyond Koja Dere] . . . I may find this difficult, however, as Mal Tepe is likely to be commanded by guns from all directions and I shall really not know in which direction to expect attack . . . I have great hopes of my being able to effect my first landing in the dark without any great opposition, but I am afraid we may come in for a baddish time of it when it gets light.[27]

The orders Birdwood then issued to Major-General William Bridges, the commanding officer of the 1st Australian Division, reflected these scenarios:

> The objective of the covering force and the subsequent action of the Army Corps is to secure a position covering the Kaba Tepe—Fisherman's Hut Landing Place; the landing of the Army Corps; and an advance to cover the enemy's North and South communications in the vicinity of Mal Tepe . . . When this situation has been secured, you will be guided by the situation as to whether you make a further advance, or consolidate your position until the landing of the bulk of the Army Corps permits the development of an advance towards its objective—Mal Tepe.[28]

In turn, Bridges instructed his four brigade commanders—MacLaurin, McCay, Sinclair-MacLagan and Monash—on their separate objectives, concentrating on establishing a beachhead and entrenching along what became known as Third Ridge from its heights at Chunuk Bair to its coastal termination at Gaba Tepe.

Any advance from this defensive position towards Mal Tepe would depend on a number of factors, from the speed and strength of the enemy's response to the Z Beach incursion to the British success at Cape Helles.

Some idea of the fighting capabilities of their enemy, the Turks, was gained by the Anzacs from a report about the war on another front in Mesopotamia—modern day Iraq, involving the British and the same foe. On 19 April 1915, General Sir Ian Hamilton received the following intelligence from Lord Kitchener, warning Hamilton and his troops of the Turks' fighting qualities:

> Following extract may be of interest to you, describing the recent fighting at BASRA:—
>
> The Turkish troops were well disciplined, well trained and brave. Their machine guns had been well concealed, and were used with great effect, and their trenches were admirably (? situated) part at 1100 yards, and part at 800 yards, at foot of slope leading from us down to them. Turks had no idea of being shot out of their trenches, and had to be turned out by a charge of the whole line with the bayonet. If pluck and determination of our troops, both British and Indian had not been of the sternest, and if they had not been handled with initiative and decision, battle would not have been won. Trenches were finally captured about 4.30 p.m. and being so well concealed, brunt of taking them fell on the Infantry.[29]

Needless to say, this report was widely circulated amongst the Anzacs in the days leading up to the invasion. Les De Vine's diary entry for 22 April showed the dissemination of such intelligence to the troops:

> Birthday today [Les turned 29], nearly forgot it, rather a quiet day, two parades as usual. Lecture this afternoon by Maj McNaughten [Major Macnaghten was the 4th Battalion's deputy commanding officer] on the Turkish position in Gallipoli & where we might have to land, he showed us a very fine military map of the country. Warned for guard tomorrow.[30]

A footnote to the Kitchener report—the Anglo-Indian force operating in Mesopotamia in 1915, emboldened by earlier successes such as the one in Kitchener's report at Basra, drove the Turks back towards Baghdad throughout 1915. In attempting to reach Baghdad, the British and Indian troops were checked at Ctesiphon, 24 miles south of Baghdad on 22 November 1915. The British force withdrew to Kut al Amara on the Tigris River and was surrounded by a superior

Turkish force under General Nur-ud-din by 9 December 1915. The British commander, General Townshend and his 11,600-strong garrison were then besieged by about 25,000 Turkish soldiers for the next five months. Despite British attempts to relieve their harrowing situation, the result of the siege was a humiliating surrender by Townshend and his emaciated army to the Turks on 29 April 1916.[31]

The following perspective, published in *The Sydney Morning Herald* on Wednesday, 1 September 1915, was written by Corporal Howard McKern of the 4th Battalion at some point before the Landing. It showed the men were well aware of the importance and gravity of what they were about to attempt, not just personally, but also in relation to the place Australia would occupy in the world and in history as a result of their efforts. It showed the mindset of the Anzacs as they steamed towards Z Beach and their date with destiny:

> Corporal Howard Taylor McKern, who died of wounds received in the recent attack of the First Brigade on Lonesome Pine, Dardanelles, enlisted at the start of the war. He finished his course of agriculture at Wagga experiment farm, prior to engaging in wheatgrowing in which he was occupied just prior to the war. He was the fourth son of Mr and Mrs James McKern, of Mosman, and had reached the age of 22 years.
>
> The following extract from one of his letters to his parents on leaving Australia indicates the spirit in which he and his comrades of the Brigade went to war, and made them fight with such valour:– 'We are able to go out and fight in a cause which we are proud to do our little to uphold. May God help me and all of us to do our little bit thoroughly and well. We have a very strong cause to fight for; we have the backing of our nation's grand past history behind us; and we have the knowledge that this Australian army marks practically the first attempt of any importance that Australia has made to assert herself amongst the nations of the world. Any failure on the army's part means a blot on Australia's future history; while we should make our mark, be it ever so small, we will be happy in the knowledge that Australia has fought and been of assistance in a good and righteous cause.

Lieutenant-General Sir William Birdwood reiterated McKern's hopes and concerns in a message to each and every man in the corps on the eve of their invasion. This was one of a number of messages read to the troops on their respective ships as they made their way to Z Beach. Other communiqués from General Sir Ian Hamilton, King George V and Colonel Henry MacLaurin were read by Lieutenant-Colonel Onslow Thompson to the 4th Battalion, assembled on the deck of the *Lake Michigan* at about 7.30 p.m. on 24 April. This was Birdwood's message:

> **Officers and men**
> In conjunction with the Navy, we are about to undertake one of the most difficult tasks any soldier can be called upon to perform and a problem that has puzzled many soldiers for years past. That we will succeed I have no doubt, simply because I know your full determination to do so. Lord Kitchener has told us that he lays special stress on the role the army has to play in this particular operation, the success of which will be a very severe blow to the enemy, indeed, as severe as any she could receive in France. It will go down to history to the glory of the soldiers of Australia and New Zealand. Before we start there are one or two points which I must impress on all, and I most earnestly beg every single man to listen attentively and take these to heart.
>
> We are going to have a real hard and rough time of it until, at all events, we have turned the enemy out of our first objective. Hard rough times none of us mind, but to get through them successfully we must always keep before us the following facts. Every possible endeavour will be made to bring up Transport as often as possible; but the country whither we are bound is very difficult, and we may not be able to get our wagons any where near us for days, so men must not think their wants have been neglected if they do not get all they want. On landing it will be necessary for every individual to carry with him all his requirements in food and clothing for three days, as we may not see our Transports till then. Remember then that it is essential for everyone to take the very greatest care not only of your food, but of ammunition, the replenishment of which will be very difficult. Men are liable to throw away their food the first day out and to finish their waterbottles as soon as they start marching. If you do this now, we can hardly hope for success as unfed men cannot fight and you must make an effort to try and refrain from starting on your water bottles until quite late in the day. Once you begin drinking you cannot stop and a water bottle is very soon emptied.
>
> Also as regards ammunition you must not waste it by firing away indiscriminately at no target. The time will come when we will find the enemy well entrenched in positions from which we shall have to turn them out, when all our ammunition will be required; and remember—
>
> - Concealment whenever possible.
> - Covering fire always.

- Control of fire and control of your men.
- Communication never to be neglected.

W. R. Birdwood[32]

General Sir Ian Hamilton's message was more succinct, but equally daunting for the men aboard ship waiting to go into action, the overwhelming majority for the first time:

General Headquarters
21/4/15.

Soldiers of France and the King.
Before us lies an adventure unprecedented in Modern War. Together with our comrades of the Fleet we are about to force a landing upon an open beach in face of positions which have been vaunted by our enemies as impregnable.

The landing will be made good by the help of God and the Navy; the positions will be stormed and the War brought one step nearer to a glorious close.

'Remember,' said Lord Kitchener, when bidding adieu to your Commander, 'Remember, once you set foot upon the Gallipoli Peninsula you must fight the thing through to the finish.'

The whole world will be watching our progress. Let us prove ourselves worthy of the great feat of arms entrusted to us.

Sgd. Ian Hamilton.
General.[33]

King George's message was relatively brief, but no less important to the men:

The King wishes you and your Army every success, and you are constantly in His Majesty's thoughts and prayers.[34]

The final message the 4th Battalion heard came from Colonel Henry MacLaurin, commanding officer of the 1st Brigade, who was also to the point:

Men:
You are soon to go into action. Your training has made you fit for it and I have the greatest confidence in your courage and resolution.

Just one word—keep a cool head, and listen to fire orders of your officers. When you shoot, let every bullet find its mark; when you use the bayonet, see that you stick it in.

Good Luck.

Mudros Bay, H.N. MacLaurin, Colonel,
April, 1915.
Commanding 1st. Infantry Brigade.[35]

After a false start on 23 April due to gale force winds, the date for the invasion was fixed for Sunday, 25 April. Les De Vine noted the beginning of the fleet's much anticipated move:

> 23/4/15 Bn guard all day 7–11 am 7–11 pm the transports begin to move out this afternoon, & all steam us up ready for moving at once. 9 or 10 ships leave during the afternoon after 4.30. We are under orders to move off at 12 am tomorrow, our landing will probably take place early on Sunday morning, we are now awaiting orders.[36]

The 4th Battalion war diary simply stated:

> Saturday 24th April, 1915 Lemnos. Left Mudros Harbor 12 Noon. Arrived anchorage North East side of Island 7.0 pm.[37]

Captain Arthur Tebbutt, the 4th Battalion's medical officer, described the preparations the officers of the battalion undertook as the *Lake Michigan* began the historic journey to Z Beach:

> . . . when the battalion left Mudros in the late afternoon on the *Lake Michigan*. This transport steamed round to the northern part of the Island of Lemnos where it lay off till after darkness had set in and then steamed towards the Gallipoli Peninsula. That evening was spent in putting finishing touches to our maps and most of our officers had coloured in contours and the Turkish trenches, redoubts and battery positions as far as our information went.[38]

Howard McKern was quite excited as he described leaving Mudros Harbour and the men's last night aboard the *Lake Michigan*:

> Served out with rations for three days. Left the harbour [Lemnos] at midday. Great sight as we passed *Q.Elizabeth, Triumph, Askold*, a couple of French boats and our old friend HMS *Euralyus* and also a great number of transports. Our pipe band played us out and attracted great attention. Sailors, marines etc. all swarmed out on decks of warships as we past. Outside we steamed through the waiting fleet but we went straight on and passed the *Jean Damour* and several French destroyers. This afternoon we were all lined up and the Colonel read us messages from Colonel Maclaurin, Sir Ian Hamilton and the King. Then the Colonel gave us a short and very appropriate address and included a eulogy to ourselves. The old Colonel showed us again the gentleman he is. We are having a merry evening of it. I forgot to mention the very successful 'Last Concert' Capt. MacKenzie got up last night. Perhaps it was the most enjoyable we have ever had and everyone was in very good spirits A fleet of six battleships steamed slowly past us where we are anchored—on the North of Lemnos—on their way to the Gulf for tomorrow's big affair . . . Just making sure by sharpening my bayonet as we are the first supports sent in tomorrow.[39]

Chaplain McKenzie, the heart and soul of the 4th Battalion, wasn't allowed to land with his boys. The chaplains' war diary recorded on 25 April that 'All chaplains were specially warned not to leave their ships so they did not land then'.[40] In McKenzie's case, Lieutenant-Colonel Onslow Thompson justified not allowing McKenzie's participation in the Landing: 'We need all the rifles we can cram into the boats, Padre. You wait your turn.'[41] However, at least one chaplain did land on 25 April. Father John Fahey, a Catholic priest, explained his presence with the 3rd Brigade: 'I was the only chaplain to land with the first lot. I believe an order came out that we were to land only the second or third day, but it never reached me.' His firsthand account of the Landing makes riveting reading—narrow escapes, death all around him and the heroism of the covering force in driving the Turks back and establishing the beachhead: 'No doubt it will bring sorrow and mourning to many a home, but it was a feat of arms Australia has every reason to be proud of . . .'[42]

McKenzie did comment on the last 36 hours with his boys as they prepared for battle:

> We held a wonderfully successful concert on Friday night. It was among the very last held. The troops were in great fettle. We sailed from Mudros Harbour at 12 noon on Saturday April 24th sailed to a point around the island of Lemnos and anchored. All lights were hooded. We retired early.

> The ship again sailed for the landing place about midnight. We steamed slowly meanwhile. Everybody was awake by 3 a.m. and had breakfast at half past.[43]

Corporal Charles Bosward remembered the concert and showed the regard the men of the battalion had for Bill McKenzie:

> Friday . . . Had a glorious concert on board for the last night led by Salvation Army Chaplain Capt. W. MacKenzie who is a champion . . . Everybody is cool and not showing least sign of fear.[44]

Les De Vine was equally effusive about the day's events:

> Under orders to sail at 12 am, iron rations for three days served out—two tins of bully beef, tea, sugar, biscuits, & cubes of 'Bovril', also rations for the first day of landing, bully beef & biscuits, we had to rearrange our packs to get all the food in, also an extra ration of water securely corked in an empty lemonade bottle in case of emergency. Had to hold my overcoat & sweater and secure same to my belt under pack. Full parade at 7.30 pm when an address was given by the Colonel Onslow Thompson, who explained our operations for tomorrow viz—We are to sail at 12 am to meet the rest of the transports at a prearranged meeting place in another bay further North, we are to remain there until midnight, when we are to be joined by the fleet, and proceed to the point of disembarkation where we are to force a landing, covered by the guns of the whole fleet. The 3rd Brigade are to land first to form a covering part for the rest of the army. He also read a letter from the Brigadier Col McLauren one from General Sir Ian Hamilton, one from Gen Birdwood and one from the King. The men are all very light hearted & gave three cheers for the Colonel & the Major. Special tea served tonight, bully beef & eggs, the men were especially excited during tea time and sang all the time, kicking up a terrible noise no smoking or striking matches allowed after 7.30 pm and all lights were put out. Filled water bottles which is to last three days, also small soda bottle as an extra ration Am under orders to report to Captain Christian on landing to be held as ammunition carrier to the firing line if wanted We all carry a small supply of wood, obtained by breaking up small boxes, each man tying a bundle on the top of his pack, this is a precaution to be taken in case we are unable to find any suitable fire wood after landing to boil our 'billies' I feel very fit and very anxious to set about the job. All

the boys tonight are singing and are in great spirits, bayonets are sharpened and everything ready for tomorrow. Went to bed early evening tired, we are all anxiously awaiting tomorrows events.[45]

Staff Sergeant-Major John Sloan was more measured in his appraisal of what they were about to undertake. In a letter home from the 'Karpa Teta Firing Line', dated 22 May 1915, he wrote:

> On the evening of the 24th we received our orders; The Aust Division were to land at Karpa Teta. The plan of landing was to be a surprise, the fleet of transports were to move to a position near the shore four abreast 300 yds interval and all lights out; At 8 p.m. every light was switched off on deck and every porthole screwed below. The 3rd Brigade was ahead of us, their boats were to be in position at 3 am and were to land and endeavour to take and hold the hills that rise from a sandy shore. Slowly and silently into the gloom this great fleet moved each ship in its allotted place, every man in his section ready for an accident or mine.[46]

~

Jack Collyer, as a member of No. 12 Section, No. 15 Platoon, D Company, 4th Battalion, was about to land as part of an amphibious invasion of an unknown, remote shore thousands of kilometres from Australia. In his diary Jack referred to their destination, Z Beach, as the 'Gollipoli Peninsular', Anzac Cove having not yet entered the troops' vernacular. It was their *esprit de corps* at each level of the battalion's structure—developed over the months of bonding and training in Sydney, aboard the *Euripides*, in the shadows of the Pyramids and the Sphinx on the monotonous sands of Egypt, and on land and on board the *Lake Michigan* at Lemnos—that Jack and his mates would rely on in action. However, in the immediacy and urgency of battle, it was the section and platoon that dominated the experience. The actual members of the section changed over the battalion's period of training. The Egyptian leg of the AIF's journey saw the restructure of its battalions from eight companies to four companies, with individual soldiers changing companies and, therefore, platoons and sections. As well, men were sent home from the Australians' desert camp in early 1915 as medically unfit and for disciplinary reasons. Their replacements were drawn from the First, Second and Third Reinforcements who arrived in Egypt during the first few months of 1915. Each AIF section was a mixture of these ingredients.

Who were Jack's mates in No. 12 Section with whom he would share this life-changing and dangerous experience?

Jack, fortuitously, wrote down the names of most of No. 12 Section in his third diary during a lull in training on Lemnos. There were probably another five names missing from his list of seven. Jack did not include Corporal Charles Macquarie (495) in the list, but two brief references by Macquarie in a letter from the front about events in early May 1915—'my section consisting of Jack & 10 others' and 'we, No.12 Section of D. Co'[47]—left no doubt about his participation and role.

Macquarie had been appointed as an NCO in No. 15 Platoon as part of the battalion's restructure on 1 January 1915. The 28-year-old, who enlisted at the end of August 1914, was single, Sydney born, a wool classer by trade who had served with the NSW Scottish Rifles.[48]

The following were the other members of No. 12 Section who Jack recorded in his third diary.

Private Clyde Bock (230) was 24 years old, single, Tasmanian and, at just 5 foot 9 inches, the equal tallest member of the section. Clyde was a mechanic who lived in Sydney prior to enlisting on 23 August 1914. His previous military experience was limited to Cadets at school.[49]

Private William Bound (1090) was a 20-year-old coalminer who joined on 1 September 1914. He was also single and had previously served in the 41st Infantry for two years. Bill was another Tasmanian, born in Launceston.[50]

Jack listed himself next—Mudgee born and bred, he was single, a 24-year-old labourer who had served in the militia.

Private Ernest 'Snowy' Robson (1088) was the section's youngest member, having enlisted on 4 September 1915, aged 19. By the time he was heading to Gallipoli on the *Lake Michigan*, he was 20 years old. Snowy, as the fair-haired Robson was known, was a bushman by calling, hailing from Uralla, born and raised on the New England Tablelands of New South Wales. He was also single and had not received any previous military training.[51]

Private Alfred Robins (1426) was a member of the Second Reinforcements for the 4th Battalion who enlisted on 12 December 1914. Alf was the shortest member of the section, being only 5 feet 4½ inches. A shearer from Junee, he was single, aged 25, and also had had no previous military training. Alf was the least experienced, sailing from Sydney on 11 February 1915 on HMAT *Seang Bee*, before undergoing a short period of training prior to the Landing. The brevity of his formal training was best shown by Alf only being allocated to the 4th Battalion at Mena Camp on 30 March. Within days the Australian and New Zealand Army Corps departed Egypt for Lemnos.[52]

Private Leslie Lott (1397) was another of the Second Reinforcements who only joined the battalion on 30 March in Egypt. Les, like Alf, had had no military experience before enlisting on 24 November 1914. He, at least, had a couple of weeks' more training in Sydney than Alf prior to embarkation. Les was 23 years old, and the same height as Clyde Bock—a towering 5 foot 9 inches! He was, like the rest of his mates in No. 12 Section, single. A wood machinist by trade, Les was born in Moruya, New South Wales. He was the only Roman Catholic in their ranks, the others being various Anglican denominations.[53]

Private Thomas Thomson (1115) was a 25-year-old Scotsman from Dumfries, a Doonhamer, just over the border from England. Tom's military experience was of a different calibre to that of the rest of the boys, as he had served four years in the King's Own Scottish Rifles in Britain. Like the rest of the section, Tom was single. Only 5 foot 5 inches tall, he was a joiner before his military service, having spent five years as an apprentice in Dumfries learning his trade. Tom had only recently arrived in Australia before enlisting.[54]

These eight men were a microcosm of the greater battalion, brigade, division and corps—in many ways a typical AIF section of the First Contingent. They were between 5 foot 4½ inches and 5 foot 9 inches tall, two of them being under Charles Bean's minimum height of 5 foot 6 inches. The average height in the section was just over 5 foot 7 inches. Half of the section had had no previous adult military training. Only one—Tom Thomson, the Scotsman—was born overseas; however, this was at odds with the rest of the battalion: nearly half the men were born overseas. They worked at a wide variety of occupations before enlisting: wool classer, mechanic, coalminer, labourer, bushman, shearer and wood machinist. The men came from the bush and the city, although a majority were born in country towns. They were relatively young, the oldest being Corporal Macquarie, aged 28; Snowy Robson, at just 20, was the youngest, some six months younger than Bill Bound, who was also only 20. Their experience of life was limited. The boat trip from Australia and the training in Egypt was the highlight of their lives thus far. What they were about to attempt on the 'Gollipoli Peninsular' on Sunday, 25 April 1915, would surpass all that.

~

In the early hours of Sunday, 25 April, the *Lake Michigan*, with the 4th Battalion on board, steamed towards Z Beach. The men were given strict orders in regard to their conduct in the boats taking them to the beach. Service dress was to be worn and the following instructions closely followed:

> In boats.
> A. Silence will be observed.
> B. No one is to stand up.
> C. Rifles will be carried in the hand, not slung.

> D. Rifles will not be loaded.
> E. Equipment will be loosened and shoulder straps unbuttoned.
> F. A military officer will be in the bows of each boat, and will be the first to land.
> G. On arrival at the beach all troops are to remain seated in the boat until the Naval officer or petty officer in charge of the boat gives the order to land, the military officer in the boat will consult with him as to this.[55]

The war diary of the 4th Battalion summed up the battalion's part in the initial phase of the ANZAC's invasion:

> Sunday 25/4/15 KABA TEPE. Arrive at point about 1 mile north of KABA TEPE. First shot fired from shore 4.50 A.M. First tow left *LAKE MICHIGAN* 6.45 A.M. containing beach party 1st Infantry Brigade Head Qrs. Battalion Head Qrs. and Brigade Signal Section.—1.5 p.m. Landing of 4th Battalion complete.[56]

The 4th Battalion, like most of the invading Australian and New Zealand force, landed in the northern section of their designated area, Z Beach, at the soon to be famous Anzac Cove.

Jack's diary recorded the tumultuous day, although his version of events as they were towed towards the shore was very calm:

> Was roused out of bed at 3 a.m. to find ourselves surrounded by our battle ships, including Queen Elizabeth. We were supposed to have been the first to land, but arrangements had been altered, + we were nearly the last brigade. Long before daylight we were almost deafened by the firing of our battle ships, booming out shrapnel on the enemy. The fire was returned by the enemy, but they did no damage, their shrapnel may have killed a few fishes, nothing more, for their shots all fell in the water. Then, towards daylight, we heard the crackle of rifle fire on the shore, + it was evident that our boys were about to prove their worth. This continued all day. Boats full of troops were continuously being landed, + we were watching them anxiously waiting our turn to go off the ship. Shrapnel was falling all round the little boats, but no one was hit, as far as I know. At about 10.30 a.m., our turn came, + we loaded on to the pontoons. Everyone was cool, calm, + collected, + smoking as contentedly as if they were looking at a football match or on a picnic boat. All went well until we got close to the beach, when a couple of shells flew past us,

+ fell a few hundred yards away, doing no damage. The ships were still at them. We eventually landed, + were taken up along a gully, which was full of Turks a few hours previously, + was cleared by a splendid charge by our Aus. 3rd brigade. We carried our water-bottles full, 3 days rations, 200 rounds of ammunition, + our full packs.

Clyde Bock, also of No. 12 Section, gave a brief reference to the Landing in a document written some time later:

> I was with Capt. Fanning when he left Australia and landed at Gallipoli with him on the memorable 25th April 1915. We landed in the same open boat from the Ship [*Lake Michigan*].[57]

At the time of the Landing, Fred Fanning was a lieutenant in charge of No. 15 Platoon, one of four platoons that constituted D Company, and it was under his watchful eye from the bow of the boat that the troops moved towards the shore. Jack and his mates were one of the last boatloads of the 4th Battalion to land.

Les De Vine also landed later in the morning and had a similar experience to Jack's:

> The transports about 11 o/c came under a heavy shell fire and were compelled to move to a safer position, nobody being hit. The 4th Bn landed between 11 & 12am under a hot shrapnell fire, we left the *Lake Michigan* and embarked on a destroyer, being packed like sardines, we are now under shell fire continuously shells fell all around us but none actually hit us while the destroyers raced for the beach, when within a few hundred yards we eased down and were transferred to ships boats, in which we were rowed through a curtain of shrapnel fire, safely landing on the beach, there being no casualties on my boat.[58]

It was on the way to the beach that the other significant officer in Jack's military career, Major James Heane, in charge of D Company, 4th Battalion, earned his enduring and endearing sobriquet, 'Cast Iron Jimmy'. The nickname was a tribute to his calm, almost cavalier demeanour under fire, beginning that morning at Anzac Cove on 25 April 1915 as Heane and the men of his company were taken towards the shore:

> As the boats slowly moved towards the Gallipoli shore . . . he and another quietly discussed the personal responsibilities of the occasion. Heane

frankly admitted his dread of fear, but resolved that, so far as he himself was concerned, this emotion must be made impersonal, and it is in keeping with his character that henceforth he gave no sign of his inward feelings. A few moments later, when the first bullets splashed around his lighter, he thrust from himself all thoughts of personal safety, and concentrated his every faculty on the job at hand. From that day onwards he became known as 'Cast Iron Jimmy'.

> Those who were with him were amazed by his courage and imperturbability. He seemed to think the Turks could not hit him.[59]

Once ashore the troops were required to clear the landing place immediately and proceed in silence, without forming up, to a rendezvous, where reorganising into platoons, companies and battalions would take place. From there the units would be deployed as needed. Unfortunately, the desperate nature of the early fighting precluded many battalions from following the script too assiduously. Not so the 4th Battalion, which landed in daylight, suffering few casualties. A famous photograph of the beginning of their arrival about 8 a.m. showed an orderly, almost casual scene, the men calmly disembarking from their boats, which were close together and packed with troops. One body, that of an Australian engineer, Sapper Fred Reynolds of the 1st Field Company Australian Engineers,[60] lay almost forgotten at the water's edge. There was no sense of urgency; it could have been a training exercise, although the ever-present Turkish artillery and rifle fire punctuated the air, occasionally finding its mark. By the time the battalion assembled on the beach in the early afternoon, the momentum of the invaders had stopped and they were digging in along Second Ridge, staving off Turkish counterattacks. The Anzacs certainly drew Turkish forces to their landing at Anzac, thereby fulfilling a requirement of Hamilton's orders. Regrettably, the high ground leading to Chunuk Bair, on the Anzacs' left, was lost during the late afternoon and with it any immediate chance of further progress.

Captain Tebbutt's medical section was also one of the last to land:

> Disembarkation. This did not begin from the *Lake Michigan* until about 10 a.m. and proceeded by companies, and I disembarked with my stretcher bearers and A.M.C. Details and the last batch of infantry of the 1st Echelon onto a Destroyer. Here I attended to a number of naval personnel wounded on previous trip shorewards. Arriving a short distance from the shore, we transferred to rowing boats and rowed till we touched the shingly beach where we waded ashore and found the remainder of the battalion at the mouth of a small Gully, afterwards Headquarters Gully, in Anzac Cove.

> The actual place of landing was about halfway between 'Ari Burnu' point and Hell Spit. Whilst waiting for orders here I remember dressing 1 casualty in the 4th Battalion (from Shrapnel fire) but I saw a number of cases from other units which had made their way down the hillside apparently from Plateau.[61]

Once again Sergeant-Major Sloan gave a concise account of the 4th's movements that morning:

> As morning broke we heard the rifle fire of the 3rd Brigade who were carrying out their great purpose, later we saw plainly the hills of Gallipoli and fleet of transports in their proper positions each guarded by a man-of-war. Our Regiment was selected to be the first to land in daylight . . . We landed and moved up a gully where we rested as reserves.[62]

The 4th Battalion was the divisional reserve for the 1st Division to be deployed as the need arose. For part of the morning and much of the afternoon some members of the battalion were used as ammunition carriers. Les De Vine, A Company, was one who did this valuable work:

> Reported for duty to carry ammunition to the firing line for the rest of the day under heavy shrapnell fire. We had vy many casualties but fortunately was not touched myself although had many escapes from the concealed snipers behind our lines, during my many trips backwards & forwards.[63]

In his diary, Les Lott, one of Jack's section mates, recounted a story involving a Turkish sniper on that first day:

> One amusing incident I saw. an Indian [presumably from the 7th Indian Mountain Artillery Brigade that landed on 25 April] lead in a mule with store(s) when his mule was shot by a sniper. he takes his big knife and sets off up the hill. the way he move(d) was marvellous. Couldn't see him at all till a glitter of a blade shone out. The Indian returned with a smile all over his face carrying a Turkish Rifle and a head held by the hair. he had avenged his mule[64]

Lance Corporal Howard McKern was another to carry ammunition:

> Landed at 12. Took ammunition up, got under fire at once. We were under shrapnel fire most afternoon. Lost none. Queen Lizzie had one or two beautiful shots. Carried ammun. to several brigades. Going to 2nd our party was followed by shrapnel for half an hour.[65]

From Jack's account it appeared that the rest of the battalion marked time, spending at least some of it in Long Valley, soon to be renamed Shrapnel Valley or the Valley of Death. The position the Anzacs had seized was later described as:

> consisting of one main gully about a mile long running in a North Easterly direction from the sea, the sides of the gully were steep slopes running up to a well defined ridge with numerous smaller gullies of different lengths branching from the main gully. The country was wild covered by a very thick undergrowth which found most excellent cover for Turkish snipers who got within our lines and on several occasions held up all traffic along the only pathway, which was the dry riverbed at the gully bottom . . . the water supply was small.[66]

There the battalion witnessed the tracks to and from the firing line, choked with the traffic of the wounded and dying descending to the beach and medical help, and the passage of troops carrying ammunition, messages and supplies ascending to the firing line. Jack's account of the next few hours showed the uncertainty of their role:

> We stayed in the gully for an hour, + enemies shells were bursting around us but no one was hit in the halt. We then marched up to the hill, halting a few yards from the crest. Here the shrapnel was very thick, + all of us had narrow escapes.

From Gaba Tepe and Anderson Knoll to the south and dotted along Third Ridge and Sari Bair, Turkish artillery batteries, most newly arrived as the ANZAC threat unfolded, rained shrapnel and some high explosive shells on the Anzacs throughout the morning and the afternoon, from the beach to the firing line being established on Second Ridge. Corporal George Mitchell of the 10th Battalion in the covering force from the 3rd Brigade was one of the first to experience a shrapnel explosion. As he was making his way uphill from the beach, Mitchell heard a:

> weird shrieking note somewhere in the air, which increased in volume every fraction of a second. It culminated in a deafening report and a cloud

of smoke some thirty yards on my right, and thirty feet high. Simultaneously there was a swishing sound as the bullets beat down bushes and swept the earth and a devilish scream. The scream was caused by large pieces of the case, as they spun through the air.[67]

Each shrapnel shell contained between 230 and 375 cast-iron balls and was able to be timed to explode at ground level or in the air, propelling its deadly contents in advance of the shell burst. According to the *1909 Field Service Regulations*, the width of the area of the ground struck by the bullets of an effective shrapnel is about 25 yards [about 23 metres]. The limit of the forward spread of the bullets of shrapnel burst at effective range is about 200 yards [about 183 metres].[68] The effect of numerous artillery pieces firing was a curtain of lethal enemy fire that could be spread over a wide area or concentrated on a particular position along the length and breadth of Anzac. Many narrow escapes and casualties were inflicted on the Anzacs, who were desperately trying to establish a foothold on the peninsula as at least 30 Turkish artillery pieces fired sustained rounds into the ANZAC beachhead that afternoon. The sound alone was unnerving, let alone the impact on the inexperienced troops.[69]

Jack, like his mates, was amazed by the stoicism of the wounded and their display of 'true British spirit'—to remain positive in the face of adversity:

At 5 p.m. we were brought back to the beach, + just as we began to move, our Serg-major [Freeman] was wounded in the arm by a spent bullet, + put out of action. We got some awful sights while in the gully, wounded men from the firing line being brought past us on stretchers, others with legs + arms shot through, wounds in the head, hobbling down past us to the red cross depot. It was marvellous, the happy disposition of those men. All had a re-assuring word for us, + many assured us that they would be back with us directly, when they got their wounds dressed. We knew this was impossible but it showed the true British spirit. Even those whom we could see would never recover from their awful wounds, tried to smile.

Les Lott in his account of the first day ashore also commented on the remarkable fortitude of the wounded:

The way our wounded bore up was the most marvellous thing heard of. to see a chap crawling back with his leg or arm shattered, a smile on their face and cheering us on. some with slight wounds wouldn't go back.[70]

Snowy Robson, the youngest of Jack's mates in the section, later claimed:

> The bravest thing I saw was a young fellow crawling down to the beach with his hand and half his leg off, refusing to be helped, saying that there were plenty needed it more than he. 'Anyhow,' he said, 'I don't think I'll last more than an hour.' What became of the lad I don't know.[71]

It was almost certain that this encounter occurred during that first day in the valley as the 4th waited and watched, eyes wide open.

Private Michael Quigley of A Company, 4th Battalion, graphically described his first hours ashore:

> Successfully landed after miraculously dodging shrapnel and a scalding rifle fire from the right and left. The first feelings when under fire are not easily described but you can imagine my feelings to see hundreds of dead and dying—some moaning quietly, others suffering their unattended wounds in silence. We knew not when it was our turn next and from bushes on all sides snipers, artfully concealed, wrought terrible havoc in our ranks as we rushed madly up the slopes.
>
> Suddenly they found our range and shrapnel followed shrapnel in soul-terrifying quick succession and our ranks were further depleted. I was knocked over but not badly hurt. They dropped a few more and we rushed for cover only to find that they had machine-guns trained on us in our new position.[72]

Mick Quigley, known as 'Quig', had a well-developed sense of the ridiculous, as many of his letters and diary entries describing his experiences showed, even though this account of his baptism of fire was decidedly serious. Two of his letters from Gallipoli were published in a local newspaper in 1915 with the accompanying comments by the editor: 'Dear old "Quig."—he simply can't be serious. In the midst of a vivid word picture of the inferno he will break off to get in a humorous remark',[73] and, '"Quig." Simply can't write a serious letter, but he writes a very interesting one.'[74]

Quig wrote another version of the landing to Cecil Carr, a friend in Dubbo, on 13 May. It was vintage Quigley, entirely from left field:

> A Turk's no gentleman. There we goes and lands—a kind of visitin' party with medicine for the poor Sick Man of Europe. It wasn't none of your tasty, haughty medicine prescribed by a third year student at the Dubbo

High School Medical Faculty Class. But it was still stuff of a beneficial and salutary effect. And what does 'e do? I shriek again. Why treat us as charlatans, and our medicine as a nostrum—and here's where he showed his lack of culture and his benightedness and his hebetude—and proceeds without no invitation from us, to pour down our dignified and stately necks the remedies we were bringing to him! It quite upset me I tell you.[75]

In another letter Quig referred to the Anzacs' place of landing and occupation as a 'Turkish Goat Farm', explaining that 'This, I understand, is what the country is used for—goat farming, not blood spilling'.[76]

~

In the late afternoon the 4th Battalion eventually deployed to what became known as Bolton's Hill, named after the commanding officer of the 8th Battalion, Lieutenant-Colonel William Bolton, the 8th having occupied the position earlier in the day. Bolton's Hill was on the far right of the ANZAC firing line on Second Ridge at the southern edge of 400 Plateau. (See the map of Anzac on the day of the Landing on page 109.) A series of phone calls during the late afternoon between Colonel James McCay, the 2nd Brigade commanding officer, and Major-General Bridges, the 1st Division commanding officer, convinced Bridges of the greater need for the 4th on his right flank. His left flank under Colonel Sinclair-MacLagan, the 3rd Brigade commanding officer, had retreated from the hotly contested Baby 700 to positions around the head of Monash Valley and was holding on as dusk fell.

McCay had spread his battalions across 400 Plateau and onto Bolton's Hill as the day unfolded; however, his order at 3.30 p.m.—for his Victorian battalions to consolidate and entrench along Second Ridge from Bolton's Hill to the head of Owen's Gully[77]—disclosed the peril his men faced in fulfilling it. In the confusion and chaos of the morning, the units of the 2nd Brigade, apart from the 8th Battalion, had become intermingled and dispersed, and there was a major gap in the firing line between the 8th Battalion on the right of Bolton's and the next units from the brigade further north on 400 Plateau. Earlier in the afternoon Major-General Bridges had despatched one of his staff officers, Major Thomas Blamey, to liaise with Colonel McCay and report on the situation on the Australians' right flank. At 3.30 p.m. Blamey rang Bridges at Divisional Headquarters and confirmed the need for reinforcements. An hour later, with no sign of further troops, McCay himself telephoned Divisional Headquarters at 4.45 p.m., Blamey having returned to the beach. In an interview with Charles Bean in 1920, McCay explained the dire circumstances:

> As a result of the fight drawing the 5th, 6th and 7th Bns to Lone Pine there was a gap of 500 yards at least in which I had no men at all . . . I discovered it pretty early. I tried to get the troops to fill it. I made the 8th Bn extend as far as it could and then rang up DHQ. White said: 'The general has only one Bn left, and General MacLagan has been very hard pressed and the general is loath to dispense with this Bn until other troops come ashore to-night.' McCay said: 'I cannot manage it. I cannot extend the 8th anymore. Unless I get reinforcements the Turks may come through at any time.' In a minute or two Bridges' voice came through the phone: 'White tells me you want reinforcements,' he said, 'I have only one battalion left.' I said; 'I must have that or they can come in right behind the right.' He asked me to speak to him not as subordinate to general but as McCay to Bridges. I assured him that the need for these troops was absolute.[78]

With Major Blamey acting as guide, the 4th Battalion left the beach around 5 p.m. and headed towards the gap in the firing line being established on Bolton's Hill and 400 Plateau. After crossing White's Valley and McCay's Hill, the battalion entered Victoria Gully and, turning left, made its way through thick scrub up the valley to the heights above and occupied the northern end of Bolton's Hill. Headquarters for the 4th Battalion were established near the head of Victoria Gully at Brown's Dip. It was only 'about 10–20 yards behind the front trench'.[79] According to Colonel McCay, the 4th was just in time: 'Half an hour after the gap was filled the Turks came against it.'[80]

The 4th's war diary continued:

> 4.55 P.M. Received orders Prepare to move to support 8th Battalion on right of position—6.45 P.M. took up position and entrenched line 224-R-4 and N.E. Corner of 224-R.[81]

During the eventful first 24 hours of the ANZAC invasion, Bolton's Hill was pounded by Turkish artillery batteries to its south at Gaba Tepe and on the southern and central parts of Third Ridge, including those at Anderson Knoll and near Scrubby Knoll, all of which had a clear field of observation and fire at the Australians hurriedly entrenching on Bolton's and along Second Ridge.

Jack's take on their eventual deployment was missing any place names at this early stage. He was also oblivious to the tactical reasons for their move, apart from their role as divisional reserve. It took nearly two hours for the battalion to negotiate the unfamiliar geography and dense scrub from the beach to the firing line on Bolton's:

> We eventually re-organised on the beach, + marched up towards the right wing of the firing line. We halted on a knoll, under cover from rifle fire, but very much among the shrapnel to get rid of our packs. Directly we halted, a shell burst amongst us, + our sergeant of no. 12 section was hit by the case, + went over, + I, as second in command of the section, took charge.

This was the last entry made by Jack in his Gallipoli diary. The knoll in question was Bolton's Hill. The diary concluded with a dramatic statement about Jack taking control of No. 12 Section as the men began their baptism in the firing line, revealing Jack was the back-up to Corporal Macquarie. Once the sergeant was hit, Corporal Macquarie took his place and Jack stepped into the breach left by Macquarie. Jack's platoon, No. 15, under Lieutenant Fred Fanning, was positioned on the far right of the battalion's extended line, with only No. 16 Platoon between it and the extreme left of the 8th Battalion, also on Bolton's. Jack probably updated this diary during the battalion's abbreviated beach bivouac on 30 April. While they were on the beach, a call to arms came from Regimental Sergeant Major Henry Pearce, meaning the diary had to wait and the men had to hurriedly fall in. That could explain its abrupt ending.

The first night ashore was an arduous one. The battalion was occupying an unknown position on foreign soil, it was raining, it was dark, it was cold, there were only the most basic of earthworks offering scant protection for each man, and the Turks fired at them incessantly and counterattacked repeatedly. In Snowy Robson's words:

> My worst twenty-four hours was the first twenty-four hours on Gallipoli—wet through, cold, hungry, thirsty, and everyone growling.[82]

After their deployment along Bolton's Hill, which the Turks named Kel Tepe or Bald Hill,[83] the 4th Battalion experienced attacks from two contrasting Turkish regiments: the 27th Regiment, a Turkish unit, and the 77th Regiment, a mainly Arab unit. A Turkish regiment consisted of three battalions of 1000 men; in turn each battalion contained four companies of 250 troops, and every company had four 60-man platoons. Every regiment also had a machine gun company of four Maxim machine guns.[84] Just as the Australians and New Zealanders were known as Anzacs and the British as Tommies, the Turkish troops were called *Mehmetciks* or *Askers*. Anzac slang for the enemy included 'Abdul', 'Jacko' and 'Johnny Turk'.

Elements of the 27th Regiment, commanded by Lieutenant-Colonel Mehmet Sefik—later known as Sefik Aker—were the troops driven back by the 3rd

Brigade covering force of the Anzacs at daybreak that morning. Three companies from the Turkish regiment's 2nd Battalion were in place, covering the coast from Gaba Tepe to Fisherman's Hut north of Ari Burnu. The fourth company was held in reserve near Gaba Tepe.[85] The remaining two battalions were also in reserve, bivouacking at nearby Maidos. These battalions, mobilised early on Sunday morning, were used by Sefik in a counterattack that afternoon on the Anzacs' southern flank. They certainly attracted the attention of the Australian commanders, who ordered their mixed units to dig in along Second Ridge as part of the 27th Regiment prepared to attack Lone Pine in the afternoon.[86]

The use of the term 'Turkish army' is something of a misnomer. The Turkish troops—volunteer and conscript—were recruited from virtually every part of the diminished Ottoman Empire. In its ranks were Greeks, Armenians, Syrians, Palestinians, Iraqis, Kurds, Lebanese, other Arabs and Turks, particularly Anatolians from the heart of the mother country, Turkey. The Ottoman Empire itself was declining, its European vassals having mostly achieved independence, and its African possessions plundered by European powers in the five decades leading to World War I. Libya, Tunisia, Egypt, Serbia, Macedonia and Cyprus were some of the nations that exited from the empire during that time. Turkey had laboured under the Russian Tsar Nicholas I's gibe as the 'sick man of Europe' from 1853[87] and had been treated accordingly by the European powers—by the outbreak of war a slow dismemberment had reduced the empire to Turkey, a European rump and a series of nearby Arab provinces. Edward Erickson, a noted expert on the Ottoman army in World War I, summed up the type of soldier either forcibly or voluntarily recruited into the Turkish army on the eve of war:

> The Turks had a multi-ethnic peasant army composed of largely illiterate and non industrialized soldiers. Sometimes the Ottoman soldiery could not speak Ottoman Turkish and many even had interests overtly hostile to the empire's continued existence.[88]

Lieutenant-Colonel Mehmet Sefik wrote a detailed profile of his regiment in 1935. He went to great lengths to describe his men, beginning with a flattering appraisal of the officers:

> Most of the officers were brave young men, zealous and devoted to their duties and they made a good impression on the staff by their power of command and sincerity. Above all they were so highly esteemed that they could be relied upon in every way. But among them there were one or

two who by their nature lacked courage and purpose. But even they acted like the rest . . .

Of the soldiers in the three Bns and the machine gun Coy of our Regt., 50% were inhabitants of BIGA district, 15% the GALLIPOLI Peninsular, 15% LAPSEN district and 20% were from the villages and small towns of various other districts close to central ANATOLIA and CANNAKALE. These were all mixed up together. 99% of them were agricultural workers. About three-quarters of them were married, with families, and one quarter were bachelors. Their ages were between 21 and 35. In general one could see at a glance their tough faces and robust bodies and the exceptional qualities of our brave race could be read in their serious looking eyes. Those who are able to read these qualities in them are left with the impression that they are men who cannot bear to be defeated by their enemies, are not afraid of the harshness and cruelty of war, are loyal to the national character and to their beloved country and are bold, zealous and sincerely devoted to their duties. They have been well brought up for war, and their good marksmanship has carried them forward.

In the whole of the Regt. there is discipline, friendliness and an air of harmony and also throughout the Regt. there is a spirit of self-respect which seems to say, 'Why should I be overcome by the enemy? I will certainly defeat him!'

The men were armed with MAUSER rifles. Just as there were no machine gun organisations in the Bns, so also there were no light machine guns. Each man in every section was equipped with two grenades. Other men had portable digging implements. Large digging implements were also carried in A echelon transport. The guns of the machine gun Coy attached to the Regt. Command were of the MAXIM type. (four guns) . . .

As regards the men's clothing, the situation was not too bad. But it cannot be said they were well clothed. There was a proportion of our loyal minded young men who carried with them their own personal civilian clothes. It was beyond the power of the Regt. to make good deficiencies of this kind. For the cause of these deficiencies one had to look to the shortcomings of the Government of the day . . .

I should like to say this, that in this Regt. there is such mutual confidence and such an enduring unity of spirit has been established that a firm resolve has been emplanted upon the minds of all in the Regt. from the highest to the lowest that if necessary for the sake of the Regt. we will fight to the last man but there will be no retreat.[89]

The Turkish Mauser rifle had a five-round magazine and a maximum effective range of up to 2000 metres. The Lee-Enfields wielded by the Anzacs had a similar maximum effective range of about 2000 metres, but had the advantage of a ten-round magazine. Both rifles' optimum effective range was under 1000 metres, ideal for the confines of Anzac. Maxim machine guns, used by the Turks and the Anzacs, were capable of firing up to 500 .303 rounds per minute with a maximum range of 3600 metres. Each one was operated by a team of four to six men, who were responsible for assembling, sighting, firing, carrying and supplying 250-round belts of ammunition as well as cooling the gun's mechanism via a water jacket surrounding the barrel.[90]

The men of the 27th Regiment were Turkish peasant farmers used to hardship and the rigours of war. They were well armed and had a strident sense of nationalism, especially when defending their homeland. Struggling to cope in an outpost of the empire was one thing, but invading the motherland was something entirely different. However, not all of Sefik's Askers were happy with their lot in the 27th Regiment. Three members—Ali Said, Hussein Ahmed and Mustafa Riza—were captured by the Anzacs on the day of the Landing. This was the subsequent report of their interrogation by lieutenants Price-Gordon and Hay that was forwarded to Lieutenant-General Birdwood:

> Three prisoners all Turks from Asia Minor were examined. They are from the 1st and 2nd Battalions of the 27th Regt of the 9th Division of 3rd Army Corps. Halil Sami Bey is in command of Division. There are no Germans in the battalion . . . The men are Mustahfiz and surrendered willingly. They were called up three months ago and recently came up from Chanak as part of 400 mustahfiz. They are tired of war having been fed only twice daily on wheat porridge and beans. They have no pay. They were unarmed as being telephonists. The telephone has broken down. They understand the troops have 150 rounds per man. Christians are employed in non combatant services.[91]

The other regiment to attack the 4th Battalion that first night was the 77th Regiment, a so-called Syrian Arab unit. It was a product of the Ottoman Empire, a mostly conscript force that did not have the same sense of nationalism or drive of its Turkish counterparts. Recent research showed that, on 1 November 1914, the 77th Regiment had 64 officers and 3179 men from a variety of ethnic and religious backgrounds enlisted in its ranks. The officers were largely Turkish, but the other ranks were Syrian Arabs—Yezidi, Nusayri—along with 1000 Turkish reserves from Thrace.[92] The Yezidi and Nusayri were minority communities in the Ottoman province of Aleppo in Syria. One of the regiment's biggest problems was the inability of the majority of the troops to speak or understand Ottoman Turkish. When the regiment received its colours at Catalca, Turkey, on 6 November 1914, the formalities were translated into Arabic as well.[93]

The 77th certainly underwent an intensive training regimen on an individual, regimental and divisional basis from the end of September 1914 until its deployment to the Gallipoli Peninsula on 25 February 1915, where it came under the command of Lieutenant-Colonel Mustafa Kemal, the commanding officer of the 19th Division. By then it had been training hard for five months and the men were toughened up. Training continued under the demanding eyes of Mustafa Kemal.

That first night ashore the Turks attacked the Anzacs' right flank, with two battalions of the 77th Regiment featuring heavily. At 10 p.m. these troops launched a major assault squarely at Bolton's Hill; like earlier attacks, it was unsuccessful. (See the map of Anzac on the day of the Landing on page 109.) The 8th Battalion and the 4th Battalion were caught up in the fighting, repelling these attacks. The 8th Battalion's war diary gave a succinct account:

> The enemy attacked heavily during the night on our left but were repulsed, heavy firing throughout the night.[94]

The 4th's war diary described a similar tense experience:

> Pressed hard most of night but held on. All companies in firing line and support none in reserve. Apprx 60 Casualties.[95]

Individual diarists in the 4th Battalion also wrote of the fighting they endured during their initial experience in the firing line. Les Lott, from Jack's section in No. 15 Platoon, noted in his diary:

> All night they attacked our position, but we managed to hold out. in between attacks we dug our trenches, the work being very hard. to start our trenches we had to be on our stomach and scratch with anything at all, mostly entrenching tool without the handle, for to stand up to dig would have been a sudden exit.[96]

Private Michael Quigley from No. 3 Platoon, A Company, recorded the deployment with his usual clarity:

> Then under a scalding fire we rushed a Turkish trench on the right flank. The boys were dropping everywhere but we got there. Then it was our turn and cries of 'Allah' were to be heard in all directions. Those of them who were not killed broke and ran for their lives followed by the boys in little groups acting on their own. Later we all joined hands in the trenches we captured on the first crest and proceeded to dig furiously. The Turks counter-attacked several times through the night but we made it too hot for them and they retired.[97]

However, Quigley's alternative account of this action in his letter to Cecil Carr was more colourful:

> In the original advance I took cover at one stage behind one of the trenches from which they had retired. They had anticipated such action, and it was not long before I discovered that they had a machine-gun trained on the trench, with the range to a T. The bullets whizzled and zizzled and frizzled (the magazines and papers speak of the 'crackle' of rifle fire and the 'scream' of a shell). I differ a little from their author blokes, but I'm a private; got to eat 'umble pie; and it aint for me to raise my weak, puny voice in dissent. We made a headlong rush forward 100 yards or so, and there we stayed till night fell—under a cruel, relentless fire from the Unspeakables. I squirmed myself into a surprisingly small target, and the chap two feet on my left got a bullet through his brain. That evening we entrenched on the crest.[98]

Private Bill Hutchison wrote cursorily of their deployment:

> The 4th took up a position on the heights + started dig ourselves in + during the night kept up a very hot fire on the enemy.[99]

Private Richard Edwards remembered the enemy attack:

> The enemy tried to rush this position we gained, but our fire was too heavy. The fighting spirit of the men is splendid.[100]

Charles Bean also wrote about the enemy fusillade that first night:

> All shellfire had ceased with the fall of night. But from the hills overhead the roar of rifles continued without an instant's intermission; for three days and nights it never ceased—such rifle fire as few ever heard again.[101]

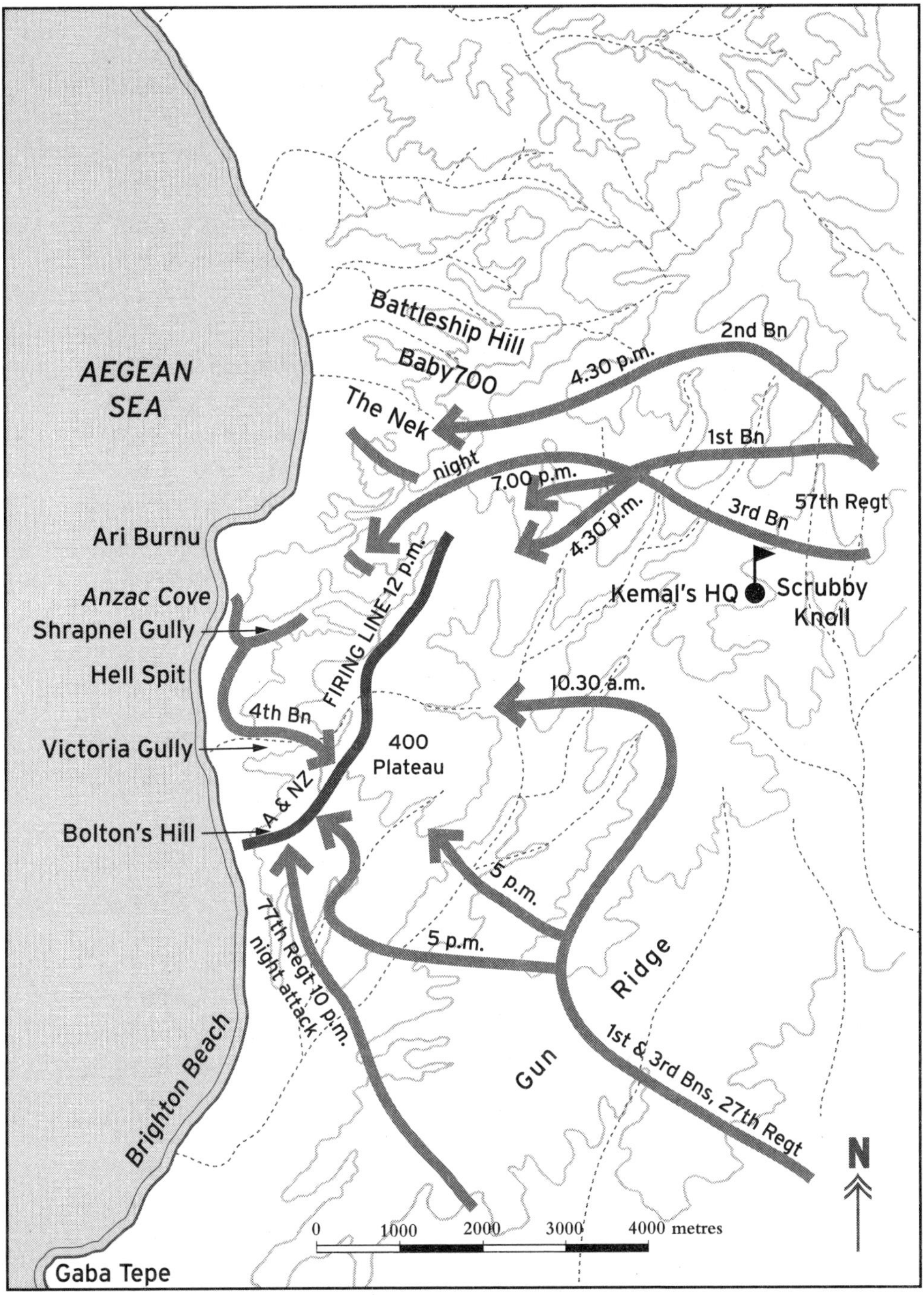

4th Battalion, 25 April 1915

Anzac on the day of the Landing, showing the movements of the 4th Battalion and the Turkish assaults.

The Turkish attacks the men repelled began soon after the 4th deployed along the ridge, filling the gap between the Victorian battalions of the 2nd Brigade. Although, as Les Lott admitted:

> The way our line was thinned out was awful. in [places] there were over 50 yards without a live man to defend it. if the Turks had only [known] what part of our line to attack they must have got through, as no one there to stop them, but they lost their chance that night.[102]

The earlier Turkish attacks that began as the 4th Battalion deployed were made by the 27th Regiment. The Turks gained a foothold on the Johnston's Jolly lobe of 400 Plateau as a result of these attacks. The later incursions came from the 77th Regiment.

The performance of both Turkish battalions on the night of the Landing showed the inherent differences between them. According to Turkish military sources, their counterattacks during the evening of 25 April had mixed fortunes:

> Although, definite developments have been achieved in the 27th Regiment's attacks and the whole of Kirmizitepe [Johnston's Jolly] was seized, the Kanlisirt [Lone Pine], was abandoned as an outcome of an event occurred in the southern flank.
>
> This event stemmed from the deserting Arabian soldiers, who formed most of the troops of the 77th Regiment. They had hidden themselves in the dense heath and upon the intensive bombardment of the English battleships they fled the battleground.
>
> In fact, many Turkish soldiers and few young Arabs had fought against the English bravely side by side.
>
> The darkness of the night, the unending bombardment of the fleet, irregular formation of the terrain had increased the dispersion of the troops. The control was lost, everything was out of control. The random firing of the Anzac troops and the deserter Arabs had adversely affected the units fighting in the southern sector of the 27th Regiment; and the beginning of the desertions have rendered this night attack useless.[103]

This analysis was harsh, but it did contain references to significant reasons for the failure of the 77th Regiment's attack. It was dark and the terrain was unfamiliar. It was raining as well. What it doesn't mention were other important factors, namely the communication problem between the officers and the men, exacerbated by the darkness and rough geography. In light of these conditions it was hardly surprising that the attack became disorganised. The regiment's commanding officer, Major Saip, also came under close scrutiny for his role. According to Mustafa Kemal, the regiment made a number of operational errors, hardly the fault of the men. Kemal pointed the finger at Saip for being responsible for his regiment's poor performance on the night of 25/26 April.[104] The Anzacs' elevated defensive position, aggressive tactics and firepower on Bolton's Hill were very significant in defeating the counterattacks of the 77th Regiment.

The 8th Battalion, bearing the brunt of the Turkish attacks, used a forward echelon to break up the Turks. As well, Sergeant Charlie Traill's machine-gun section kept up a withering fire, thwarting Turkish attempts to form up and storm the Anzacs' line. A bayonet charge by elements of the 8th finished off the 77th Regiment's disjointed assault and scattered the enemy troops.[105] The 4th Battalion was also involved with No. 15 Platoon, including Jack and No. 12 Section, adding their Lee-Enfields' considerable volume of fire, shooting at the waves of attacking Turks. As the attack faltered and failed, some of the troops from the 77th Regiment were guilty of deserting their positions; however, plenty of them were still in place in the ensuing days to counterattack the Anzacs.[106]

~

Monday, 26 April, was largely spent by both sides consolidating their positions. Turk and Anzac were exhausted, diminished and desperate to hold onto their hard-won ground. The territory the Anzacs had seized was 'only a mile and a half [2.4 kilometres] in length from extreme north to south, and exactly 1000 yards [914 metres] from the sea to the furthest point inland. Its area was less than three-quarters of a square mile [just under 2 square kilometres]'.[107]

The Anzacs' disjointed firing line ran from Walker's Ridge, Russell's Top and then Pope's Hill in the north, along Second Ridge, encompassing MacLaurin's Hill, the western edge of Johnston's Jolly and Lone Pine, across Bolton's Hill, terminating on Brighton Beach to the south. Battle outposts were established in Wire Gully and in the rugged foothills north of Walker's Ridge. The Turks held the all-important high ground on Third Ridge in front of and to the Anzacs' left. They began to establish posts, using the favourable lie of the land to threaten the invaders' tenuous position. On both sides entrenching began in earnest, lines straightening and gaps closing where possible. Such was the lot of the 4th Battalion until a most remarkable and injudicious decision was made during the afternoon by Lieutenant-Colonel Onslow Thompson and his righthand man, Major Charles Macnaghten.

The 4th Battalion war diary's entry for Monday, 26 April 1915, began benignly enough:

> Weather Calm clear day admirably suited for disembarkation. Sea chop calm. Battalion temporarily attached to 2nd Inf Brigade—Day spent in improving the fire trenches also supporting trenches and Communication trenches. Snipers very troublesome all day—good supplies of ammunition + water brought up during the day.[108]

Les Lott's take on the start of the day was less serene:

> As soon as it was light a terrible sight met our eyes. dead bodies laying every where. but worse of all were to see the wounded trying to get back, some mangled of all shape.
>
> The Turks were to be seen moving back to prepare their badly broken line. Then our chance came to show what kind of Snipers we were and we easily held our own.
>
> And at daylight the Shrapnel which had eased off through the night starts again. our trenches now are about 18 inches to two ft deep and we have to crouch down, the look out being the only one exposed to any extent . . . all the time we are competing as snipers against the Turks. every one is very cool and the remark was often made by the Officer, (")[Les was recalling the observations of his platoon commander, Lieutenant Fred Fanning, encouraging the men as he made his way throughout the sections of No. 15 Platoon holding the firing line on Bolton's.]
>
> You are a cold blooded lot. any(one) would think that you were just shooting rabbits instead of human beings.(") A conference was held with the Admiralty and they wanted to withdraw us, but we wasn't having that as we were into it now and here to stop.
>
> The Artillery and machine gun fire is heavier than yesterday and played havoc with our lines. it is marvellous how anyone came out alive. nearly all day we worked and with bent back digging our trenches. we kept busy sniping as well till 2 pm.[109]

Les refererred to an extremely important decision made by General Sir Ian Hamilton, the commanding officer of the Mediterranean Expeditionary Force, in the early hours of Monday morning. In response to a late night entreaty from an anxious ANZAC hierarchy, seeking guidance to re-embark or remain after the chaos and heavy casualties of the Landing, Hamilton ordered his charges to stay:

> There is nothing for it but to dig yourselves right in and stick it out . . . Make a personal appeal to your men and Godley's to make a supreme effort to

> hold their ground . . . P.S. You have got through the difficult business, now you have only to dig, dig, dig, until you are safe. Ian H.[110]

Hold their ground and dig the Anzacs did—for the next eight months.

Michael Quigley also gave a clear picture of the appalling conditions that Monday morning:

> I am now a perfect object of misery, covered with powder, oil, dirt and blood; as I write this bullets are splattering around me like hailstones and only a friendly mound of dirt saves me from being riddled. I am supposed to be having a spell after a day and night of solid going, but there are dead and dying everywhere and one continued screech of lead through the air till it seems there is not a place on earth where one could lay down and have a sleep.[111]

Throughout the day the Turks and Anzacs traded heavy rifle, machine-gun and artillery fire. An inertia gripped most of the combatants, until the 4th Battalion undertook a disastrous sally onto 400 Plateau during the afternoon, mistakenly believing that a general advance had been ordered.

Major-General Bridges had been inspecting the Australian line to the north of Bolton's Hill on the edge of 400 Plateau early in the afternoon and gave orders to straighten part of it. He wanted the 5th, 6th and 7th battalions and part of the 15th Battalion to advance towards the Daisy Patch, joining the firing line of the Fourth to the south and the Tenth to the north.[112] To complete the manoeuvre, the two northernmost 4th Battalion platoons were required to move as well. However, the order received at 4th Battalion Headquarters was for a general advance. The 4th's war diary described the fiasco, which began in the late afternoon:

> 4.30 P.M. Got word for General Advance, evidently in error. Turks cleared from line of trenches in front, after which no orders as to movements could be obtained. Advance moving to left approx. 1 mile. Shrapnel fire opened up on us, we were compelled to retire.[113]

In Volume 1 of the *Official History*, Bean wrote an absorbing account of the moment the 4th's commanders acted decisively on Bridges' supposed order:

> Further south, where the 4th was holding the line along Bolton's Hill, a messenger burst in, flushed with haste, upon the battalion headquarters.

> 'Order for a general advance,' he said. 'The line is to make a general advance.'
>
> Major Macnaghten, the brave, hot-headed, forcible trainer of the Woolloomooloo cadets, sprang to his feet. 'I'll take the right, Colonel, if you'll take the left,' he said. Colonel Onslow Thompson and he hurried out. Both were strong, impulsive men, and at that time they saw nothing strange in such an order. The troops had been trained to act on words of command passed down the line . . . Onslow Thompson and Macnaghten did not wait to issue operation orders; they simply went out and led the men forward from the trenches. The left had already begun to move; Macnaghten went to the right and set it in motion. It swung to the left slightly behind the Colonel and formed a sort of second line. So, led by two of the bravest and most highly-trained officers in the force, without the vaguest instruction or any idea as to an objective, the 4th—the one whole and intact battalion in the 1st Division—went blindly on to Lone Pine. [114]

No. 15 Platoon, including Jack and his mates of No. 12 Section, and No. 16 Platoon were ordered by D Company's commander, Major Cast Iron Jimmy Heane, to remain behind as a reserve to protect the right flank of the advancing 4th and the left flank of the 8th next to them in the firing line on Bolton's.[115] According to Les Lott, they were also required to 'guard a gun which was placed just in rear of us'.[116] This was a gun from the 7th Field Artillery Battery from the 3rd Artillery Brigade manhandled into position, 224R4 (the map reference), behind Bolton's around 3 p.m. on Monday.[117] The gun was an 18-pounder weighing over a tonne. The lack of artillery support for the Anzacs on the day of the Landing was being redressed as suitable gun positions were found. (See the map of the 4th Battalion's ill-fated Lone Pine advance on page 116.)

So sudden was the movement of most of the battalion that the 4th's Medical Officer, Captain Arthur Tebbutt, stationed in the Regimental Aid Post near the valley floor of Victoria Gully nearly 200 metres behind battalion headquarters, had no idea it had occurred:

> I received no information from Battalion Headquarters that the battalion were going forward, but I learnt afterwards that the C.O. had no warning of the operation and had no time to let me know.[118]

In 1935, Mehmet Sefik, the commanding officer of the 27th Regiment, positioned opposite the 4th Battalion, wrote the following account, which gave the Turkish perspective of the 4th's startling manoeuvre that afternoon:

> The guns which the Australians had placed with great secrecy behind KANLISIRT [Lone Pine] were also adjusted for fire. Infantry and machine gun counterfire was also heard very intermittently. At just such a moment the Australians were seen advancing on KANLISIRT and from CELALDERE [Owen's Gully]. Both sides intensified their fire. When the Australians did not see the new attacks which they had been expecting from us on the night of 25/26 April 1915 and the following day, 26th April, and when they did not see our infantry which they knew had been close by opposite them on KANLISIRT, they must have been hopeful that a part of their force could go over to the offensive. Our firing had inflicted losses on the advancing Australians and had shaken them.[119]

The Turks believed their failure to attack led the Australians to take a chance and attempt to seize 400 Plateau. With the 4th to the fore, the Anzacs seized most of the Lone Pine lobe of the plateau, established a headquarters in Owen's Gully and reached the southern crest of Johnston's Jolly. The Turks reacted with heavy shrapnel, rifle and machine-gun fire. The majority of the battalion was pinned down, with no further orders or objectives in mind. (See the map of the 4th Battalion's ill-fated Lone Pine advance on page 116.)

It was at this point that the 4th's fortunes went awry. In a letter to *Reveille* in 1936, Major Harry Mann, then an NCO in the 4th Battalion Signals Section, described what happened next:

> On the afternoon of 26th April when in response to a then mysterious message the 4th Battalion left their pot hole trenches at the top of Victoria Gully and advanced vaguely into the scrub. I was attached to Colonel Onslow Thompson, and when the astonished Turk opened with shrapnel, we lay down and wondered what it was about. It was then that Major Heane strolled over while Jacko was sniping at everything he could see, and said to the Colonel—'You're the senior officer present, sir, what orders do you give?' Colonel Thompson said—'I give the order to retire' and jumped up and started off but was shot after a few steps.[120]

At dusk the lieutenant-colonel was fatally shot by a burst of Turkish machine-gun fire as he began to move towards the battalion's original position. Lieutenant Jack Massie, the battalion adjutant and writer of the 4th's war diary, was with Onslow Thompson and vividly remembered the circumstances of his death:

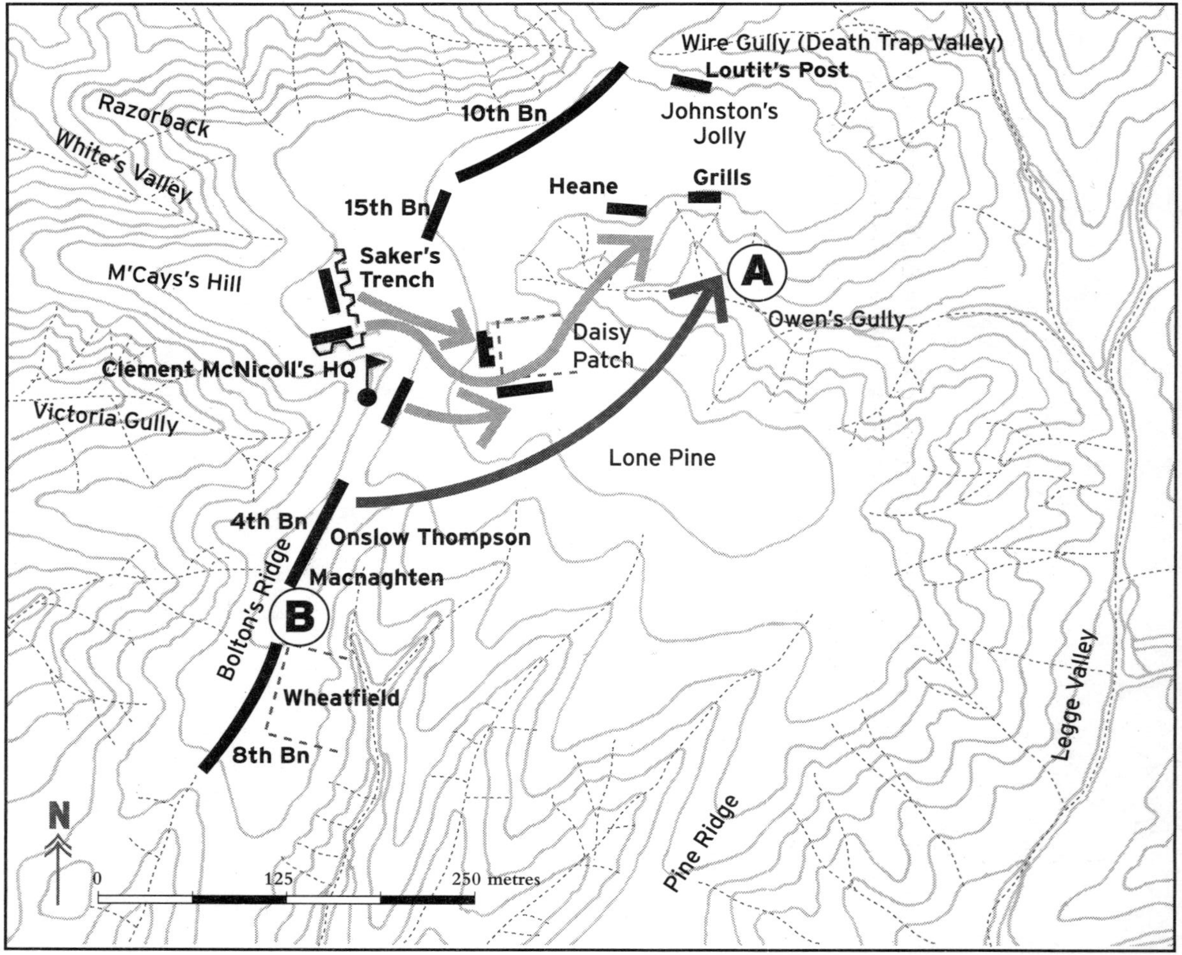

Ⓐ Late afternoon on 26 April, 4th Bn reach Owen's Gully. Posts maintained until midnight. Rest of Bn retreat at dusk. Lt-Col Onslow Thompson killed during retirement.

Ⓑ No. 15 and 16 platoons, including Jack, remain in trenches, guarding the flank. The rest of the 4th Bn mistakenly advance mid-afternoon.

The 4th Battalion's ill-fated Lone Pine advance, 26 April 1915

> I remember the sun was just about half below the horizon, and as we moved back towards it I could see the glint of the machine-gun bullets as they passed from behind and caught the light of the sun—a thing which sounds incredible but nevertheless remains clearly stamped in my mind.[121]

Massie carried Onslow Thompson's body in the retreat, but the Turkish fire was too heavy and he reluctantly left it in No Man's Land. It was later recovered on 11 May and interred by Chaplain McKenzie. Jack Massie wrote to his mother on 4 May, praising his former commanding officer:

> Dear Mother,
> I must write to the Colonel's people . . . He was loved by every officer, N.C.O. and man in the regiment and the mess regarded him as their best friend. It was a great shock when he was killed . . . It was great to see him with a rifle and bayonet, which he had picked up somewhere in the rush, in the lead.[122]

Unfortunately, Major Macnaghten, the battalion's second in command, was badly wounded late in the afternoon during the advance on Lone Pine. Bean's description of Macnaghten's plight that afternoon showed the major's fortitude:

> Macnaghten, shot through the chest, was leading forward some men whom he had rallied, when he was hit again in the throat. He staggered back to the dressing station, grateful for any helping hand, yet cursing because he wanted to lie down and die where the line had been. As he lay in the aid-post, he heard McNicoll's voice speaking to some stragglers. He struggled to his feet, drew his revolver, and started off again with three stragglers—all he could find—then he fainted, and was sent to the rear.[123]

Macnaghten wasn't to return to his beloved 4th until early June. On 14 July he was appointed commanding officer of the 4th Battalion; the incumbent, Lieutenant-Colonel Alf Bennett, transferred to the 1st Battalion as its new commanding officer.[124]

The 4th Battalion war diary continued its account of the unfortunate events of Monday afternoon:

> Advance re commenced but were mostly repulsed. A mixed party approx. 200 men became isolated under Lieut Col Onslow Thompson was shot dead during retirement. Battalion eventually re occupied its original position. Casualties estimated at approx. 150. Lieut M.P. Smith Signalling officer killed. His conduct was conspicuous having been wounded in the

knee and left to return to trenches he collected a number of men and almost succeeded in capturing a Machine Gun when he was killed by a sniper. The following officers were wounded severely Major C.M. Macnaghten, Captain S. Milson. Seriously wounded Lieuts P.F.V. Turner and R.T.F. Seldon. Trenches kept under continuous fire from snipers the whole night. Defences assisted by Artillery on extreme right and H.M.S. Bacchante the latter illuminated the enemy's position by searchlight and gave considerable assistance with her guns.[125]

Mehmet Sefik also described the conclusion to the Australians' spontaneous assault:

With the advance of our own infantry under the command of Captain ISMAIL HAKKI, who had counterattacked from the southern ends of EDIRNE ridge [Mortar Ridge], the Australians in the CELALDERE [Owen's Gully] fell back and the Australians who were moving forward on KANLISIRT [Lone Pine] suffered losses from our effective fire and they, too, withdrew and entered the positions to the west of KANLISIRT which they had tried to fortify the previous day and night and there they remained.[126]

In a letter to his mate, Cecil Carr, Mick Quigley had his own take on the afternoon's events:

We tore out and rushed about wildly. No one knew where we were going. The henemy 'ad unostentatiously and quietly retired. My platoon—50 of us—being the crack shooting crowd, was detailed off to scout the Valley, as the Brigade [the 1st was the only one in this attack on Stambool] whizzed past them. We shot three or four, and got one prisoner who kissed the sergeant fervently. It confirmed my worst suspicions of Turks. When we rejoined our battalion they had advanced about 1½ miles, and our platoon must have done at least two more diving around bushes and glens, looking for strays, as you would goats in your orchard. And then the thunderbolt! From a 1000 points we were fired on—shrapnel, machine-guns and rifles to an ad nauseum degree. We had been beautifully ambushed! And what a debacle it was! Back we bolted and for a few hundred yards my celerity would have been the envy of Altria, but it wasn't for long. The advance had told its tale, and I became very wearied—wearied to an alarming degree. Imagine my disgust at having to walk back, with shrapnel screaming

> all around, and everybody else scurrying at a goodly bat. Dead beat, I paused for a drink from a dead man's waterbottle, and then hurried on. It was a pitiable object that crawled back into the trench.[127]

The first inkling Captain Tebbutt had of the disaster that befell the battalion came with an increase in the sounds and sights of battle:

> In the afternoon there suddenly broke out an extremely hot burst of machine gun and shrapnel fire and I was wondering what it could mean when a number of wounded men from the 4th Battalion mostly, were brought into the R.A.P. amongst whom the 2nd in command of the Battalion [Major Macnaghten], and I was informed that the Battalion had just advanced from their position taken up the night before. From that time on through the night, we were kept continually at work dressing and carrying to the beach, with the aid of the 1st Field Ambulance bearers and nearly all the cases were from the 4th Battalion . . . the Battalion came back to the position originally taken up the day before.[128]

Even though much of the battalion retired with Onslow Thompson's party, some men remained in a series of supporting posts established by the 4th on Lone Pine and in Owen's Gully. These outposts were held until 10 p.m., when they were ordered to evacuate. The last of them was abandoned after midnight.[129]

One of Jack's mates from No. 12 Section, Les Lott, had a most adventurous and harrowing set of experiences from the afternoon of 26 April over the next few days. Unlike the rest of No. 15 Platoon, Les did not stay to guard the flank and a gun. This was what happened to him:

> I was on extreme end of our line as it stands with the rest of the Battn away. Our Officer (Fred Fanning) sent along the man on the flank (that's me) to go out and find the rest of D Coy and report what is doing. then starts my stiffest job as scout. After an hour's scouting among the hills I find them [and] reports back nothing doing. I no sooner reach back to the line as word comes for 15 platoon to follow. I lead the way. I rush up the hill from where the order comes from and find myself alone. The reason I find out a couple of days later was as soon as I moved off the order was cancelled. They called to me to come back but [I] never heard. So on I went alone, going up the hill. It was hell, the shrapnel falling like rain and snipers were everywhere. I no sooner top the rise and 'sip sip' am under machine gun fire. In the distance I see a party of our Boys which I

am making for. To reach them I have to go over a clear patch. To do so I have to run the gauntlet of machine gun. I get about halfway before they see me. Then the machine gun starts. God knows how they missed me for the air seems alive with bullets. I run as if the Devil is after me and reach them without a scratch. After I join them I find out the move has been organised by the enemy, who have spys in our lines, and that is how they had all the artillery trained on the way we came and machine guns ready as we topped the rise. I no sooner reached the party when word came along that a party of Turk(s) were advancing on our right flank. We were about 75 to 100 strong, 25 of them being Officers. Our Colonel who was with us after finding it has all been a hoax, gives the word to fall back on the line we occupied last night and hold them. He with about half our party starts off. He hardly goes 20 yards before he is shot dead. As I move to follow an Officer catches my sleeve and says 'For God's sake lads don't go back. Give them a chance to fix up our lines. We must hold them if to the last man.' So there we stay, about 50 all told. Twice the Turks came at us, but were surprised at the opposition they met (our numbers being only 30 odd) for they retired and our lines were saved. About midnight we were ordered to return to our lines. It being pitch dark we got split up. I find myself all alone. Not knowing which way to go I stay in a dugout I find. At day light I try to take my bearings. Seeing some Turks close by I decide to lay low for a while.

April 27th All day I lie in the dugout for there is nothing else to be seen but Turks. I do some sniping but have to be careful. At night I make as I judge back to our trenches, which I reach early next morning.

April 28th . . . so I decide to find my own unit, which I find after much manoeuvring to dodge snipers, in the same place I left them on Monday. I rejoin them about 3 pm.[130]

Snowy Robson was another from No. 12 Section who took part in the attack. In a letter to his sister he wrote:

I have had my cap shot off by a bullet from a machine gun, and my rifle smashed in my hand. All this happened in a charge the second day after we landed. We hunted the Turks off the hill, but about two hundred of us were cut off from the rest of the battalion, and the way they poured the shrapnel into us was awful and we had to retire.[131]

Private Bill Hutchison also recorded an account of the 4th's ill-fated charge:

During the afternoon at 2 o'clock we were called on to charge + the 4th gave a good account of themselves but lost a lot of men.

The Enemys machine gun fire was deadly to those who returned we had to retire to our old position very lucky. I believe the 4th Battn was mentioned in despatches—after the charge we had a great number of our men missing besides the Killed + Wounded.[132]

Some accounts, Charles Bean's in particular, claim the 4th Battalion was decimated during this action. This was not the case. Approximately 12 men died and about 60 men were wounded as a result of the action.[133] The battalion was not decimated; just badly shaken, having had its commanding officer killed and its second in command severely wounded. Major Storey was temporarily placed in charge. The battalion resumed the position it vacated earlier that afternoon; the unauthorised advance that promised so much having achieved so little. It was a debacle.

Mehmet Sefik had to deal with his own tragedy on 26 April:

An unfortunate incident happened on that day when three of us were standing almost in a line and a rifle bullet coming from the right of the Australians apparently have wounded all three of us, but it happened I was out of the line by about the thickness of three or four fingers, which saved me from being wounded, but severely wounded in the face and jaw my faithful batman BIGALI and my adjutant 2/Lt CEVDET and deprived me of their valuable service and help.[134]

~

Tuesday 27/4/15 Fine day until 4.30 p.m. when rain squall passed over—sniping heavy all day. A few casualties reported—8.0 p.m. enemy appeared to be going to make an attack and opened heavy fire, later they made use of British Bugle Calls 'Charge' 'Retreat' 'Cease Fire'. Artillery opened fire then till 4.0 A.M. 28/4/15 when sniping became very hot.[135]

This was the report of the 4th Battalion's war diary for Tuesday, 27 April—the day of the second Turkish attempt to overrun the ANZAC positions on Second Ridge and force them to evacuate their beachhead under fire.

At 7.30 a.m. a series of Turkish assaults began across the ANZAC firing line, including 400 Plateau. According to Bean, at 11 a.m. the Turks attacked in force across Lone Pine towards the lines of the 4th and 6th battalions.[136] The 4th Battalion diary didn't record these attacks. By 12 p.m. they were repulsed. By 6.30 p.m. the Turks, nursing casualties of up to 40 per cent in their battalions, called off the attacks and regrouped for a night assault. The 4th's diary referred to this, claiming the preparatory artillery barrage began at 8 p.m., the attack itself at 9 p.m.[137] Despite some limited success, the Turks were eventually beaten back; heavy casualties, darkness and their exhaustion conspiring against them. The 4th Battalion suffered at least 13 casualties during the course of the day—six men were killed in action and at least seven men were wounded in action; two men died of wounds as well.[138]

The bugle calls that the 4th's war diary and Les Lott mentioned were also noted by Charles Bean:

> That night was full of the tension following a great attack—of Turkish bugle-calls, shouts of enemy officers rallying their men, and cries of the men seeking to urge themselves to enthusiasm by calling upon Allah, while all the time maintaining a furious fusillade.[139]

All this was to no avail—the second Turkish counterattack failed.

On that Tuesday Snowy Robson had another close call, this time from enemy artillery:

> Three shells struck the trench I was in, and completely smothered me, and I had to be dug out . . . Barring little bruises about the body, I was none the worse.[140]

Turkish attempts at more subtle tactics to unsettle the Anzacs were given short shrift by their officers, Cast Iron Jimmy Heane epitomising their response. Mick Quigley described the Australian reaction in a letter home:

> It is not an infrequent occurrence to see a white flag hoisted gingerly in front of the Australians. The next ten seconds are occupied by our lads in speculations as to the range and then—exit white flag. It is done with the permission of the Australian officers, Major J. Heane being a notable transgressor in this respect. 'It is only a ruse,' he yelled out one day, and immediately 50 Australian rifles made the Turkish conspirators regret that in their bush jokes they had encountered an enemy bushwhacker capable of returning the joke.[141]

In another letter, this time to Cecil Carr of Dubbo, Quig praised Heane's demeanour: 'Major Heane was superb under fire—absolutely cool, calm, determined, self-possessed and reliant; the best man in the Battalion.'[142] Private Quigley and Major Heane were well acquainted with one another, both being Dubbo boys. Heane would regularly pass on his copies of *The Dubbo Liberal* for Quig to peruse. Early in the invasion the two crossed paths. Quig later recalled their encounter:

> 'More exciting than billiards, Quigley,' he [Heane] said as he bustled past one day.
>
> 'Yes,' I replied, with a modest droop of the eyelids, as is becoming to a private when replying to an officer.[143]

The following day, Wednesday, 28 April 1915, the 4th Battalion war diary recorded:

> Fine clear day till 6.0 pm when rain storm sprang up which lasted to 4.0 A.M. 29 /4/15 intermittently. About 20 casualties due to sniping on morning of 28/4/15 mostly in the head. Artillery reported having a good bag HMS *Baccante* shelled Turks entrenching in position approx. 700 yards in front of our trenches with high explosive shells. Results excellent. Everything very quiet during the night. One machine gun was put out of action during the morning by a sniper breaking the lock. New one supplied by the Navy.[144]

Les Lott was back in the embrace of his section:

> the trenches are now between 3 and 4 ft and are some protection now. Though we still have to keep low to dig it is not so hard as the first 2 days. it rained very heavily through the night and is bitterly cold, having no great coats or waterproof sheets to keep out the rain as they were in our pack which we dropped as soon as we put foot ashore.
>
> Through the night the Turks made some very severe counter attacks and we had hard fighting to keep them from breaking our line, but morning came and we still held our own.[145]

On Wednesday, 28 April, two other Turkish prisoners gave further insights into the morale of the enemy. Dimitri Papasoglu, an Orthodox Turkish-speaking Greek member of the 20th Regiment, revealed that an Arab-Syrian regiment, the 77th, 'has bolted and is now scattered all over the place—hiding'. Two days earlier an Armenian officer from the 77th Regiment who claimed to be a volunteer, and Onbashi Abdullah Oghlu Ismail, a Turk from the much-vaunted 57th

Regiment, were also interrogated. According to their interviewers, lieutenants Price-Gordon and Hay: 'In both cases they allow that the Turks are much shaken by our shell-fire and by our refusal to retire. The Arabs of the 19th Division are heartily sick of the war.'[146] Such was their view of the situation on part of the Turkish side of the Gallipoli fence.

Relief for the depleted ANZAC battalions arrived, with the Royal Marines Light Infantry landing on Wednesday. The Marines began replacing the Anzacs as dusk fell. However, as noted in its war diary, the 4th Battalion was not relieved:

> Thursday 29/4/15 Everything very quiet during the morning. No fresh developments. Got word at about 9.0 pm that Battalion would be relieved at 9.0 a.m. 30/4/15 by 3rd Inf Brigade. The work done with entrenching tools of web equipment was almost incredible. The position fortified almost entirely with this tool and proved satisfactory.[147]

More Marines arrived on Thursday; more ANZAC battalions straggled back to the beach—but still not the 4th.

Les Lott's version of events on Thursday was poignant and revealing. He described just how hard it was to man the firing line and dig continuously with no sleep, little rest, a paucity of food, the putrid smell of the decomposing dead and the extreme cold of the nights—let alone the relentless enemy artillery, rifle and machine-gun fire. Whatever the men had trained for was easily surpassed by the actual conditions of war. Even going to the toilet was hazardous:

> Through the day the Turks kept out of sight, but the Shrapnel without ceasing, causing us to keep low, but it caught a good number.
>
> To answer the call of nature was dangerous having no communication trenches, and snipers being all around us, was the cause of a good number of casualties. We had to climb out the back of our trenches and run the gauntlet for about 100 yds behind our lines, till too many were shot. So we then had to do the best we could with the use of tins and shovels.
>
> The War ships kept up a continuous bombardment, firing over our heads, the noise almost deafing everyone. In fact it was the cause of a big percentage of those invalided for deafness.
>
> Our most strenuous work being digging. day and night we had to dig. our only rest when we went on the look out. sleep was a thing unheard of. we are all dog tired and hungry, all the food we carried being gone. to keep our selves going had to crawl out after dark and take what there was on the dead bodies lying around. by this time the stench being awful and

> no way of shifting the dead, for now we have most of the Turkish army in front of us and to show a head in daylight or expose too much at night meant a bullet knocking one out of time.
>
> Again tonight the Turks attack us and again we beat them back. the amusing feature of a Turkish attack. They always came blowing bugles and beating kettle drums and calling 'Alla Alla', so giving us a hint of their coming, but it never lasted long as [they] no doubt thought it wiser to come without a sound, so giving us a surprise attack, that giving us more work for we had to keep a sharper look out.
>
> The country now looks like a battle field, dead lying every where, bent smashed rifles and different articles strewn all over the place, schrub torn and scattered by big gun fire, and fresh dug soil mounds from the now maze of trenches.
>
> The cold by night and early mornings went right to the marrow. it brought tears as we tried to use our feet or shift our fingers from rifle or shovel and pick.
>
> The life is very hard but the excitement of battle makes up for it all.[148]

Private Les De Vine commented in his diary on Thursday about the importance of Shrapnel Valley to the ANZAC cause:

> 'Shrapnel Gully' or as we call it 'The Valley of Death' heavily shelled today, this is the main artery that feeds the firing line. all food, water, ammunition, wounded etc must pass up the gully to reach the front line, so the Turks managed to keep it pretty warm, passed through several times without a scratch.[149]

On Thursday Private Richard Edwards mentioned in his diary the fine work the stretcher-bearers were doing:

> The Stretcher bearers with their mules are doing splendid work which is the only means of transport as the country is here is very rough & hilly & covered with small scrub.[150]

The 4th Battalion finally saw some relief on Friday, 30 April, when they rested at what was known as Brighton Beach, a shingled 'sanctuary' on the Aegean shore. Although even here, 'Beachy Bill'—the nickname given to Turkish artillery batteries that fired on the beach, particularly those guns located around Gaba Tepe and the Olive Grove, both to the south of Anzac—waited and threatened to ruin their much-needed rest. However, while the relief by the 12th Battalion commenced mid-morning, the 4th Battalion didn't reach the beach until late afternoon. Some of the battalion's northernmost platoons were relieved by the Deal Battalion of the Royal Marines. Their deserved stint at the beach was very brief; events and orders conspired against them.

The 4th Battalion war diary recorded:

> Friday 30/4/15 All quiet. Relieved by 3rd Brigade at about 10.15 a.m. Moved into rest camp on beach in rear of position where reorganisation commenced. 7.20 ordered to Reinforce R.M.L.I. [Royal Marine Light Infantry] Bde in centre.[151]

For Les Lott, Friday began with the unending task of digging:

> This morning being like all others, digging and dodging shrapnel till 12 noon when a party came to our relief. we go back to the beach, arriving there about 4.30 pm, as we had to go steady on account of snipers who are hidden behind our lines. we lost a couple before we reached the beach and also caught 4 Turkish snipers hidden in the scrub who were promptly shot, we having no inclination to take prisoners. the reason of that we thought to receive such treatment, but later on we learned to respect the Turk and treat him as a clean fighter, and all the rumours to the contrary are all rot. He 'is a good clean fighter.'
>
> On reaching the beach we have a swim, a pleasure which cost us dear, being fully exposed to the distant hills, and the shrapnel soon fell fast and furious, causing us to take cover behind the hill, leaving a number at the bottom of the sea, also a few on the beach. the wounded were brought in but sad to relate they were greatly in the minority.
>
> Then we turn in for a sleep behind what little cover we could find, but fate was against us having a night's sleep for we had hardly got settled when '4th Battn fall in. Rifle and equipment.' the Turks have broken our line where the R.M.L.I. are holding. again we take the hill at the double, this time about ½ mile to the left of the position we just left, to take part in the scrap.[152]

After the furious conditions of the firing line, Private Richard Edwards enjoyed some simple pleasures on the beach:

> Friday 30th We were relieved yesterday & got down to the beach where we made ourselves a hot cup of tea. I think it was the best I have ever

tasted, & I went for a swim heedless of the bullets that kept dropping in the water around.[153]

Corporal Charles Bosward was disappointed by the brevity of the battalion's stay on the beach:

> Friday 30th April 1915. 10 a.m. Relieved by 3rd Brigade who had 2 days spell. We were only on the beach a few hours, when we had to march away up hills galore to the centre of the position. It was no rest for us at all.[154]

Private De Vine also gave an account of their fortunes that day, lamenting the lack of sleep:

> 30/4/15 Heavy dg [digging] today . . . we leave the trenches today for a rest. The first time since the landing on last Sunday, we are relieved by the Marines, feeling done up & pretty well exhausted, have as yet no sleep since the landing. We have a bathe in the sea at Brighton Beach, and a general clean up we have all lost our packs which we dumped on the day of landing so we have lost everything only leaving what we stood up in. I am the only man in the Coy that has an overcoat as I did not carry it in my pack but on my belt, after a swim we dig ourselves a little shelter to sleep in, when we are suddenly called out in fighting order to reinforce the centre so had to remain in close support all night. There is continuous firing all night, the marines held their line so we were not actually required, got very little rest or sleep. Lt Col Bennett assumes command of the Bn.[155]

Captain Arthur Tebbutt, the battalion's medical officer, recalled:

> The battalion moved out and assembled on the beach near the mouth of Victoria Gully where a roll call was being held when we received orders to move off again.[156]

In a letter to Jack's father, George Collyer, Corporal Charles Macquarie recounted how once they'd reached the beach:

> Things came about in a peculiar style Friday night, we were all having our tot of rum, when along the beach (spot where we landed in Gallipoli) came our sergt major—calling out all hands, 'Battle order', 'Battle order'.

> We at once jumped into kit, grabbed rifles and what food was at hand, and away we went. we climbed up hills until one thought a lot of nasty things re officers and the army in general.[157]

Incredibly, despite being one of the last of the battalions who landed on 25 April to be relieved and have a 'spell' at the beach, the 4th was called on to reinforce the firing line as preparations for the third Turkish counterattack unfolded.[158] They had barely rested before being ordered back to the centre of Second Ridge to unfamiliar territory at night. The Marines who were currently occupying MacLaurin's Hill—the Chatham Battalion—and Johnston's Jolly—the Portsmouth Battalion—were being threatened and required support, hence the need for reinforcements. Rumours of a Turkish breakthrough fuelled the urgency of the situation. The Chatham Battalion war diary recorded that on 30 April trenches were lost to the Turks but regained later that night.[159] This might have been the catalyst for the 4th being hurriedly sent back to the firing line.

Remarkably, the 3rd Battalion was not called on to reinforce the line in the Central Sector. Not only had the 3rd been bivouacking on the beach for at least 24 hours longer than the 4th, it was from the very positions being pressed that the 3rd Battalion had first deployed after landing on 25 April and then been relieved; they knew the ground. Surely military thinking dictated that it would be the 3rd Battalion who rushed to the aid of the Marines. The only possible explanation was that the 4th had suffered fewer casualties than the other battalions who landed on 25 April. Although the 3rd Battalion suffered more casualties than the 4th, it was able to return to the firing line 24 hours after the 4th in the evening of 1 May, when it was ordered to relieve the Marines on the Jolly next to the 4th Battalion and adjacent to their former trenches on MacLaurin's Hill. According to Charles Bean, the beach roll call of the 3rd Battalion showed 40 men killed in action, 194 men wounded in action and 81 men missing by 29 April. The 4th Battalion's figures were 28 men killed in action, 95 men wounded in action and 67 men missing by 30 April.[160]

The state of the men in the 4th, such as Jack and No. 12 Section, must have been one of utter physical and psychological exhaustion as they did indeed curse and course their way up Shrapnel Valley and then Bridges' Road 'at the double' to the firing line. Some idea of their mental and physical state can be gauged from an entry in the 10th Battalion war diary as its remnants made their way out of the firing line on the Jolly to the beach on Thursday, 29 April, after being relieved by the Portsmouth Battalion. The suffering of the men of the 10th was common to all the ANZAC troops who landed the previous Sunday and had fought since:

> 29.4.15
> Our men were thoroughly exhausted + their nerves shattered after 96 hours continuous fighting in the trenches with little or no sleep, the dreadful anxiety of not knowing how the battle was progressing, especially on our left, every night just before dusk the enemy shelled our trenches + fired heavy bursts of rifle fire at our trenches which gave us the impression that they intended to rush our position, at no time during the 96 hours did their firing cease, altho' it raised in volume at times the fusillade was simply deafening, but it did little damage for our men by this time were well dug in.[161]

Prior to their relief, the 4th Battalion had spent 24 more debilitating hours in the firing line than the 10th and most of the other battalions, but after a brief rest at the beach they were required to return to the firing line.

After winding its way uphill through Shrapnel Valley, Bridges' Road—the main ANZAC access route to the centre of the firing line from the beach—terminated near Scott's Point, which overlooked the gap at the head of Wire Gully on Second Ridge. Engineers constructed Bridges' Road early in the ANZAC occupation, 'probably following an old Turkish pad'.[162] Not only did the 4th Battalion have to struggle uphill to reach their new position, they also had to contend with heavy artillery fire as the Turks softened up the Marines and the Anzacs for their third counterattack, to be delivered early the next day. Turkish artillery batteries had the range of the track and often peppered it with shrapnel, night and day. Knowing that reinforcements of men and supplies of materiel were being sent to Second Ridge on the eve of their attack, the Turks hammered it with shrapnel on Friday night just as the hapless 4th negotiated their way towards the firing line above them. The 4th's diary noted the intensity of the enemy fire on their return journey to Second Ridge: 'Snipers and Artillery very hot.'[163] By Friday evening three field and seven mountain batteries of Turkish artillery were in place to support the Turkish infantry's planned counterattack.[164]

Corporal Charles Bosward experienced that hazardous journey:

> M guns Matins howitzers etc. Shrapnel bullets shrieked + roared + were hurling thro' the air in showers . . . It was HELL coming up the gully to position. A lot of R.M.L.I. were hit + a few of ours + a few killed. I think we are in for a hot night.[165]

On an eventful day that began in the firing line on Bolton's Hill, and included a brief interlude at Brighton Beach and concluded on MacLaurin's Hill and the

Jolly, the 4th, under fire the whole time, suffered considerable casualties. Thirteen men were killed in action and at least 26 men were wounded, the men being hit while digging, shooting, swimming, walking and just plain resting.[166]

Bosward's diary entry for 1 May also contained a heartfelt reflection on the fighting feats of the Anzacs during their first week in action:

> Major Bennett is now in command of our Battn. + promoted to Lieut. Colonel. Heard that Kitchener sent the message 'Well done Australia. The world is proud of you. Hold on—Reinfs coming.' It is a treat to know that we poor devils in hell (It is nothing else than hell) who are fighting as well as humans can are congratulated on our maiden battle. If you could only see the hills + gullies we have to contend with + consider that we drove Turks (+ Germans) at the point of the bayonet up these hills right from the beach after landing in open boats under the very nose of the enemy under heavy fire + gained this high ridge you would do as I do consider it the equal of any feat of arms I have ever heard of or read of.[167]

PART 2

Destination

4 Death Trap Valley

This little post in Wire Gully was peopled throughout its short but all-important existence by men of all brigades. Perhaps no other isolated position on the whole of the Peninsula suffered more, or put up a more heroic defence.

Captain Eric Wren, *Randwick to Hargicourt: History of the Third Battalion*, 1935[1]

Death Trap Valley, also known as Death Gully and the Death Trap, was grimly and colloquially named by the members of the 4th Battalion after their experiences there on 1 and 2 May 1915. Officially known as Wire Gully, it was located in the heart of the ANZAC firing line on the Hellespont or Dardanelles side of Second Ridge. Even Charles Bean declared it a death trap in his book, *Gallipoli Mission*, after visiting the Anzac site in 1919.[2]

The valley straddled Second Ridge, crossing it to the right of MacLaurin's Hill and to the left of Johnston's Jolly. There was a gap in the ridge at this point, separating the halves of the valley. The seaward half of the valley was named after Bridges' Road, which wended its way through it from Shrapnel Valley to Second Ridge.[3] Bridges' Road was the main ANZAC access route to MacLaurin's Hill in the centre of the ANZAC firing line. In some sources the seaward half of the valley, which was an extension of Shrapnel Valley, was also referred to as Wire Gully. (See the map of Death Trap Valley on page 165.)

The Turkish name for Death Trap Valley was the innocuous Gedik Dere, or Hole Valley; the hole being the dip in the ridge line.[4] The equally bland ANZAC name, Wire Gully, was coined in May after the gap was filled with barbed wire to deter any stray Turks. Trenches weren't practical owing to the steepness of the dip in the ridge where the valley crossed it.

Death Trap Valley's position, virtually in the centre of hostilities, made it very significant tactically. A Turkish breach at this point would have led to a splitting of the ANZAC line and a direct route to the beach—both disastrous scenarios. Also, the prospect of individual Turkish infiltration was a concern. On Sunday, 30 May, Private Les De Vine, 4th Battalion, noted in his diary:

> 3 Pn detailed to mount an observation post at the top of the gully which we have named 'Wire Gully' as it is full of barbed wire . . . This post is a vy important one as isolated scouts etc seeking information have many times attempted to pass through & so reach the top of Shrapnel Gully which is about the centre of our line on the R flank, if successful they would have a clear observation right down Shrapnel Gully to the beach and could direct artillery fire, the approach is well hidden by bushes etc on their side, this part of the line is only patrolled at night as our frontline is broken here by the gully.[5]

Charles Bean recorded such an incursion:

> On a day in May men sitting in their dugouts above Bridges' Road [the valley on the Anzac side of this gap] saw a solitary Turk with a number of waterbottles slung round him standing in this 'nick' above them and looking down on the scene as if dazed. He had evidently been sent to bring water to the Turkish trenches, and, making his way up the wrong gully, had found himself in the Australian lines. He dived back and escaped down the enemy's side of the hill, a few shots ringing after him.[6]

The Turkish commanding officer of the 19th Division, Lieutenant-Colonel Mustafa Kemal, based his headquarters on Kemal Yere (Scrubby Knoll), having established himself behind its northern shoulder late on 25 April,[7] about 1500 metres away from the Anzacs' firing line. From the knoll's height of 165 metres,[8] Kemal had an uninterrupted view above Mortar Ridge of Gedik Dere and its environs, almost straight in front of him; in fact all the enemy's positions along Second Ridge, from Lone Pine to Quinn's, were open to scrutiny from his eyrie. So from late afternoon on Sunday, Mustafa Kemal, field glasses at the ready, was able to see the construction of the ANZAC entrenchments. Charles Bean, after climbing Scrubby Knoll in 1919, described it in *Gallipoli Mission* as 'a perfect panorama' of the ANZAC firing line along the central part of Second Ridge.[9] Major Zeki Bey, who served at Ari Burnu in 1915 and as Bean's Turkish liaison officer in 1919, called it 'a dress circle view'.[10]

As a result a number of Turkish attacks were sent into Gedik Dere during the first month of the enemy occupation, notably in early May and on 19 May. Kemal was able to direct accurate and concentrated fire from a range of weapons into the whole valley and most of Second Ridge. At his immediate disposal was a mountain gun battery of four guns, which was positioned just north of Kemal Yere, late morning during the Turkish reaction on the day of the Landing.[11] On 26 April a further two mountain gun batteries were positioned nearby.[12] They had a clear field of fire towards Second Ridge, as did the Turkish batteries at Anderson Knoll, and the Olive Grove and Gaba Tepe to the south of Anzac, although the latter was also an observation post for the former. Telephone communications via lengthy cables enabled Kemal to call in artillery support from other Turkish batteries dotted along Third Ridge. The Anzacs christened Third Ridge 'Gun Ridge'; the Turks called it Topculuk Sirt or Artillery Ridge.[13] Safely ensconced behind the ridge line, Turkish batteries fired with virtual impunity night and day, occasionally suffering counter battery fire from Indian mountain gun batteries and then ANZAC artillery in the days after the Landing.

Death Trap Valley was overlooked on three sides—MacLaurin's Hill at its head, Johnston's Jolly on its right and German Officers' Trench to its left. Even the mouth of the valley opened onto Turkish positions from Sandbag Ridge in front of Mule Valley to Mortar Ridge and Scrubby Knoll beyond it. Importantly, some of the valley, including Loutit's Post, was also clearly visible to Turkish positions on the ANZAC left, on the high ground running along Second Ridge leading to Baby 700 and Battleship Hill.

Death Trap Valley was approximately 200 metres wide near the head of the valley where Loutit's Post, most of the outposts in the valley and Snipers Post aligned across it. It was about 300 metres long from the ANZAC trenches—some 15 metres in front of the crest of MacLaurin's Hill—to Turkish trenches near its mouth at Sandbag Ridge. The valley's sides were so steep that, in *Gallipoli Mission*, Bean referred to it as a ravine.[14] Robert Rhodes James, in *Gallipoli*, his classic account of the Dardanelles Campaign, also called it 'a deep ravine'.[15] The sketch of Death Trap Valley made during Bean's pilgrimage in 1919 gave a real sense of the valley's depth. It also showed how open the valley was to Turkish observation, fire and attack. (See the sketch on page 157.) The Jolly side of the valley was particularly precipitous, the slope falling rapidly to the watercourse at its base between 20 and 30 metres below. On the floor of the valley was a continuation of the dip in the saddle on Second Ridge, described by Bean as a 'V-shaped, 12-feet deep, channel of the valley-bed', snaking its way towards the mouth of the valley.[16] A spring, emptying into a small pond,[17] was near the channel, close to and below the ANZAC firing line, although it had no field of fire.[18] Equally, this part of the valley could not be fired on except by artillery. Holding the valley was dangerous from the beginning of the ANZAC occupation. A thick covering of scrub on the valley's steep sides and floor afforded some protection for the Anzacs, and then the Royal Marines during the first week; however, occupying the high ground surrounding it was crucial to the survival of the position and its occupants.

During the chaos of the morning of the Landing on 25 April, a series of battle outposts was established by a mixed force of Anzacs in Death Trap Valley, about 50 metres or so in front of the firing line on MacLaurin's Hill. They overlooked the valley and ranged up and down its sides and across its floor.

In his role as the honorary historian of the battalion, Captain Eric Wren certainly knew of the outposts' short but tumultuous history. Wren landed at Anzac on 25 April as a lance sergeant and briefly experienced the fighting in the valley before being wounded and evacuated. In the 3rd Battalion history, *Randwick to Hargicourt*, he claimed that from the early hours of the invasion:

> This little post in Wire Gully was peopled throughout its short but all-important existence by men of all brigades. Perhaps no other isolated position on the whole of the Peninsula suffered more, or put up a more heroic defence.[19]

The purpose of the outposts was to act as a tripwire for the main firing line being hurriedly formed in front of the crest on MacLaurin's Hill and on Johnston's Jolly behind them. The outposts provided a number of distinct advantages. They were advanced listening and observation posts and a first line of defence against the Turks and any surprise moves the enemy initiated. There was a real fear the Turks could form up in considerable numbers behind German Officers' Trench in Mule Valley, out of sight of the Anzacs, and flood the valley, overwhelming the embryonic ANZAC line on Second Ridge, which was particularly vulnerable during its first few days. There was also the threat of small parties or even individual Turks entering Gedik Dere.

In theory the outposts should also have been reconnaissance bases, from which patrols could have sought out the enemy, reporting their finds to the main firing line. The close proximity of the Turks negated this role. In fact, the *1909 Field Service Regulations* specified that the first duty of an outpost was reconnaissance and the second one was resistance. The regulations stipulated that one of the first principles of outpost duty was 'to see without being seen . . . All troops on outpost duty must, therefore, be carefully concealed'.[20]

In the case of the Death Trap Valley outposts, reconnaissance wasn't an option, the Turks having closed to within 70 metres of them before the end of the first week. As the week progressed, resistance became the sole purpose of the outposts' garrison. Unfortunately, because of the high ground held by the Turks to either side and in front of the outposts, the troops stationed in them were in a fishbowl, with a vigilant enemy doing all the observing. Survival dictated careful concealment by the Anzacs and then the Marines; movement attracted heavy Turkish fire.

Outposts at Anzac were not unique to Death Trap Valley. In the wild, tortured geography north of Walker's Ridge, both sides established outposts. The three ANZAC outposts were established on 30 April by the Nelson Company, under Major Brereton of the Canterbury Battalion, in the largely Kiwi fiefdom of North Anzac. According to Bean, 'They were precisely opposite the three boats of the 7th and 12th battalions which had been riddled at the Landing, and the knolls occupied by Brereton were those from which these boats had been fired upon.'[21] Christopher Pugsley, the New Zealand historian, described each of these northern outposts starting 'as a smattering of shell scrapes, where movement was impossible by day, but now each in turn was developed into a small fortress, cut off by day but capable of matching Turkish fire'.[22]

In early May reconnaissance, so lacking in the closeness of the opposing lines of the Central Sector, was underway in the Northern Sector under the experienced Major Percy Overton, a Boer War veteran whose scouting skills were well known in the New Zealand Expeditionary Force.[23] Manned by the Canterbury Mounted Rifles, the outposts limited Turkish attempts to infiltrate the New Zealand positions but allowed Overton and his scouts the opportunity to roam the comparatively lightly defended rugged hills and gullies of the Sari Bair Range overlooking them. Valuable intelligence about the enemy's dispositions and possible routes for attacking troops was gathered and used later during the ANZAC August offensive. Compared to the outposts in Death Trap Valley, these northern outposts were able to operate in a far more orthodox mode. Turkish outposts were scattered throughout the heights above the ANZAC trenches in the Northern Sector, more as points of resistance than reconnaissance.

Some of the first ANZAC positions in Death Trap Valley were established by Lieutenant Noel Loutit and Lieutenant James Haig of the 10th Battalion and the remnants of their platoons on the morning of the Landing. Retreating from Third Ridge in the face of increasingly heavy Turkish fire and considerable enemy reinforcements pouring into Legge Valley, they escaped their pursuers via Death Trap Valley. They met up with the ANZAC main force establishing itself along Second Ridge in the late morning. Here they chose to dig in on the lip of the southern crest of Death Trap Valley—on what was to become known as Johnston's Jolly—and face the enemy. Charles Bean gave a graphic description of their retirement:

> The withdrawal across the final flat shortly after 10 a.m. was a race between the Turks and the Australians. By the time the Australians were half-way over the open the Turks were reaching the spur which they had just

> quitted. The fire was intense. With the bullets raining about them the Australians raced into Wire Gully, which bounded the northern side of 400 Plateau. The gully was scrubby, broken and narrow, and gave them shelter as they made up it. Near its upper end they climbed a steep gutter on their left onto Johnston's Jolly. And there, on the northern edge of the plateau, near the top of Wire Gully, Haig and Loutit turned and dug in.[24]

In a later interview Loutit claimed it was 'closer to 10.30 or 11' when they judiciously withdrew from Third Ridge.[25] The Australians established two posts overlooking the valley, each manned by the survivors of their platoons under their direction. These were about 50 metres in front of the main firing line on Johnston's Jolly. Around this time, possibly earlier, a further three outposts were placed in the valley itself.

Loutit's Post was to play a key role in the ensuing dramatic days. It was from Loutit's that most troops made their attempts to reach the outposts below, although it was a gamble. Loutit's Post overlooked the valley, as did its northern equivalent, Street's, which the 3rd Battalion established. Both posts were soon to be threatened by the steady encroachment of the Turks as they sapped their way towards the ANZAC firing line on Second Ridge during the first week.

~

By 8.30 a.m. on the morning of the landing the 3rd Battalion had landed on the beach and was initially ordered to reinforce the troops fighting to reach the crucial high ground on the ANZAC left.[26] Private Les Wright, a stretcher-bearer in the 3rd Battalion, described their hazardous journey to the firing line:

> Whilst advancing up the gully 'Shrapnel Gully' we lost the first man of the 3rd Battalion being Sgt Cavell. It was a death trap advancing up the gully what with machine gun fire and shrapnel bursting over head from all directions.[27]

Walter Cavill, a popular NCO, was one of the few 3rd Battalion veterans who had been under fire before, having seen active service in the NSW Lancers during the Boer War.[28] He died from his wounds later that day. About four platoons, drawn from two companies under the command of Major Malcolm Lamb, continued to the end of what was to become known as Monash Valley, climbed to its crest and set about establishing themselves on seaward spurs of Mortar Ridge.[29] However, as the rest of the battalion made its way along the valley, it was hastily sent to the posts being formed high on the ridge to their right.[30] These men, arriving in the vicinity of MacLaurin's Hill mid-morning, were deployed along the ridge from Courtney's Post to MacLaurin's Hill. Captain David McConaghy of the 3rd Battalion had established a similar post to Loutit's on the edge of the valley, overlooking it on the northern slope in front of the main firing line on MacLaurin's Hill. Eventually this post, known as Street's Trench, anchored a series of rifle-pits leading to the hollow of the valley near the spring, which provided water only for the men in the immediate vicinity. From there further scrapes and rifle-pits dug into the valley's steep southern shoulder ended on its crest at Loutit's Post on Johnston's Jolly; all these positions were well forward of the main ANZAC firing line. Some posts were formed even further down the valley.

When Lieutenant George McDonald from No. 3 Platoon, A Company, 3rd Battalion, reached the left side of MacLaurin's Hill during the morning, he seized the initiative:

> . . . anticipating his platoon would not be required there [on MacLaurin's Hill], McDonald dived down Wire Gully ensconced himself in a little watercourse and established a post that was destined to play one of the most important parts in the fight that was to follow.[31]

McDonald and another 3rd Battalion subaltern, Lieutenant Bill Carter, and their platoons, stayed in the valley until they were both wounded in the days following the Landing. The outposts they established ranged up and down the valley's sides and along its floor towards its mouth.

It was now midday on 25 April and in the Central Sector—from Lone Pine to Quinn's—the Australian battalions, many of them mixed together, began to dig in, their momentum halted by the heavy fire and numbers of the enemy, and the uncertainty surrounding their role. Attempts to cross 400 Plateau by ANZAC units were met by withering Turkish fire. Pockets of Anzacs scattered on the eastern side and to the south of 400 Plateau were either eliminated or retreated as the afternoon wore on. Any forward movement in the Central Sector of the ANZAC line was repulsed or stopped as the security of Second Ridge was sought instead.

Turkish infiltration of the valley late on the first day caused Lieutenant McDonald to seek reinforcements, and a further platoon from the 3rd Battalion, Lieutenant Bill Beeken's, was despatched. An attempted enemy ruse proved the value of the outposts during the confusion of the Landing. Captain Eric Wren set out what occurred:

> Just as twilight came to the Gallipoli scrub, there was a great movement of troops in the gullies below where McDonald with his handful of men

lay hidden. As indicated previously, the spirits of the assaulting troops in places had been raised during the day by whispers of help from Indian regiments presumed to have landed with the 29th Division farther south.

Now from out of the approaching darkness came voices shouting: 'For God's sake don't shoot: we are Indians.' It was a critical moment. All that could be seen were shadows moving in the scrub. McDonald and his men lay with bayonets fixed, sceptical but not daring to fire. Crouching low, the better to get a silhouette against the now fading light, McDonald saw a tall officer undoubtedly in the uniform of a Turk. Quick to realize the significance, he grabbed a rifle, and, by a gentle persuasion of the bayonet, brought the Turk in but unfortunately not before his prisoner had given some rapid monosyllable instructions to the figures moving about in the scrub behind him. Then did McDonald realize that his suspicions had been well-grounded. The Turks had planned a counter-attack through Wire Gully, in the guise of Indian troops.

As his little company poured volley after volley into the scrub at short range, there came frantic cries from the Australian line above, exhorting him to stop firing. 'You are firing on Indian troops.' Shouting back the information that the supposed Indians were Turks, the by now more slender garrison rapidly slipped and slammed the bolts on their almost red-hot rifles.

It was indeed a stroke of fortune for the precariously placed Australian invaders that this tiny 'battle out-post' stood in the way of the advancing pseudo-Indians. Had it not been there, and had not Lieut McDonald acted with promptitude, the odds are that some hundreds of Turks—who could guess the number?—would have penetrated unobserved through Wire Gully, and by morning the Australians would have been fighting both to their front and rear.[32]

The battle outposts were formed under heavy Turkish fire. Occupation of them became increasingly hard; however, even more hazardous was reaching them, especially during daylight hours. Charles Bean described the treacherous route:

The posts in Wire Gully were most difficult to reach, even by night, with ammunition or water. One 3rd Battalion post lay all Tuesday afternoon with bayonets fixed, but without a cartridge. For water some crept to McDonald's spring by night. In Loutit's post, as no water came, two of the men on Monday morning collected water-bottles from the remaining seventeen and tried to crawl back to the line to fill them. Both were killed by snipers from Mule Valley, and one of them could be seen for days afterwards upon the skyline, still on his hands and knees, with the bottles slung round him. The post eventually obtained water on Monday night from the line of the 10th Battalion, under Lieutenant Todd, behind it. Goldring's post in a hollow of Wire Gully was entirely without water, but on the second day there reached them from the line, despite the deadly risk, a stretcher-bearer with a bottle.[33]

Lieutenant Eric Goldring's post was formed on Monday, 26 April. Goldring was ordered into the valley, and that afternoon his small detachment from the 3rd Battalion moved deeper into the valley to connect with other outlying positions. With him he took Corporal Tom Louch and his section from the 11th Battalion, who were already near the head of the valley. Unfortunately, Goldring was wounded in the abdomen and chest during this move. Joining his platoon in the valley was another 3rd Battalion detachment, commanded by Lieutenant Don Moore. Tom Louch gave a detailed description of the deployment and the dangers associated with occupying the battle outposts:

> Goldring was wounded. There was little room in our pot-hole but we dragged him in. He implored us to give him a drink, but we had been told this would be bad for anyone with an abdominal wound, so we refused. He became delirious, but after dark when a stretcher bearer arrived he pulled himself together and walked back. The possie into which we had stumbled was anything but a home from home. It was overlooked from the higher ground of Johnston's Jolly, where there were snipers who fired at any sign of movement. After dark there was a lot of movement in front of us, the Turks were shouting 'Allah, Allah!' blowing bugles like those used by the tram drivers in Cairo, and we stood to expecting an attack. But after a time we fired a few rounds in the direction of the noise and the Turks departed. We were too worked up and tired to get any sleep, and the night wore on. At first light we saw Turks digging in on Johnston's Jolly, about 200 yards away on our right, so we opened up on them. But they were being covered by snipers, and in no time Clayden, in the next pit, was shot in the head and my rifle was knocked out of my hand by a Turkish bullet just as I was about to fire. My face was spattered by steel splinters which drew blood; but though a sorry sight, I was more frightened than hurt. On Tuesday night the 3rd Battalion man who had been with us went off to try and get

> some water, and we did not see him again. Since the Sunday morning when we landed Dick and I had had nothing to drink other than the water in our water-bottles. We had little sleep, so by Wednesday we were so dazed that we hardly knew what we were doing.[34]

As Tom noted, the Turks were starting to creep into the valley and out onto the heights of Johnston's Jolly above the Australian right, and onto German Officers' Trench on the left. From there the Turks sniped at the Australian positions in and around the valley.

On Monday night Corporal Bert Smythe of A Company, 3rd Battalion, had a narrow escape in the outposts, which he related in a letter to his family:

> Just near dark Maj Brown went down to the outpost trench to lead a bayonet charge but things were so hot that he got down into the trench & I did so also, crouching behind Elbel. Well shrapnel began to come our way so I squeezed in alongside Elbel instead of behind him. A little after a concussion shrapnel tore bits out of Elbels haversack which was on his back & exploded in the ground 3 feet behind us & right on top of it another one landed in the same place & the only damage both of them did was to cut Maj Brown's face a little. Elbel was a bit dazed for a few seconds. If I had remained where I was I would have got it fair in the chest which would have made an awful mess to say the least of it.[35]

During the second Turkish counterattack on Tuesday night, two of the casualties from the 3rd Battalion were wounded by enemy snipers watching the valley and the outposts. Bert Smythe, perched above the outposts, recorded this disconcerting incident in his letter:

> Shortly after a chap from the outpost trench tried to rush back to us & reached us moaning horribly with an awful hole in his stomach. You see it was bright moonlight the whole night long. A chap named Cox—a letter carrier & also A co's head cook—was the connecting file between the outpost and the main body. He was in a deep dugout & had to pass orders back and forward. The outpost couldn't raise him after awhile so a man sent to waken him but it was no use he'd died at his post—a sniper got him in the head.[36]

Bean also described the primitive method of communication some of the outposts used during those first few days:

> All day long messages were passed along the line of posts, at first verbal, afterwards written on paper and folded in a cartridge clip. The men threw these from left to right or from right to left, and those near the creek bed, who had no field of fire, came to imagine that this was the duty for which they were holding on.[37]

This practice was necessary, as any movement by troops between posts incurred the wrath of the watching Turks. The increasingly dangerous Turkish presence was noted by Bert Smythe, again in his letter:

> Just below us out of sight of the Terrrrrrible Turrrrrrk was a little deep gully in which there was a nice spring & we used to slip down and make ourselves some tea or beef tea or both according to fancy. There were 4 beef tea squares in our rations. The only thing about it we had to get down like a streak of lightning & back the same way or else have a dozen snipers on to you. On the Wednesday the Turks must have taken a tumble as they made it impossible for us to stay in the gully at all so the tea making had to be abandoned but during the Monday & Tuesday there was quite a quantity of tea made.[38]

At least two enlisted men from the 3rd Battalion received a Mention In Despatches for their courage under fire in the valley during the 3rd's initial occupation of the battle outposts. These men were Corporal Ralph Moore and Corporal Roy McGregor, both of whom belonged to A Company. Moore's recommendation read:

> Corporal Moore had charge of a section of No. 2 Platoon and held a position in the gully from Sunday night 25th to Thursday morning 29th. Whilst in this position Corpl. Moore and his section were under a continuous fire from the enemy, especially at night from snipers, who were within 30 yds. of the trench. On two occasions Moore moved forward about 20 yds. to obtain a better view of the snipers; on the second occasion he accounted for five. (Reported by Lieutenant Beeken)[39]

Roy McGregor's recommendation was as follows:

> Corpl. McGregor had charge of a section from No. 1 Platoon and held a position in the firing line about 100 yds in advance of the support trenches. On 27th April the supply of ammunition had run out in Lieut. Beeken's

portion of the firing line and he sent two messages for ammunition. One messenger was killed. Cpl. McGregor under a very heavy fire succeeded in reaching the support trench where he found two boxes of ammunition waiting to be taken up to the firing line. He carried these to Lieut. Beeken. (Reported by Lieut. Beeken)[40]

These incidents showed the precariousness of operating in the outposts from the very beginning of the ANZAC occupation of Second Ridge on 25 April. During this time the outposts had been under constant enemy observation and fire. Disturbingly, new Turkish positions, called Snipers Post and German Officers' Trench, appeared during the week on the knuckle of German Officers' Trench, poised just to the left above the valley and about 70 metres from the outposts. A short communication trench connected these new positions. Loutit's was open to fire from German Officers' Trench and its offshoot, Snipers Post, directly across the valley. As well, it was open to observation and fire from Turkish positions on its left above German Officers' Trench, from the heights rising along Second Ridge to Baby 700 and Battleship Hill. Artillery batteries and machine guns were positioned in these enemy positions, well within range. Enemy trenches on Turkish Johnston's and Mortar Ridge covered Street's Trench and MacLaurin's Hill, while protecting Snipers Post.

~

The Australians' tenure in the valley ended with the arrival of the Royal Marines on Second Ridge in the early hours of Thursday, 29 April. The Royal Marines—in the form of two battalions from the Royal Marine Brigade, the Portsmouth and Chatham battalions, under the command of Brigadier-General Charles Trotman—began to land at Anzac at 4 p.m. on Wednesday, 28 April. A further two battalions—the Deal and Nelson battalions of the 1st Naval Brigade—commanded by Brigadier-General David Mercer, landed from 8 p.m. on Thursday. Also in their ranks were the Bearer Division of the 3rd Field Ambulance and the No. 1 Field Company of the Divisional Engineers. Their purpose was to relieve some of the exhausted and diminished 1st, 2nd and 3rd Australian brigades who had been in action continuously since landing on the morning of Sunday, 25 April. Remarkably, the first of these units to land, the Portsmouth Battalion, did so with just a few stores, the understanding being they would only be required for 48 hours. It was to be two weeks before the Marines left Anzac.[41] By then they, too, were exhausted and diminished.

The Anzacs were delighted to have such a renowned body of Britain's regular armed forces come to their assistance. Since 1664 the Royal Marines had been carving a fine tradition as seaborne fighting men throughout the British Empire. Their motto, *Per Mare Per Terram*—By Sea By Land—and their use of the 'Great Globe itself' as their colours,[42] instead of individual battle honours, with the exception of Gibraltar, showed their versatility, endurance and success. Their battle honours by 1915 included Gibraltar (1704), Bunker Hill (1775), Trafalgar (1805), Balaklava (1854) and The Boxer Rebellion (1900).

Private Les De Vine of the 4th Battalion commented in his diary on Wednesday, 28 April:

> Large force of the R.M.L.I.'s landed during the night, receiving a great reception from everybody, they went at once into the firing line.[43]

De Vine added on Thursday, 29 April, that '2000 marines landed tonight'.

Corporal Charles Bosward of the 4th Battalion was also pleased: 'More troops landing to reinforce. What a treat to see them.'[44]

There were men in the ranks of the 4th Battalion who had served in the Royal Marines Light Infantry. Private Tom Farndell was one, as was Lance Corporal John Pritchard, who spent more than 12 years in Marine colours prior to migrating to Australia before the war. Sergeant George Thomas of the machine-gun section was another 12-year veteran of the Royal Marines.[45]

In late February and early March 1915, the Royal Marines were involved in a series of raids by British Naval demolition parties on the Turkish forts guarding the entrance to the Dardanelles. These were a limited success. It was hoped that a combination of naval bombardments and the raids would neutralise these Turkish defences. The largest raids—on 4 March on the forts at Kum Kale, on the Asiatic side of the Hellespont, and at Sedd el Bahr, on the European shore—encountered significant resistance. One company from the Plymouth Battalion was landed at each site to support the demolition parties. However, both parties were eventually withdrawn in the face of sustained Turkish resistance. The demolition parties achieved little on these raids. The retirement of these detachments was assisted by covering fire from destroyers lying off each of the landing places.[46] Twenty-two men were killed and 22 were wounded in these sorties.[47]

Then, on the day of the ANZAC, British and French landings on the Gallipoli Peninsula and at Kum Kale, most of the Royal Naval Division conducted a feint or demonstration landing off Bulair, which was inland from the Gulf of Saros, to the north of the actual landing sites. This was part of the deception to keep the Turks and their German cronies guessing the Mediterranean Expeditionary Force's intentions. In this they were successful. Substantial Turkish forces, under the command of General Liman Von Sanders, moved to secure the Bulair Lines against possible invasion.

The principal unit occupying the outposts prior to the Marines' relief of the firing line was A Company from the 3rd Battalion. In the 3rd Battalion war diary for 28 April, the newly appointed acting adjutant, Lieutenant Owen Howell-Price, recorded that:

> About midnight the R.M.L.I. were brought up to relieve us. Our men were completely exhausted having been 4 days + 4 nights under the strain of a fierce battle.[48]

Howell-Price's relief was palpable in a letter he wrote to his parents on 9 May, which described the first week:

> We had four days [from landing] the like of which I never want to go through again. It was nerve racking and practically sleepless. We were quite done when relief arrived + we got a few days rest.[49]

In his letter Bert Smythe gave an indication of the strain of these conditions:

> Wed night was comparatively quiet and a little wet. Tho I'd had practically no sleep since Saty night I couldn't sleep. The strain & worry was awful & my head was singing & buzzing awfully. Before I went to bed got a hint that the 3rd were going to be relieved in the morning so I gathered all my things together . . . we were relieved by the 'Tommies' at daybreak on Thursday morning.[50]

On 29 April the 3rd Battalion war diary noted the relief:

> The R.M.L.I. commenced our relief at 4 a.m. which owing to the difficulty of access to the trenches was not completed till late that date. As relieved the men proceeded to a rendezvous on the beach.[51]

Unfortunately Bert Smythe was shot during the relief:

> We had to cross about 100 yards of fire swept ground & we rushed it. Just near the safety trench I stopped to walk and got a knock in the shoulder like a kick from a horse. I tumbled into the trench pretty slick & Sgt Harris dressed my wound.[52]

Suffering a gunshot wound to his right shoulder, Bert was put on a hospital ship and sent to Alexandria to recuperate.

Charles Bean gave a moving firsthand description of the Anzacs as they came out of the firing line during the relief:

> A concentration area was fixed at the mouth of Shrapnel Gully and on the folds south of it, and to this for two days there straggled along the Beach or down various tracks from the hilltops individual men, men in twos and threes, men in platoons, with or without officers. Bearded, ragged at the knees and elbows, their putties often left in the scrub, dull-eyed, many with blood on cheeks and clothes, and with a dirty field-dressing round arm or wrist, they were far fiercer than Turks to look upon . . . Officers were often indistinguishable from men; buttons were gone, and stars scored in indelible pencil on shoulder-straps became a recognised badge of an officer's rank . . . Many wandered in a half-sleep, like tired children.[53]

Corporal Tom Louch of the 11th Battalion was one such Anzac, having emerged still in one piece from the battle outposts during the relief. Bean sketched his lethargic, bedraggled appearance:

> He started along the Beach to Hell Spit, dragging his rifle through the sand by its sling and trailing in the other hand the overcoat . . . which he had dragged from his pot-hole. His face, cut by a bullet, was caked with blood, and he had a four day's beard.[54]

Louch slept for 30 hours after he reported to the 11th Battalion's depleted roll call and had a tot of rum.[55]

In a report written on 14 May, Lieutenant-Colonel Owen, commanding officer of the 3rd Battalion, who was temporarily in command of the Central Section of the ANZAC line after the death of Colonel MacLaurin on 27 April,[56] described the relief:

> On the 28th April 1915 after 3 days and nights of continual fighting which began at the landing on Apl 25th the Central Section of our position in Gallipoli was taken over from me by the Royal Marines Light Infantry under General Trotman . . . General Trotman's Brigade began to arrive before dusk and the tired Australians were relieved Company by Company during the night. It was dark and drizzly and the Turks kept a constant

> fire varied with local attacks making the operations most difficult particularly as the RMLI had only just landed and the ground was unknown to them.[57]

Early on Thursday morning, the Chatham and Portsmouth battalions took over the Anzacs' MacLaurin's Hill and Johnston's Jolly positions. They were joined on Second Ridge by the Deal Battalion on Thursday evening, extending the relief to Brown's Dip on the right of the Anzac position.

The Marines were thrust into a firing line, about which they were largely ignorant, against a relentless, determined enemy in wet weather at night. In their ranks were a large number of recent recruits, possibly as high as 75 per cent of each battalion.[58] Some Anzacs, including the Official War Correspondent Charles Bean, were not impressed by the Marines' physical appearance:

> Yet some of those who saw the two new battalions lined, in their great sun helmets and faded khaki, along the Beach could not but feel a doubt. These men seemed strangely young and slender to represent the old seasoned regular Marines.[59]

The terrain was a challenge in itself, particularly as the battalions had been aboard ship for at least two months, some for three months, with only a few opportunities to train on terra firma.[60]

Bean vividly described their initiation at Anzac:

> All through the night the relief continued. It was a cold, dismal evening. A black storm of rain descended at sunset, followed by a drizzle lasting till dawn. The Marines, each man laden with his blankets, water-proof sheets, ammunition, and rations as well as his rifle, were exhausted before they reached the hilltops . . . Some had but a few weeks' training; most only a few months' . . . They had no conception of the conditions of the fight at Gaba Tepe. Expecting to garrison definite trenches—one asked the way to the officers' mess—they were led over the top to the worst sectors of the line, to trenches of which those who had held them for days did not realise the badness, to wretched, isolated pot-holes from which the fight on MacLaurin's and the 400 Plateau was still being carried on . . . They knew nothing of what was ahead of them or on their flanks . . . From the dark came the distant sounds of Turkish bugle-calls. Close in front of them from the dense scrub flashed the occasional rifles of snipers; overhead the bullets cracked; machine-guns sent the mud of

> the parapets in showers upon them. Up and down the line came the same wild messages that had passed for days.[61]

Private Thomas Baker of the Chatham Battalion was one of the Marines who landed and commenced the relief of the Australians. His account echoed Bean's previous description:

> We had to relieve the Australians, who were slightly to the right. The position held by the Australians and New Zealanders was a huge ravine. They had run right up this ravine without very much opposition and they had manned the whole of the position at the top of the ridge. This was as steep as a railway embankment, but very much higher. The position was like a horseshoe the Australians had named the ravine Shrapnel Valley.
>
> Anyway we took up positions in the dark along the top of this ridge. This was in a tiny ditch, about two feet deep, which the Aussies had dug along the top and a kind of a trench. But you see there was very little protection there, and every few yards lay dead men. So you had to crawl over them to take up your position. There were quite a number of dead men, you could feel them in the dark and see them as well. It's not a very nice experience, but self preservation was the main thing, so you tried to keep your head down as much as possible. The lower you got the better it was but I can assure you it was very steep all round. There were scrub, bushes and trees, not very big trees, oddly enough a number of trees like our Scotch Firs.
>
> They had not managed to clear up the snipers, who were still in this bush, behind what was really the front line. They used to pick quite a number of men off, till they got wiped out, as they could not get out once they were behind our front line, so we picked them off gradually. What you used to watch for in the dark was where the flash came from. That's how they betrayed where they were. We picked out quite a number like that.
>
> We did not try and make the trench any deeper, for one thing we had only got entrenching tools. We hadn't got ashore with a lot of shovels and things, as a matter of fact I can't say I dug anything at all in the few days I was there. The natural shape of the land itself gave some natural protection, for as long as you kept your head down you were fairly safe except from shrapnel.[62]

This was the situation the Royal Marines faced when they assumed control. General Trotman relieved Lieutenant-Colonel Owen in his Scott's Point headquarters on the southern side of MacLaurin's Hill.[63] Trotman and the commanding officer of the Chatham Battalion, Lieutenant-Colonel Cunliffe McNeile Parsons, whose men initially occupied the firing line from MacLaurin's Hill to Courtney's Post, deemed the occupation of the battle outposts lying in front of his lines in the valley as necessary.

Unfortunately Parsons' battalion was stretched, the battalion war diary describing the relief:

> The section allotted to the Chatham Bn was rather extended and for the first two days it was impossible to relieve all the Australians in the centre trench on this account.[64]

So two thin platoons from the adjacent Portsmouth Battalion on the northern part of the Jolly were lent to the Chatham Battalion and ordered to occupy the battle outposts in the valley. This deployment occurred despite the advice of Captain McConaghy, 3rd Battalion, who felt that the main firing line was almost complete and his outpost, let alone the ones in the valley, was no longer needed.[65]

The two platoons, No. 9 and No. 10, from C Company, Portsmouth Battalion, numbering about 60 men, deployed into the outposts which some English accounts described as a 'detached fire trench'.[66] The two subalterns in charge of these men, Richard Empson and Alan Alcock, were only 18 years old, although Empson had been in action in Belgium at Antwerp in 1914. He had also seen active service at Lille and Lierre.[67] Empson, having enlisted in October 1913 at the age of seventeen and a half, was commissioned as a 2nd Lieutenant.[68] He had been serving the Marine colours for nearly a year longer than Alcock. Empson was promoted to Acting Lieutenant on 19 September 1914, while Alcock received the same promotion on 27 April 1915, only days before deploying into Death Trap Valley.[69] Thus Empson was in charge of the detachment.

In a number of letters written to his family before, during and after his northern European war service in late 1914, Richard Empson detailed his experiences, particularly the Marines' hastily enacted Belgian operation. His letters revealed an exuberant personality, a penchant for detail, an innate sense of duty and an eye for the ladies—a young man in the prime of life. He was obviously close to his parents, addressing them as 'My dear Mother & Daddy' and signing off with 'Yr affect son Richard' in every letter.[70] Educated at Marlborough College in Wiltshire,[71] Empson, very much a product of the English public school system, was revelling in his military career. Many junior officers in the British armed services were of a similar background, particularly early in the war.[72]

The other officer in the Marine detachment was Lieutenant Alan Alcock, who enlisted on 29 August 1914. He spent the first few months of his service at a Royal Marine Depot in England, undergoing training. Alcock was later described by Brigadier-General Trotman as being 'conscientious and reliable', while another senior Marine officer reported him as 'a very charming, gentlemanly young officer'.[73]

The adolescent lieutenants, Empson and Alcock, and their men began their occupation of the outposts at 2 a.m. on Thursday, 29 April, using the cover of night to facilitate their deployment. The full moon was obscured by clouds. Dawn revealed the intimidating lie of the land they had been forced to occupy. Over the next two days and nights, despite the close attention and fire of the Turks, the outposts' Marine garrison hung on; their supplies of food, water and ammunition steadily dwindled as the Turks ramped up the pressure on the British firing line, preparing the ground for their third counterattack. The Marines' presence in the valley became increasingly untenable. Their position had become isolated, cut off from the main firing line behind them as the Turks took control of the heights around the valley. Bean described their trench as having:

> . . . now been transformed into a continuous one climbing the northern slope of Wire Gully. Its right ended in the spring in the gully bed; its left, at the top of the hill, was blocked by a small barrier of earth forming the end of Street's Trench, which lay on the summit.[74]

Loutit's Post above the battle outposts on the edge of the Jolly was garrisoned by the Marines.

While no Marines in the detached fire trench in the valley appear to have been killed in action on Thursday, 29 April, a small number of men—including the officer commanding the detachment, Lieutenant Empson—were wounded and required medical attention. According to his service record, Empson was wounded on about 29 April.[75] Other sources state that he was wounded on 30 April.[76] A messenger, Private Frank Hunt, was sent on Friday night, 30 April, requesting assistance in the form of ammunition, medical supplies, food and water for the outpost's occupants. Despite the brightness from an all but full moon, Hunt successfully negotiated his way uphill from the valley to his battalion's lines on the Jolly.[77] Regardless of his wound, Empson fought on, bravely leading his men in their resistance to the Turkish pressure as it intensified in preparation for their attack the next morning.

British accounts of the Marines in the outposts in Death Trap Valley over the weekend of 1 and 2 May made no mention of ANZAC involvement, apart from two ambiguous references. Firstly, to the bodies of Australians strewn on the path to the outposts, having failed to reach the Marines during the early hours of 1 May and, secondly, to the aggressive antics of an Australian officer towards a marine, again early on 1 May. Apart from these, there was nothing in British sources connecting the Anzacs to Empson's beleaguered detachment.

5 The Battle of Death Trap Valley, 1 May 1915

The Turks were watching for us and as soon as one tried to get across down he went . . . the boys falling almost as fast as one could count.

Private Les Lott, 4th Battalion, Gallipoli diary, 1 May 1915[1]

At the end of the first week of the invasion the third Turkish counterattack was unleashed—it was a massive force. The Turks concentrated their efforts on the centre of the ANZAC and Marine positions along Second Ridge,[2] initially focusing on those posts between Quinn's and German Officers' Trench—Bombasirt and Merkeztepe. The ensuing struggle for control of Second Ridge devolved into a series of battles spread across the ANZAC Central Sector on Saturday, 1 May, and Sunday, 2 May.

One of these battles was the epic encounter in Death Trap Valley in which Turk, Marine and Anzac fought for the valley. For the Turks, it was an opportunity to threaten the very heart of the enemy position. Control of the valley would enable them to attempt to take the heights behind it and, if successful, split the invaders' line and drive them back to the beach. In order to accomplish this, the Turkish objectives in Gedik Dere were to dominate the valley and deny the Marines in the outposts any reinforcements of men and munitions. Next they would attack the outposts and then threaten the British firing line on MacLaurin's Hill and Johnston's Jolly on Second Ridge.

For the Anzacs and Marines, the battle was simply for survival.

The Turkish units committed to the Central Sector, German Officers' Trench (Merkeztepe), were six fresh battalions from the 14th and 15th regiments under the command of Lieutenant-Colonel Ali.[3] There were significant flank attacks planned as well. On the Turkish right flank four battalions—the 3rd battalions from the 57th, 64th, 72nd and 77th regiments—were to attack from the Nek (Cesarettepe) to the Sphinx (Yukseksirt), under the direction of Major Avni. On the left flank the Turkish attack was to target Lone Pine (Kanlisirt) and the ridges on its sides. Troops from the 27th, 33rd and 72nd regiments were to participate. Lieutenant-Colonel Mehmet Sefik was given command of this sector. Two additional regiments—the 125th and the 13th—were to be held in reserve.[4] Another source had seven battalions from four regiments on the right flank, six battalions from the two fresh regiments in the middle and six battalions from four regiments on the left flank partaking in the huge assault.[5] Regardless, this was to be a major Turkish offensive, second only in size to the failed mass attack of 19 May. A total of nearly 18,500 Turkish troops had been assembled, positioned, provisioned and given specific instructions by their commanders.

During the build-up to the third Turkish counterattack, Kemal insisted his men close the gap between the firing lines. By the end of the week newly created Turkish trenches appeared markedly closer to the Anzac and Marine firing line on Second Ridge, from Quinn's Post to the Jolly. By Friday, 30 April, the Turks were firmly ensconced on Turkish Johnston's on the Jolly to the south of Death Trap Valley, and in new positions on its northern side on German Officers' Trench and the ominously named Snipers Post, which overlooked the outposts in the valley below. It was only about 70 metres away. German Officers' Trench and Turkish Johnston's, bristling with Mehmetciks, were within 100 metres of the outposts, again on high ground. According to Bean, 'Sniping squads of ten, twenty, or even fifty men were pushed forward by every (Turkish) unit.'[6] A machine gun, newly positioned on German Officers' Trench by the Turks, was to play a key role in the ensuing conflict.[7] As the 4th Battalion found on their way up Bridges' Road on the evening of 30 April, a feature of this attack was an intensifying of Turkish artillery fire preparatory to the infantry attack. Up to 40 Turkish artillery pieces were involved.

A divisional order sent on 30 April by Lieutenant-Colonel Mustafa Kemal, who was in charge of the attack, encapsulated the Turkish aims, mood and preparations:

> Such being the case I am convinced that we ought to drive the enemy, who is now in front of us into the sea. Our front in comparison with the enemy is not weak. The enemys morale has been completely broken down. In continually digging trenches, he is seeking for a refuge for himself. You have seen with your own eyes the immediate flight of the enemy when a few shells fell near his trenches. There is no need to scheme (or think) much to make the enemy run away. I do not expect anyone amongst us, or amongst the soldiers we command could be found who would not rather die here than repeat the shameful story of the Balkan War. But if there are such men among us, we should at one lay hands upon them and

set them up in line to be shot. With a view to complete the triumphs we have already achieved a new regiment composed of fresh and sound troops has been put under my orders, and this regiment has just arrived in the firing line. We have still two other battalions which have not yet been in action. I am expecting the arrival of two other battalions tonight. On the other hand the enemy who is waiting to receive reinforcements cannot be supposed to have received the same amount of reinforcements as ourselves, or even to have any reinforcements whatever. Therefore with this new reinforcement and with the help of Almighty God I intend to attack the enemy tomorrow. Preparations should be made in the following way for the proposed attack:– The snipers who are to be found in our infantry line, should engage the enemy afresh. Our artillery should keep up continual fire on the fronts which I personally indicated to the batteries and thus they should cover the fire of our infantry and completely silence the machine gun fire of the enemy. The Commandants of zones should personally come to me today at 2 pm, to take further instructions from me re the plan of tomorrows attack.

Sd M. Kamel [*sic*], Lt Col.
O.C. 19th Divn[8]

Kemal was determined his men would be victorious over the Anzacs and Marines. He demanded that his commanders pay great attention to detail, insisting the attacking troops be fed hot food and be well rested before the assault. Any supply officer failing to provide adequate hot food would face a court martial. He also required each regiment to prepare properly for the coming attack. Kemal imparted these concerns at the final briefing of his senior officers at his Scrubby Knoll headquarters on Friday afternoon:

I strongly recommend you to further strengthen tonight, the positions you are holding, to see that your detachments are in touch with each other and in good order, that greater attention be paid to their order and command; that your reinforcements and reserves be so posted as to be readily available when needed, and that you continue to display your wonted zeal as you did in the past.[9]

Further instructions to the officer commanding the 1st Battalion of the 33rd Regiment from his regimental commanding officer showed the seriousness of the task ahead:

> There is no need to dwell on the necessity for completely carrying out the attack tomorrow, on which the very existence and safety of the nation depends. With the help of God and continual spiritual support of our Prophet this attack must be carried out tomorrow.[10]

Invoking Allah and the Prophet Mohammed was a traditional method of inspiring the overwhelmingly Islamic fighting troops of the Turkish army. National identity and religious fervour joined as one to steel the Mehmetciks in their duty to their nation. Certainly the Turkish and Arab troops often went into battle shouting their God's name and their spiritual devotion to him, '*Allahu Akbar!*'—'God is the Greatest!'

By 1 May Anzacs and Marines wanting to reach the outposts from Second Ridge via Loutit's Post had to firstly traverse 50 metres to reach Loutit's and then another 50 metres of open ground downhill to the valley floor and the outposts. An English report referred to the latter track as 'a fire swept ground of about 40 yards'.[11] This was the ground Private Hunt negotiated the previous night with Empson's urgent request for help. Many Turkish positions had fields of fire that incorporated the valley and, in particular, the tracks to the outposts. The Turks had pinpointed some of their arsenal—artillery batteries, a number of machine guns and numerous snipers—on both these pieces of ground, especially the track leading to the outposts from Loutit's. The Turkish firepower of the first few days was now considerably augmented by a locally based machine gun on German Officers' Trench. Other machine guns were located on the higher slopes on Second Ridge to the ANZAC left, overlooking its line. From Battleship Hill to Snipers Post, Turkish positions dotted along Second Ridge had commanding views of the approaches to the outposts. There were also Turkish artillery batteries, rifles and Maxim machine guns in front of the outposts. These were in layers of Turkish trenches, ascending from near the mouth of the valley, from Sandbag Ridge to Scrubby Knoll.

Another English account later described the exposed ground joining Loutit's Post to the outposts as 'an open passage, upon which, day and night, Turkish machine guns were ceaselessly playing . . . a deadly trap'.[12] The Marines' Lieutenant Alcock concurred, afterwards reporting that the approach to the outposts had 'no cover at all, and was marked by the enemy'.[13] This was the centrepiece of the Turkish plan in Gedik Dere—a killing ground—prepared by them as their new positions evolved in and around the valley during the second half of the last week of April. The Turks were determined to isolate the outpost's garrison by denying them any reinforcements or munitions. To reach the Marines necessitated running the gauntlet of the death trap.

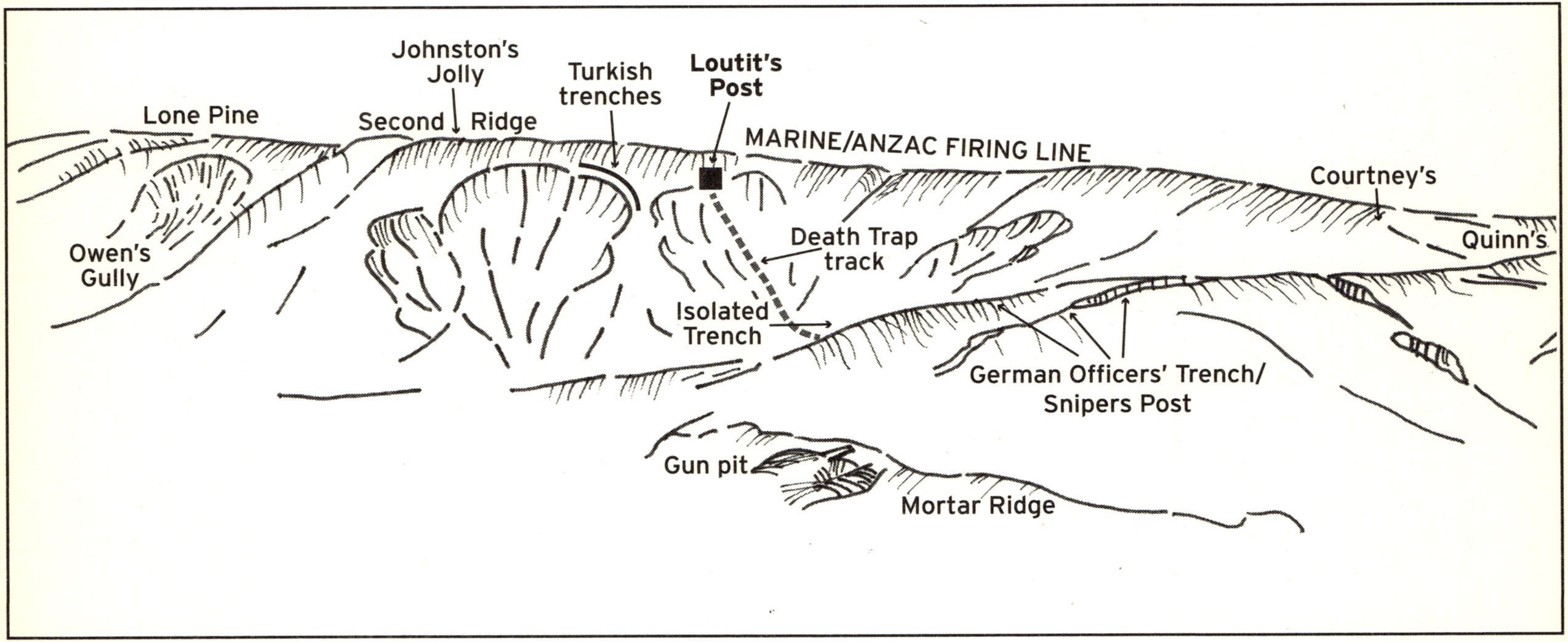

Turkish view of Death Trap Valley

This view of Death Trap Valley, from a Turkish position on Mortar Ridge, was originally drawn by Charles Bean during the Historical Mission to Anzac in 1919. This is a similar perspective to the one enjoyed by Mustafa Kemal's headquarters on Scrubby Knoll, although it was further away and slightly to the left. The valley was open to observation, fire and attack from any number of Turkish positions around it.

Of course, reaching the battle outposts provided little respite from the incessant and accurate Turkish fire. Trapped in the valley with limited cover, the garrison of Royal Marines was pinned down in rudimentary earthworks—fire coming from Snipers Post and German Officers' Trench looming over them to the left, enemy infantry attacks from their front, and fire also coming from Turkish positions in front and on their right from the Jolly. Compounding their plight were the artillery strikes that pounded their position with shrapnel. The Turks had turned the whole valley into a death trap, with their focus being the steep approaches the troops entering or leaving the outposts were forced to use. These tracks were perilous by night; deadly by day.

Arguably, the whole of the extended ANZAC beachhead was a death trap. Nowhere was safe from Turkish fire. Men were hit regardless of their location. The Turks held the high ground overlooking many ANZAC positions and if their machine guns or sniper fire couldn't hit you, then their artillery could. A number of Anzacs' accounts refer to death traps, starting from Quinn's Post, the most dangerous position in the firing line, to the rearmost position on the beach. The term 'death trap' was used in regard to many parts of Anzac; however, some positions were particularly exposed and deadly.

~

On 30 April the 4th Battalion's war diary made no explicit reference to where the battalion was sent, merely acknowledging they had been 'ordered to reinforce R.M.L.I. Bde in centre' and that on 1 May, 'A.C. + D Coys were in support and in trenches most of the day. B Coy returned at 4.0 pm + held in reserve'. Even though the ferocity of the Turkish fire was noted on 1 May, there was no mention of Death Trap Valley or of any casualties at all on 30 April, 1 May and 2 May. The battalion war diary entry for 2 May was equally lacking in regard to the situation in Death Trap Valley.[14] As events later proved, the adjutant, Lieutenant Jack Massie, was rather remiss in not recording these details, particularly the casualties.

There were four main chroniclers of the 4th Battalion's actions in Death Trap Valley on 1 and 2 May 1915. Remarkably three of them—Corporal Charles Macquarie, Private Ern 'Snowy' Robson and Private Les Lott—were from Jack's section—No. 12, No. 15 Platoon, D Company. The fourth chronicler, Private Les De Vine, was from No. 3 Platoon, A Company. A fifth member of the battalion—Private Michael 'Quig' Quigley, A Company—offered some additional insights. All of them were participants in the battle.

The 4th Battalion, having been abruptly ordered to return to the centre of the firing line, rested in support behind MacLaurin's Hill from around midnight until 3 a.m. on Saturday, 1 May, still under heavy enemy artillery fire. Corporal Macquarie recounted in his letter to Jack's father:

> Anyway, as we came well within range—Jack—was close at hand, I asked him how things were. It was midnight by this time we spelled for 3 hours.[15]

About the time the 4th Battalion reached the firing line on MacLaurin's Hill to reinforce and relieve the Marines, Private Hunt arrived with his urgent message from the battle outposts—Empson's men needed assistance. Adjacent to the newly arrived A and D companies of the 4th Battalion was the Portsmouth Battalion on Johnston's Jolly. Major James Heane, the commanding officer of D Company and very much a senior figure in the battalion that was missing its commanding officer and deputy, dealt with the RMLI authorities as they organised support for Empson's Marines.[16] Heane immediately volunteered his company's services, in the form of Captain Fred 'Maud' Fanning's No. 15 Platoon, to enter the valley and reinforce Empson's outpost. They did so at 3 a.m. with Heane and Fanning at the helm, and Jack and his mates of No. 12 Section in tow, along with the three other sections that constituted No. 15 Platoon. At this point in the campaign No. 12 Section was intact, all of its members having survived their first week under fire, despite many nerve-racking close shaves. The deployment occurred under a waning gibbous moon, which had risen hours earlier at 8.46 p.m. on 30 April—95 per cent of the moon was visible, casting a lunar wash over the battlefield.[17]

The 4th Battalion war diary stated that 'only 42 men went to the trenches' late on 30 April. This entry probably referred to events early on 1 May, considering that on Friday evening, 30 April, the 4th were slogging their way up from the beach and only arrived at MacLaurin's Hill at midnight.[18]

Les Lott's version ominously recorded:

> Arriving at 3 a.m. the battle is going hot and strong . . . We press in, 56 of us going to the left into what is now known as Death Trap Valley, the rest of the Battn going to the right.[19]

This party of 56 men that Les referred to was the first of four parties sent into Death Trap Valley over the next 24 hours to help the Marines. Heane's detachment became a rescue party as the day unfolded. (See Appendix 2 for list of probable participants.) The party's first objective was to reach Loutit's Post about 50 metres in front of the British firing line on the northern edge of the Jolly, which they did, relieving the Marines who held it. In a later interview with *The Sun*, Snowy Robson reported that they reached the trenches 'just before daybreak'.[20]

Corporal Macquarie described their chaotic deployment in far more detail in his letter to Jack's father:

> . . . then went forward, to what, well *was a death trap* so things appeared 12 hours later. We relieved a company of *Royal Marines* they got out as quickly as possible, our company taking up their place. At 5 a.m. my section consisting of Jack & 10 others, got mixed up with other sections and the *platoon* generally. eventually under heavy fire we, No. 12 Section of D. Co, *4th Battalion* found our men tallied more than the trenches hold, so, along we scooted through the scrub passed a dug out and finally into a large trench, which was commanded by St *Wright D* company. Here again we were more than the trench had room for, so Jack with 5 others of the section hopped back into the dug out that we passed en-route. [Snowy Robson was one of these men. Jack, as second in charge of the section, took control of this post.] In this position they did splendid work saving *lives* to some good extent. [Note: Words in italics previously deleted by censor.][21]

Meanwhile as dawn approached, in response to Empson's plea for help Colonel Frank Luard and Captain Alfred Syson—the Portsmouth Battalion Commanding Officer and C Company Commanding Officer, respectively—detailed a replenishment party of 11 NCOs and men under the leadership of Sergeant Marcus Minter to resupply the men in the valley via Loutit's, where Heane and his men were now located. This was the second detachment to enter the valley on 1 May to support the Marines. Minter was a veteran who had enlisted in the Royal Marines in 1896 and had also been fighting the German Army in northern Europe the previous autumn.[22]

While nearly all the members of the party were loaded with much-needed supplies of food, water and ammunition, one of them carried medical supplies. He was Lance Corporal Walter Parker, a 33-year-old stretcher-bearer who had enlisted in September 1914.[23] Since landing at Anzac on 28 April, Parker had distinguished himself as part of Surgeon Basil Playne's medical section in the battalion. He led the stretcher-bearers, repeatedly evacuating wounded men under heavy fire and, at times, in exposed positions.

When the request came for a volunteer stretcher-bearer to join Minter's party, Parker readily chose to go:

> 'We were in and out,' says Parker, 'both night and day, attending to the wounded, and rendering first-aid to the injured. Having been at work at

> the Hospital some time, Col. Luard, Capt. Syson, and Capt. Morton came in quietly and called for a volunteer to go down to one of our own companies which was enfiladed. All of us realised the task was super-human.[24]

Surgeon Playne, the battalion's medical officer, was already occupied attending to wounded men in other trenches. Playne was awarded a Distinguished Service Order for his bravery at Anzac. The platoons marooned in the valley contained wounded men who desperately needed medical help. According to Captain Syson, Parker 'immediately volunteered to go with the medical stores'.[25]

But unbeknown to Parker and the rest of the Portsmouth Battalion, the gallant teenage subaltern, Richard Empson, leading the defence of the outpost's garrison, was killed during the first Turkish assault about the time the replenishment party was preparing to enter the valley.

Captain Syson recalled what happened next when the detachment left the relative safety of Loutit's Post at dawn:

> The party consisted of 10 N.C.O.s + privates and Lce Cpl Parker, and in attempting to emerge from the nearest trench [there was no communication trench] one man of the party was wounded. Lce Cpl Parker stayed and organised a stretcher party to carry him back.[26]

After instinctively performing this initial act and, unaware of the fate of the rest of Minter's party, Parker remained determined to attempt to reach Empson's position, now under the command of Lieutenant Alcock. Alcock, in a later interview, described Parker's state of mind:

> There is no doubt whatever that Lance Corporal Parker knew, as soon as he started, that he was taking the greatest risks possible and that his one idea was to succour the wounded in the isolated trench.[27]

As it was daylight he would have seen evidence of the gravity of what he was about to attempt in the number of Australian bodies, probably from Heane's party, littering the track between him and his goal. According to Surgeon Playne of the Portsmouth Battalion, in a later report, 'a party of Australian troops had [already] been wiped out in the attempt' to reach the Marines.[28] Equally disturbing was the apocryphal threat from an unknown Australian officer to shoot him unless he abandoned his mission.[29] This officer might have been Major 'Cast Iron Jimmy' Heane or Lieutenant Fred 'Maud' Fanning, both of whom were present in Loutit's Post at the time and had probably just witnessed their own men being hit and Minter's party also suffering casualties. At the time either of these officers would have been incredulous upon hearing of Parker's plan to go on his own in daylight. Minter's party's attempt had the watching Turks on high alert, ready to fire on any further troops foolhardy enough to try to reach the Marines in the isolated trench.

However, Parker's inordinate sense of duty prevailed and, somehow, despite the close attention of enemy marksmen, he climbed out of Loutit's and ran and stumbled his way downhill to the isolated trench. Such was Parker's momentum that he fell into a pond at the bottom and may have injured himself. According to reports, 'The next thing that aroused his failing sense was the tremendous cheering of the outpost's occupants.'[30]

Of the 11 men who set out in Minter's replenishment party from Loutit's, only Parker made it through to the outposts. C Company Sergeant Major Fred Chapman, the senior NCO and second in command of the detachment in the valley after Empson's death, later wrote that 'Lance Corporal W.R. Parker was entirely alone, + the only one to reach the trench.'[31] The rest of Minter's men, including the original messenger Frank Hunt, became casualties or were frustrated by the ferocity and accuracy of the Turkish fire as they tried to reach the exhausted Marines. Sergeant Minter later claimed to have made three attempts to breach the death trap that day, all of them unsuccessful. Current research has shown that none of Minter's party was killed in action during their brave attempts to help their fellow Marines; some of them were certainly wounded in action, although not Sergeant Minter.[32]

Once Parker made it to the trench, the doughty Marine treated the wounded. According to Alcock, 'The extreme courage with which he carried out his work was excellent and he remained calm and collected under very trying circumstances.'[33] The wounded were moved to a relatively safe part of the hollow of the valley near the spring. While Parker set about establishing an aid post, the overall position of the Marines became increasingly desperate due to a shortage of ammunition. Sergeant Major Fred Chapman verified that, 'There were no ammunition or water carriers who reached the trench'[34] from Minter's detachment, which did not help the already dire situation.

~

At around 5 a.m. the Turkish attack began with an artillery barrage on the British lines, followed 15 minutes later by the infantry. In the crucial Central Sector encompassing Death Trap Valley, the assault by the 14th Regiment bogged down in the face of fierce resistance and the combination of well-sited ANZAC and Marine machine guns and 200 metres of open ground in No Man's Land.[35]

The Chatham Battalion war diary recorded that 'The position was again attacked at dawn on May 1st but without result.'[36] Private Bertram Wilson of the Chatham Battalion in trenches on MacLaurin's Hill behind the outposts experienced the Turkish assault:

> At dawn the Turks attacked in mass and the situation looked critical, but before arriving at the trench they retired with heavy losses. My machine gun officer was killed; he was using his rifle during the attack and got a bullet through the head. I borrowed a periscope from one of my subalterns to try and spot a machine gun that was worrying us considerably. As soon as I got it in line with the top of the trench a bullet smashed it in my hands. I went to inform the officer, but he had just been killed. Snipers are a menace, they seem to be everywhere and are very clever at concealing themselves. The sun and flies are terrible and one cannot obtain water to quench the thirst. The dead Turks in front and our fellows lying at the back of us are beginning to smell. The din was terrific: shouting and blowing of bugles and the whole place was lit up with fires that were raging in the scrub. During the attack I caught about thirty of them coming towards our gun position. I emptied a belt of ammunition into them at 60 yards with good effect.[37]

The 14th Battalion was now stationed at Courtney's Post to relieve the pressure on the Marines. Their war diary recorded the ineffectual attack:

> 1/5/15 about 5 AM Another attempt on part of enemy to break through the section of trenches on our Right held by the R.M.L.I. 14th Battalion stood to arms in case assistance was wanted, but were not required. Portion of this attack launched against Courtney's Post and enemy estimated at about 500 were repulsed and retired in great disorder losing many casualties.[38]

Charles Bean also described the early morning attack:

> At 4 a.m. the enemy, about a battalion strong, advanced against MacLaurin's Hill. The Marines and the 14th Battalion met them with a tremendous fire. When 200 yards distant, the Turks broke and fled, losing heavily. They were rallied, and advanced again; but the heart had gone out of the attack. It swerved to the right towards Courtney's and withered.[39]

However, it was not only the Marines who were suffering the effects of the Turkish onslaught. Major Heane's party was in Loutit's Post and nearby dugouts above the isolated trench, and had been since the early hours of 1 May in their quest to support and supply the besieged Marines. (See the map of Death Trap Valley on page 165.) They were the nearest support troops. In this position they were subjected to heavy continuous enemy fire throughout the day. Conditions in the valley deteriorated as the long day wore on. Some idea of the intensity of the Turkish fusillade can be gained from comments made by the 4th's adjutant, Lieutenant Jack Massie, in the war diary on 1 May: 'Artillery fire "Hell" M.G.s very hot, also sniping all the afternoon',[40] keeping in mind Massie was in trenches in the comparative safety of MacLaurin's Hill.

In a report written some days later, the newly promoted commanding officer of the 4th Battalion, Lieutenant-Colonel Alf Bennett, reiterated Massie's observations: 'May 1 . . . The enemy brought very heavy artillery and machine-gun fire to bear on position. Sniping was also very severe.'[41] Charles Bean noted, 'The Turkish shrapnel fire on the whole area was heavy all day.'[42] The sensory assault for both sides that began just before dawn on Sunday, 25 April, and continued unabated all week, intensified during the Turkish attacks that weekend. The unrelenting sights, sounds and smells of battle must have been overwhelming for the participants. Michael Quigley described the Turkish shrapnel fire early on 2 May in the valley:

> They have been literally raining shrapnel on us this morning. I saw as many as seventeen shells burst in a few minutes over one section of our trenches making my head ache with their confounded noise.[43]

Multiply that shrapnel snapshot many, many times for the first week across the length and breadth of Anzac, about 200 hectares in size, and the result was a curtain of enemy artillery, machine-gun and rifle fire that continued day in and day out.

Also acknowledging the intensity of the Turkish fire was Major-General Sir Alexander Godley, the commanding officer of the New Zealand and Australian Division, who made the following observation in an order of 2 May: 'It is noticeable that the superiority of fire all along the line belongs to the enemy.'[44]

Corporal Charles Saunders of the New Zealand Engineers, who was awarded a Distinguished Conduct Medal for his fighting on Walker's Ridge on 27 April, agreed with Godley's remarks in his diary entry for 3 May:

> The Turks have a very strong position slightly above us and we have not enough men by half to shift them. I am sure they have two armies, one for fighting and one for digging, as their fire is ever so much heavier than

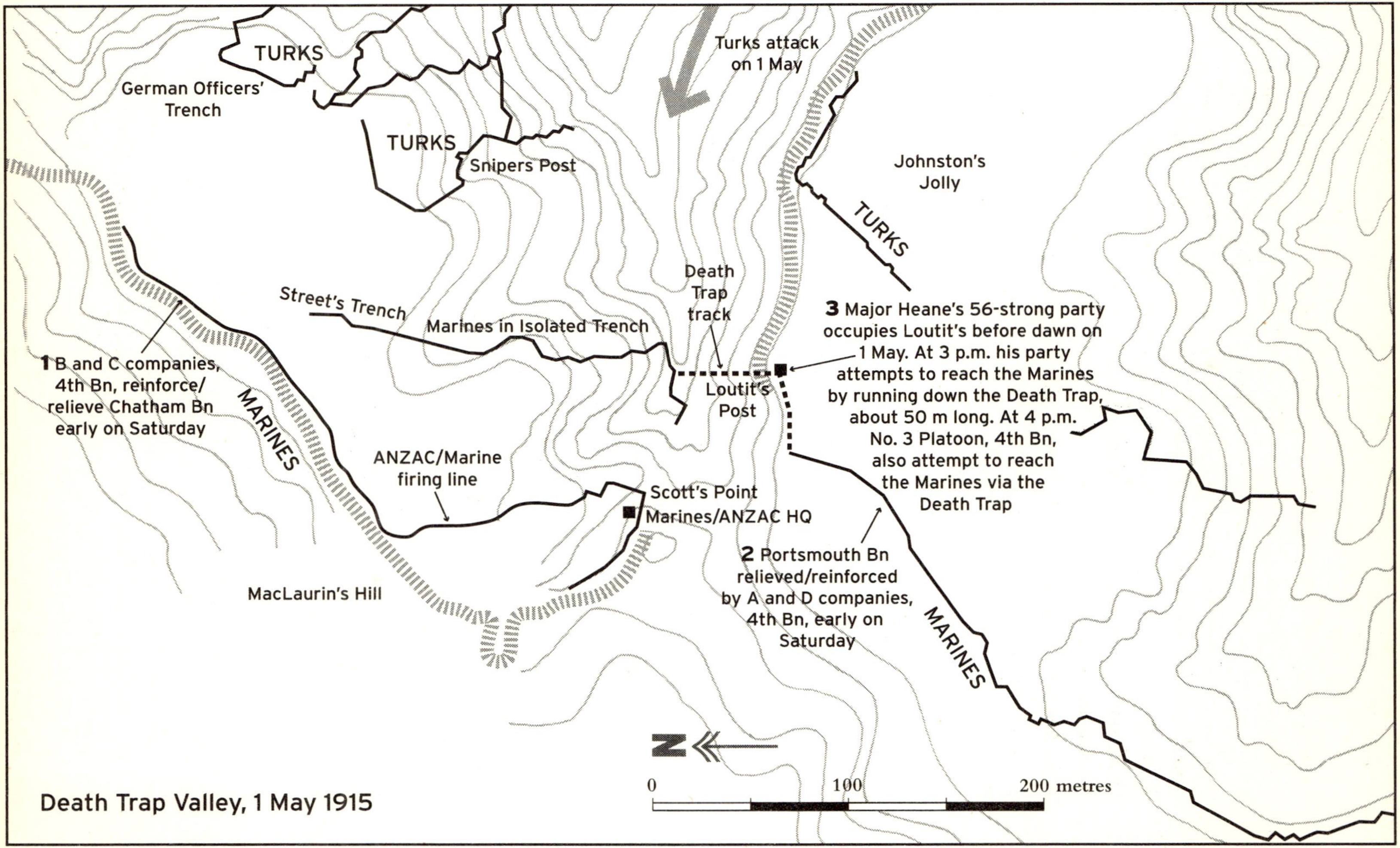

Death Trap Valley, 1 May 1915

> ours and also for every shovel full of earth that we pitched up, they pitched up three ... [45]

The Marines in the valley and Heane's party in Loutit's were now experiencing the full might of the third Turkish counterattack. While other attacks by the Turks occurred during the day, particularly in the late afternoon across the Central Sector of the British firing line, the epicentre of their counterattack seemed to be in and around Death Trap Valley.

Throughout the day, attacks from the Mehmetciks of the 14th and 15th regiments further depleted the outpost's resources. It was later reported that 'at one point ammunition was reduced to about 15 rounds per man'.[46] The Portsmouth Battalion's commanding officer, Lieutenant-Colonel Luard, described their difficult and dangerous situation:

> On the 1st instant a platoon of the Portsmouth Battalion [temporarily lent to another unit] was forced to be in an isolated trench without any means of reinforcements, replenishment, or of retreat. The trench was exposed to constant hostile fire, and infantry attacks of the enemy were with difficulty repulsed by rifle fire.[47]

The three No. 12 Section chroniclers described the awful conditions in the valley and the ferocity of the fighting during their occupation of Loutit's Post above the isolated trench. In these accounts they also referred to the Marines in the outposts below them. Jack and his mates were in the thick of the action, fighting for their lives and the lives of the Marines in the isolated trench.

Les Lott recorded in his diary:

> The fight turns out to be one of the severest for our Battn previous to Lone Pine ... The R.M.L.I. only being a pack of Boys they were badly rattled. At daylight the Turks are still pressing heavily, we were in the Valley bearing the Brunt of it, getting very little assistance from the Marines, who were calling 'for God sake send us reinforcements and ammunition'.[48]

Snowy Robson wrote about the ferocity of the battle in a letter to his sister:

> A few days later we got into a place named by the lads—'The Death Trap.' I was in a dug-out a little apart from the others. We had some fierce fighting all that day, and the lads below us were calling out for water and ammunition.[49]

Corporal Macquarie's letter to Jack's father also referred to the plight of the Marines below them:

> At three o'clock *the Royal Marines* lost confidence in themselves, losing ammunition & calling on we Australians to get them reinforcements. [N.B. Italicised words censored from letter.][50]

By mid-afternoon the Marines' situation in the isolated trench was dire indeed. Apart from Lance Corporal Parker, no reinforcements, food, munitions or water had reached them for days. They had been in the valley and under fire since 2 a.m. on Thursday morning. It was now 2 p.m. on Saturday afternoon. Sixty hours had elapsed since they were forced to occupy the battle outposts. The only word of their parlous situation came via Private Hunt on Friday night. Little wonder that, as their position became more desperate, the embattled Englishmen called out for help to Heane and his men, who were the nearest support troops.

Cast Iron Jimmy Heane now ordered his men to undertake what was a suicidal but desperately needed mission to save the Marines and their post. He instructed them to reinforce the Marines with men, ammunition, food and water by running the gauntlet of the death trap in broad daylight at the height of the Turkish attack. Unfortunately for Heane's men, any movement in the valley provoked the ire of the vigilant Turks. The fate of Minter's party and some of their own 56-strong force, both of which Heane's detachment had witnessed, was testament to that. Marcus Minter's 11-man party also attempted to reach the outposts in the valley in daylight.

A critical moment had been reached in the battle for the valley and in Jack's journey. Again the accounts of Les Lott, Snowy Robson and Charles Macquarie provided dramatic recollections of what then followed for Fred Fanning's No. 15 Platoon and Jack. It was now mid-afternoon on Saturday, 1 May 1915. The battle for the valley and the outposts was in the balance.

According to Les Lott:

> We then endeavoured to reach them (ie. The Marines) bearing ammunition which cost us dear. The Turks were watching for us and as soon as one tried to get across down he went. Only 6 of us managed to get across without a serious scratch . . . the boys falling almost as fast as one could count.[51]

From Snowy Robson there were two accounts. Firstly, in his letter to his sister he wrote:

> From where we were to them (ie. The Marines) was a clear track of about 40 yards swept by machine gun, shrapnel and rifle fire. Thirty-one of our lads tried to go down there, but the farthest any of them got was about ten yards before they were shot down.[52]

Secondly, in his interview with *The Sun*, Robson said:

> From the position I had in the trench I could see a clear track ahead to the trench in front. It was about 60 to 70 yards away. The Turks were entrenched about 50 yards in front of that. At about 2 or 3 o'clock in the afternoon 34 men were sent up to reinforce the trench along this track. The Turks had a machine-gun turned on to it, and the 34 men were dropped in no time. The last man to fall had a box of ammunition with him.[53]

Corporal Macquarie's account of what happened next concentrated on Jack:

> At 3 o'clock . . . Twas cruel *to see* what then took place. Men were dropping around me by the dozen. Jack could bear their cry (the Marines) no longer, and left his position to fall in alongside of your humble. Just at the moment of his seeking a place to jump into the trench, he got hit, poor fellow—took it game too. Then out of that trench I hopped, as a duty to a friend and comrade, to find a great big wound caused by a soft-nosed bullet, received below the hip, in his left thigh. I did what experience of wounds taught me, patched him up and all this under heavy shrapnel and machine-gun fire. Jack said he was not long for this world. This upset me more than being hit, and I could not help standing upright and gazing at him for a second or two. Then I told him that he was fit for a longer life than people imagined. The battle was raging very hot at 3.30 p.m. of the 1st May, so I used my shoulder and assisted by two marines, got poor Jack under cover, where he was forced to wait . . . [54]

Jack was shot by a sniper probably operating from the high ground on the ANZAC left, possibly in Snipers Post or German Officers' Trench. He was one of the many men from No. 15 Platoon the three eyewitnesses reported being hit as they attempted to reach the Marines caught in the valley. All three described many casualties dropping and falling around them. Turkish artillery and machine-gun observers and snipers had zeroed in on the track, targeting man after man. Jack, having fought hard for a week, was now out of the fight, suffering a gunshot wound that was possibly caused by a dumdum or explosive bullet. The bullet not only left a gaping wound but also shattered his femur below his left hip. Undoubtedly, he was in great pain, suffering severe shock.

Still no water or ammunition had reached the Marines, despite the sacrificial attempts of Heane's party. Snowy Robson, who was in the same dugout as Jack during the fighting that day, having observed the slaughter of his mates, noted that the last of the 34 men hit was carrying a box of ammunition. It lay in the open on the death trap, among the dead and wounded Australians adorning the track in a ghastly, sanguinary tableau. Snowy now made a momentous decision, one that each man braving the Turkish fire to reach the Marines had also made:

> As soon as all the boys dropped I said to myself, 'Oh well, damn it! I might as well be in it, too.' I rushed out and picked up the ammunition box. As luck would have it, the machine-gun stopped firing. Whether they were putting in a new belt, or the gun got jambed, I don't know. I wasn't hit, anyway but there were six bullet holes put into the ammunition box. (The box, containing 1000 rounds, weighed 1 cwt [51 kilograms].) After that I went back and got all the water bottles from the boys who had fallen and took them to the front trench.[55]

Snowy later rather humbly reflected on his survival:

> How I got back was a miracle . . . the bullets fairly ploughed the scrub up around me. The enemy was entrenched only 150 yards away, and I still came back alive.[56]

In fact, he had defied the death trap three times to deliver vital ammunition and water to the desperate Marines. Snowy's heroics were very significant, certainly influencing the outcome of the battle in the valley.

The handful of survivors from Heane's party now joined the Marines in their defence of the outposts. One of these men was Les Lott, who was clearly traumatised by his experiences. The fighting was desperate and continuous. There was no respite from the Turks, who were determined to break the enemy hold on Second Ridge. Les gave a detailed account of the fighting in his diary:

> All day we fought to keep them back . . . soon our trenches were full of dead and wounded. Some of my worst experiences were that day. One of my mates [possibly Private Thomas Davis] fell along side of me with the

top of his head blown off and lingered about 10 hrs when he died. to hear his moans was sickening. Our water being low, and we shared with the wounded in most cases we went without till our tongues were like a bit of rag. The Turkish snipers doing deadly work, and they had plenty of area to work in, while we are cooped up in a small place . . . The Marines, now being practically useless having lost heart, so we put them to hold a smaller space of the line.[57]

In his letter to George Collyer about the events that day, Corporal Macquarie had one last comment to make, which showed he was also suffering from his experiences in Death Trap Valley:

> I cannot mention more, as the things that I witnessed were terrible, & hope not to see again.[58]

~

The appalling cost to No. 15 Platoon that afternoon resulted in Major Heane requesting another platoon to reinforce his decimated detachment. No. 3 Platoon, A Company, 4th Battalion, was now ordered to enter the valley at 4 p.m. to support the men in the isolated trench. This was the third party to enter the valley to help the Marines on 1 May. (See Appendix 3 for list of probable participants.) A member of that party, Private Les De Vine, commented on the very heavy shrapnel fire he and his mates endured while waiting in reserve earlier that day.[59] This was but a taste of the hellish conditions in the valley itself.

The commander of the platoon, Lieutenant Percy Turner, and one of his sergeants, Robert Cranmer, had been wounded on 26 April, probably during the 4th's ill-fated Lone Pine gambit. Neither man was present on 1 May. Cranmer was in Egypt receiving treatment for a gunshot wound to his right arm. Sergeant Walter Oakes of No. 3 Platoon was present. Snowy Robson, now in the outposts, was selected to act as a guide for the 50 reinforcements. A report written by Lieutenant-Colonel Bennett of the 4th Battalion on 4 May described the next phase of Snowy's heroics:

> Robson went ahead of the reinforcing party, returned, showed the way, and as the officer commanding reinforcing platoon was wounded, he acted as guide and subsequently controlled all men in the vicinity.[60]

The officer in charge of No. 2 Platoon, A Company, Boer War veteran Lieutenant John Christie, was wounded in the throat and shoulder by shrapnel on 1 May.[61]

He might be the officer mentioned in Bennett's report, possibly acting in Turner's place. There were no other officers from A Company wounded that day.

Bennett's account belied the danger the men faced in carrying out the order. Like the previous two parties, this one had to run the gauntlet of the death trap to reach its objective. Like the previous two parties, many casualties were inflicted on them as they leapt the parapet of Loutit's Post and charged down the hill in daylight. Les De Vine described their attempted passage: 'Went into the firing line about 4 p.m. under a heavy hail of shrapnel, we received many casualties, had a machine gun turned on us but I escaped.'[62] What was left of the platoon reached the isolated trench, their numbers thinned considerably.

About the time the third party was ordered into the valley, another Turkish attack was launched in the Central Sector. The Chatham Battalion war diary briefly referred to this late afternoon Turkish foray, the battalion's former sergeant major, Lieutenant A.F. Hayward, being 'wounded during an attack on the evening of May 1st'.[63]

On Johnston's Jolly the indefatigable Major Duncan Glasfurd, one of the senior officers on the 1st Division's Headquarters Staff, witnessed the enemy action at 4 p.m. on Saturday. Charles Bean caught the moment:

> Across Johnston's Jolly about 1000 made a spirited attack upon the Marines' line, jumping over the bushes on the plateau and advancing in a manner which called forth the admiration of the gallant Glasfurd, who was making another of his many journeys along the line. The machine-guns and rifles of the Marines opened, and, when 200 yards distant, the advance broke down.[64]

Private Thomas Baker of the Chatham Battalion, which was positioned behind the valley from MacLaurin's Hill to Courtney's Post, experienced such an attack when 1000 Mehmetciks attacked his battalion's lines at 4 p.m. on Friday. Although this attack occurred on the previous day, it was indicative of the nature of their later assaults. It also vividly described the experience and perspective of the defenders on Second Ridge during such an attack. The rifle and machine-gun fire of the Marines, which began when the Turks were about 180 metres away, stopped them well before the Marines' trenches:

> The Turks began to attack in the afternoon in huge numbers, you know, on mass. They came out of the scrub like rabbits towards you. My word we had a real rough time repelling them. I had two men loading for me, and I kept firing the rifles when they made these mass attacks. They did not get

within more than fifty yards, as we repelled all the attacks. They had been fairly close together, staggered somewhat so they were easy targets. I reckoned if you missed one you would have the next man. Mind, you didn't get too much time to aim, you had to get on with your job. It was all over in minutes and of course they were heaped up, wounded and dead. Quite a number of our boys got killed in these attacks and being a horseshoe position it wasn't only a frontal attack for us, they came at different angles . . . The rifles got very hot until you couldn't fire them, when you can't fire your rifles you are snockered and it doesn't take many rounds before they were very hot. You had to make your own decisions in a way as, when you saw Turks you knew you had to kill. That was all there was to it.[65]

While the enemy attack unfolded late on Saturday, in the isolated trench in Death Trap Valley Snowy Robson took control of 'all men in the vicinity'.[66] Conditions were abysmal. The Turkish assault across the Central Sector, including the valley, was accompanied by heavy enemy shrapnel, machine-gun and sniper fire. However, once again the superb fire of the ANZAC and Marine machine guns and rifles foiled the Turkish intentions. The attack failed. Snowy's take on his actions was brief and typically modest:

After it got dark 50 reinforcements were sent down and I was put in charge of them. I got them to work and dug a trench, waited until it was finished and then completely knocked up, I pulled my weary bones up the hill (through the death trap yet again) and joined my platoon, where I put in a sleepless night as we had to stand all the time (in Loutit's Post.)[67]

Apart from a short interlude from the firing line at Anzac Cove on Friday afternoon, Robson, like the rest of his battalion, had been in action and continuously under fire, even at the beach, from just after daybreak on Sunday, 25 April, until Sunday morning, 2 May—some seven days and nights, with little or no rest, let alone sleep. No other AIF battalion had such demands placed on it. Snowy had diced with the death trap six times in the previous twelve hours. He must have been physically and psychologically spent.

The Death Trap Valley parties from the 4th Battalion, No. 15 and No. 3 platoons, fought heroically and unstintingly at the end of a very demanding week to save Empson's Marines and their position. The first phase of the battle for the valley was over. The Turkish attacks across the ANZAC firing line failed to dislodge the British. The Marines and their ANZAC saviours from the 4th Battalion held on grimly to the hotly contested outposts.

However, the Turks weren't finished with their counterattack or Gedik Dere. Frustrated by the stubborn enemy defence of Second Ridge, Kemal ordered a fresh attack for early on 2 May on all three fronts, part of it aimed squarely at the isolated trench. Lieutenant-Colonel Ali's 14th and 15th regiments, despite having suffered considerable casualties hurling themselves at the Central Sector for most of the day, were required to prepare for another frontal attack. In the words of the Turkish General Staff's recent analysis of the battle:

> The failure of the attacks performed during the day could discourage neither the commander of the division nor his soldiers fighting heroically. In order to raze the ANZAC forces from their positions, and to stop the bleeding in the Ariburnu before it became gangrenous, the continuation of the attacks was decided, thus it was intended to take the advantage of battle weary ANZAC troops.[68]

In the outposts under the supervision of Snowy Robson, Les De Vine and his newly arrived mates from No. 3 Platoon were keeping a close eye on the enemy:

> We take it in turns to watch for ½ hour on & 1 hour off time off taken up by digging. During the night the Turks came up in hundreds in front of our trenches swarmed across the sky line, but did not attack us merely advancing a little & dug in considerably closer to us, we had good sniping all night, as they were constantly moving about the sky line.[69]

While the Turks prepared for further assaults on the mixed force now occupying the isolated trench, the 3rd Battalion, which had been resting and reorganising on the beach since being relieved around midnight on Wednesday, 28 April, was ordered to return to the firing line on Johnston's Jolly to relieve the now struggling Marines. The battalion had suffered significant casualties during their previous occupation of MacLaurin's Hill and Death Trap Valley, revealed by a roll call held soon after arriving on the beach. Lieutenant-Colonel Owen described his battalion's condition after their relief by the Marines:

> These men had been fighting . . . continuously for 3 days were almost dropping with sleepiness & fatigue & their officers had been killed and wounded and they had lost nearly 1/3 their numbers.[70]

The 3rd Battalion war diary for 1 May gave a brief description of its movements: 'Bn in bivouac until 5pm when orders were received to prepare to move at very short notice . . . At 9pm the Bn commenced to relieve a Bn of Marines; the operation was completed by 4 a.m.'[71] The blandness of this entry failed to begin to describe the dramatic situation that unfolded during the relief for part of the battalion. The bulk of the 3rd Battalion was deployed to the right of the 4th Battalion across the Jolly on 400 Plateau replacing the Marines. During the relief Lieutenant-Colonel Owen received a report that Marines in an 'advanced' trench were being driven back. A message was sent through Major Heane that 'help was wanted by the RMLI in front of Courtney's Post'.[72] The trench in question was the isolated one in Death Trap Valley. In Owen's words:

> I told General Trotman that my men who knew the ground would retake the trench and sent two platoons of D Coy 3rd Battalion to do the job.[73]

The two platoons were understrength, having lost a third of their number during the first week of fighting. They were led by Hubert 'Bert' Meager and Tallisker 'Tully' McLeod, who were promoted to second lieutenants on 1 May. The casualty rate among the officers during the first week at Gallipoli necessitated NCOs being appointed as junior officers across the ranks of the ANZAC battalions.

Bert Meager and Tully McLeod had almost identical military careers in the AIF. Both enlisted in the 3rd Battalion within a week of one another about a month after war was declared, and both were almost immediately appointed as sergeants due to their considerable experience in various pre-war military units, including the regular British Army and the Australian militia. English-born McLeod had spent 12 years in the regular British Army, including a stint in South Africa. Prior to his promotion he was the D Company sergeant major.[74] Australian-born Meager, aged 22 on enlistment, was nearly ten years younger than McLeod, but had still served as an officer commanding a militia company in Sydney for a few years.[75] Like Lieutenant Fred Fanning, commanding No. 15 Platoon, 4th Battalion, Meager and McLeod proved to be outstanding junior officers, much admired by their men. Unlike Fanning, who died fighting as a company commander in the 56th Battalion in France, neither man survived Gallipoli. Both subalterns were promoted to lieutenant on 4 August, immediately before they were killed in the carnage of Lone Pine days later. When the Australians, including the 3rd and 4th battalions, attacked at Lone Pine, Fanning, somewhat fortuitously, was in Egypt being treated for dysentery.[76]

Owen, in an after-action report, referred to Meager and McLeod as 'gallant' and the platoons as 'willingly' going into action 'with such spirit'.[77] Theirs was to be the fourth party to enter the valley to support the Marines.

Meanwhile, the Turks were girding themselves to once again assault the

Above left: A studio portrait of John (Jack) Collyer, dated 6 November 1912. COURTESY OF THE COLLYER FAMILY

Above: This photographic portrait of Jack in uniform has been coloured with pencil. COURTESY OF ALMA COLLYER

Top: The Collyer family, dressed in black after Jack's death. Some family members are wearing black armbands. COURTESY OF THE COLLYER FAMILY

Above: Another family portrait taken after Jack's death, this time with Jack inserted. COURTESY OF THE COLLYER FAMILY

Above: A life-boat crew from the Australian cruiser HMAS *Sydney* rows to the German raider SMS *Emden* at Cocos (Keeling) Islands on 11 November 1914. C.E.W. BEAN/AUSTRALIAN WAR MEMORIAL (G01442A)

J. Collyer No 1341 D. Coy
4th Battalion, 1st Inf. Bgde.
A.I.E.F.

March 2nd 1915

I had leave to-day, my pass being made out from 10 A.M. to 9.30 P.M. but it was well after 1 before I got to Cairo. After a run round town for half an hour, I went to a restaurant & had dinner. I decided to take a run to Helliopolis, a suburb of Cairo, of which I had heard a great deal, but up to to-day, I had never been able to spare the time to take the trip. Both trams & trains run out, & I selected the tram, as it was closer to where I was in town.

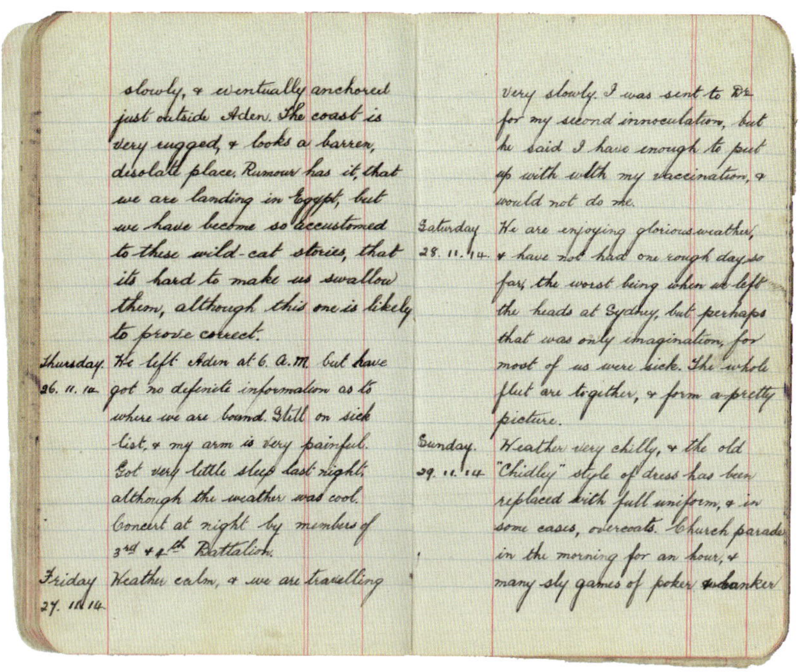

slowly, & eventually anchored just outside Aden. The coast is very rugged, & looks a barren, desolate place. Rumour has it, that we are landing in Egypt, but we have become so accustomed to these wild-cat stories, that its hard to make us swallow them, although this one is likely to prove correct.

Thursday. 26. 11. 14. We left Aden at 6. A.M. but have got no definite information as to where we are bound. Still on sick list, & my arm is very painful. Got very little sleep last night, although the weather was cool. Concert at night by members of 3rd & 4th Battalion.

Friday 27. 11. 14. Weather calm, & we are travelling very slowly. I was sent to Dr for my second innoculation, but he said I have enough to put up with with my vaccination, & would not do me.

Saturday 28. 11. 14. We are enjoying glorious weather, & have not had one rough day so far, the worst being when we left the heads at Sydney, but perhaps that was only imagination, for most of us were sick. The whole fleet are together, & form a pretty picture.

Sunday. 29. 11. 14. Weather very chilly, & the old "Chidley" style of dress has been replaced with full uniform, & in some cases, overcoats. Church parade in the morning for an hour, & many sly games of poker & banker

Opposite: Pages from Jack's diary, written during the voyage to Egypt (bottom) and while he was training at Mena, near Giza (top). COURTESY OF THE COLLYER FAMILY

Right: Captain C.E.W. Bean, possibly photographed in the communications trench known as the Great Sap. PHILLIP SCHULER/AUSTRALIAN WAR MEMORIAL (PS1580)

Below: Mena Camp, Egypt, c. 1915. The 4th Battalion, AIF, can be seen on parade. AUSTRALIAN WAR MEMORIAL (H02719)

Below: This photograph, taken in 2005 from Kemal's Headquarters on Scrubby Knoll, shows the 'dress circle' view of the ANZAC firing line on Second Ridge that Kemal enjoyed. Death Trap Valley is at the extreme right of the shot, virtually straight in front of the Turkish commander's headquarters.
COURTESY OF FAULKNER/WAKEFIELD PRESS

Bottom: In 2010 this photograph was taken from almost the same place as Bean's 1919 shot (right). Apart from the valley being heavily overgrown, the photograph shows the vulnerability of the position to Turkish fire.

Above: This view of the outposts from MacLaurin's Hill was taken in 1919 during Bean's Historical Mission. Bones can be seen in the foreground where the outposts were located. Looming on the right is Turkish Johnston's Jolly, which overlooks the valley. In the distance is Scrubby Knoll, behind Mortar Ridge. GEORGE WILKINS/AUSTRALIAN WAR MEMORIAL (G01893)

Left: This portrait of Mustafa Kemal Pasha is reproduced from the first volume of C.E.W. Bean's *Official History*. AUSTRALIAN WAR MEMORIAL (J00288)

Below: Part of the 4th Battalion and the mules for the 26th (Jacob's) Indian Mountain Battery land at Anzac Beach, at 8 a.m. on 25 April 1915. A.R.H. JOYNER/AUSTRALIAN WAR MEMORIAL (J03022)

Opposite: The beginnings of the outposts in Death Trap Valley. This iconic image was taken on the day of the Landing after platoons from A Company, 3rd Battalion, deployed into the valley. It shows a section from one of those platoons in action, well forward of the ANZAC firing line being formed on MacLaurin's Hill behind them. AUSTRALIAN WAR MEMORIAL (A01854)

This series of three photographs taken in 1919 during Bean's Historical Mission show Death Trap Valley from Loutit's Post. The isolated trench appears as a scar on the opposite side of the valley. The panoramic view shows how open Loutit's Post was to observation and fire from any number of Turkish positions. GEORGE WILKINS/AUSTRALIAN WAR MEMORIAL (G01988A, G01988B, G01988C)

Lance Corporal Walter Richard Parker VC RMLI, wearing his Victoria Cross. TRUSTEES OF THE ROYAL MARINES MUSEUM

Top: An informal portrait of Lieutenant Hubert Meager, 3rd Battalion, standing in a frontline trench and holding a periscopic rifle, July 1915. Meager was killed in action at Lone Pine on 8 August 1915. AUSTRALIAN WAR MEMORIAL (C01780)

Above: The hospital ship *Gascon*, one of the ships that carried the wounded from Gallipoli to Alexandria. AUSTRALIAN WAR MEMORIAL (H18949)

A flat-bottomed barge loaded with wounded soldiers from Anzac Cove lies alongside the hospital ship *Gascon*. AUSTRALIAN WAR MEMORIAL (A02740)

Top: Bodies of Turks, killed on 2 May as they attempted to enfilade the isolated trench below them, lie in Street's Trench. This photograph was taken on the day of the Armistice, 24 May, when the dead from both sides of the conflict were buried in No Man's Land. AUSTRALIAN WAR MEMORIAL (A01003)

Above: Padre McKenzie of the 4th Battalion buries a soldier in Shrapnel Gully as two grave diggers stand by, c. 24 May 1915. AUSTRALIAN WAR MEMORIAL (H15688)

James Quinn, *Brigadier General James Heane*, 1918, oil on canvas, 67.4 x 51 cm. Etched in Heane's face are the psychological scars of four years of fighting. AUSTRALIAN WAR MEMORIAL (ART03345)

isolated trench and its occupants, who were indeed battle-weary. Hundreds of Mehmetciks, who were also exhausted, moved into position, ready for further attacks in the valley early the next morning. Their deployment attracted the attention of the Australians and Marines in the valley who sniped at them for hours on Saturday night, particularly once the moon rose at 10.04 p.m.[78]

6 The Battle of Death Trap Valley, 2 to 5 May 1915

At daylight the Turks once more charged the section held by the Marines and captured it, there being only 6 of us left who could get into that part. Blocking up our end as now our line has been broken for the first time, we set to work to clear them out, having direct fire along the trench just captured. we cleared it out. Then our next job is to stop more coming in. with such constant firing our rifles got so hot they blistered our fingers.

Private Les Lott, 4th Battalion, Gallipoli diary, 2 May 1915[1]

Despite staging attacks that failed against other ANZAC positions in the early hours of 2 May, the Turks attacked the isolated trench around dawn. They carried out a two-pronged assault during the relief of Lieutenant Alcock's Marines and the remnants of the two 4th Battalion parties by Meager and McLeod's detachment from the 3rd Battalion. Lieutenant-Colonel Robert Owen set the scene in his after-action report of the relief:

> An isolated bit of trench was held by a party of 40 RMLI and 14 Australians [probably the survivors of No. 3 Platoon, 4th Battalion] and it became enfiladed by fire from the trench temporarily captured by the Turks and some of the enemy got a footing in one part of it and a retirement took place towards the southern end of trench.[2]

The Turks seized Street's Trench and simultaneously launched themselves en masse up the valley at the isolated trench. There is some doubt over whether the Marines manned Street's Trench when they deployed into the outposts on Thursday. Captain McConaghy, 3rd Battalion, 'advised the Marines not to take over his battle outpost as the trenches were fairly complete'.[3] What is clear is that by 1 May Street's Trench was not garrisoned. It appeared that some of the Turks, who had been espied and sniped at by Private De Vine and his reinforcement party during the night of 1 May, massing ready to attack early the next day, occupied Street's Trench during the relief on Sunday morning in Death Trap Valley. Charles Bean reported:

> . . . with shouts of 'Allah,' some fifty or sixty Turks rose from the trench [German Officers'] and rushed across No-Man's land to Street's [Trench]. For some reason, possibly connected with the relief, not a shot was fired at them, and they scrambled into the empty trench. From the barrier on their left they looked straight down the battle outpost, and at a distance of a few yards poured into it a fire against which there was no defence, killing many, including some of the wounded who still lay in it. Those of the occupants who could escape clambered up the creek bed into the main trenches, but a few Australians were seen in the outpost hugging the side of the trench in an almost hopeless endeavour to avoid the Turkish shots.[4]

Bean claimed the attack began at 2.30 a.m; however, two of the 4th Battalion accounts of the Turkish attack specifically stated the enemy assault began at 'day break' and at 'daylight'. It's hard to disregard their accounts; after all Les De Vine and Les Lott were there, and the Turks had launched their counterattack the previous day at dawn. Snowy Robson's version also began, 'The next morning', and the ensuing description of his actions almost certainly meant that it was light. The Turks did attack other Marine and ANZAC positions earlier that night without success.

The entrenchment held by the Marines and No. 3 Platoon, unfolding from Street's across the valley floor to the creek bed, could be enfiladed because much of it was straight, without any traverses, apart from one in the middle. No. 3 Platoon's effort in the valley late on Saturday evening only exacerbated the flaw in the trench. The inexperience of the Marines and the Anzacs, coupled with the pervasive fire of the enemy and the lack of light, gave the Turks in Street's Trench a clear field of fire along most of it. The Turks' enfilading fire caused a retirement at the southern end of the trench, the section occupied by the dispirited Marines. Turkish infantry attacking up the valley from its mouth were able to take advantage of the Marines' disorder and occupy a part of the southern end of the trench. Again a crucial moment in the battle for the valley had been reached. In spite of the gallant defence of the isolated trench, it was breached by the Turks. The Turks now also held Street's, which was behind an earthen barrier at the elevated northern end of the isolated trench. This meant that both ends of the trench were in enemy hands and the ANZAC–Marine force caught in the middle could be attacked from both sides. (See the map of Death Trap Valley on page 178.)

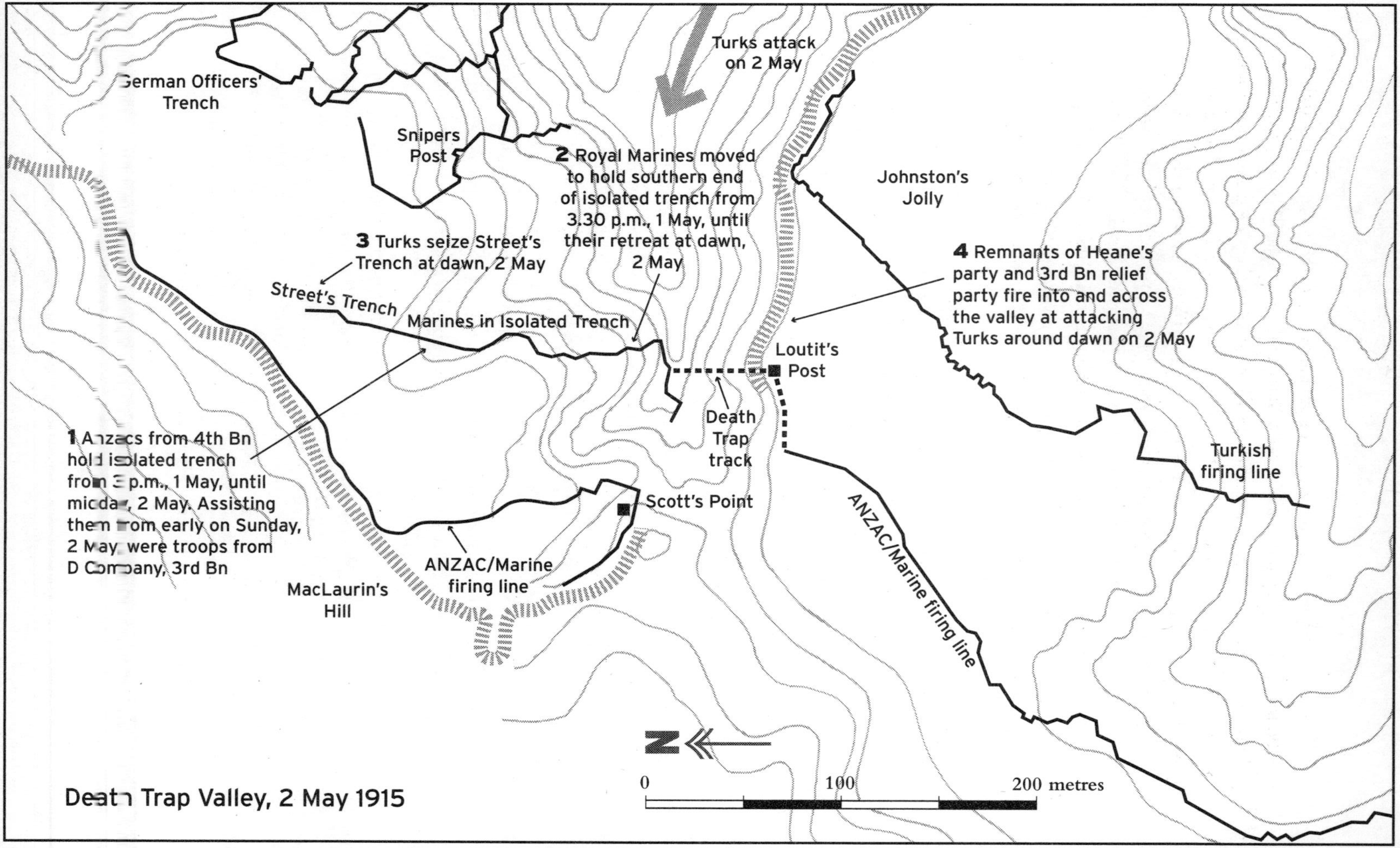

Death Trap Valley, 2 May 1915

A combination of the three Australian parties from the 3rd and 4th battalions who reached Loutit's Post and the outposts over the previous 24 hours, with some Marine support, now fought the Turks for control of the valley. Assisting them were 4th Battalion and some 1st Battalion troops on MacLaurin's Hill and the newly arrived 3rd Battalion troops on Johnston's Jolly, who had reinforced the firing line on Second Ridge next to the valley. When the Marines' line was broken and they retreated, the remnants of Heane's party were in Loutit's Post above the isolated trench, together with some of Meager and McLeod's platoons, who were relieving the Marines and the 4th Battalion parties in the valley.

They watched in horror as the Turks seized the unoccupied Street's Trench and waves of Mehmetciks advanced up the valley. However, all was not lost. Bolstered by Meager and McLeod's relief party, the remaining members of Heane's party were heavily involved in repelling the Turkish attack. The first two priorities were to eliminate the enemy troops causing chaos from Street's as well as those Turks breaching the isolated trench below. Again, a number of the 4th Battalion chroniclers gave accounts of the action. Both Les Lott and Snowy Robson, in Loutit's Post above the isolated trench, were able to enfilade the Turks across the valley in Street's as well as the Turkish breach in the trench below them.

According to Les Lott, who was in Loutit's Post:

> At daylight the Turks once more charged the section held by the Marines and captured it, there being only 6 of us left who could get into that part. Blocking up our end as now our line has been broken for the first time, we set to work to clear them out, having direct fire along the trench just captured. we cleared it out. Then our next job is to stop more coming in. with such constant firing our rifles got so hot they blistered our fingers.[5]

One of the six Les Lott mentioned was the seemingly indestructible Snowy Robson. In his interview with *The Sun* published in *The Uralla Times* on 4 September 1915, Snowy recounted how he fired at the enemy in Street's Trench from Loutit's:

> The next morning the Turks charged and the marines were compelled to retire. From the position I was in I saw 13 Turks in a trench about five yards away from our fellows, who had no ammunition. I sighted these Turks and shot the whole of them. I was about two hundred yards away, and I was just going to have another shot when a bullet got me in the back. It was an explosive bullet, and I had to have seven pieces taken out.

Finally, Private Ern Robson was eliminated from the battle. His contribution probably saved the situation over the previous 24 hours. Whether his survival was luck, fate or sheer tenacity, Snowy continually conducted himself in a brave and inspiring manner.

The lack of traverses in the trench worked against both attacker and defender, as Les and Snowy's accounts attest. Lieutenant Tully McLeod discovered this when he was enfiladed by the Turks as they exchanged shots during the early morning firefight. In a couple of letters written in the aftermath of the action, both displaying a humble brevity, Tully mentioned almost in passing:

> I had a narrow shave was enfiladed in a trench but managed to get out of the road as a bullet caught me across the back, only made a flesh wound. we gave the Turk a hot time.[6]

In an earlier letter he also briefly referred to the incident:

> Had a close shave a few days ago. Stopped a bullet in the back, it did not do any damage. I have already revenged myself and shot a bird or two.[7]

In these two accounts Tully McLeod barely acknowledged the heavy and desperate fighting he and his men experienced, although he did write that the Turks were given a 'hot time'. There was no other reference to the Death Trap Valley action in either letter.

McLeod's partner in the relief, Lieutenant Bert Meager, received praise for his leadership during his platoon's ordeal from one of his men, Private Arthur McGuirk. In a letter to his father dated 30 July, McGuirk wrote:

> I think the next four days were the worst I experienced, we were sent out on outpost duty, that means in front of our lines, + thanks to Lt. Meagher's good head-work he managed to get most of us back.[8]

Charles Bean credited Bert Meager and his men with ending the threatening Turkish occupation of Street's:

> There followed a sharp exchange of fire across the gully, by which Meager's men in Loutit's old trench eventually shot the Turks out of Street's Trench, very few escaping.[9]

In a report written on 14 May, Lieutenant-Colonel Owen praised Meager and McLeod's men for their role:

> . . . when Meager + McLeod's platoon got going they in turn enfiladed the Turks and drove them out.[10]

Clearly, they weren't the only Anzacs involved in clearing out the Turks from Street's Trench or the valley. The survivors of Heane's party and No. 3 Platoon, as well as Meager and McLeod's platoons, all participated in the action, Snowy Robson and Tully McLeod being wounded in what was a shootout across and into the valley.

Les De Vine, in the isolated trench, described the enemy assault in the valley itself:

> Heavily attacked at day break by Turks who had advanced the night before but we were ready for them & gave them a vy warm reception, not a single Turk gained our line but on our R a few got through & were dealt with, their attack a complete failure. Sgt Oakes was hit while standing by my side in one of the fire positions we were seen by machine gunners, who turned the gun on us, as we were freely exposing ourselves sniping at such good targets. I was not touched. Oakes only slightly Capt Coultman wounded also many men, we had a warm time, although the Turks didn't press their attack vy hard they came up in considerable numbers to our lines, things quietened down by midday.[11]

The Marines were on De Vine's right in the valley, holding a small section of the trench where they had been put the previous day, their morale in disarray. In their accounts Les Lott and Snowy Robson also confirmed the Turks captured the section of the isolated trench held by the Marines. Lieutenant Alan Alcock, the commanding officer of the Marines Les Lott referred to in his account, admitted that his men 'had to retreat' on Sunday morning. Other Portsmouth Battalion accounts of events that morning also describe their withdrawal as a retreat. Surgeon Basil Playne was another one who used the word 'retreat' to describe the Marines' evacuation of the isolated trench.[12]

Private Mick Quigley, also defending the isolated trench in the valley with De Vine, had his own quirky version of the morning's events:

> The trench is half full of dead and on looking around this morning I find fully half are Turks. We appreciated their company so much last night that we persuaded most of them to stay for good.[13]

From this account there seems little doubt that hand-to-hand fighting occurred. It was this desperate close-quarter fighting and the marksmanship of the Anzacs that foiled the Turkish breach in the valley.

~

Over a prolonged period on the morning of 2 May, the enemy incursion in the valley was gradually defeated. The Turks in Street's were eliminated and the hundreds of Mehmetciks attacking up the valley, some of whom held part of the isolated trench, were shot, bayoneted or gradually driven back. They very nearly accomplished what they had hoped to achieve the previous day. In one of Bean's Gallipoli notebooks he acknowledged that the combined 4th and 3rd battalions accounted for about 200 Turks during the mayhem in Death Trap Valley early on Sunday.[14]

The only mention of the Marines in these Anzac accounts was to record their retirement. The Marines played little part in repelling this Turkish attack. By the time Heane's men reached them on Saturday afternoon they were in no state to continue to hold off the Turks on their own. As Les Lott noted, the survivors of Heane's party moved the Marines to hold a smaller part of the line in the valley, and sent for more reinforcements. By late Saturday afternoon, when Major Heane sent for reinforcements, it was to his own battalion that he turned and not the RMLI. He apparently repeated this action later that night when he sent a message to Lieutenant-Colonel Owen, commanding officer of the 3rd Battalion, for part of their relief to include a detachment to relieve the Marines and what was left of No. 15 Platoon and No. 3 Platoon, 4th Battalion in the valley. After enduring the most appalling conditions for three days and four nights, the Marines still held their position in the isolated trench, although reinforced by members of three Australian parties that largely took over the defence of the trench during their last 12 hours in the valley.

By Sunday morning the Marines' confidence and fighting ability were shattered. Waves of Turks intent on their annihilation; a lack of water, food and ammunition; the loss of their charismatic commanding officer; being continuously under fire for days in the almost claustrophobic confines of the valley with little or no movement possible during daylight; and witnessing the awful fate of all three parties desperate to help them on 1 May, sapped their morale. They had held their post with only their Lee-Enfield rifles and bayonets as weapons. The Marines had no machine guns in their armoury in the isolated trench, and only minimal, if any, artillery support. They were mostly inexperienced and had received little training. The besieged garrison did have the main firing line and its attendant machine guns behind them, almost hovering over the valley.

Eventually, by midday, the relentless Turkish infantry attacks in the valley ended. At last the almost walking dead of Heane's party were able to rest, some eight days and seven nights after their baptism of fire. The last few sentences of Les Lott's diary entry for 2 May reflected the survivors' lassitude:

> Finally things settled down, and we were allowed to have a much needed sleep. The rest of the Battn digging. All my pals, except 'Pimmy' have gone under. 'Davis' is one who never came out of Death Trap Valley. that night I bury him. Little was done during the night.[15]

According to Les Lott, by midday on 2 May Cast Iron Jimmy Heane's 56-strong party, who had entered Death Trap Valley at 3 a.m. on 1 May, had been reduced to about half a dozen unscathed men. Most of the platoon had been killed or wounded. In No. 12 Section five of the eight known members were casualties. Alf Robins was shot in the head and killed while sniping in the valley on 2 May; Jack suffered a gunshot wound to his left thigh on 1 May; Snowy Robson was wounded in the back by fragments from a bullet on 2 May; Tom Thomson was wounded in the scalp; and Bill Bound was wounded on 2 May. Alf Robins was the only one killed in action. Clyde Bock, Les Lott and Corporal Charles Macquarie were three of the untouched survivors. (See Appendix 1 for list of casualties.)

The second party from the 4th Battalion, numbering some 50 men, who entered the valley at 4 p.m. on Saturday, suffered a similar fate. According to Bennett's report on Snowy Robson's actions, 'As only five men of the platoon were uninjured, the nature of the peril was obvious.'[16] Bennett was referring to No. 3 Platoon, A Company, which Snowy had guided into the valley late on Saturday afternoon to reinforce the isolated trench's garrison. Again, most of the platoon was killed or wounded. (See Appendix 1 for list of casualties.)

Most British accounts of the end of the Marines' occupation of the isolated trench do not mention the Turks breaking their defence and driving them back, leading to a retreat. One Royal Marine report in regard to the actions of Walter Parker described how 'He remained in this trench attending to the wounded and retired when the trench was evacuated on 2nd May, owing to the Turks enfilading it.'[17] This was the closest admission that the Marines were in trouble. There was nothing about the Anzacs fighting doggedly for hours to drive off the Turks and suffering appalling casualties as a result. The actions of the four AIF platoons in coming to their rescue were missing in these explanations. In fact, Fred Fanning's platoon saved Alan Alcock's men twice. Instead, British accounts talk about the Marines' stoic defence coming to an end as a result of a shortage of ammunition and therefore being forced to withdraw on Sunday morning.[18] However, one member of the 3rd Battalion's relief party, Private Bill Ward, found rifles and ammunition left behind by the Marines in their hasty exit on Sunday morning,[19] which contradicts the reason they gave for retreating.

Even though British accounts didn't acknowledge the presence, let alone the heroics, of the various Australian detachments ordered to, in turn, rescue, reinforce and relieve the Marines in Death Trap Valley, there are two Royal Marine documents in the First AIF Brigade archive at the Australian War Memorial that clearly did. These records praised Major Heane's men from D Company, 4th Battalion, including Jack and his mates of No. 12 Section, No. 15 Platoon.

A memorandum written by Lieutenant-Colonel Frank Luard, the commanding officer of the Portsmouth Battalion, specifically identified Heane's men as the saviours of his trapped platoons. He wrote it while convalescing on the hospital ship *Gloucester Castle* after being wounded at Anzac on 3 May:

> Brigade Major
> Royal Marine Bde.
>
> On the 1st instant a platoon of Portsmouth Battalion (temporarily lent to another unit) was forced to be in an isolated trench, without means of reinforcements, replenishment, or of retreat.
>
> The trench was exposed to constant hostile fire, and infantry attacks of the enemy were with difficulty repulsed by rifle fire. The Commander Lieut. EMPSON displayed great gallantry till he was killed.
>
> From this dangerous position the platoon was rescued by a most gallant effort made at heavy sacrifice by the adjacent unit 'D' Coy 4th Bn. Australian Infantry. (MAJOR HEANE)
>
> The officers and men of the Portsmouth Bn. R.M.L.I. have been greatly moved by the splendid act of Imperial Comradeship and desire that an expression of their deep gratitude may be conveyed to the 4th Bn. Australian Infantry through the Brg'r Genl. Commdg. R.M. Bde.
>
> Sgn. Luard Lt - Col.
> Commdg. Portsmouth Bn.
> Hospital Ship '*GLOUCESTER CASTLE*'[20]

The memorandum was attached to the following letter from the Royal Marine Brigade Commanding Officer, Brigadier-General Charles Trotman:

G.O.C.
1st Inf. Bd
Aust. Div.

I beg to forward to you attached memorandum from Lieut. Col F. Luard R.M.L.I. Commdg Portsmouth Battalion and to add my own expression of gratitude and admiration of the conduct of Major Heane and the N.C.O.s and men of his Company who acted so nobly.

'Most distinguished gallantry' is the only epithet by which I can describe this truly soldier-like conduct.

Sgd. Charles Trotman
Brig - Gen.
Commdg. R.M. Bde.[21]

Coming from the senior officers in the Royal Marine hierarchy, this was high praise indeed. A comment in the war diary of the Australian 1st Division on 1 May also acknowledged Heane's rescue party, abbreviating the Marine commanding officers' reports: 'To Note—gallantry of "D" Coy. 4th Bn under Major HEANE, in extricating a platoon of Portsmouth Bn. on 1st inst.'[22]

Arguably all three AIF parties—No. 15 Platoon, D Company, and No. 3 Platoon, A Company, both from the 4th Battalion, and the two D Company platoons from the 3rd Battalion—played a part in saving the Marines and the outposts. All of them displayed 'Most distinguished gallantry'.

Walter Parker was one of the Marines who left the isolated trench that morning. He assisted with the removal of wounded men up the slope to their lines, under fire the whole time from the Turks ringing the valley and from those in the valley. Unfortunately, the brave Marine was seriously wounded during the withdrawal. His service record detailed gunshot wounds to his right thigh, shin and the front of his chest on 2 May.[23] Lieutenant Alcock later wrote: 'We had to retreat and it was then I believe that he (i.e. Parker) got wounded.'[24] Found crawling on his hands and knees after being hit, Parker was finally carried to safety by other Marine stretcher-bearers.

However, not all the wounded Marines were evacuated from the valley. The remarkable story of 3rd Battalion privates Bill Ward, Bill Hatton and Bill Beal from Meager and McLeod's relief party shed considerable light on the Marines' exit from the valley. It also showed an inordinate devotion to duty. While they did not participate in driving the Turks out of the isolated trench, they did have their own extraordinary tale to tell, beginning on 2 May.

Private Ward, described by Lieutenant-Colonel Owen in his 14 May after-action report as 'the leading spirit in their brilliant little affair', related their story in the 3rd Battalion history, *Randwick to Hargicourt*:

> I was one of a squad who were detailed to go out and reinforce the Royal Marine Light Infantry at No. 1 Battle Outpost in Wire Gully. We went over at daybreak, and only five of us gained the trench. To reach our objective it was necessary to cross a very steep-sided gully. This we accomplished by sliding down the hillside. Then, under the cover of the opposite side, we crawled along to the trench.
>
> When I reached it I could see things were in a bad way. There were many dead lying in the trench, also a few wounded. It appeared the Turks had invaded and over-whelmed the defenders.
>
> This outpost trench was approximately 50 yards from our lines and about 150 yards from the Turks, with a ridge between its right flank and the Turkish lines. The trench was occupied mostly by the R.M.L.I., and as soon as we arrived they began to retire. I tried to persuade them to stay, but they were not having any. I don't know why, but I think they had had enough.
>
> We had not been there very long before one of our chaps, Pritchard, was wounded. A pal of mine, Bill Downer, carried him back to our lines. That left only three of us, Bill Hatton, Bill Beal, and myself and we settled down to make the best of things, and to look after the trench and the wounded. The dead, including an English officer, (Lieutenant Empson) were thrown over the back of the trench and covered with dirt . . .
>
> We fared all right for a while in the matter of food and water. When the Marines retired they left behind their water-bottles, packs, rifles, and ammunition. There was a little muddy pool at the end of the trench near the gully, and this cleared sufficiently to allow of drinking. Food we obtained from our lines during the night.
>
> There were three wounded Marines in the trench, so we set to work to make them comfortable and feed them. Luckily we had candles which we brought from Mena Camp. These came in handy for boiling the bully-beef and biscuits in our mess-tins. One of the wounded men had been shot in the head. Another had his leg fractured and it was tied up with puttees with a couple of rifles as splints. The third chap died shortly after our arrival. The Marine wounded in the head had to be fed with a spoon. He could not talk or do anything for himself. After a while he started to knock himself about. So, with the aid of a couple of bayonets

> driven into the ground, one on each side of him, we fastened him down to the bottom of the trench with puttees. Although our lines were within call, stretcher-bearers, they told us, were not procurable. So we had to be satisfied with things as they were.
>
> While we were in this trench the Turks made an attack on our lines, but we, being in the corner near the gully, could not see them coming from our left. We were told afterwards that they had been very close to our trench. They were repulsed and driven back to their own lines with machine-gun and rifle fire by the 3rd Battalion on the right, and by the 4th on the hill at the back.
>
> While in occupation of the trench we made it deeper and generally improved it for defence, while a strict watch was maintained night and day. On the third night a stretcher-bearer, 'Jumbo' Blackburn, was sent over to help get the wounded back to our lines. When we took them back we were told to remain with the battalion. So we left the outpost trench unoccupied.[25]

Ward's testimony covered many aspects relating to the battle outposts. He and his mates slid down the slope and crawled along the ground to cheat the death trap although, as he admitted, only five of them made it to the trench. His little band seemed to have occupied what was probably Walter Parker's aid post near the bed of the watercourse, out of the direct line of the enemy's rifles and machine guns although still vulnerable to shrapnel fire. He referred in passing to Lieutenant Richard Empson, the gallant Marine officer who was killed in action the previous day. More importantly, his other references to the Marines were quite disparaging, even though this seemed to be unintentional. The Marines' withdrawal due to a lack of ammunition lacked credibility; Ward claimed he and his mates found the rifles and ammunition they had left behind. His evidence about the dead and wounded in the trench, which left him with the impression that the Turks had indeed broken the outpost's defences, lent credence to other Anzac accounts of the fighting on Sunday morning. Finally, the haste with which the surviving Marines left tended to validate their diminished morale and retreat, Ward being largely ignorant of the Marines' experiences over the previous few days.

Vacating the trench so hurriedly and leaving behind significant quantities of equipment, including rifles and ammunition, was reprehensible enough, but to fail to evacuate all their wounded was a dereliction of duty and a failure of the Marines' discipline. This was made worse by the number of Marines who weren't wounded—up to 40—who should have been able to assist in the removal of their incapacitated brothers and any of their equipment. Walter Parker was praised for assisting in the evacuation of wounded Marines on Sunday morning; one notable account claimed he 'proved to be a tower of strength, helping all the wounded men to safety'.[26] Obviously he didn't; three suffering Marines were left behind by their platoons. The awful conditions and confusion in the valley on Sunday morning, caused by constant heavy enemy fire and the close proximity of large numbers of attacking enemy troops who broke the Marines' line, precipitated their retreat. The Marines' inexperience in battle and lack of training, having recently spent months aboard ship before being ordered to occupy for days what was one of the most increasingly dangerous positions at Anzac, also contributed to their controversial retirement.

Even though the frontal attacks of the Turks seemed to have ended in the valley, the enemy sniping did not. Les De Vine recorded on 2 May: 'Plenty of sniping all day, which cost us several men.'[27] The snipers were mainly operating from Snipers Post, German Officers' Trench, Johnston's Jolly, Sandbag Ridge and the high ground to the Australians' left, as they had done for days.

In one of the final actions in the fight for the valley, the 4th Battalion war diary reported on 2 May:

> Turks were reported to be massing in the gulley 224J. Navy shelled gulley and ridge about 6pm.[28]

Newly promoted Lieutenant-Colonel Alfred Bennett, now commanding officer of the 4th Battalion, also noted that on 2 May:

> At about 6.30 pm the Navy shelled the gulley 224J40 and the ridge behind where the enemy were reported to be massing.[29]

From these two documents it seemed the Turkish positions the navy blasted were the ones that had killed and wounded many Anzacs and Marines over the past week on the high ground to the Anzacs' left. The bombardment also incorporated Mule Valley and Mortar Ridge, where the Turks were apparently forming up. It may well have thwarted yet another Turkish foray into the valley. For Les De Vine this was a moment to savour:

> About 6pm the naval guns opened on the hills that were infilading our trenches on the left with considerable effect we saw the whole of the action from our trenches, as the position overlooks ours, their snipers causing us many casualties.[30]

Sister Muriel Wakeford, one of seven Australian Army nurses on the hospital ship *Gascon,* witnessed the bombardment from near its source. She documented the experience in a letter home:

> The fighting at *Anzac* [deleted by the censor] was terrific and we were in the midst of it . . . We arrived last Sunday [2 May] at about 5 p.m., and at 7 p.m., a terrific bombardment commenced, seven or eight battleships firing practically together made a terrifying din I can assure you. The rifle fire was continuous, and as soon as darkness sets in the flames were visible. I could scarcely believe we could be so close and feel absolutely no fear, there is just a feeling of intense excitement.[31]

The dead in the valley, who couldn't be buried, were thick on the ground, testament to the ferocity of the fighting. Les De Vine painted the disheartening scene on 2 May:

> The dead that are left unburied are tossed over the rear of the trench, and are smelling very badly being a menase [sic] to our general health, in fact the whole of the ground in front is covered with the dead who have been laying there for a week in the sun.[32]

The Armistice, ostensibly to bury the enormous numbers of Turkish dead after their calamitous 19 May attack, was still three weeks away.

Bill Ward and his mates from the 3rd Battalion maintained their vigil with the wounded in the isolated trench until Monday night, 3 May, when a sap [trench dug forward of a position] was dug through to them. Les De Vine's final entry in regard to the Death Trap Valley action on 3 May included this accomplishment:

> Returned to A Coy this morning have been with D Coy (in Death Trap Valley) for a few days to reinforce them . . . During night we sapped to some wounded men that had been left lying out in an exposed position for 3 days, we managed to get them.[33]

Lieutenant-Colonel Owen described what Ward and his mates did in a report written soon after the action:

> When the rush began we had several dead and 5 wounded and these brave fellows wouldn't leave them. They stayed with them and tended them

> from 4 am till 8.30 pm the next day. They were isolated and exposed to constant menace by the enemy and even when a narrow approach had been dug through and relief became possible they still would not come out but preferred to stay with their wounded till they too could be removed.[34]

The 'rush' Owen referred to was probably the hurried departure of the Marines during the last Turkish assault as his men relieved them. Marine detractors may well see this as another example of 'Run My Lads Imshi', a particularly vitriolic play on the initials of the Royal Marine Light Infantry. In one of his Gallipoli notebooks Charles Bean described the Marines' negligent actions on Sunday morning: 'The RMLI when they ran left some wounded in the trench.'[35] However, Empson and Alcock's men did hold the battle outposts in Death Trap Valley for a considerable time—trapped for three days and four nights until they were forced out. The Royal Marines can be proud of their part in the defence of Second Ridge on 1 and 2 May. Bean offered this praise for the Royal Marines in the *Official History*:

> The Marines bore the brunt of Mustapha Kemal's third attack. Though better timed and delivered than the last, it completely failed.[36]

On 5 May Meager and McLeod's parties were ordered back to their own lines on Johnston's Jolly and Loutit's Post was no longer manned[37] although, according to Bean, James Heane's D Company later tunnelled to Loutit's Post and incorporated it into part of the firing line, the sap leading to a sniper's position known as Tambour.[38]

The battle for the valley was finally over. Ironically, despite the heroics and large loss of men on both sides, the outposts were abandoned after the third Turkish counterattack petered out. In *Gallipoli Mission*, Bean wrote the following epitaph:

> Eventually having proved a death trap (though the scene of a series of fine actions . . .) these outposts were all given up—the last of them on May 5th.[39]

According to Turkish sources, the attack failed because of 'the carefully positioned heavy machine-gun fire of the ANZAC supported by the heavy bombardment of the fleet. The commander of the division aborted the attacks so as not to lose any more casualties.'[40] In an interview after the war Major-General Kiazim Pasha, the Chief of the Turkish General Staff, believed the superior numbers of British troops was significant in denying the Turks a 'decisive result' during their attacks over the first week, including the attacks over the first weekend in May.[41]

Once again Mustafa Kemal addressed his troops in a message distributed to them at the end of the battle:

> All the soldiers fighting with me here ought to be aware of the fact that there is no taking of a step back before we accomplish our task of honour. I hereby would like to remind you all that the desire for sleeping in comfort will not only render us devoid of sleep but our nation forever as well. I have no reservation by all means that my friends are of the same opinion and that they display no sign of fatigue before we push the enemy back into the sea.[42]

Kemal reluctantly ceded this round to the infidel. He expected further sacrifices from his men to satisfy national honour; after all, the battles were taking place on Turkish soil. Ultimately he was determined they would prevail and drive the enemy into the sea. The next major Turkish attack, on 19 May, dwarfed the earlier counterattacks. It also failed to dislodge the Anzacs.

During the first week of the invasion, the occupation of the outposts frustrated the Turks, particularly over the weekend of 1 and 2 May, when the courageous defence of the position by Marines and Anzacs played a significant role in thwarting their third counterattack in the Central Sector. The head of Death Trap Valley, at the heart of the firing line on Second Ridge, was a key objective for the Turks. The Anzacs and Marines were clinging to their newly established trenches along the ridge, knowing they couldn't allow any breach of their line because there were very few defensive positions or troops in support behind them. If the Turks could break through, their whole beachhead was vulnerable.

Initially the outposts were a viable point of resistance but, ultimately, once the position became isolated, their value diminished rapidly. The isolated trench in the valley, which became known as Marine Trench, later appeared on maps of the ANZAC firing line as such, even though it was unoccupied. The outposts in the valley were now untenable; they had indeed proved to be a death trap.

PART 3

Aftermath

7 Jack's fate

. . . hoping you shall receive your son home, with honour & credit as I believe he is somewhere between here and Australia.

Corporal Charles Macquarie, 4th Battalion[1]

Jack's part in his platoon's desperate fight came to an end when he was hit in the left thigh as he attempted to reach the Marines being attacked in Death Trap Valley. Jack's mate and section leader, Corporal Charles Macquarie, first reassured him then manoeuvred him under cover with the help of two Marines at about 3.30 p.m. on Saturday afternoon.

Macquarie attended to Jack's wound using what limited experience he'd acquired over the previous six days: he used a field dressing to bind up Jack's wound, mainly to close it and stem the flow of blood. He didn't clean the wound; that was the responsibility of a trained medical officer further down the line. This meant that fragments of Jack's filthy uniform—he'd been fighting in it for a week—were lodged in it. The most debilitating part of Jack's wound was the femur fracture in his left thigh, caused by the impact of the bullet. Corporal Macquarie might have been unaware of this complication. Jack certainly required a stretcher to be evacuated to the beach, where he would enter the care of the Australian Army Medical Corps—a chain of ascending levels of medical attention, from the firing line at Anzac to a hospital in Egypt. Each of these levels was challenged by the enormity of the casualties over the period of the Landing and the ensuing consolidation.

The battle continued to rage around Jack. He was now in shock, immobilised by his wound and in excruciating pain. He couldn't be moved during daylight because his position was too dangerous and exposed. According to Macquarie, Jack had to wait 'till the best men I know—Red Cross men [AAMC] of our own Australian Army came & picked Jack up.'[2]

The Anzacs revered the courage and fortitude of the stretcher-bearers. Major John Corbin, the second in command of the 1st Australian Casualty

Clearing Station, established his unit in the lee of the southern end of the beach after landing at 10.30 a.m. on 25 April. In his diary on 28 April he noted the stretcher-bearers' heroism:

> The courage of the men is equalled by the bravery of the stretcher bearers. They go right into the Firing Line and help their comrades under the most trying and dangerous conditions. One has to see this country to realise the mechanical difficulties they have to overcome.[3]

Throughout the war the praise and regard the ordinary Australian soldier held for them remained undiminished. The marvellous reputation they established during the Landing, battling not just the indiscriminate fire of the enemy but also the rugged terrain and overwhelming demand for their services, showed a simple philosophy based on an absolute devotion to duty—caring for their wounded mates in the firing line. On occasion they also treated and retrieved wounded Anzacs from exposed positions, at times to their own cost.

Captain Arthur Tebbutt, the 4th Battalion's Medical Officer, had established his regimental aid post (RAP) late on 30 April as the battalion came close to the firing line near MacLaurin's Hill:

> I followed the Battalion up Shrapnel Gully and turned [off] into Bridges Road which we followed up to its head and the Battalion took over a point here from a battalion from the Marines Light Infantry, 2 companies of the 4th Battalion fronting Johnsons Jolly (ie. A & D) and 2 on Steel's Post (ie. B & C). Some of the 1st Battalion seemed to be between these two halves of the 4th Battalion. I formed an R.A.P. about 150 yards behind the centre of this line towards the top of Bridge's Road and in close touch with Battalion Headquarters. A large number of casualties seemed to occur at the takeover and my bearers and myself were very busy that afternoon and evening. (ie. May 1st)
>
> The two companies fronting Johnson's Jolly were fairly easily evacuated down Bridge's Road by stationary bearers at the entrance to the trenches at the top of Bridge's Road.[4]

Under the cover of darkness during the evening of 1 May, Jack was evacuated from the valley. When he arrived at Captain Tebbutt's regimental aid post, he was one of many wounded men from the battle in Death Trap Valley. Jack probably received morphine for pain at the RAP. His dressing was checked but not changed; the initial dressing was usually left in place during the pressure of the first tumultuous days after the Landing. Following a preliminary examination, Tebbutt ordered Jack to be passed on to what had become the next part of the chain—the casualty clearing station at the southern end of Anzac Cove.

For a wound such as Jack's,[5] the next level of treatment should have been a field ambulance and then an advanced dressing station, but the ridiculously close proximity of the firing line to the evacuation point at the beach meant that the Australian Army Medical Corps was forced to adapt its usual textbook structure. The functions of the field ambulance, advanced dressing station and the casualty clearing station overlapped in what was little more than an enlarged beachhead. Wounded men were taken from their battalion's RAP to the beach—bearers from field ambulances and individual battalions sharing the arduous workload, their areas of responsibility also blurring in the chaotic conditions of the first ten days.

In theory, a casualty clearing station was supposed to be a sophisticated medical facility—akin to a small hospital, with operating theatres, x-ray machines and hospital wards, staffed by nurses and specialist doctors—located 16–19 kilometres from the firing line.[6] At Anzac, during the Landing, it operated in a most reduced form about a kilometre from the firing line, continuously under fire, certainly lacking the equipment and staff it was supposed to have. It was on the beach in the open and became little more than a holding pen, funnelling the men onto ships that themselves were often lacking basic equipment, trained personnel and an acceptable level of hygiene.

Jack needed an operation to clean his wound, set his femur and close the wound's entry hole in his thigh, none of which could be accomplished on land at that time. Only in extreme cases did lifesaving emergency surgery occur in the primitive surrounds of Anzac during those intense initial days.

~

In October 1915 the Wounded and Missing Enquiry Bureau of the Australian Red Cross was established. Under its charter it:

> . . . sought to identify, investigate and respond to enquiries made regarding the fate of Australian personnel. It investigated the majority of personnel posted as wounded and missing on official Army lists, as well as written enquiries from concerned relatives and friends.[7]

One of the men who picked up Jack was Private Tom Hyland, a stretcher-bearer in the AAMC attached to the 4th Battalion. Each AIF battalion landing at Anzac had 16 stretcher-bearers.[8] The Red Cross Sydney Bureau interviewed Hyland and produced this report in August 1916 in regard to Jack:

> Informant was a stretcher bearer attached to the 4th Battalion. He remembers about seven or eight days after the landing picking up a wounded man outside D Coy's trenches at the top of Shrapnel Gully. The man's name was Collyer and he belonged to the 4th Battalion, either A or D Coy. Collyer had been wounded and was taken down to the beach and put on a hospital ship.[9]

While Hyland's account seems straightforward, the reality of Jack's experience was vastly different; 'taken down to the beach' did not describe the hazardous journey he endured during his evacuation from the regimental aid post to the casualty clearing station on the beach. Two stretcher-bearers, Jack lying inert on the stretcher, possibly with a rifle as a splint strapped to his left thigh giving him scant comfort, struggled down Bridges' Road and then through Shrapnel Valley to the beach, a descent of about 2 kilometres along an evacuation route (see the route of Jack's medical evacuation on page 199).[10] The valley, also known as The Valley Of Death, was open to constant Turkish artillery fire, occasional sniper fire and stray bullets, and was very busy, particularly at night when it became a sea of human traffic. Troops bearing full water containers, 1 cwt (51 kg) ammunition boxes and messages headed uphill to the firing line on the crests above them. A stream of wounded men and their faithful attendants headed downhill to the beach, along with men carrying empty containers for water and on ammunition fatigues. Messengers also darted to and fro. Battalions, having been relieved, headed to the beach to bivouac; their replacements, plodding ever upward, also used the track through Shrapnel Valley, detouring to the left and right as their orders demanded, to their positions on Second Ridge.

The stretcher-bearers were trained to evacuate a wounded man in four-man teams, but this became impractical during the period of the Landing, with the medical arrangements being overwhelmed at every level by the sheer scale of the casualties. At Anzac they were forced to work in two-man teams. 'You could only carry for about a hundred yards at a time, before you had to stop to have a rest, before going on,' Bert Baker, a stretcher-bearer, recalled.[11] The rough terrain and the downhill route forced the overworked bearers to carefully manage their precious loads.

Jack reached the casualty clearing station at the southern end of Anzac Cove on 2 May. Hyland's brief conclusion in reference to Jack's experience—'put on a hospital ship'—again disguised the terrible ordeal he and thousands of others suffered, waiting to be evacuated from the beach.

At dusk, the HMHS *Gascon*, the designated hospital ship for Z Beach, was just arriving back on station off Anzac. Edward Hugo, head surgeon of the

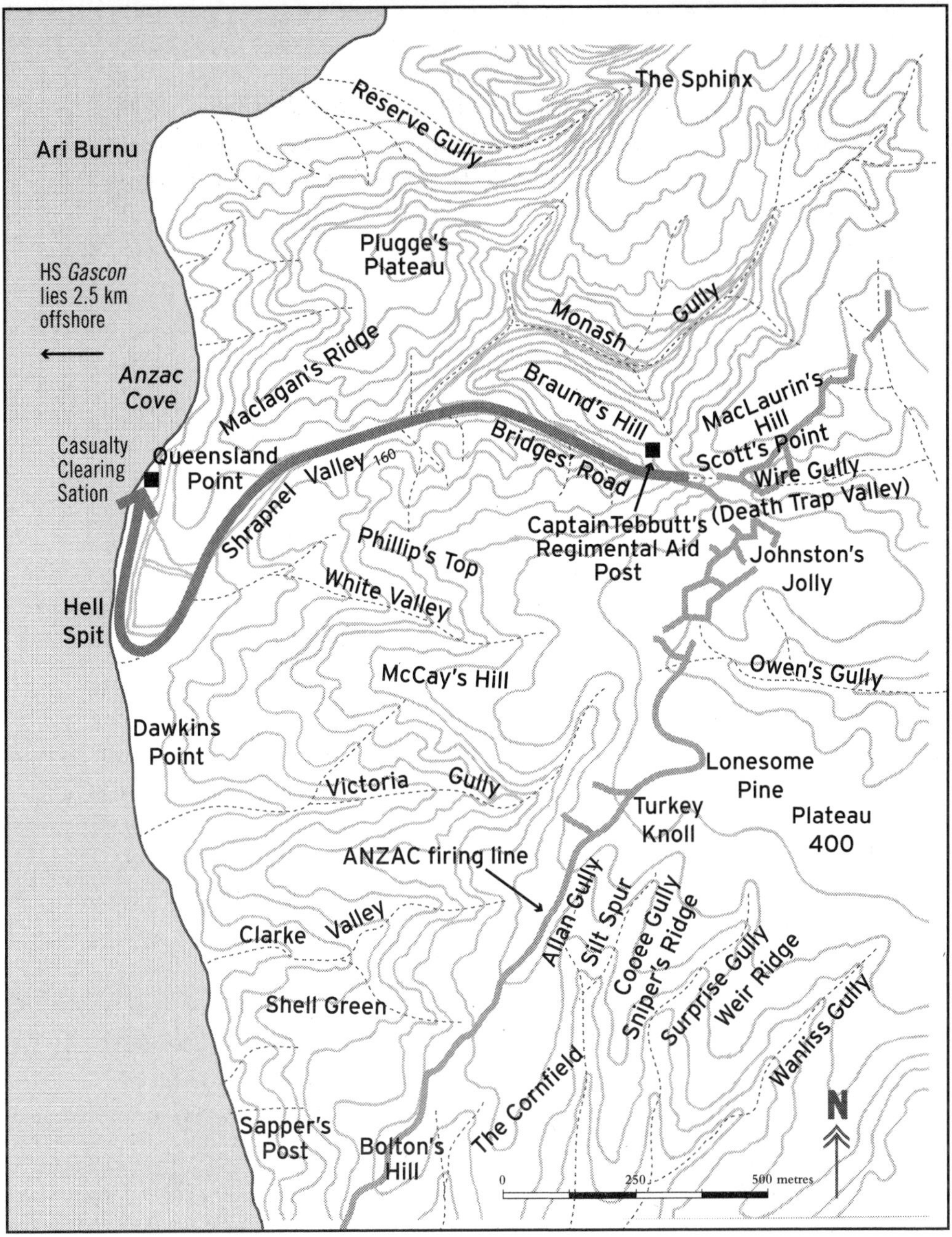

The route of Jack's medical evacuation

After Jack was wounded, he was taken from Captain Tebbutt's Regimental Aid Post behind MacLaurin's Hill to the 1st Australian Casualty Clearing Station on the beach on 2 May 1915.

Gascon, wrote in his diary: '6 pm lying one and a half miles off shore . . . shrapnel is bursting, shells in water.'[12] The hospital ship had left Anzac at 6.30 p.m. on 25 April, the day of the Landing, to take 548 cases to Alexandria.[13] In just the first few days, 3500 casualties were taken by six ships to Egypt.

The *Gascon* was unmistakable in the waters off Anzac, being 'painted white overall with a horizontal band of green, about a metre and a half wide, around the hull . . . with a large red cross on her hull, and illuminated at night by a string of green lights'.[14] The Turks respected her status and generally refrained from firing directly on her. Charles Bean wrote in May 1915: 'The white hospital ship . . . a beautiful thing with her bright motionless lights at night . . . No Turkish shot or German torpedo ever threatened her.'[15]

However, Lieutenant-Colonel Hugo did make this observation after arriving back at Anzac: 'About 1.15 [3 May] had to move away from where we anchored as large shells kept falling into the water some came too close to be pleasant.'[16] In her letter Sister Muriel Wakeford also described this close shave: 'The shells from the enemy splintered a piece of the deck, so the captain promptly moved away a short distance, and we had just got away when a shell fell where we had been.'[17]

The *Gascon* did not start taking on the wounded until 3.30 a.m. on 3 May. Jack was not among them. He lay amid a vast swathe of hundreds of wounded and dying men, Colonel Monash's ill-fated attacks of 2 and 3 May swelling the ranks of the casualties on the beach enormously.

The diary of the 1st Australian casualty clearing station gave a clear picture of the fortunes of the Anzacs and the congestion on the beach over the first week or so:

> April 25th—Owing to pressure of work + the necessity of keeping the beach clear of wounded (in event of having to retire) it was impossible to keep record of all cases treated . . . about 700 cases passed through hands of Clearing Hospital.
>
> April 26th—Wounded continued to come in very freely all day and the same difficulties experienced in getting them first aid + rapid evacuation. The only position possible was open beach 20ft by 20ft in which to treat a large number of cases many of very great severity. Evacuated about 700 cases.
>
> April 27th—The position of Casualty Clearing Station exposed to shrapnel fire several people being hit but not dangerously. Evacuated 659 cases.

> April 28th—Still working at high pressure but great decrease in number of cases compared to first few days. Evacuated 398 cases.
>
> April 29th—The Field Ambulance of R.M.L.I. landed and assisted in medical work in the Clearing Hospital giving my staff a very much needed rest as they had been working about 20 hours a day since landing. Evacuated 225 cases.
>
> April 30th—A quiet day . . . Evacuated 199 cases.
>
> May 1st—Conditions the same. Evacuated 304 cases.
>
> May 2nd—Much busier owing to an attempted advance on our front. Evacuated 205 cases.
>
> May 3rd—Evacuated 658 cases.
>
> May 4th—Evacuated 220 cases.[18]

An astonishing total of about 4270 wounded men were evacuated over the course of the first ten days from the rudimentary environs of the Australian casualty clearing station at the southern end of Anzac Cove. The conditions on the beach's southern end were far from ideal for treating wounded men. Enemy shrapnel raked it and did not spare the staff or wounded located there. At the northern end of the beach, the New Zealand field ambulance had established its own clearing station, operating under the same awful conditions.[19] On 27 April Major Corbin described his experience of this difficult situation:

> As I write this I am crouched against the side of the hill. Shrapnel is raining down. Two stretcher bearers have been hit within two yards of me. Standing up on a small piece of ground on which our Clearing Station stands this morning I got smacked in the side by a shrapnel bullet. It didn't go through my pocket book, just gave me a stunning smack. No harm done.[20]

Corbin also described what happened when his staff and wounded men awaiting treatment and evacuation were hit:

> They had to be redressed . . . several of our men were put out of action by shrapnel bullets. The shelter-shed for wounded was pierced by a huge

> high explosive shell, which killed a sick man lying on a stretcher, wounded another and so shattered the leg of a member of our unit that it had to be amputated two days later on a hospital ship and he died.[21]

During the first four days of the casualty clearing station's existence, John Corbin and his staff attended 'roughly 3300 casualties since the Landing on Sunday, 11.30 am. Not bad for five men, one of whom does practically nothing'.[22] The figure was closer to 2500; regardless, the numbers were astonishing. Eight officers and 77 other ranks were listed in the unit;[23] Corbin was only referring to the officers in his aside.

The diary entry of the 1st Field Ambulance for 3 May also noted the endless shrapnel and the difficulties posed by the climate for the wounded lying on the beach:

> Campsite of unit receiving considerable shellfire from 'OLIVE GROVE'—Days fairly hot but nights exceedingly Cold—wind from snow on SAMATHRACE very searching—any wounded lying out at night will suffer continuously.[24]

Jack was one such incapacitated soldier, unable to move and having to cope with his wound, enemy artillery fire and the fluctuating temperatures prevalent at the time: it was spring in the northern hemisphere, which meant very cold nights and warm days. In all likelihood, Jack didn't have his greatcoat to keep out the cold.

Another problem for him was the lack of anaesthetics available on the beach. Major John Corbin wrote about this after the ANZAC attacks of 2 May flooded the casualty clearing station with casualties:

> About 8 pm the first wounded began to come in and they kept coming in, just like the first day, dreadfully wounded and mangled, arms and legs, shattered heads, crushed in chests and abdomens. A most hateful procession. The courage of the troops is marvellous. They don't groan or complain, and bear the biggest dressings with equanimity and cheerfulness. No chance of giving anaesthetics, and one end in view, to get them to the ships without delay.[25]

During the first days of the invasion the classification of the wounded at the casualty clearing station was haphazard or non-existent; the primary focus of the medical staff was to expedite the patients' removal from shore to ship. The tagging of patients as seriously or lightly wounded, with red or white labels, respectively, foundered from the day of the Landing. The sheer weight of numbers and the disconcerting and dangerous enemy artillery fire prevented it from happening.[26]

On 3 May conditions at the clearing station weren't any better. According to Major John Corbin:

> All the morning the wounded dying + dead coming in just one continuous effort to cope with it. The attack was not successful we hear our losses must have totalled 1000 . . . I've been at it one way or another all day, either dressing cases or getting them off to the ships.[27]

From the clearing station, the wounded were carefully loaded onto an overcrowded horse barge, an improvised water ambulance, then towed by a small steam launch about a one and a half kilometres to the designated ships. Corbin, who oversaw the embarkation of casualties from Anzac, was critical of the loading and transfer of patients to ships during the early days ashore. The pier he claimed was:

> a movable + flimsy structure made partly of rough stones + earth with a narrow wooden bridge (unfixed) over a drain at its inner end. The outer portion is in two parts consisting of boards upon barrels, the two parts being at a different level. Even with careful stretcher bearers it is difficult to avoid jolting patients more especially at night when the only light is provided by lanterns.[28]

Corbin was also unhappy about the vessels used to transport the wounded from the beach:

> Boats for conveying the wounded are ships cutters launches etc. It is an extremely difficult + slow matter to place stretchers on the seats of these boats with any degree of safety, when there is a swell + at night it becomes a matter of considerable danger to the wounded + nothing but the care which has been exercised by the boats crews has prevented serious accident from time to time.[29]

A shortage of vessels for this purpose meant further delays in transferring casualties from shore to ship.

Jack was one of the uncomplaining casualties who waited to be evacuated. His timing could not have been worse—he became lost in the huge numbers of wounded generated by the invaders' first real sally, on 2 and 3 May, against the Turkish siege of their foothold on the peninsula.

Finally, on 4 May, came Jack's turn to be transported to the hospital ship.

~

The *Gascon* had been converted into a first-class hospital ship. The senior medical officer on board was Lieutenant-Colonel Edward Victor Hugo, who had most recently been professor of surgery at King Edward's Medical College in Lahore, then part of British India. Hugo was a 60-year-old decorated veteran of Britain's North-West Frontier Expeditions of the 1890s, in which he had extensive field experience as a regimental medical officer. He volunteered to return to the army's medical service once war was declared in 1914.[30]

Lieutenant-Colonel George Syme, appointed surgical consultant to the *Gascon*, remembered it as an impressive facility:

> The conditions on H.M. Hospital Ship *Gascon* for dealing with those wounded at the landing and fighting at Gallipoli on April 25 were as favourable as possible. The *Gascon* was well equipped with a good operation theatre, having full provision for sterilization; a fair supply of ordinary instruments and apparatus; and a good X-ray plant. The staff consisted of the Officer in Command, Lieutenant-Colonel Huy [*sic*. Hugo], who was Professor of Surgery at Lahore, and a most excellent surgeon and operator, three majors and one captain, all belonging to the I.M.S., and two Hindus of the subordinate Indian Medical Service, one of whom gave anaesthetics, and had charge of the X-rays department. The nursing staff consisted of a matron and seven sisters, with a number of R.A.M.C. orderlies, and also Indian attendants. The *Gascon* was fitted up for 350 patients. By putting mattresses in the smoking room and on the floors, hatchings and decks, we arranged to accommodate 150 more, and actually took on board 540 . . . we had the equivalent of a well-equipped base hospital practically close to the firing line.[31]

In Butler's *Official History of the Australian Army Medical Services 1914–18, Volume 1*, the staff on the *Gascon*'s second trip consisted of six officers (presumably the surgeons), 38 other ranks (mainly Indian orderlies) and seven nurses (and a matron).[32]

Surgeon General Charles Snodgrass Ryan, the Assistant Director of Medical Services of the 1st Australian Division with the rank of colonel, was a vastly experienced doctor. In 1878 he served in the Russo-Turkish War and had even been decorated by the Turkish Sultan.[33] The 60-year-old veteran, who examined the ships being used to evacuate and treat the wounded during the Landing at Anzac, inspected the *Gascon* about the time Jack was hoisted aboard. He also described it in glowing terms:

> I then went on the *Gascon* which was a perfectly equipped hospital ship belonging to the Indian Government. The commanding officer, Colonel Hugo, Professor of Surgery at Lahore, had a most excellent staff of four Surgeons and the nurses were all Australians. Colonel Hugo was an extremely capable surgeon and was extremely courteous and kind to me and we both attended the cases, he assisting me and I assisting him. It was on this boat that General Bridges was brought shot through the thigh . . . Most of the wounded on the *Gascon* were cot cases; they were nearly all cases for operation . . . few cases were operated on within 10 or 12 hours of receipt of injury. Many were dying on admission.[34]

Apart from their boss, British-born Matron Woolley, the nurses on the *Gascon* were from the Australian Army Nursing Service. They included Sisters Ella Tucker, Clementina Marshall and Elsie Gibson, and Staff Nurses Muriel Wakeford, Ethel Peters and Sophie Durham.[35] They worked tirelessly over many trips, at times under fire. For their stalwart service during the war these dedicated women received many accolades and decorations. Muriel Wakeford epitomised the exemplary attitude of the nurses:

> We have seven Australian Sisters on board; and the Imperial people we have dashing temperaments. I can assure you there is no time for anything but dash, and we often wish they had more than they have. Any way we all do our best, and wish we could do more. Our patients tell us that they prefer their own jobs to ours and really sometimes I would too . . . It is a wonderful thing for us to be so near the scene of action. Not many women have the chance.[36]

Sister Elsie Gibson's diary entry for 26 April demonstrated the onerous workload:

> There is no end to the work you just leave off when it is impossible to work more or get orders to go off duty. To wash helpless ones, dress wounds & feed them is all one can aim at & if ev dressing is finished 10 p.m. you are lucky indeed. Making beds is an unheard of luxury. We give Morphia ad lib.[37]

Keep in mind, too, that the nurses did all this while wearing a uniform that had evolved from Victorian England's climate and social mores. This included a long grey dress, heavily starched white cuffs, collars and apron, belt, red cape, heavy black or grey stockings, and laced black walking boots or shoes; Army nurses also wore white veils on their heads.[38] It was decidedly impractical for the Mediterranean climate and active-service nursing in a war zone.

Private George Rowden, 6th Battalion, who was wounded on the day of the Landing, was fortuitously sent to the *Gascon* for treatment and transportation to Egypt. He was part of the first trip the *Gascon* made from Anzac. His experiences highlighted the benefits of having a properly equipped hospital ship to care for the wounded and, like many other patients, he gratefully acknowledged the nurses' courage and devotion to duty:

> My arm was useless, I couldn't go on, so back to the beach. Here there were lots of unfortunates shot everywhere from the feet to the head. I was feeling real weak from loss of blood by this time and was glad to get some attention. The shrapnel was still falling thick on the beach—they were trying to get our reinforcements as they landed. After waiting some time we were put on board some barges and taken to the beautiful hospital ship S.S. *Gascon*. It was good after nine months to get into a bed again and get your wounds dressed by the Sisters. They couldn't do enough for us—all Australian girls and they were under fire; the guns were booming all round us. One of the warships fired a broadside alongside over our ship and I thought she'd rattle to bits.[39]

Rowden was one of many fortunate Anzacs sent to the *Gascon* on 25 April. Sister Ella Tucker had a different view of the patients' lot that day:

> There are 557 patients on board and only 7 nurses so that we can't attempt to do anything else for the men, except their dressings, it nearly breaks your heart, to see them lying, looking hot & dirty, & not be able to sponge them, & make them comfortable.[40]

Lieutenant-Colonel George Syme also described the avalanche of wounded that inundated the ship on 25 April:

> Just after breakfast a transport came alongside with wounded, & they kept pouring on board from launches & lighters & torpedo boats & we were as busy as possible attending to them. I began operating almost

> at once but then Col. Hugo said I must wait as everyone was wanted to attend to the wounded as they arrived. After things got settled down a bit I got to work in the theatre & was at it till 1.30 a.m. next day. I had no lunch, & just snatched a bit of dinner—On Monday I started again & was operating & dressing cases all day—In the afternoon of Sunday we were as full as we could be—540 cases & sailed back to Mudros Bay.[41]

Ironically, George Syme became a casualty himself, developing an infected knuckle on his right hand after performing an operation. Eventually on Friday, 7 May, he was sent to hospital, despite Hugo operating on the injury on 6 May.[42]

The *Gascon*'s orders for its first trip to Egypt entailed sailing to Mudros Harbour on Lemnos. Lieutenant-Colonel Hugo described the farcical events that followed:

> Arrived back at Mudros Bay at midnight. Everyone hard at work. Finished dressing officers at 12.45 am. Turned in at 1. Monday 26th April. Waited at Mudros Bay for orders. When a dispatch boat came alongside ordered us to start for the Dardanelles ignorant of the fact that we were full of wounded. Eventually the skipper went in the ships boat saw the S.H.O. we got permission to proceed to Alexandria.
>
> Accordingly we left at 6.30 pm and at 7.10 pm consigned to the deep 6 of our dead.[43]

In other words, more than 18 hours were lost while the ship trod water in an anchorage far removed from the desperately needed facilities available in Egypt. Ten of the wounded died en route to Alexandria. It also meant that the *Gascon*'s arrival back at Anzac was delayed. Instead of arriving on 1 May, the ship reached its old anchorage at 6 p.m. on 2 May. This first return trip took three days, five and a half hours, thanks to its Mudros detour. By comparison the *Gascon*'s second trip to Egypt and back to Anzac took a day less—two days, five and a half hours.[44] While the *Gascon* lost precious time in Mudros Bay, Corbin's casualty clearing station filled up with men like Jack requiring urgent medical attention beyond the capability of the primitive beach facility.

What a contrast the *Gascon* was to the transport ships being used as improvised hospital ships or ambulance carriers—often known as black ships. During the Landing the enormous number of casualties meant the arrangements for transporting the wounded to Egypt were insufficient. Ships used to carry the invasion force were pressed into service as temporary solutions. The *Lutzow* was such a ship. Surgeon General Ryan's description of the *Lutzow* was scathing. He was horrified by what he found:

> The next boat I went on was the *Lutzow*, which was a captured German boat and the dirtiest and nastiest boat I have ever been on, and why she should ever have been chosen to carry wounded men passes my comprehension. In every other boat the captain and crew were English. In this boat the Captain was a German and the crew were Levantines, Greeks, Italians and Turks. (!) The food was bad. In all the others the food was good. Colonel Marshall was on board when he was wounded, and his remarks will not bear repetition. The row kicked up by these frantic horses kept everybody from sleeping . . . We had no Australians on board. There was not one bed pan in this boat, and no paper, and the men had to defecate in their breeches, and this is the state the boat was going on to Australia (?) in with about 700 to 800 wounded on board; there were no nurses . . . I did my level best to stop her . . . As far as I know there was a very decent British Medical Officer in charge of the boat; I do not remember his name, but his personnel seems to have been very inadequate. In this boat I did all the operations and everything. In many of these boats were only general practitioners and they had no experience of surgery.[45]

Indeed the 'very decent British Medical Officer' Ryan encountered on the *Lutzow* was a 'veterinary officer, helped by an orderly and a few combatants', according to Butler in his *Official History of the Australian Army Medical Services 1914–1918*.[46] Butler also revealed there were 130 horses on board,[47] no doubt frightened by the awful noises of war echoing in and around the ship. This made them agitated and panicky, and they kicked up a ruckus.

The *Lutzow*'s personnel and equipment were deficient, mainly because the allocation of Australian medical staff and stores from the 2nd Australian Stationary Hospital didn't arrive before the transport sailed. The *Lutzow* and the *Ionian* had already sailed for the front on 25 April, minus the three officers, 20 other ranks and stores that were to be provided by the Australians.[48] It seems almost incomprehensible that the care and transportation of wounded Anzacs was entrusted to enemies—a German captain and a crew largely made up of the dregs of the Ottoman Empire. The state of the ship showed how little regard they had for what to them was cargo, albeit a wounded and suffering human cargo.

~

Sister Ella Tucker, on board the *Gascon,* described the preparations as they neared Anzac on their second trip:

> On the return journey to Gaba Tepe we work hard getting our wards ready, can't get clean pyjama suits; pick out the cleanest, & about forty pairs of bloodstained ones, with the orderlies assistance, we do our best to wash in Salt water, and then dry on the deck, every spare minute is spent in cutting up dressings & padding splints which the ship's carpenter is making for us.[49]

Muriel Wakeford wrote about the demanding conditions when they arrived:

> At 3.30 a.m. [3 May] patients started to come on board, and we were working from then on continuously till now [7 May] with just enough time to get a few hours sleep. So many more doctors and nurses wanted, I cannot understand why more do not come from Australia . . . I had 100 patients, and dressed the biggest part of them myself, so you can imagine how busy I was. Occasionally I felt the futility of things. The little bit we do seems like a drop in the ocean, and yet I suppose it means something.[50]

Jack, crammed into a flat-bottomed boat called a lighter, reached the sanctuary of the *Gascon* early on Tuesday, 4 May, having endured the agony of waiting on the beach since Sunday, 2 May. There were important implications for Jack's condition as a result of this unfortunate delay, which was caused by two unrelated circumstances: the tardy return of the *Gascon* to Anzac after its first trip, and the wave of wounded Anzacs and Marines that flooded the beach's inadequate medical arrangements from 2 May. Jack became lost in this morass. The walking wounded were able to access and board the barges and other vessels used to transport casualties far more easily than patients like Jack, who were dependent on the awareness and compassion of others.

As a consequence, Jack's wound had become infected with gas gangrene. Gangrene was bad enough; gas gangrene, its rapacious sibling, was particularly virulent and deadly unless treated expeditiously. Dr Michael Tyquin in his book, *The Medical War: The Australian Army Medical Services in The Dardanelles Campaign of 1915*, described the causes, course and cure of gas gangrene at Gallipoli:

> The incidence of gas gangrene was never as serious at Gallipoli as it was on the Western Front. It was not frequent at Gallipoli as the necessary anaerobes were not present in the largely uncultivated (and therefore

> unmanured) soil. However, as most open wounds contain one or more types of bacteria or anaerobic organisms (which can cause gangrene), such bacteria were often present in situations where bandages had been applied too tightly, dressings changed too infrequently, or where wounds had not properly drained.
>
> Gangrene may commence as a local infection with spread of gas through the tissues, and especially the subcutaneous (ie. Situated beneath the skin) tissue around the wound, or the whole limb can be rapidly infected and may die en masse in a few hours. Treatment consisted of removing as much of the blood clot and dead tissue as possible, providing the wound with free access to the air, and ensuring efficient drainage of the wound. Any wound that showed signs of gaseous cellulitis (ie. Inflammation of tissue caused by gas bubbles leading to fever, pain and swelling.) was freely opened under an anaesthetic, dead skin or muscle completely cut away, and the whole wound cleansed by mopping it out with gauze and an antiseptic such as hydrogen peroxide.[51]

Amputation of the affected limb was also needed at times, otherwise the infection would spread rapidly, resulting in kidney failure, which would lead to the patient's death. The nurses felt powerless in the face of men afflicted with gas gangrene. One of the few salves the nurses could afford such cases was the simple act of wiping their faces. Later in the war, while nursing in France, Sister Alice King commented on this after receiving a parcel of linen from Penzance Red Cross: 'Beautiful fine linen sheets cut to large handkerchief size. Scented with lavender. Such a boon! Poor old gas gangrene patients can have their sweating faces wiped.'[52]

Gas gangrene, also known as moist gangrene, had an unmistakable smell due to the decomposing tissue around the wound. At this early stage of the war it was relatively unknown, but the Gallipoli experience changed that: 'In bad cases, nurses could detect the overpowering "swamp" gas odour as soon as the patient came into the ward or theatre, long before the staff saw the rotting flesh and odious frothy brown fluid when they removed the field dressings.'[53] An effective antiserum for gas gangrene wasn't developed until 1918.[54]

Poor Jack. At best he would have been administered morphine at Tebbutt's RAP. By the time he was placed on board the *Gascon* his wound was smelly, suppurating and acutely inflamed, enveloping him in a feverish pain. The dressing on Jack's wound, applied by Corporal Charles Macquarie in the field on Saturday afternoon, had probably not been changed. It was now Tuesday morning. Over 60 hours had elapsed, long enough for gas gangrene to take effect. Macquarie did what experience of wounds had taught him and patched Jack up; however, in doing so, he may have inadvertently precipitated the onset of gas gangrene by applying the dressing tightly to stop the loss of blood. The corporal wasn't to know that Jack would not receive the specialist care he needed for days. Before he reached the *Gascon*, Jack's wound wasn't operated on, and the dressing was not changed. At Gallipoli, as Tyquin observed, 'even the smallest cuts and abrasions were likely to become infected'.[55] Jack's life now hung in the balance.

Firstly, Jack had to be winched aboard the *Gascon*. Sister Elsie Gibson described the difficult process in her diary:

> A box large enough to hold a stretcher & patient is lowered, 2 [Red Cross] Orderlies stand ready to lift stretcher into the box, it is hauled up by pulleys, 2 more orderlies lift out the stretcher, carry it to a lift about 12 yds off an iron bedstead which looks just a large another iron box in which the Stretcher fits easily. The patient is lowered to the hospital in this lift & as the lift reaches the lower deck 2 Indian orderlies lift out stretcher & carry it to the bed (all the beds are swinging beds) 3 other Indian Orderlies stand ready to lift the patient off the stretcher onto his bed. One side of the bed is let down & swings just like side of a cot & the moment the patient is lifted off the stretcher, the stretcher bearers drop one side of stretcher & is held by only one pole so as the orderlies who are lifting the patient may step forward & place patient in bed.[56]

Once on board Jack was examined by Lieutenant-Colonel Hugo. Hugo's diary entry for 4 May showed compassion and concern for his severely wounded patients:

> Got to bed at 2 am, was up again at 3.45. Taking in wounded and was kept hard at it all day so I have hardly had time to see the wards . . . we were to have started for Alexandria about 7. But now, 1.15 am, we haven't started yet and I'm afraid they will try to get more wounded on board although we are quite full nearly 500. The mortality has been very heavy. To 12 am there have been 29 deaths. Poor fellows such fine men but the wounds are horrible. The Turks must have been using some sort of explosive bullet.[57]

One of those 29 deaths was Jack. The closeness of the wound in his thigh to his torso and vital internal organs meant that once gas gangrene began when he was on the beach, an immediate operation would have been Jack's only chance of survival. The surgery would have involved the cleaning, aerating and draining of his wound—none of which was possible or practical at Anzac at the time. As it was his condition deteriorated during his enforced stay on the beach on 2 and 3 May. For Jack the delay at the casualty clearing station proved fatal, as it did for countless other casualties during the first week or so at Anzac.

Like Hugo, Muriel Wakeford was also aghast at the state of the men taken on board during the second trip: 'The men were in a much worse condition this week than our first lot and many more deaths occurred.'[58] Ella Tucker concurred, writing in her diary that: 'We are two days anchored off Gaba Tepe, taking on patients, mostly at night, we had not so many this trip, but they were very severely wounded, had over 40 deaths on our 3 days trip.'[59]

Surgeon George Syme described another gas gangrene case from the *Gascon*'s second trip, with the wound also being close to the patient's torso:

> In one case of very lacerated wound near the shoulder, gas gangrene set in almost immediately, and spread rapidly on to the chest and trunk; the patient died in spite of free incisions and the pumping in of hydrogen peroxide. I think this case, however, occurred in our second trip, after the men had been in trenches for a week, and was a shrapnel wound. The cases seen then had been wounded a longer time before being sent on board, and were much more infected.[60]

Syme was referring to the many soldiers whose evacuation from the beach was delayed—Jack among them—in his final comment.

~

Jack Collyer's death resulted from a gunshot wound that was most likely caused by an explosive bullet. Unfortunately, at Anzac both sides suffered deaths and wounds from them.

Lieutenant-Colonel Hugo commented in regard to the Turkish use of explosive bullets on successive days. On 3 May he wrote: 'Started taking in wounded at 3.30 a.m. Some very bad cases. Continued with short intervals all day until 11.30 p.m. Many wounds very large as if made by explosive bullets . . .'[61] On 4 May he made similar remarks, and on 5 May he further noted: 'The wounds are very bad variety this time.'[62] Hugo's concerns were interesting. He was a very knowledgeable surgeon with considerable field experience.

In Jack's case, Hugo's remarks were identical to those of Corporal Macquarie, who referred to Jack's wound as 'a great big wound caused by a soft nose bullet'.[63]

Sister Muriel Wakeford also witnessed the effects of the explosive bullets and assertively condemned the enemy use of such ammunition:

> I would use a dum dum bullet on every German and Turk I could get a shot at. It is time Britain gave up fighting like gentlemen and paid Germany back in some of her own coin. Fresh evidence of their 'kulture' comes to light daily.[64]

The use of dumdum—expanding or explosive bullets—in international warfare was banned by the Hague Convention of 1899.[65] Many early accounts of the fighting at Anzac refer to their use by the Turks. Snowy Robson claimed to have been hit by an explosive bullet during the fighting on 2 May in Death Trap Valley: '. . . a bullet got me in the back. It was an explosive bullet, and I had to have seven pieces taken out.'[66] Bert Smythe in his 9 May epistle was critical about this enemy tactic:

> They use 'dum dum' & explosive bullets. The 'dum dums' are made by sawing the point off or by turning the bullet back to front. In either case the result is the same. One of Kiplings poems describes the work of a 'dum dum' perfectly, 'A small blue hole in his forehead & the back blown out of his head.' Cpl Watson one of A co's reinforcements had half his head blown away with one bullet. It was awful. The wounds these bullets make are terrible. They are enough to unnerve a man.[67]

In a letter published in *The Tamworth Daily Observer* on Thursday, 15 July 1915, Private Bill Flannery wrote:

> Lots of the killed, wounded and captured Turks had 'dum-dum' bullets in their possession. The service bullet of Turkey is sharp-pointed and a trifle heavier than our own, and the ones I saw had the points filed off about a quarter of an inch from the top. When these are fired and strike flesh they 'mushroom' and make a bad wound. Being contrary to war rules the possession of 'dum-dums' is enough to justify the possessor being shot on sight, so a good many were dealt with that way, while others will be kept apart from ordinary prisoners with a view to being more severely dealt with when the time comes.

This preoccupation with Turkish use of such banned ammunition was later explained away as the troops' inexperience and lack of understanding of the dreadful impact such modern high velocity projectiles could have on the human body. During the Armistice of 24 May, Anzacs were horrified when they saw firsthand the carnage their bullets inflicted on the enemy. Charles Bean commented directly on this issue in newspaper articles published across Australia after the Armistice:

> The conditions of the burial armistice the other day were on the whole very honorably observed. Our wounded in the enemy's hands are said to be well cared for. A few stories of atrocities are current, and may reach Australia. I can only say the principal one which I have tested proved to be wholly untrue. Some dum-dum bullets have been picked up, but the stories of the use of explosive bullets by the Turks are quite foundationless, and are due to the men misunderstanding the curious double crack of a Mauser rifle. Some of the wounds are terrible, and I would put them down to expanding bullets had I not seen wounds quite as terrible in the heads of Turks lying just outside our trenches.[68]

Regardless of Bean's testimony, in which even he conceded some of the banned projectiles had been found, other evidence indicated that both sides transgressed.

In the ANZAC ranks, Harvey Jones, a member of the Wellington Battalion, acknowledged using explosive bullets while fighting at Quinn's Post. In an interview in 1982 he readily admitted:

> We split bullets—in the way we weren't supposed to, as dumdums—so that when it struck it branched out and made an even bigger mess.[69]

~

At 12.30 a.m. on Wednesday, 5 May, the *Gascon* left its station off Gaba Tepe with 446 cases throughout its decks.[70] Butler's *Official History* cited slightly different figures, claiming there were 475 cases embarked from Anzac Cove and that 41 of them died by the time the ship reached Alexandria.[71] In her diary Elsie Gibson noted the figure was 514 wounded men.[72]

Jack's body was laid to rest on 5 May:

> At Sea Between Gallipoli Pen + Alexandria . . . Principal Chaplain . . . Buried by Lieut Col Hugo.[73]

George Syme described the burials at sea that took place on the *Gascon*'s first trip; presumably the same procedure was followed on the second trip:

> On Monday, just at sunset we buried the dead. The bodies were placed on boards at the stern of the vessel, covered with the Union Jack, & those of their comrades able get about stood around, with the officers & men of the ship. The Captain (W.F. Stanley) read the burial service very impressively & separately for each man—as he came to the part where the body is 'committed to the deep', the propeller was stopped, the sailors tilted the end of the board & the body fell into the sea & immediately disappeared.[74]

Jack's journey had ended. His war was over.

~

While the agony of Jack's last days had ceased, his family's agony was just beginning. A series of unfortunate events conspired to delay the final confirmation of his death for months. This was a common problem for many anxious families during the war; some unfortunate grieving families even waited years for official news, living in a traumatised limbo. For too many families, their loved one was simply listed as 'Missing In Action'. Although Jack's parents, George and Jessie, or Janet as she was formally known, and siblings had not heard from him for many, many weeks, they lived in hope.

Jack's fate was played out in *The Mudgee Guardian*. His family, friends and the local community were very proud of him, as he was one of the first men to enlist from the district. He certainly went with their blessing and high hopes. Any news from Gallipoli about any one of the local boys was often found in *The Guardian*. This was true of every community across the country. A significant part of the social media of its day, the local newspaper printed local, regional, state, national and international news. It was the major avenue for advertising and wasn't complete without at least one gossip page. Newspapers also provided the perfect forum for letters, the other integral form of early 20th century social media, and Gallipoli letters were a prized source of information. The other relatively fast form of communication was the telegram, but during the war it came to be dreaded by the families of men and women serving their country.

In Jack's case, his family didn't receive the telegram informing them that he was wounded, even though there is a copy of it in his personnel dossier:

> MRS JANET COLLYER MUDGEE (NEW SOUTH WALES) REGRET REPORTED SON PRIVATE J COLLYER WOUNDED WILL ADVISE UPON RECEIPT FURTHER PARTICULARS SECRETARY DEFENCE 22/5/15.[75]

The first word that something was wrong came in the form of a letter to Jack's father written by Charles Macquarie to reassure the family that their boy, although wounded in action, was making a good recovery and was probably on his way home:

> Well, sir—must now close, hoping you shall receive your son home, with honour & credit, as I believe he is somewhere between here & Australia.[76]

Macquarie wrote the letter while recovering from a bout of gastritis on Mudros. He fell ill early in June and was admitted to No. 2 Stationary Hospital on Mudros on 15 June.[77] Jack's parents had not heard from their son for four months, nor had they heard from the authorities about him. Macquarie's plea to George Collyer to keep the 'hard part from Jack's mother as it may upset her'[78] was ignored by George, who not only shared the letter with Jessie but also had it published in its entirety in *The Mudgee Guardian* on Monday, 28 August 1915. This was the first piece of correspondence that gave them false hope.

Jack's family received Macquarie's letter on 20 August and immediately wrote to Senator Pearce requesting further information:

> Mudgee
> 20.8.15
>
> Senator Pearce
> Minister for Defence
>
> Dear Sir
>
> I would be very pleased if you would inform me where my son John Collyer is at present, I got word privetly today that he was wounded some time ago, I have not heard from him for 13 weeks now, please let me know where [he] is, + if wounded the nature of his wounds, + his present condition, I have never seen his name in any of the lists of wounded, nor have I had any official word from the military authorities of him been wounded, there was a John Collyer Eastwood reported as wounded in the papers about May the first there may be a mistake about his address, trusting you will give me some information about him as I + his mother are very anxious about wellfair
>
> Yours faithfully
> G.T.Collyer
> Mudgee
> (PS. he left with the 1st Brogade + 4th Battallion)[79]

Jack's parents were thrown by the 24th Casualty List in *The Sydney Morning Herald* of Friday, 28 May 1915, stating that a John Collyer of Eastwood was wounded on 1 May. *The Daily Telegraph* of the same day also listed Private J. Collyer 4th Battalion as wounded, but did not give his place of residence. Presumably the Collyers did not see *The Daily Telegraph* issue.

The next day, Jack's mother wrote her own plea for information to the senator:

> Mudgee August 21st
> 1915
>
> To Senator Pearce
> Minister for Defence
> Sydney
>
> Dear Sir
> I am writing you a few lines, in regard to my son Jack who is on active service, + as I heard from a brother soldier that my boy has been wounded; but not having been officially notified of the fact; + also not receiving word from my boy himself since the landing of our troops at Gallipoli; I am very anxious about him. Would you please find out his whereabouts + let me know as soon as possible.
> Yours truly
>
> J.Collyer
>
> Address
> Mrs G.T.Collyer
> Redbank
> Mudgee[80]

In addition, Jack's family sent a telegram on 26 August to the Minister of Defence's office in Melbourne:

> Please reply by wire any information asked in my letter very anxious about my son,
> Collyer Portland.[81]

On 1 September, a close family friend also made an enquiry concerning Jack:

1.9.15
The Secretary of Defence
Melbourne

Dear Sir

Being closely interested in the welfare of Private John Collyer who I have known from childhood. I should be very glad to know if there is any way of learning particulars of his condition and whereabouts he was reported seriously wounded receiving his wounds May 1st his father George Collyer of Mudgee has heard nothing of his son since then.

Trusting you will be able to put me on the right track
I am yours respectfully

F.P. Edwards
Inverell
N.S.W.[82]

The result of these requests for definitive information about Jack's welfare was given in *The Mudgee Guardian* on Monday, 6 September 1915, in the following article:

PRIVATE COLLYER DEAD
Sad Circumstances
Word has been received by Mr. and Mrs. George Collyer that their son, Private Jack Collyer, was wounded on May 1st and died on May 4th. For four months the parents had received no word from their soldier son, and became anxious. The first intimation that their boy had been wounded was received per medium of a letter from a friend name Macquarie—which communication was published in our column a couple of weeks ago. On receipt of this missive Mr. Collyer wired to the defence authorities asking for news and received a return wire last Monday to the effect that Private John Collyer had been wounded, not seriously, stating that from the known nature of the wound satisfactory progress could be expected, but that no particulars were available. A couple of days later the Defence Department wrote that they were trying to obtain particulars. On Saturday the period of suspense ended. The Rev. Morris Yates received a wire to inform Mr. and Mrs. Collyer that their son had been wounded on May 1st, and died

> on May 4th. We tender our sincere sympathy to the bereaved parents on the death of their soldier hero.

Reverend Morris Yates had the unenviable task of breaking the news to Jack's family. By now the local minister had become an integral part of the process of managing the death of a loved one at war and its effect on the family. Jack's family had their worst fears realised; their boy was dead.

In *The Sydney Morning Herald* on 9 September, Jack's photograph appeared as one of the 'Heroes of the Dardanelles', the caption reading 'Private Jack Collyer (Mudgee). Died of wounds'.

On the same day under Local Brevities in *The Mudgee Guardian*, this notice appeared:

> Owing to the death of Private Collyer in Gallipoli the proprietors of that old-established boarding house, 'The Zoo,' in Gladstone street, decided to close up the establishment. As a result, the numerous boarders have sought accommodation elsewhere, and 'The Zoo' has become a memory.

Jack resided at The Zoo before joining the Australian Imperial Force. It sounded like the boarding house was something of a local institution, and Jack a popular resident. Once he joined up, the other boarders and the owners followed his travails in *The Mudgee Guardian* with interest. This was a compassionate gesture on the part of its proprietors, in keeping with the fine reputation Jack had in Mudgee.

On Thursday, 16 September 1915, the following notice appeared in *The Mudgee Guardian*:

> **MEMORIAL SERVICE**
> A memorial service for the late Private 'Jack' Collyer, who was killed in action at Gallipoli, will be held in the Salvation Army Hall at 7.15 p.m. on Sunday next.

No doubt his distraught family, dressed in black, led the mourners on what would have been a very sad occasion. Their anxiety about their son's fate had been replaced by a sense of grief and loss.

In the same edition of the paper a eulogy of sorts was written:

> From information to hand it would appear that Private Collyer, particulars of whose death under distressing circumstances were recently published, was buried at sea. It would appear that the young Mudgee hero was

wounded at Gallipoli, and was in a serious condition when taken aboard the hospital ship. He gradually sank, and died while en route to the hospital. His remains were then consigned to the waves after an impressive service had been held over him. 'Jack' was a fine, young fellow. May he sleep quietly beneath the blue waters of the Mediterranean.

On Monday, 11 October 1915, in *The Mudgee Guardian* a further communication the family received from the Defence Department was published:

MISSING TELEGRAM
News of Jack Collyer's Wounds
Since Mr. and Mrs. Collyer of Mudgee received word of the death of their son, Jack, they have written to the Defence Department, asking why news of the wounding of their son had not been sent to them. In reply to their representations they have received the following letter from the Officer in Charge of Base Records, Melbourne:—

Dear Madam,— In reply to yours of the 21st ult., I beg to inform you that a telegram, as per attached copy, was despatched from this office on the 22.5.15 intimating your son was reported wounded, and it appears strange that you have not received same, as when a telegram remains undelivered, the Telegraph Branch notifies me to that effect and as such no notification was received in this office it would be assumed that same had reached you. You will already have been advised through the Military Commandant N.S.W. of the regrettable loss of your son, who is now reported as having died of wounds. No further particulars will be known until the receipt of the official despatches from the Front, when such details as refer to him will be immediately transmitted to you. All further communication will be addressed herein.

Jack's family, shattered by their loss, joined the ranks of thousands of other families across Australia mourning the deaths of their sons. Jessie Collyer, exploring any avenue for news about Jack, had earlier written to Chaplain McKenzie, seeking information. In mid-November she received a startling reply, which was printed in *The Mudgee Guardian* on 18 November:

PRIVATE JACK COLLYER
Is He Killed?
A Strange Letter.
There seems to be hope left that Private Jack Collyer is still alive. Some time ago Mrs Collyer received a reply to a letter of inquiry she wrote to

the Defence Department stating that her son was killed on May 1st. Mrs Collyer also wrote a letter to Brigadier McKenzie, who is the chaplain of the 4th Battalion. The following is a copy of the letter received from Brigadier McKenzie:—

> Gallipoli Peninsula.
> Turkey 25th September, 1915.
>
> Dear Mrs Collyer I have just received your letter of inquiry re your son, Private J. Collyer, No. 1241, D Company, 4th Battalion. I may say that your boy was wounded on the 1st May, the sixth day after we landed on the peninsula, and was taken away on a hospital ship to a hospital. He was not severely wounded. He later went to England, and he is still there, and will now be at Weymouth (Eng.), where the Australian boys are having a remarkably good time. Probably you have heard from him ere this. Your letters have come along to the regiment here safely, and have been re-addressed to your son at the hospital, and I guess he has received them safely. I hope that you have heard from him and looked upon his handwriting once more, as I can readily believe you are having a very anxious and trying time. This is a terrible war, and I pray to God that it may end soon—Yours faithfully,
>
> William McKenzie,
> Chaplain, 4th Battalion.

The cruellest irony of Jack's fate was that this letter was from the hand of Chaplain McKenzie—a high-ranking fellow Salvation Army member as well as the 4th Battalion's adored chaplain. Jack had written about 'Fighting Mac' in his diary and probably also in his letters to his family. Jack's mother, Jessie, was a devout Christian and Salvationist, and would have undoubtedly admired the influence and presence of Bill McKenzie in her son's life. The Collyers had every reason not to believe the contents of his letter; however, it gave the grieving family and the local community false hope that Jack was not dead, but alive and recuperating in England. This was the second time the family received a letter from a member of the 4th Battalion that led them to believe Jack was alive. Obviously, the word in the battalion was that Jack had survived his wound; Macquarie and McKenzie were only trying to reassure his relatives.

Once again, the family contacted the relevant authorities, seeking clarification of Jack's status and whereabouts:

Mudgee Red Bank
Nov 16 1915

Hon Minister for Defence

Dear Sir
Some time ago I communicated with you in reference to my son John Collyer, having heard privately that he had been wounded. You replied that he had been wounded on or about May 1st. Later I again wrote you + you informed me that he had died of wounds on the 4th of May. I now wish you to make further inquiries having had a letter from Brigadier McKenzie Salvation army Chaplain who went away in the same boat with my son, informing me that he was wounded on May the 1st + sent to a Hospital at Whymouth + that he was not dead or severely wounded. This information was written by Brigadier McKenzey on 24 September + I received it on Nov 13th of course you will understand we feel very curious having got the above information, + are hoping it is true. I would therefore be thankfull if you would inform us if your wire sent me has been confirmed + guaranteed from the home departments, or if we may have any hope of any information from Mr McKenzie being correct. I trust you will make further inquiries + inform me again when you get a reply.

I remain
Yours Faithfully
George Collyer
Red Bank Mudgee[83]

Final irrevocable confirmation came in a letter from the Defence Department dated 25 November 1915:

Dear Sir,
In reply to yours of 16th instant, I have to state that official confirmation of the death of your son, No. 1241 private J. Collyer, 4th Battalion has been received, not only in the shape of a confirmation of the cabled advice, but also a British Army Form containing the following particulars;—

No. 1241 Private Collyer J., 4th Battalion, 1st Infantry Brigade, Australian Imperial Force, died of wounds on H.M.S. '*Gascon*' at sea on 4th May 1915.

This Army Form is signed by the Officer Commanding Australian Records Section of the Head Quarters of the Mediterranean Expeditionary Forces at Alexandria and I'm afraid leaves little doubt but that your son has given his life in the service of his country. In addition I venture to think that ample time has elapsed for your son to communicate with you himself.

Yours Faithfully
Mr G. Collyer, Capt.
Red Bank, Officer i/c Base Records
Mudgee, N.S.W.[84]

Nearly seven months had passed since Jack's death. Finally, his family could lay him to rest. In the years to come Jack was remembered in a number of ways. In successive years the following notices were published in *The Mudgee Guardian*. Jack was 24 when he died; he would have been 25 at the time of the first notice.

May 4th, 1916.
IN MEMORIAM COLLYER—In loving memory of our darling son and brother, Jack, who died on May 4th, 1915, aged 25 years.
Thy voice is now silent, the earth is now cold,
Where thy smile and thy welcome, oft met us of old;
We miss thee, we morn thee, in silence unseen,
And dwell on memory of joys that have been.
(Inserted by his loving parents, brothers and sisters.)

May 3rd, 1917.
Roll of Honour
COLLYER—In loving memory of our dear Jack, who died from wounds at Gallipoli May 4th, 1915.
Do not ask us if we miss him,
There is such a vacant place;
Can we e'er forget his footsteps
And his dear familiar face?
Time has passed, and till we miss him,
Words would fail our love to tell;
But in heaven we know we'll meet him,
Jesus doeth all things well.
Inserted by his loving parents (George and Jessie Collyer) and brothers and sisters.

Jack's grief-stricken family remembered him in another way as well. They had two family photographic portraits taken after Jack's death. In both shots the family were dressed in black, with Jack's youngest brothers, Charles and Bert, donning black armbands on their left arms. The family's expressions were sombre; muted smiles creased their faces. In one of the photographs there was a gap in the back row between Minnie and Andrew, signifying Jack's tragic absence. In the other photograph, Jack appeared, filling the aforementioned gap: an earlier formal shot of Jack was inserted—the family was complete again, at least for posterity.

The George Collyer family bible had two entries relating to Jack's death. The first entry was:

> Jack left Australia on October 20th 1914 in *Euripides* for Egypt. Left Egypt in April 1915 for Gallipoli, was in the firing line for 6 days and was wounded on May 1st in the left thigh, + died May 4th.

The second poignant entry was:

> Our precious boy Jack died May 4th 1915 on board *Gascon* and was buried at sea.

Jack's descendants—numerous nieces, nephews and their offspring—have all heard his story and have remembered his sacrifice. Like many families, some of them have made the pilgrimage to Gallipoli. Jack's nephew, Ray Warry, has made the trek twice, in 2003 and 2005, and is hoping to be at the Dawn Service at Anzac on the centenary of the Landing in 2015. In 2003 Ray laid a wreath below the panel bearing Jack's name at the Lone Pine Memorial with the simple but evocative message, 'Jack Collyer Still Remembered', on it. Along with more than 4900 other fallen Anzacs with no known grave, Jack's name is recorded on the Lone Pine Memorial.

Finally, in Robertson Park in his home town of Mudgee, there is the Mudgee District Fallen Soldiers Memorial, an imposing stone obelisk recording the names of 144 men who lost their lives in World War I, World War II, Korea and Vietnam. Among the 96 names of fallen soldiers from World War I is Jack Collyer. Similar stone sentinels stand in towns and cities across the country, silent testimony to the wartime sacrifice of so many sons and daughters. The Mudgee memorial was unveiled on 25 April 1925. Fittingly, it is at this memorial that Mudgee's Anzac Day ceremonies are conducted.

8 Casualties

It is deeply regretted that almost the whole platoon fell in doing what was but their simple duty . . .

Lieutenant-Colonel A.J. Bennett, Commanding Officer 4th Battalion, 8 May 1915[1]

It was most unfortunate that the 4th Battalion war diary did not record any casualty figures for 30 April, 1 May or 2 May, despite the battalion's considerable losses on these days. It was remiss of the 4th Battalion's adjutant, Lieutenant Jack Massie, to fail to record them.

On 30 April, as the battalion marched from the firing line on Bolton's Hill to the beach to the firing line on MacLaurin's and the adjacent Jolly, 13 men died and at least 26 others were wounded.[2] Approximately 104 men from the 4th Battalion were killed and wounded on 1 and 2 May, most of them on 1 May. On Saturday, 1 May, 34 men from the 4th Battalion were killed in action (KIA), two other men died of wounds (DOW) incurred previously. On Sunday, 2 May, a further seven members were killed in action. Of the 63 men from the 4th Battalion wounded in action (WIA) over that weekend, eight later died of their wounds.[3]

More men from the battalion were killed on 1 May than on any other day at Gallipoli, apart from the 4th's horrendous Lone Pine losses of early August, when hundreds of them were killed and wounded. On 26 April, during the 4th's foray on 400 Plateau, when the battalion was supposedly decimated, only 11 men were killed and approximately 60 men were wounded in action. Most of the losses on 1 and 2 May occurred in Death Trap Valley. Significantly the 4th's toll—particularly the number of men killed in action—was a lot higher than the 3rd Battalion or the Marine's Portsmouth Battalion on these days; however, the Turkish casualty figures were very high, far heavier than the Anzacs and Marines. This demonstrated the defensive advantages of the battle at Anzac, soon to be reinforced by Monash's unsuccessful attack and the Turk's 19 May offensive.

There is no list available showing the names, number and circumstances of the Death Trap Valley casualties or the members of any of the four parties who ventured into the valley that weekend. The Turkish casualties are not listed either. The use of a variety of sources, mainly personnel dossiers, allowed a detailed list of the 4th's killed and wounded to be compiled. The same lists cannot be composed for the 3rd Battalion or the Portsmouth Battalion. However, estimates of their men killed in action in Death Trap Valley can be made, and the names of some of their wounded have also come to light.

In regard to the 4th Battalion's heavy losses, personnel dossiers offered a unique insight into the date, type of wound and company, occasionally platoon, of the casualty. Although the casualty form in each personnel dossier was dependent on the whim and style of the clerk who wrote it, the availability of reliable reports and the conditions at the time—remembering that the duration of the Landing was a fairly chaotic period under fire—the level of detail recorded was remarkable and generally accurate. The 4th Battalion's clerical staff at Gallipoli recorded sufficient information to enable the casualty figures for that weekend to be determined. In contrast, during the first week or so the 3rd Battalion's clerks were less scrupulous in recording details about soldiers' companies and the specific dates on which men were wounded.

By examining nearly every personnel dossier of the members of the 4th Battalion from the First Contingent and the first three batches of reinforcements—some 1377 records—a reasonably accurate picture of the battalion's casualties in the valley can be assembled. It was from these troops that the Anzacs of the 4th Battalion, who landed on 25 April and who were still fighting a week later, were from. The first reinforcements after the Landing reached the battalion on 2 May, too late to be part of the fight in Death Trap Valley. Logically, casualties in the 4th Battalion from A Company and D Company, from which No. 3 Platoon and No. 15 Platoon, respectively, were from, were probably incurred in the valley while assisting the Marines. Based on the B and C companies' casualties, a few casualties from A and D companies would have occurred in the battalion's trenches on MacLaurin's Hill and Johnston's Jolly on 1 and 2 May, but the majority would have occurred in the valley itself. Equally, some of the casualties in B and C companies might have been related to the events in the valley.

According to Les Lott, Heane's party was 56-strong. A number of sources attest to most of this detachment becoming casualties that weekend. Les claimed in his diary entry for 2 May that 'only 16 out of the 56 who went down came out alive, 10 of who were wounded'.[4]

Lieutenant-Colonel A. Bennett, the newly promoted 4th Battalion's commanding officer, later lamented in a heartfelt reply to the praise of the RMLI brigade's hierarchy for Heane's men's actions: 'It is deeply regretted that almost the whole platoon fell in doing what was but their simple duty.'[5]

Each of the three No. 15 Platoon chroniclers—Les Lott, Snowy Robson and Charles Macquarie—clearly recollected the carnage the Turks inflicted, particularly mid-afternoon on Saturday, 1 May. There were 13 men from D Company KIA on Saturday and a further two on Sunday, 15 in all. As well, 23 D Company men were WIA on those days, the bulk of them on Saturday. Three of these men later died of their wounds. This meant that 18 men in D Company died and at least 20 were wounded as a result of the fighting on the first weekend in May, a total of a minimum of 38 casualties.[6]

However, a further 10 men from the 4th Battalion were WIA that weekend, but their company can't be ascertained from their personnel dossiers. Arguably, most of these would have been either in A or D company, who provided the platoons for Death Trap Valley. The number of casualties in D Company increased to at least 40, given that the overwhelming casualties that were known in the 4th Battalion for that weekend were nearly all related to Death Trap Valley. For example, only three men from B Company and five men from C Company were killed in action that weekend, compared to 15 men from D Company and 18 men from A Company.[7] Clearly, the Death Trap Valley parties from D Company and A Company suffered a far higher rate of casualties. It would follow that the majority of the men wounded in action whose company couldn't be determined from their personnel dossiers were from D or A companies and were probably hit in Death Trap Valley.

So how many of the 4th's fatalities derived from the fighting in Death Trap Valley? One indication is the men's burial place. According to their personnel dossiers these D Company men were buried in Wire Gully immediately after the battle, two during the Armistice on 24 May:

Private N. Brand, KIA 1/5, Lone Pine Memorial
Private K. Chambers, KIA 1/5, Lone Pine Memorial
Private T. Davis, KIA 2/5, Lone Pine Memorial
Private J. Farnsworth, KIA 1/5, Lone Pine Memorial
Private K. Gillies, KIA 1/5, Lone Pine Memorial
Private R. Heaslip, KIA 1/5, Lone Pine Memorial
Private W. Holder, KIA 1/5, Lone Pine Memorial
Private T. Hollands, KIA 1/5, Lone Pine Memorial
Private A. Robins,* KIA 2/5, Lone Pine Memorial
L/Sergeant L. Sherburne, KIA 1/5, Lone Pine Memorial
Private W. Wilkinson,* KIA 1 or 2/5, Lone Pine Memorial
[*Buried during the Armistice.][8]

Red Cross evidence points to Alf Robins being buried in Death Trap Valley on 24 May. Private Bill Wilkinson was officially listed as being killed in action on 30 April, but the evidence from his Red Cross file firmly places him in Death Trap Valley when he was hit.

As their graves remain unmarked and unknown, all these men are remembered on the Lone Pine Memorial. The casualty forms in their personnel dossiers showed they were initially buried near where they fell—in this case Wire Gully—which meant they were involved in the Death Trap Valley fighting.

Macquarie's letter to Jack's father offered a detailed description of the circumstances surrounding Jack's fatal wound, but very few other accounts provide the same detail about the fate of the other members of No. 15 Platoon. The Australian Red Cross Society Wounded and Missing Enquiry Bureau files provided evidence of the fate of at least two men from Heane's party for their families. These two—Private Bill Wilkinson, who witnessed Jack's will, and Private Alf Robins, who was in Jack's section—were missing after the battle. These Red Cross enquiries not only helped determine the circumstances leading to their demise but also revealed the whereabouts, actions and identities of members of No. 15 Platoon on 1 and 2 May 1915. In the case of Bill Wilkinson, Private Esmond Brunker testified in a statement sent to the Red Cross:

> Sometime in early May in the old Marine trenches at top of Shrapnel Gully, Anzac, he saw Wilkinson shot through the eye and killed. Informant was about the 4th man from Wilkinson say 10yds away. This was in trenches. Lieut. Fanning of XV Platoon who has returned to Australia could confirm.[9]

Another informant, Corporal Bill Upjohn, stated that 'on 24th May, 1915 (the Armistice), at Anzac I saw one of the men (Pte. J. Newstead of same Coy.) who buried Wilkinson. Newstead knew Wilkinson personally.' Upjohn added that 'Newstead, D. Coy., brought in Wilkinson's identification disc after the Armistice on May 24th'.[10] This was further confirmation of Wilkinson's presence and subsequent death as part of No. 15 Platoon in Death Trap Valley over the first weekend in May.

The other Red Cross investigation, involving Private Alf Robins, revealed similar evidence of the platoon's actions. One of the witnesses was Snowy Robson:

> On the 2nd May Informant was in firing lines—Robins passed me and he was wounded in the arm. We were in Death Trap Gully at the time. This ground was afterwards evacuated, and it was only later that bodies could be recovered.[11]

The other notable testimony came from Corporal Sydney Bartle of No. 15 Platoon:

> Witness states that he knew Robins well. He was known as 'Alf'. They came with the same reinf., the 1st. [Actually the second reinforcements.] Robins was killed on 2/5/15, while sniping at a place called Death Gully or Death Trap. He was shot through the head. Witness was there and actually saw it. Robins was buried during the Armistice.[12]

Evidence of the latter came from Corporal Frank Ponting, also a second reinforcement:

> On 24th May an armistice had been arranged and informant was one of a Burial party that went into 'Death Trap Gully'—a continuation of Shrapnel Gully. On one of the bodies buried there was a circular pocket compass, about the size of a watch, bearing the name, 'A.A. Robins'. The body was not capable of identification.[13]

Ponting was chosen for the burial party for one reason—his height. At 5 foot 11 inches he was deemed suitably tall enough to impress the Turks in No Man's Land during the Armistice.[14] Many of the ANZAC burial party were similar in height or taller.

Another clue as to the identity of the fallen men in Heane's party came from the platoon to which they belonged. Most sources don't specify the men's platoons; however, using Jack's Gallipoli diary—in which he listed the names of 11 members of his platoon and their sections—together with incidental references in other sources, allowed the collation of the following list of members of No. 15 Platoon who were killed and wounded during the fighting in Death Trap Valley:

Private B. Bathurst, WIA 1/5
Private W. Bound, WIA 2/5
Private J. Collyer, WIA 1/5, DOW 4/5
Private A. Fuller, WIA 1/5
Corporal C. Lawler, WIA 1/5
Private A. Robins,* KIA 2/5
Private E. Robson, WIA 2/5
Private T. Thomson, WIA 1/5 or 2/5 DOW 11/5
Corporal R. Usher, KIA 1/5
Private W. Wilkinson, KIA 1 or 2/5[15]

The first five members of this list were from Jack's section. (See Appendix 1 for a list of D Company soldiers who were killed or wounded that weekend.)

The second detachment from the 4th Battalion, No. 3 Platoon, A Company, largely controlled by Snowy Robson in the late afternoon and evening of Saturday, 1 May, also suffered heavy casualties. Privates De Vine and Quigley of A Company both referred to many dead and wounded mates in their accounts. As in D Company, a considerable number of men in A Company were killed and wounded that weekend, most of them from No. 3 Platoon, in Death Trap Valley. In reporting Snowy Robson's heroics, Bennett wrote: 'and as only 5 men of the platoon were uninjured the nature of the peril was obvious'. Bennett was referring to the reinforcing platoon (No. 3 Platoon) that was guided and controlled by Robson.[16]

There were 35 documented casualties, including 22 fatalities, in A Company that weekend. A total of 18 men from A Company were killed in action—17 of them on Saturday. The number of men wounded in action was 17; most of them (at least 15) were hit on Saturday, with four of them later dying from their wounds. This meant that 22 men from A Company died as a result of the fighting on the first weekend in May and at least 13 men were wounded, a total of at least 35 casualties. Some of the 10 men who were wounded in action from the 4th Battalion on that weekend, and whose company could not be determined from their personnel dossiers, must have come from A Company. The number of A Company casualties would have been about 40 with the addition of some of these men.[17]

The majority of the casualties from No. 3 Platoon, A Company, occurred late afternoon on Saturday, 1 May, in Death Trap Valley. Evidence for this again comes from the time and place of the burials for the men killed in action from A Company. All these men are commemorated on the Lone Pine Memorial (LPM):

Private W. Andersen,* KIA 1/5, buried Valley of Death, Armistice, 24/5, LPM
Private T. Bann,* KIA 1/5, buried Valley of Death, Armistice, 24/5, LPM
Private S. Beer, KIA 1/5, buried Head of Wire Gully, LPM
Private J. Clancy, KIA 1/5, buried Head of Wire Gully, LPM
Private F. Cooke, KIA 1/5, buried Shrapnel Valley, LPM
Private G. Craig,* KIA 1/5, buried Valley of Death, Armistice, 24/5, LPM
Private E. Cusack, KIA 1/5, buried Shrapnel Valley, LPM
Private E. Edmondson, KIA 1/5, buried Wire Gully, LPM
Private L. Edwards,* KIA 1/5, buried Valley of Death, Armistice, 24/5, LPM
Private H. Murr, KIA 1/5, buried Wire Gully, LPM

Private F. Richards,* KIA 1/5, buried Valley of Death, Armistice, 24/5, LPM
Lance Corporal W. Smith, KIA 1/5, buried Wire Gully, LPM
Private M. Stackpool,* KIA 1/5, buried Valley of Death, Armistice, 24/5, LPM
Private J. Stewart,* KIA 1/5, buried Valley of Death, Armistice, 24/5, LPM
Private F. Waine,* KIA 1/5, buried Valley of Death, Armistice, 24/5, LPM
Private E. Ward, KIA 1/5, buried Shrapnel Gully, LPM
[*Buried on Armistice Day, 24 May.][18]

(See Appendix 1 for a list of A Company men who were killed or wounded that weekend.)

The presence of these men in Death Trap Valley was confirmed by their burials during the Armistice. They lay in the valley in front of the firing line in exposed positions that could not be safely accessed. Like their mates in D Company, today these men are commemorated on the Lone Pine Memorial, their original graves also being unmarked and unknown.

Bill 'Fighting Mac' McKenzie, the 4th Battalion's revered padre, arrived at Anzac on 10 May. He conducted the burials of the men on the day of the Armistice, 24 May, fulfilling his duty to his beloved battalion.

However, for about three weeks the bodies of these fallen men lay where they fell, in exposed positions or rudimentary resting places, dictated by the amount of fighting that was occurring. Once the outposts were abandoned, the only chance of retrieving their bodies and giving them a decent Christian burial was during the Armistice. The protracted nature of the fighting meant survival came first for the troops. Private Geoff Leslie from the 3rd Battalion, in a letter home, wrote:

> We were at the beach for two days and then went back to relieve the Marines but to a different part of the line. The poor Marines had been slaughtered and dead were lying everywhere. The bodies in the trenches were just tossed out. There was no time for burials.[19]

Bill Ward's account admitted he'd done the same to the dead he and his mates found in the battle outposts on 2 May.[20] Les De Vine also confirmed the practice was commonplace—the corpses were tossed behind the trench where they remained unburied. He added that those who had been killed in No Man's Land were thick on the ground, as they could not be buried.[21]

One of the A Company men who died on 1 May was Private Frank Cooke. According to a letter in his personnel dossier, Frank was in No. 11 Section, A Company. This meant that he was in No. 3 Platoon, there being four sections to a platoon. Most letters on file in personnel dossiers dutifully mentioned the regimental number, company and battalion of a soldier for identification purposes, but very few included the platoon and section. The letter, written on 9 May 1915, was from Miss Ethel Way; Frank was her 'intended husband'. In it Ethel set out her concerns about hearing from the military authorities: 'If anything serious should befall him . . . I would like to know if he has arranged that I should hear from the authorities. Can you please relieve me of this anxiety as I am afraid to read the lists as they come forward?' Ethel, like so many relatives and friends of the Anzacs, feared reading the lengthy casualty lists in newspapers and their blunt, grim contents. Tragically for Ethel, Frank was already dead, a casualty of the fighting in Death Trap Valley. She eventually received the dreaded Base Records telegram on 17 June: 'Dear Madam, It is my painful duty to advise you that No. 640 [*sic*] Private Frank Newton Cooke, 4th Battalion, is reported as having been killed in action at the Dardanelles.'[22] Unfortunately, the circumstances surrounding Frank's death remain shrouded in the fog of war.

Approximately 80 men from the 4th Battalion, probably more, were killed or wounded while rescuing and reinforcing the Marines in Death Trap Valley. About 40 lost their lives and 40 or more were wounded.

The 3rd Battalion's Death Trap Valley casualties were harder to ascertain. On 1 May the 3rd Battalion began the day still at their beach bivouac and ended it at the firing line once again, only this time on Johnson's Jolly. Remarkably no one in the 3rd Battalion was killed in action on Saturday, 1 May.[23] Equally remarkable was that in all likelihood no one from the two D Company platoons sent into Death Trap Valley from the 3rd Battalion early on 2 May was killed during their deployment over the next few days. The two men killed in action from the 3rd Battalion on 2 May—Private Leonard Hammond[24] and Private Walter Heylen—were from C Company and B Company respectively.[25] In the ensuing days a small number of 3rd Battalion men died from their wounds, including some D Company members, but their personnel dossiers indicate they were wounded earlier than 1 or 2 May, or were officers, or were not in D Company. Possibly only one member of the 3rd Battalion lost his life as a result of relieving the Marines and occupying the battle outposts. He was Private Charles Bass, a second reinforcement, who died of wounds during the week ending 9 May; however, his personnel dossier revealed neither the company to which he was allocated after arriving in Egypt nor the date on which he was wounded.[26]

It was almost impossible to determine the names and numbers of 3rd Battalion men wounded in action in Death Trap Valley. Firstly, there was no record of the members of the two D Company platoons who occupied the isolated trench and, secondly, during the early days at Anzac 3rd Battalion casualty forms were weak on company and specific casualty details. Obviously there were 3rd Battalion men wounded in action in the valley. Bill Ward noted that *only* five of his squad reached the Marines after braving the deadly track to the isolated trench.[27] Arthur McGuirk commented in his letter that Lieutenant Meager's fighting skill saw *most* of his party return intact from their stint of outpost duty.[28] Two men who were wounded were Private Cyril Pritchard and Lieutenant Tully McLeod, both on 2 May. They also suffered the same wound—a gunshot wound to the back. Pritchard's casualty form states that he was wounded between 25 and 30 April,[29] contrary to Bill Ward's recollection. McLeod's wound was not even recorded, the lieutenant preferring to stay with his men rather than seek treatment. These two examples demonstrate the difficulty of gauging casualties for the 3rd Battalion.

The men who died in each AIF battalion on 1 May gave some idea of the whereabouts and strength of the Turkish attack these units faced. This was the most intense day of the third Turkish counterattack. The full range of munitions as well as thousands of troops were hurled at the Anzacs and the Marines from first to last light and into the night across Second Ridge. Some of the AIF battalions, like the 3rd and 5th, were still in bivouacs on or near the beach; however, others, like the 4th, 1st and 14th, were in the thick of the action. No other battalion suffered to the extent of the 4th on 1 May, with 30 of its 36 deaths resulting from men in D and A companies, which provided the Death Trap Valley parties, killed in action.

The numbers of men Killed in Action or Died of Wounds (KIA/DOW) from each of the AIF battalions at Anzac on 1 May were:

1st Battalion—14
2nd Battalion—1
3rd Battalion—none
4th Battalion—36
5th Battalion—1
6th Battalion—1
7th Battalion—2
8th Battalion—5
9th Battalion—none
10th Battalion—1
11th Battalion—none
12th Battalion—3
13th Battalion—5
14th Battalion—15

15th Battalion—12
16th Battalion—7[30]

Among the Marines, there were casualties in the Portsmouth Battalion's No. 9 and No. 10 platoons, under lieutenants Empson and Alcock, and in Sergeant Minter's replenishment party; however, the sources are by no means complete. According to a report published in *The London Gazette* on 13 September 1915, Empson and Alcock began their occupation of the battle outposts with 'with two platoons, numbering in all 60 men' early on Thursday, 29 April. By the time the isolated trench—as the position had become—was hurriedly evacuated on Sunday, 2 May, there were about 40 unwounded Marines left, according to Lieutenant-Colonel Owen and Lieutenant Alcock. Alcock described being in 'the trench, where I was with about 40 men, and a number of wounded'[31] when Lance Corporal Walter Parker, as part of Sergeant Minter's early morning replenishment party, unexpectedly arrived on Saturday morning. Owen, in a report detailing the actions of the 3rd Battalion during the period of the Landing, wrote about 'an isolated bit of trench [that] was held by a party of 40 RMLI and 14 Australians' on Sunday morning.[32]

The disparity in these two figures—60 and 40—indicates up to 20 Marines might have become casualties by the time of their retreat around dawn on Sunday. The best known and most significant was the death of the garrison's 18-year-old commanding officer, Lieutenant Richard Empson, early on 1 May during the beginning of the Turkish attack. However, despite up to 60 Marines occupying such an exposed position for three days and four nights, very few men were killed. Most of the Marines survived unscathed, weathering the third Turkish counter-attack and even the chaotic relief on Sunday morning, during which they were heavily attacked.

Current Marine records show that there were no deaths in the Portsmouth Battalion on 29 April. On 30 April two enlisted Marines from this unit—Private George Lowe and Private John Parker—were recorded as being killed in action. These men might have been in Empson's detachment.[33] On Saturday, 1 May, the three Portsmouth men killed in action were all officers, with only Empson being in the valley.[34] On Sunday, 2 May, only one Marine from the Portsmouth Battalion—Private Albert Smart—was killed in action.[35] Assuming all these men—Empson and three enlisted Marines—were killed defending the outposts, the total number of Empson's men to fall in battle was four. However, three of these deaths could well have occurred among the greater part of the rank and file of the Portsmouth Battalion, defending positions on Second Ridge from enemy artillery, rifle or machine-gun fire.

According to current research, no enlisted man in the Portsmouth Battalion was killed in action on Saturday, 1 May, when Sergeant Minter's party made their suicidal attempt to reach the men trapped below.[36] This means that no member of Minter's party was killed outright during their attempt to reach the Marines. British accounts often refer to all of his party, apart from Walter Parker, being killed or wounded. This error stems from reports compiled in relation to Parker's heroics. A member of Empson's detachment, veteran C Company Sergeant Major Fred Chapman, in verifying that only Parker reached the isolated trench, wrote that '. . . the water + ammunition carriers being killed, + wounded, trying to reach the trench'.[37] This has become the basis for English accounts of the Marines' experiences in the valley on 1 May. Douglas Jerrold in *The Royal Naval Division* concurred: 'all the water and ammunition carriers being killed or wounded.'[38] Blumberg in *Britain's Sea Soldiers* used virtually the same phrase.[39]

A total of 13 Marines from the battalions present at Anzac were killed in action during the Turkish counterattack on the first weekend in May.[40] Those units were the Chatham, Portsmouth, Deal and Nelson battalions. As well, a small number of Marines might have died from wounds received in this action over the next few weeks. How many of them were hit in Death Trap Valley is not known.

Amongst Minter's party was a Marine who was wounded immediately, and it was well documented that Lance Corporal Parker attended to his wounds before taking on the death trap. Despite making three attempts to reach his brothers-in-arms, Sergeant Minter's service record does not show him being wounded on 1 May.[41] Undoubtedly other members of Minter's party were hit; some may even have died from these wounds.

There were a number of wounded Marines in the isolated trench. Empson himself was hit, probably on 30 April, before he sent a message for assistance, including medical help to treat the wounded. Lieutenant Alan Alcock later reported a number in his force had been wounded. According to his service record, Walter Parker was wounded in action on 2 May, sustaining multiple gunshot wounds.[42] Bill Ward's testimony described three wounded Marines left behind by their compatriots; one died of his wounds, probably on 2 May. Between 30 April and 6 May, 22 Portsmouth Marines died of their wounds, most of them on hospital ships.[43] It would be reasonable to assume that some of these fatalities were a result of the fighting in Death Trap Valley. However, no casualties were evacuated from the Marines' outpost before 2 May and they wouldn't have reached the sanctuary of a ship before 3 May at the earliest. It followed that the Marines from the Portsmouth Battalion who died from their wounds on ships before 3 May were not present in the valley.

Further complicating this situation was Monash's assault of the evening of 2 May, in which the Portsmouth Battalion became involved on 3 May, suffering more casualties. Over the next few days Portsmouth Marines continued to die from their wounds; however, where they initially received those wounds cannot be determined.

As such it is impossible to accurately surmise how many Marines were wounded or died from wounds sustained in Death Trap Valley. At most, a dozen Marines from the Portsmouth Battalion lost their lives as a result of their occupation of the outposts in Death Trap Valley. Equally, perhaps only six Marines died. A similar number, between six and 12, might have been wounded. An indication of the difficulty in establishing these figures came in the contradictions about Alan Alcock being wounded at Anzac. His service record showed he was wounded on about 7 May, suffering a superficial wound to the knee which did involve hospital treatment in Cairo.[44] However, in *Britain's Sea Soldiers* Sir Herbert Blumberg listed Alcock as having been wounded on 1 May at Anzac.[45] Even though there was no list identifying either figure, it was likely that up to 20 Portsmouth Marines were killed, wounded or died of their wounds as a result of their occupation of the isolated trench. Further casualties were suffered by Sergeant Minter's replenishment party on Saturday morning.

Turkish casualties for their third series of attacks against the Anzacs and Marines were very heavy. Unfortunately, it is not known if there is a list of these men's names and their respective units. Even the total Turkish casualty figures were disputed. What was not in dispute was the enormous number of Mehmetciks who gave their lives or who were wounded on 1 and 2 May, spearheading the final Turkish assaults of the 'Battle of the Landing'. Thousands of them were killed and wounded. The official Turkish figure was 6000 dead compared to the Allies' estimate of 10,000 Turks killed in action.[46] Either figure is appalling—and testament to the courage, discipline and resolution of the Turkish troops to drive the invaders from their land. The machine guns of the Marines and the Anzacs in the firing line exacted a terrible toll.

A Turkish study, *Brothers in Arms: Turkish Officers in the Canakkale Campaign*, also concluded that the Turks suffered heavy casualties in their ranks on 1 May and during the early morning attack of 2 May at Anzac.[47] In the 13th, 15th and 33rd Turkish infantry regiments, 25 officers and 1885 other ranks became casualties as a result of their attacks that weekend.[48] Each regiment consisted of three battalions, so even though their losses were spread over up to nine battalions, they impacted significantly on the Turks. These figures included 960 officers and men from the 15th Regiment killed and wounded attacking the central part of the enemy line, encompassing the crucial action in Death Trap Valley on 1 and

2 May.[49] The commanding officer of the 27th Regiment, Lieutenant-Colonel Mehmet Sefik, whose regiment was heavily involved, later wrote:

> In the attacks made up to the evening of 1 May 1915, it was essential losses be endured in order to meet the Turkish resolve which was full of hope, and the doomed situation of the enemy at ARIBURNU invited the attack. But these attacks could only have been justified for gaining experience. It would not have been right to repeat under similar conditions this experience which was gained at the cost of heavy casualties.[50]

Unfortunately the Turks repeated these tactics of massed attacks against entrenched positions only two and a half weeks later on 19 May, with worse results.

Specific Turkish casualty figures for the action in Death Trap Valley over the course of the first weekend in May were hard to ascertain. Charles Bean in his April–June 1915 notebook described the repelling of the Turkish attack of 2 May in an abbreviated account—it was a notebook. He claimed that 'They [i.e. 3rd and 4th battalions] got some Turks cut off + as they tried to get back thro a whole night they were shooting them until abt 200 shot.'[51] In this final encounter Snowy Robson was credited with shooting between 13 and 20 Turks, while Les Lott in the same action recorded that the constant firing of rifles blistered the defenders' fingers. Michael Quigley commented on the large number of dead Turks sharing his trench in the valley on Sunday morning.

Bean's estimate of 200 Turkish casualties indicated the severity of the situation and the pressure the Turks applied once they breached the enemy line in the valley on Sunday morning. Movement by either side in exposed positions, such as those existing in Death Trap Valley on 1 and 2 May, resulted in heavy casualties. The defensive advantages of machine guns, volleys of rifle fire, sniping and sustained shrapnel bursts allowed both sides to inflict numerous casualties on enemy troops, whether they were attacking or reinforcing. The Turks undoubtedly suffered the most casualties, hundreds of them being killed and wounded in Death Trap Valley alone.

In summary, the 4th Battalion and, in particular, the two parties sent to support the Marines on 1 May, experienced significant casualties. These two parties totalled 106 men—about 80 or more of them were killed and wounded by the time they left the valley late on Sunday morning. Both platoons were nearly wiped out. By comparison, the two platoons from the Portsmouth Battalion and the 3rd Battalion's relief party emerged relatively unscathed, with fewer men being killed and wounded in each of them, although the Marines did suffer more casualties than the 3rd Battalion.

In letter published in *The Illawarra Mercury*, Sister Muriel Wakeford wrote an emotional epitaph for the men killed during the period of the Landing:

> I can quite imagine what a sad Australia it will be when the casualty lists come out and the roll of honour will be a very long one. People will begin to realise this is war in earnest. The poor men in the trenches living for a week at a time without sleep or a wash, and very little food and eventually getting these terrific wounds, makes one wonder if it is worth the cost. The Australians are spoken of highly in every quarter. They are called the 'Die Hard Australians' and I tell you they are too. There should not be one person in Australia, not doing his or her part to save the burden of these men, for no one knows except those who see it how hard it is.[52]

9 Recognition

Thanks for the congratulations, but it was more luck than anything else, and it happened to come through an English General. But always in war the best things done are never seen. So you see it is all luck and as to whether or not the big ones take a fancy or not.

James Heane, in a letter dated 28 July 1915 to his brother Ted[1]

The awarding of medals for bravery under fire was a contentious issue; contentious because of the men who did not receive recognition for their courage in that most extreme condition of human behaviour—battle.

James Heane acknowledged as much in his letter to his brother Ted. Lieutenant Lawrence Street, 3rd Battalion, writing about the period of the Landing, was also philosophical, praising the human spirit in adversity:

> The men stuck at it with a courage that I think could not have been excelled by any troops. One saw every hour deeds of bravery such as I hardly thought possible and it opened my eyes as to the possibilities of the human character.[2]

Men who were awarded medals for gallant actions in battle generally deserved them. However, due to a variety of circumstances, other examples of bravery went unrewarded, such as the acts of heroism Lawrence Street noticed regularly. The death or wounding of officers who would have otherwise reported such acts was a key reason. As well, a lack of records, or records being lost, and overworked, inexperienced staff contributed to the lack of recognition for some. As Heane said in his letter, just having a witness to gallantry was part of the recognition lottery. Charles Bean alluded to this controversy in a letter to Major John Treloar, the director of the Australian War Memorial, on 28 February 1928, regarding titles and medals being included on the Honour Roll at the War Memorial:

> . . . the War Memorial Committee was against the inclusion of ranks, I feel that the same applies to decorations, which were sometimes given to a degree which aroused comment and bitterness, to staff officers, and which, if generally well earned, were certainly not received by a proportion of those who deserved them. I strongly feel this: that the visitor, not knowing the conditions of the front, will stand before these lists and, seeing the DSO's and MM's, will say to himself 'Ah, those are brave men' (or, perhaps, 'the bravest')—a conclusion which is not true, how far from true only those who were actually through heavy fighting can realize.[3]

Bean himself was recommended for a Military Cross for his courage in helping to evacuate a wounded man under fire during the 2nd Brigade's valiant but futile attempt to capture Krithia at Cape Helles on 8 May 1915. As an honorary captain, Bean was ineligible for the award. He was Mentioned In Despatches for this brave act. Arthur Bazley later expanded on Bean's actions that night at Cape Helles:

> Throughout the dreadful night of 8th May Bean wandered backwards and forwards over the battlefield, carrying tins of water and succouring wounded officers and men despite the steady machine-gun fire and the protests of some who recognised him and told him that this was not his job.[4]

Five gallantry medals—a sixth was proposed—were awarded to Marines and Anzacs for their heroics in Death Trap Valley over 1 and 2 May 1915. Three went to Royal Marines of the Portsmouth Battalion and two went to members of the 4th Battalion. No member of the 3rd Battalion was awarded a medal. Other participants from these units might have deserved medals, but not everybody could receive such recognition.

Many of these men were reported for their bravery in reports written by senior officers in each of these battalions. These early reports covered the period of the Landing, from 25 April to 5 May 1915. They were forwarded to General Sir Ian Hamilton, the general commanding the Mediterranean Expeditionary Force, who approved the awards, which were then published in *The London Gazette*. These men were then said to have been Mentioned In Despatches (MID) or gazetted. As a rule, one had to be Mentioned In Despatches as a precursor to being awarded a medal, although as the war progressed this protocol changed. To be MID was in itself an acknowledgment of bravery in action. Post-war, veterans wore their multi-leaved oak leaf, signifying the award, on the riband of their Victory Medal.[5] From these initial reports, recommendations for higher honours from senior officers were submitted, with some men receiving medals. King George V signed off on medal winners, his approval being largely ceremonial.

~

One of the medals given as a result of the fighting in Death Trap Valley over the first weekend in May was the Victoria Cross (VC), the highest honour for bravery awarded to soldiers of the British Empire. It is a small bronze cross with the inscription 'For Valour' on it. Apparently, after December 1914, the bronze used to manufacture the medals came from antique Chinese-made guns, not from, as legend would have it, Russian cannon captured during the Crimean War.[6] The recipient of the Victoria Cross was Lance Corporal Walter Parker. While this was the first Victoria Cross given at Anzac, it was the last to be gazetted, not being formalised until Friday, 22 June 1917.[7]

The citation for Walter Parker's Victoria Cross was published on that date in *The London Gazette*, the official mouthpiece of the British government during the war. It read:

> The King has been graciously pleased to approve of the award of the Victoria Cross to the undermentioned:—
>
> Lce.-Corpl. Walter Parker, R.M.L.I., No. Po/S. 229, Royal Naval Division.
>
> In recognition of his most conspicuous bravery and devotion to duty in the course of the Dardanelles operations.
>
> On the night of 30th April/1st May, 1915, a message asking for ammunition, water and medical stores was received from an isolated fire trench at Gaba Tepe.
>
> A party of Non-commissioned Officers and men were detailed to carry water and ammunition, and, in response to a call for a volunteer from among the stretcher bearers, Parker at once came forward; he had during the previous three days displayed conspicuous bravery and energy under fire whilst in charge of the Battalion stretcher bearers.
>
> Several men had already been killed in a previous attempt to bring assistance to the men holding the fire trench. To reach this trench it was necessary to traverse an area least four hundred yards wide, which was completely exposed and swept by rifle fire. It was already daylight when the party emerged from shelter and at once one of the men was wounded: Parker organised a stretcher party and then going on alone succeeded in

reaching the fire trench, all the water and ammunition carriers being either killed or wounded.

After his arrival he rendered assistance to the wounded in the trench, displaying extreme courage and remaining cool and collected in very trying circumstances. The trench had finally to be evacuated and Parker helped to remove and attend the wounded, although he himself was seriously wounded during this operation.

Parker's heroism was noted from the first; however, these early reports were lost. Unfortunately, the commanding officer of the Portsmouth Battalion, Lieutenant-Colonel Frank Luard, wounded at Anzac, was killed in action on 13 July 1915 at Cape Helles. The battalion adjutant, sergeant major and Parker's own C Company commanding officer, Captain Syson, were wounded as well. This meant their new reports, acknowledging Parker's inordinate devotion to duty and courage under fire, weren't collated until late 1916.[8] An important criterion for the award of the Victoria Cross to Parker was his 'sole and devoted efforts' to bring assistance to Empson's beleaguered garrison. In August 1916 the Royal Marine Adjutant General was quite specific in ascertaining how many of Minter's party made it to the isolated trench. The fact that Parker was the only one made his actions worthy of consideration for the Victoria Cross.[9] A final scrutiny by the War Office meant that it wasn't until 24 May 1917 that the Army Council granted its final approval. Parker was a civilian by the time King George V awarded him with the Victoria Cross at Buckingham Palace at 10.30 a.m. on 21 July 1917. He was invalided out of the Marines because of the lingering effects of his wounds and illness.[10]

In the preface of the revised second edition of the *Official History of Australia in the War of 1914–18, Volume 1, The Story of Anzac*, Charles Bean wrote a footnote acknowledging Parker's bravery:

For a very gallant action in carrying succour to this trench at dawn on May 1, L/Cpl. W.R. Parker (of Stapleford, Notts, Eng.), a stretcher-bearer of the R.M.L.I. was awarded the Victoria Cross. Parker stayed in the trench and, though wounded, helped eventually to remove the wounded from it. This was the first Victoria Cross awarded for action at Anzac.[11]

Many years later, in *Gallipoli Mission*, Bean qualified his acknowledgment of Parker's award, noting:

It [i.e. 'first Victoria Cross to be won at Anzac'] was won by a British marine, Lance-Corporal W.R. Parker. Others were deserved, as the reader

> will see at *Vol. 1, pp. 540–2, and Preface to 2nd Edition, pp. xix–xxii*; but that battle left the inexperienced staffs far too busy, with the task of rebuilding their units and carrying on, to attend to recommendations for awards; also witnesses were dead or in hospital, and records almost non-existent.[12]

Bean was referring to the 3rd Battalion.

There are a number of furphies about the story of Parker's Victoria Cross that have gained currency, although only one of them originated from his medal citation published in *The London Gazette*. One common one is that Parker was wounded on 1 May on the way down to the outposts, after setting out in daylight on his own. However, his service record clearly shows under 'Date wounded' '2nd May 1915'.[13] Also, the officer commanding the Marine detachment by the time Parker arrived, Lieutenant Alcock, stated in his testimony for Parker's Victoria Cross that he believed it was during the Marines' retreat on 2 May that Parker was wounded. Surgeon Basil Playne of the Portsmouth Battalion's medical staff, and Parker's commanding officer, concurred in his reply to an official enquiry concerning Parker's reported heroics:

> He went in full daylight the morning of Saturday 1st May (as far as I can remember) and stayed in the trench treating the wounded until the trench was evacuated on Sunday 2nd May when he helped bring in all the wounded, being himself wounded in the retreat.[14]

Parker might have been injured when he landed in a 'pond' after charging downhill through the death trap to the outposts below on 1 May. This would explain the repeated references in secondary sources to Parker being wounded as he made his way downhill.

Another report, written by Lieutenant-Colonel F.R. Godfrey, one of the commanding officers of the Portsmouth Battalion after Luard's death, stated unequivocally that Parker 'was wounded during the evacuation' of the isolated trench on 2 May. This report was a 'Recommendation for Meritorious Service', which probably assisted the case for Parker being considered for a Victoria Cross.[15] Parker's VC citation confirmed that the gallant stretcher-bearer was seriously wounded during the Marines' withdrawal from the valley on Sunday, not on Saturday, as he gambled with the death trap to reach his comrades.

Another furphy is that Parker carried ammunition to the Marines. The evidence of Company Sergeant Major Fred Chapman, who was the senior NCO in Empson's party in the outposts, clearly showed otherwise:

> Lance Corporal W.R.Parker was entirely alone, + the only one to reach the trench, the water carriers + ammunition carriers being killed, + wounded, trying to reach the trench.[16]

Parker was detailed to carry *only* medical stores. The adjutant general of the Royal Marines wrote in a report in August 1916, 'I have personally interviewed Lieut. A. Alcock D.S.C. R.M.L.I., who was in command of the trench to which Lce Corpl. Parker made his way with *medical stores* [emphasis added] after Lieut. Empson had been killed.'[17] The C Company commanding officer, Captain Syson, also reported that Parker had promptly volunteered 'to go with *medical stores*' [emphasis added] when he was organising Sergeant Minter's replenishment party.[18] Both of these reports were used to prepare the case for Parker's Victoria Cross. The citation for his medal mentioned in part: 'Parker . . . going on alone succeeded in reaching the fire trench, all the water and ammunition carriers being either killed or wounded.'

The last statement that 'all the water and ammunition carriers being either killed or wounded' is actually false. Parker's VC reports were responsible for this mistake, British historians taking their cue from them. Most conspicuous among these reports was Company Sergeant Major Fred Chapman's submission that all the ammunition and water carriers were killed or wounded.

Current Marine research indicates that no member of the replenishment party was killed in action trying to reach the Marines and, as noted earlier, no enlisted man of the Portsmouth Battalion was killed outright on 1 May 1915. A number of the detachment were wounded and some might have died of their wounds. The leader of the replenishment party, Sergeant Marcus Minter, later claimed to have tried to reach Alcock's position three times. His service record showed he wasn't hit on 1 May.

The final furphy was that Parker helped all the wounded Marines to safety during the retreat on Sunday morning. Undoubtedly, Parker was helping wounded Marines to the firing line and relative safety during the Marines' chaotic withdrawal. He was wounded himself during this time. What is in grave doubt is the assertion that he helped *all* the wounded Marines out of the valley. Private Bill Ward's account of his occupation of the isolated trench after taking the Marines' place made the following observation: 'There were many dead lying in the trench, also a few wounded . . . There were three wounded Marines in the trench, so we set to work to make them comfortable and feed them.'[19] Ward and his mates, Privates Bill Beal and Bill Hatton, stayed with the wounded Marines for the next couple of days until a sap was dug to make the removal of the wounded men more feasible. Parker did not assist *all* the wounded Marines to safety and, judging by Bill Ward's account, it was impossible for him to have done so.

~

One of the other Marines to be awarded a gallantry medal was Lieutenant Alan Alcock. After initially being Mentioned In Despatches, he received the Distinguished Service Cross (DSC), which was announced in *The London Gazette* on 13 September 1915. It read:

> The King has further been graciously pleased to give orders for the award of the Distinguished Service Cross to the following officers:—
>
> Acting Lieutenant Alan Bennis Fennel Alcock, R.M.L.I., Portsmouth Battalion.
>
> For gallantry and good service near Gaba Tepe, between the 28th April and 1st May, 1915. Accompanied by Lieutenant Empson, of the same regiment, with two platoons, numbering in all 60 men, he defended an isolated trench against overwhelming odds. Lieutenant Empson was wounded early in the day on April 30th, and was killed on 1 May, and Lieutenant Alcock was finally compelled to withdraw, after having held this ground for four nights and three days. During this time no food or water could be conveyed to the trench, and at one time ammunition was reduced to about 15 rounds per man.

Obviously the citation was missing crucial details, such as the significant support provided by the Australian troops and their sacrifice to save Alcock's men. Food, water and ammunition were conveyed to the trench by the parties from the 4th and 3rd battalions on 1 and 2 May.

The other Marine medal recipient was Private Frank Hunt, who was awarded the Distinguished Service Medal (DSM) for his bravery and resource under fire in risking passage of the death trap to deliver Empson's message for help on Friday night, 30 April. Hunt then volunteered to return, acting as a guide, for Marcus Minter's replenishment party just before dawn on Saturday, 1 May. Like the majority of the party, he did not reach the isolated trench; only Walter Parker did. Hunt's award was announced in *The London Gazette* on 6 September 1916.

Another Marine to be Mentioned In Despatches was Lieutenant Richard Empson, who would have received the Military Cross if he'd survived Death Trap Valley. His commendation was announced in *The London Gazette* on 5 November 1915. An extract from the despatches of the GOC (General Officer Commanding) the Royal Naval Division, dated 16 June 1915, read:

> Acting Lieutenant Empson behaved with the greatest gallantry & devotion to duty in holding an advanced & isolated trench at Gaba Tepe, Gallipoli Peninsula, from 2 am 29/4/15 until killed at dawn 1/5/15. Had he lived he would have received the Military Cross. He was wounded 30/4/15 but continued duty until he was killed.

The bravery of other Marines in the action was acknowledged by being Mentioned In Despatches. One such recipient was Sergeant Marcus Minter,[20] who was in charge of the replenishment party from the Portsmouth Battalion that attempted passage of the death trap around dawn on 1 May. Of the 11 Marines in the detachment, only Parker made it. Despite repeated attempts to reach his chums in the isolated trench, Minter failed to successfully breach the Turkish fire.

~

The Distinguished Service Order (DSO) was awarded to Major James Heane, the commanding officer of D Company, 4th Battalion. The DSO was second only to the Victoria Cross as an acknowledgment of displaying courage in action by an officer, although early in the war it was sometimes awarded to staff officers who weren't in the firing line. Not so in Cast Iron Jimmy's case. His DSO was announced in *The London Gazette* of 1 June 1915. The citation read:

> On 1st May, 1915, during the operations near Kaba Tepe [Gaba Tepe], for displaying conspicuous gallantry in leading his Company to the support of a small force which, in an isolated trench, was without means of reinforcement, replenishment, or retreat. He obtained his object at a heavy sacrifice.

The full text of Heane's longer recommendation is virtually identical to the memorandum and letter of commendation and thanks Lieutenant-Colonel Luard and Brigadier-General Trotman sent to ANZAC headquarters, reproduced on pages 184–5. These documents praised Heane's leadership and his men's courage during the difficult and dangerous rescue operation of Empson's detachment they undertook on 1 May, despite a terrible toll of casualties. Trotman and Luard recommended Heane for his decoration.[21]

In one of his notebooks Charles Bean wrote:

> Heane of 4th Bn was in (nearest Coy) of 4th Bn + as the R.M.L.I. authorities dealt with him they—to his gt surprise—recommended him for a D.S.O. for this work—wh he got.[22]

Bean was hardly being laudatory, attributing Heane's medal to his fortunate proximity to the RMLI commanding officers.

Heane's 'gt surprise' was more a product of the almost universal humility of ANZAC medal winners. James Heane put his medal into perspective when he wrote to his brother Ted in a letter dated 28 July 1915:

> Thanks for the congratulations, but it was more luck than anything else, and it happened to come through an English General. But always in war the best things done are never seen. So you see it is all luck and as to whether or not the big ones take a fancy or not.[23]

Cast Iron Jimmy Heane had just seen one of his platoons, No. 15, virtually destroyed while saving the Marines in Death Trap Valley. Heane didn't just deal with the Royal Marine authorities; he and his men fought hard and died all day and all night on Saturday and into Sunday to save the Marines and secure the valley, thereby denying it to the Turks. In a letter to his mother written in May, which was published in one of the local newspapers, *The Dubbo Liberal and Macquarie Advocate*, on Friday, 9 July 1915, Heane praised the men of his company:

> We got rather a hot time for some days after we landed . . . and our boys are as happy as larks, and I would never wish—nor would any other officer wish—to lead a better lot of men. They are brave and would follow anywhere. I thank God I have not been behind them. Although I can say it now, I was deadly afraid I should be. It has been said that every man who went into his first battle was afraid, but I went into it without any feelings, and it has been the same ever since. And I have to think nearly all the men were the same way, and there is no doubt our boys have made a great name for themselves.

Heane and his men were also officially acknowledged in the Summary of Operations of the 1st Australian Division for May:

> To note—gallantry of 'D' Coy. 4th Bn. under Major Heane, in extricating a platoon of Portsmouth Bn. on 1st inst.[24]

In early June 1915, after the announcement of his award, Heane was the talk of Dubbo. One of the local newspapers reported that: 'Mrs Heane mother of Major Heane, was the subject of numerous congratulatory messages when it was learnt that her son was included in the roll of honour.'[25] It was an unfortunate choice of words by the journalist, the roll of honour being a record of the fallen, not medal winners.

On 23 July *The Dubbo Liberal and Macquarie Advocate* published an article by the special correspondent of *The Argus,* Charles Patrick Smith, detailing how James Heane earned his DSO. Smith, another journalist Bean trumped in the vote for the coveted Official War Correspondent's position, languished on Lemnos until given a month-long window by General Sir Ian Hamilton to report from Anzac itself. Finally, after feeding on second- and thirdhand accounts, Smith and Peter Schuler were able to experience Gallipoli firsthand from 20 July to 20 August. During this time they were able to interview men from the firing line to the beach in regard to the previous three months. Smith's article was remarkable for its jingoistic embellishment. He wasn't going to let the facts get in the way. Perhaps it was just as well that Bean triumphed in the 'official correspondent' stakes. This is what Smith wrote:

> **MAJOR J. HEANE, D.S.O.**
> **How He Won Imperishable Fame**
> The special correspondent of '*The Argus*' tells how the peerless Major Heane, of Dubbo, won his D.S.O., at Gaba Tepe. Now that the complete story of the Australians' heroic attack on Gaba Tepe (he writes) is being pieced together, the various little incidents, tragedies and personal touches, which go to make a great achievement, are being thrown into bold relief for the first time. In the fierce glare of battle these phases are overshadowed by more brilliant combinations of effects, but they are interesting enough when time is available to sort out the tangle and pick the gems from the debris. For instance what could be more human than the message of appreciation communicated to Major Jam. Heane, commander of D Company of the 4th (N.S.W.) Infantry Battalion, by Brigadier-General Trotman, who was in charge of the Royal Naval Brigade. It read as follows:—
>
> 'Officers and men have been greatly moved by your splendid act of Imperial comradeship, and desire that an expression of their deep gratitude should be conveyed to the 4th (Australian) Battalion.'
>
> The story is simple enough, but it indicates in some measure the splendid spirit of the Commonwealth troops. In the early fighting a platoon of the Portsmouth Battalion of Royal Marines Light Infantry was temporarily attached to another unit, but in the thick of the struggle found itself in an isolated trench, without means of reinforcement, or retreat. The position was exposed to fire from three sides, and on the fourth a body of Turks lay waiting for the men to expose themselves. Commander Empson was at the

head of the little party, and succeeded in keeping the enemy off for some hours, but he was killed, and the situation then became desperate in the extreme, every new assault being repulsed with increasing difficulty. The news of the fearful adventure came along to the 4th Australian Infantry Battalion. Major Heane was the first to hear the story, but it was quickly passed from mouth to mouth in the line, and the same determination seems to have entered every mind, because when that gallant officer intimated that he intended going to the rescue of the embarrassed force with such soldiers as dared to follow him, every man in D Company jumped forward.

An Australian Charge.

The rush that followed could not be stayed by Turkish guns. A khaki line of 250 yelling Australians, with set faces and bayonets fixed, charged right into the danger zone. They caught the waiting line of Turks quite unprepared, and smashed down that side of the square almost in their stride, leaving not a single man unwounded. On the wave rushed to the left. For a moment the enemy held its ground, and poured a hail of bullets on the charging furies that were coming to overwhelm them—but only for a moment. Then followed a disorderly scuttle for safety that almost resolved itself into a panic, and crying out 'The Australians are coming!' the Turks slipped away from their position, and raced for the next line of trenches, where greatly superior numbers guaranteed them some measure of temporary relief from the bayonets and bullets which were always spurring them to greater efforts from behind.

Attention was subsequently directed to other positions, which the Portsmouth men, now with renewed hope, kept under constant fire. In the end the Turks were beaten off, and the platoon, with sadly diminished strength, made its way back from impending total destruction to the main firing line, the Australians covering their retirement from the trenches which the enemy had obligingly provided for them. As they passed their rescuers the Marine Infantry cheered, and in the cheers there was a note of genuine sincerity. Major Heane congratulated his men on the work they had done in the face of tremendous difficulties, and was not disposed to accept any of the credit for himself. He was paid a pretty compliment, however, a few days later, when the whole of the official correspondence relating to the incident was published in 'divisional orders'.

What a load of bellicose propaganda! Just who did Smith talk to when framing his story? What sort of impression of the war was Smith giving the readers in

Australia? The people of Dubbo would have been incredulous, amazed by Heane's feats. By the time Smith wrote the article, the Anzacs had been bogged down for months in the quagmire that constituted Anzac. The Australian public were beginning to understand that the position was a stalemate. Clearly the Turks were largely in control of the situation, although frustrated by the stubborn resistance of the enemy. The awful battles of August, in an attempt to break out, were just around the corner. Smith rightly praised Heane and his men for their courage, but his artistic licence concerning the actual events belied the grim reality of the situation, Death Trap Valley on 1 and 2 May being a microcosm of the greater Gallipoli morass. At the end of the battle the outposts were abandoned; ultimately the Allied positions on the peninsula were also abandoned.

~

The other 4th Battalion recipient of a bravery award for his heroics in Death Trap Valley on 1 and 2 May 1915 was Ernest 'Snowy' Robson, who received the Distinguished Conduct Medal (DCM). The DCM, the second highest award for bravery after the Victoria Cross that a member of the other ranks could receive, was awarded for acts of courage in action. In Snowy's words, in December 1916:

> Being a discharged member of the AIF serving in the 4th Battn. during the operation at Gallipoli during the engagements at Death Trap Valley I was awarded the D.C.M. for services rendered.[26]

The medal was announced in *The London Gazette* on 3 June 1915, two days after James Heane's award. Robson's citation read:

> On 1st May, 1915, during the operations near Kaba Tepe, for distinguished conduct in the command of a platoon, guiding and controlling the men after the Officer Commanding the platoon had been wounded. Although in an exposed position, he personally carried up ammunition and freely exposed himself.

His longer recommendation read:

> In connection with the assistance rendered to the battalion of the Royal Marine Brigade by 'D' Company, 4th Battalion, Robson went ahead of the reinforcing party, returned, showed the way, and as officer commanding reinforcing platoon was wounded, he acted as guide and subsequently controlled all men in the vicinity. His position was one of open exposure

> but he personally carried ammunition to the Marines, whose supply was exhausted, and kept up a steady and very effective fire on the enemy, killing at least 20. All accounts agree that this soldier's conduct largely saved the situation on the 1st May, and as only 5 men of the platoon were uninjured the nature of the peril was obvious. [Reported by Lieut.-Colonel Bennett, Commanding 4th Battalion.][27]

Although both the citation and the recommendation for higher honours only mentioned 1 May, it was clear that Snowy's feats encompassed the morning of 2 May as well.

In *Anzac Memorial*, a publication of the Returned Soldiers Association to commemorate the first anniversary of the Landing, Snowy was typically brief:

> I got the D.C.M. for carrying water and ammunition under heavy fire, taking charge of 50 men and shooting 13 Turks with a rifle.[28]

In his report Lieutenant-Colonel Bennett claimed Snowy shot 20 Turks.

Snowy was invalided home after suffering a gunshot wound in the right arm on 6 June at Gallipoli; it caused paralysis of the median nerve. He arrived home on the *Hororata,* berthing in Sydney on Monday, 30 August 1915. Snowy was big news whether he liked it or not. He had survived the Landing and been decorated for his bravery in action. Snowy knew the fortunes of war had favoured him. He'd been witness to, participated in and survived the vagaries of war—heroic, mundane and tragic. He'd lived where others had died, surviving many close shaves with death.

The following extracts from *The Sun* and *The Sydney Morning Herald* highlighted the humility of ANZAC medal winners, alluded to earlier. Almost without exception these men played down their role and praised others. Snowy Robson was the epitome of this.

In *The Sun* it was reported that:

> Every other soldier on board the *Hororata* knew him as Snowy, and he appeared to be highly popular. He was modest also, and the story of his deed, which won him his distinction was dragged out of him gradually.[29]

The Sydney Morning Herald ran the following story on Tuesday, 31 August 1915:

> **OUR FIRST D.C.M.**
>
> The man who has done things is, as a rule, the hardest man to get the story of his deeds from, and Corporal E.J. Robson, of Tamworth, D

Company, 4th Battalion, who has returned wearing the coveted Distinguished Conduct Medal ribbon, is no exception to the rule. He is only 20 years of age, and is modesty personified. When asked to tell the tale of how he won the decoration he remarked—'There are heaps of men here can tell you more thrilling stories. They have done great things.' 'Don't you believe it,' said another wounded man by him, 'he's all right and besides that he's been wounded five times.'

The corporal, thus prompted, said that he landed on that Sunday night in April, which has done more to advertise Australia than all the posters in the United Kingdom. 'I got through the landing O.K.,' he remarked, 'and kept at the game some weeks. On and off I did get wounded as you might say. One bullet got me in the back, another in the hand, a third in the body, a fourth in the arm, and then I was blown up by shells exploding close to me twice running. The D.C.M.? Oh, I got that, according to the official report, on the sixth day after we landed. The Royal Marine Light Infantry were being driven back by the Turks, and it was necessary that they be supplied with ammunition and water, and so I took it on. The despatch stated that I was to be decorated for conveying ammunition and water to the troops under heavy fire, and for taking charge of 50 men of the 4th Battalion and inflicting heavy losses on the Turks. I've got the ribbon but have not received the medal yet. That'll come later on, I suppose.'

Snow's reference to his medal is almost an afterthought. He certainly didn't tell the whole story. His reticence about his valour continued in his home town of Uralla and also nearby Tamworth; both towns wanted to honour him. Snowy's family had recently moved to Tamworth, where 3000 people turned out at Ison's open-air picture show on Monday, 6 September 1915, to welcome Snowy. There were speeches by the mayor, local clergy and a local politician. The town band played patriotic songs and two local singers performed. The war was in its infancy and the horror of France and Flanders was yet to come. The Australian public clamoured for news of heroic deeds; to have a hero such as Snowy among them was a significant moment in their lives and in the history of the district. The mayor, Alderman W. Green, according to *The Tamworth Daily Observer*, spoke along these lines:

With regard to Corporal Robson they were all acquainted with the remarkable deed of heroism which had gained for him great distinction. He had won on the battlefield the D.C.M. (Applause.) They all recognised that

> every man who was fighting on the blood-stained peninsula was a hero. When a man distinguished himself amongst such a band of heroes then indeed he must be a kind of super-hero. Corporal Robson had seen distinguished services on the battlefield, and they were all proud of the fact that he belonged to this part of the country. (Applause.) . . . His record, however, would stand for ever. It would be remembered for all time how Corporal Robson won the D.C.M. (Applause.)[30]

In reply Snowy gave a speech, beginning with an apology. He was supposed to have fronted the same crowd some days earlier, but might have got cold feet; he was suffering from neurasthenia:

> I cannot express my thanks for this magnificent reception. I must apologise for not turning up the other night. Of course, being a stranger to the town, I did not expect the reception. I am very sorry I disappointed you. No matter where I may be I will always remember your reception tonight. Ladies and gentlemen I have been blown up with shells two or three times, and this does not improve one's nerves.[31]

In his speech he concentrated on the Landing and Turkish tactics. His only reference to his medal was to say, 'He thought that they had all heard the description of Death-trap valley and how he won the D.C.M.'[32]

~

Charles Bean felt that members of the 3rd Battalion should also have received gallantry awards for their work during the relief in Death Trap Valley on 2 May. His *Gallipoli Mission* footnote, in regard to Walter Parker's Victoria Cross, stated this unequivocally. Lieutenant-Colonel Owen, the 3rd Battalion's commanding officer, agreed. In his report of 14 May 1915, he singled out Privates Ward, Beal and Hatton:

> I recommended them for some recognition of their good work. But I fear credit did not always go where it was due as no reward came to these brave men of the 3rd Battalion.[33]

At a recruitment rally in Wollongong on 4 December 1915, Lieutenant-Colonel Owen gave a garbled version of the heroism of members of lieutenants Meager and McLeod's relief party in Death Trap Valley on 2 May 1915. Owen was Wollongong born and bred, and after suffering from neurasthenia in early July at Gallipoli, was ruled unfit for active service and transferred to home service.[34] In the course of his address, 54-year-old Owen revealed he had recommended the VC and two DCMs for three members of the relief who had stayed, fighting the Turks and caring for wounded men for a considerable time and that 'the reward had not yet been granted, but he hoped they would'.[35] Surely these men were Ward, Beal and Hatton. And yet there is no record of this report in the file of 70 unsuccessful official Victoria Cross recommendations from World War I held by the Australian War Memorial. In fact, there are no 3rd Battalion members on the list at all.[36]

Private Richard Humberstone of the 3rd Battalion was awarded a DCM on 1 June 1915.[37] Initially he was the recipient of one of Hamilton's Special Mentions, which on further investigation led to the DCM. His citation read:

> On 25th April, 1915, and subsequently during operations near Kaba Tepe, for conspicuous coolness and bravery in volunteering on many occasions for dangerous missions, and for judgement in carrying them out.[38]

This was one of the first DCMs to be given for service at Anzac. Bean's earlier comments in regard to the problems confronting the awarding of medals sounded almost hollow in the light of Owen's explanation and Humberstone's decoration. After all, lieutenants Meager and McLeod were still present at Anzac and therefore were still available to provide evidence. Undoubtedly, most of the staff of the AIF battalions were inexperienced and pressed for time during these early days, but perhaps it was simply a case of Owen's interpretation of the course of events that 'credit did not always go where it was due'.[39]

~

A number of men in the 4th and 3rd battalions were Mentioned In Despatches—also known as Special Mentions—which were announced for the period of the Landing, 25 April to 5 May 1915.

Lieutenant Fred Fanning was one. In a report written by Major David Storey, temporarily in command of the 4th Battalion, covering the period from 26 April to 1 May 1915, Storey noted:

> 2nd Lieut. F. Fanning for his coolness and judgement in leading his Platoon, directing operations in a very difficult situation.[40]

The 'very difficult situation' was his platoon's unenviable task of saving Empson's Marines in the hellish conditions that prevailed in Death Trap Valley on 1 and

2 May 1915. This was reported to Storey by Major Heane, Fanning's D Company commander, who witnessed Fanning at close hand.

The wording on the promulgation of these Special Mentions was:

> 153 COMPLIMENTARY. The Army Corps Commander has very much pleasure in publishing the name of the Junior Regimental Officers, Warrant Officers, N.C.O.'s and men, in the attached supplement, which have been brought to his notice for having performed various acts of conspicuous gallantry or valuable service during the period from 25th April to 5th May, 1915. We cordially thank them for the good work they have performed, which more than ever testifies to their devotion to duty towards King and Country. His only regret is that they cannot be all rewarded.
> Lieut. F. Fanning.
> 4th Battalion.[41]

The announcement was made by the Base Records Office AIEF on 29 November 1915 and was sent to, in Fanning's case, his father, Lieutenant-Colonel F.G. Fanning, 'Coomeragee', Casino NSW.

The king's 'regret' was an acknowledgment of the other acts of bravery that went unrewarded for any number of reasons, particularly during the Landing.

In the 3rd Battalion, privates Bill Hatton, Bill Ward and Bill Beal received Special Mentions for their efforts as part of the relief party on 2 May in Death Trap Valley. Lieutenants Meager and McLeod wrote the following report:

> These three men of D. Co. 3rd Bn. who formed part of the section which reinforced the R.M.L.I. a few minutes prior to the trench being evacuated most pluckily remained behind in the trench succouring four wounded men. They collected them from various parts of the trench into the lower end, which they deepened for safety. No assistance could be rendered them all day. Constant messages were sent for stretcher-bearers during the ensuing night but owing to tactical reasons it could not be rendered. They remained in this precarious situation until nightfall on Monday, 3rd May. One had meanwhile succumbed to his injuries. The conduct of the men was most creditable.[42]

It was on the basis of this report, as well as other accounts, that Charles Bean and Lieutenant-Colonel Owen thought Ward, Beal and Hatton deserved medals.

Lieutenants Meager and McLeod were also the recipients of Special Mentions. The report written by Lieutenant-Colonel Robert Owen, Commanding Officer, 3rd Battalion stated:

> Did fine work in going to the assistance of the R.M.L.I. Have since been promoted 2/Lieutenants.[43]

This was a rather abbreviated version of what Meager and McLeod and their men did during the relief of 2 May 1915. Their contribution was significant in relieving the Marines and helping to repel the final Turkish attack, thereby securing the battle outposts. It was only later, on 5 May, that the outposts were relinquished by the 3rd Battalion.

Owen wrote another report in which he put the whole Death Trap Valley episode into perspective. His comments were in regard to the heroics of Bill Ward, Bill Beal and Bill Hatton; however, they applied equally to the actions of the Marines under Empson, Alcock and Minter, the two parties from the 4th Battalion under Heane and Robson, and the other members of Meager and McLeod's detachment:

> This is only one of the memorable, gallant deeds of the old 1st Brigade a small thing in lists but the fighting was made up of small affairs by small parties and the aggregate was a good defence with the most difficult conditions in which the Junior Officers + the N.C.O. + men proved themselves and made the name ANZAC immortal.[44]

The Turks were a courageous enemy, with their own heroes to laud from the Battle of Death Trap Valley. The records of their 'memorable, gallant deeds' and awards for this action are probably buried in a Turkish archive, or are available in Ottoman Arabic and haven't been translated. Tim Travers, a prominent Gallipoli historian, set out the difficulties he encountered researching Turkish sources:

> Almost all of the papers in the ATASE [General Staff Archives, Ankara,Turkey] are in Ottoman Arabic. Some papers are in German, a very few in English or French, and a considerable number in modern Turkish, but the vast majority are in Arabic. This requires either dedication in learning the language or a translator. If one succeeds in overcoming these two hurdles, other difficulties emerge. There are no personal diaries of key individuals, because this was not an Ottoman tradition. And there

are no war diaries as such, but there are *jerredesi,* or war reports, often small pieces of paper stuck onto larger sheets, that represent the actions of individuals or units at certain times. Finally no index to the Gallipoli/Canakkale campaign exists as yet.[45]

While the names of the Turkish heroes haven't been revealed, the feats of the regiments of Mehmetciks who fought the Anzacs and Marines for Second Ridge on 1 and 2 May were prodigious. Over a period of about 30 hours their infantry, supported by snipers, machine guns and artillery, repeatedly attacked across open ground marked by well-sited British machine guns and riflemen in entrenched positions along the ridge. Most of these attacks were launched in daylight and some of them were directed at the isolated trench in Death Trap Valley. As well, the Turks maintained an accurate and heavy fire during the third counterattack, especially on the afternoon of Saturday, 1 May. They eventually called off their attacks on Sunday because of the awful extent of their casualties.

10 Combatants

We have been in the trenches now for 10 days without a spell. The men were very done for a few days as just as we had dug in one place we were shifted to another place and redig all over again. They practically had no sleep for 8 days but are better again now.

Lieutenant R.J. Massie, Adjutant, 4th Battalion, letter to his mother, dated 4 May 1915[1]

For the men in the 4th Battalion, life went on regardless of losses and who was killed. The unexpected death of its commanding officer, Lieutenant-Colonel Onslow Thompson, on 26 April did not cripple the battalion. Nor did the deaths of 40 men and the wounding of 40 more in Death Trap Valley on 1 and 2 May weaken its platoons. Reinforcements from the 4th Battalion's holding party began to arrive on 2 May.

In early May the 4th Battalion was firmly ensconced on MacLaurin's Hill and the adjacent Johnston's Jolly. Private Richard Edwards described the deployment:

> We relieved the Marines early this morning under very heavy shrapnel fire. The trenches we went into were awful death traps. Whatever the Marines had been doing, we suffered much because of them, but we very soon got to work with pick and shovel and got them safe from the terrible shrapnel which causes the majority of casualties.[2]

On the Jolly the Turkish trenches were about 110 metres away. The remnants of Fred 'Maud' Fanning's platoon were now bolstered by a steady stream of reinforcements. By 9 May 99 men had joined the battalion's ranks,[3] including 44 who joined D Company,[4] most of them filling the gaps in No. 15 Platoon.

What the remaining men of the 4th Battalion, particularly the Death Trap Valley survivors, desired and needed more than anything was sleep. As Lieutenant

Massie pointed out, they had been on the go and under fire for about a week and a half, apart from a very brief beach hiatus on 30 April. Even this was under fire and necessitated two fatiguing journeys—from the firing line to the beach and back again—incurring casualties along the way. All this in about 12 hours—not much of a rest. Virtually every other AIF battalion had an extended break on the beach by the start of May.

In their diaries and letters, a number of 4th Battalion men mention the fatigue they were suffering by early May. On 2 May, in the immediate aftermath of the battle, Les Lott enjoyed 'a much needed sleep' and 'little was done during the night', such was his exhaustion.[5] Massie, in a letter to his mother dated 4 May, pointed out the lack of sleep, the arduous nature of the fighting and the unending digging the men were subjected to during the early days at Anzac:

> We have been in the trenches now for ten days without a spell. The men were very done for a few days as just as we had dug in one place we were shifted to another place and redig all over again. They practically had no sleep for 8 days but are better again now.[6]

In another letter written on 5 May, also to his mother, he had similar complaints:

> Dear Mater . . . We have had a pretty rough time since we landed. We have been in the trenches for 10 days now without a spell and are not likely to get one for a considerable time I think. The men had to dig day and night at first for a week and were very done at the end of it . . . and if it were not for the damned noise would get a good sleep. It gets cold at night but we really have had perfect weather since we landed here.[7]

The noise at Anzac, certainly over the period of the Battle of the Landing, was unrelenting and loud. It was a deliberate tactic on the part of the Turks, designed to make the ANZAC occupation as uncomfortable and dangerous as possible.

Corporal Charles Bosward touched on the weather and a new menace for the Anzacs—lice—in his diary entry of 9 May:

> Have not had clothes off for 15 days. Nor had a wash. Had only one shave since landing. I must look an awful wreck with long growth of whiskers + dirty face and hands + body etc + would like a change of clothes badly. These trousers nearly done, very threadbare + full of lice. Itchy all over, very hot in the daytime + very cold at night.[8]

However, according to Les De Vine, things were looking up. On 5 May he noted in his diary:

> 2 oz tin of tobacco issued today, tried to find where I dumped my pack on the first day of landing but had absolutely no hope, everything scatted & could find nothing, everything being lost, night very cold, tot of rum issued tonight for the first time.[9]

And on 8 May he was almost upbeat about his lot:

> Had a shave today for the first time since the landing, not so cold tonight, we had a hot meal sent up to the line, the first since the landing.[10]

Battalion after battalion left their packs on the beach or as they advanced up Long Gully on that first day. Obviously the men could move far more easily unencumbered by their packs; however, the packs were never to be retrieved, so the creature comforts the men had hoarded were lost. Unfortunately, greatcoats were also discarded en masse, which meant the men suffered acutely from the cold nights. Lieutenant Lawrence Street of the 3rd Battalion, in a letter to his mother on 16 May, summed up the anguish the men felt at the loss of these two important items of kit:

> Away we went panting under heavy loads, up steep hills and down precipitous dales, all the time through thick scrub . . . and that was the last we ever saw of our precious packs. Mine contained all my treasures, changes of clothing, my beautiful great coat, warm sweater, torch, a pound of Imperial Ruby in stick form which I had been treasuring, a good supply of matches, everything, in fact, required to make a comfortable home.[11]

Later in the letter he listed their diet: 'We get plenty of bully beef, bacon, jam, cheese, tea, sugar, and biscuits and latterly potatoes have been available.'[12]

There was one member of A Company, quite possibly the only one in the 4th Battalion, who did have his greatcoat. Les De Vine boasted in his diary:

> We have all lost our packs which we dumped on the day of landing so we have lost everything only leaving what we stood up in. I am the only man in the Coy that has an overcoat as I did not carry it in my pack but on my belt.[13]

In a letter to his mother in mid-May, Major Heane was quite informative about life for him and his men of D Company:

> There is always an argument as to what is the day of the week or the date. One day is the same as another, and we have been here over three weeks . . . the trenches we are in now are the second lot we have made, and are a very good lot. I have lived most of the time in a very shallow dugout in the firing line, but now we have more time, I have a good one built about 18 feet from the firing line where I sleep, and all the officers of D Coy. come for meals. It is a palace compared to anything any of the Coy officers have, but I had to 'shake' some timber to cover it with from the artillery. We are all living like fighting cocks—splendid weather, no rain.[14]

~

In early May word about recognition of what Cast Iron Jimmy Heane and the battalion's two parties had done in Death Trap Valley started to filter through to the ranks of the 4th Battalion. Corporal Howard McKern reported in his diary on 9 May that:

> R.M.L.I. sent thanks and appreciation to D and A. Coy for relieving them in isolated trench under heavy fire. The platoon relieving them came back only five strong.[15]

He was referring to the reports written by the Royal Marine hierarchy that only referred to D Company. McKern, not being privy to the actual documents, assumed they included No. 3 Platoon from A Company in their praise.

On 9 May in the 4th Battalion war diary, Adjutant Jack Massie noted: 'No. 1088 Pte E.J. Robson promoted Cpl for distinguished conduct in the field on 1st May.'[16] In a letter to his mother dated 10 May, Massie wrote: 'Some very good work has been done here. One of our boys called Robson has been recommended for D.C.M.'[17]

The newly promoted 4th Battalion commanding officer, Lieutenant-Colonel Alf Bennett, wrote two responses in regard to the recognition of his men's Death Trap Valley exploits. There was a certain obsequiousness about both pieces of writing; however, they were genuine expressions of his feelings on behalf of the battalion. The first one was a heartfelt reply to the memorandum and its accompanying letter penned by Lieutenant-Colonel Frank Luard and Brigadier-General Charles Trotman, respectively, of the Royal Marines soon after the action. Bennett replied:

I desire to express through you the grateful appreciation of all ranks of the 4th Bn. for the generous terms in which the G.O.C. R.M.Bde and the Comg officer of the Portsmouth Bn have written of the assistance a platoon of the Bn was so fortunate as to be able to render their Comrades of the R.M.L.I.

It is deeply regretted that almost the whole platoon fell in doing what was but their simple duty but the kindness of feeling evoked is the greatest compensation those left could desire.[18]

The news of the decorations awarded to James Heane and Snowy Robson, and the awarding of a Military Cross to Boer War veteran Captain Jasper Magee for an action not related to Death Trap Valley, was officially announced in early June. Bennett was moved to write in Battalion Routine Orders on 3 June a copy of his reply to Brigadier-General Harold 'Hooky' Walker, Birdwood's chief of staff's congratulations on the awards to Heane, Magee and Robson:

Will you please accept the warmest thanks of the Officers, N.C.O.'s and men of the 4th Battalion for your kind expression of pleasure in the inclusion of the names of Major Heane, Captain Magee and Corporal Robson in the Honours and Awards List.

So early an expression of His Majesty's favour will pass into the records of the battalion as its most cherished tradition and act as an incentive of appreciation of the privilege permitted us of serving our Common Empire.[19]

~

On the night of 8 May the first official AIF trench raid occurred. This was the beginning of what was to become a common practice, especially on the Western Front. Such raids, like the first one, were fraught with danger and not always successful. In the days leading up to the raid the Turks were spotted sapping their way forward on the northern edge of Johnston's Jolly about 110 metres away from the 4th Battalion's lines. A party of 30 volunteers from the 4th Battalion led by Lieutenant Fred Fanning, now a relatively experienced officer after two weeks in the trenches, set off at 10 p.m. to investigate and, if possible, raid the enemy trench. The raid was timed to take advantage of the darkness before the moon rose later that night, at 2.39 a.m. on 9 May. Lieutenant-Colonel Bennett's report on the operation was finished at 7 a.m. the next morning:

Report on night operation: At 10pm (8/5/15) 30 men under Lieut Fanning advanced from D Coy trenches in direction of enemy's advanced trench. They moved by everything very slowly. Men on left fell back and lost touch and afterwards acted alone. About 17 men reached within 10 yds of enemy's trench which runs irregularly parallel to ours at 120 yds. Voices of Turks talking, laughing + singing could be heard along their trenches apparently from fully occupied trenches. Exact estimate is difficult but most men agree that the Turks very much outnumbered our men and the officer leading decided that he would not be justified in charging with his reduced force so he returned to our lines.

Time absent 1¾ hrs. The going was rough.

Casualties: one man was wounded by an unaimed bullet. Corpl Cliff started back with him saying he could manage easily but neither has returned—They may have lost direction and got into enemy trench.

Information obtained:—

1) The enemy's trench is 120 yds [110 metres] from ours.
2) The enemy's trench is fully occupied.
3) The enemy's trench is not vigilantly guarded.
4) From direction of flash men in Turkish trenches fire their rifles unaimed in the air at intervals.
5) There are a few snipers firing from fixed rifles.
6) There are many dead bodies in front of our lines.

Some men report hearing a rumbling sound as of a truck on rails underground coming towards our trenches.

The operation may be regarded as an instructive experiment.[20]

The report contained a number of fascinating details. It gave a human dimension to the enemy, who were 'talking, laughing + singing'. At this stage of the campaign the Turks certainly weren't expecting any late-night visitors; their guard was down and had Fanning's party remained intact, raiding rather than just reconnoitring the trench might have been possible.

The mass attack by the Turks on 19 May was more than a week and a half away. The Armistice to bury the dead, ostensibly from that action, was still two and a half weeks away, yet No Man's Land was already an open-air mortuary, fetid with the bodies of Anzac, Turk and Marine. Negotiating dead bodies was an unexpected hazard for the raiders. Their smell must have been overwhelmingly putrid.

Les Lott was one of Fred 'Maud' Fanning's raiders. His account dovetailed with Bennett's more formal one in many respects:

May 8th 1915

Through the day things were very slow. A call for volunteers to go out and investigate the enemy's trenches in front. 30 of us under Lieut Fanning vollenteered to go. the object being, we go to the trenches, bayonet everything in it, but we musn't fire a shot, see what fortifications they have, and return, it being explained to us after we had vollenteered and it seemed like sudden death, 30 of us to take a position which the whole Battn had tried to take.

10 pm creeping along to the enemy trenches we reach within 10 to 15 yards of them still without being heard. the night being pitch dark there was little chance of being seen. the trenches were full of Turks, and after being out about 1½ hours the officer decides to return as the numbers were too great to attempt the ruse. a slight noise aroused the enemy when we were about halfway back, and they opened fire. lying flat on the ground all bar one missed being hit.[21]

The two missing men, Corporal William Cliffe and Private Alan Campbell, were captured by the Turks. There was much conjecture about their fate at Anzac and at home in Australia. Initially, Cliffe and Campbell were listed as missing on 9 May. This was the start of a saga that lasted until after the end of the war, although for the Campbell and Cliffe families the effects of their capture would continue indefinitely.

On 10 December 1918, Corporal Cliffe, a recently repatriated prisoner of war, gave a statement regarding their capture. On 8 May 1915, he was a newly promoted corporal, having been raised in rank from lance corporal on 2 May.[22] Cliffe's elevation came as a result of his impressive work after the Landing, for which he was Mentioned In Despatches. The recommendation read: 'General distinguished conduct and leading and instructing their men in the attack and the construction of trenches under fire.'[23]

This was the corporal's recollection of that night:

No. 482.
Rank Cpl.
Name. Cliffe William.
Platoon. 13.
Company. 'D'
Battalion. 4th.
On the night of the 8th May 1915 I was in charge of a party who's [sic] duty it was to find out the Turkish movements.

Allan [sic] Campbell was with this party at about 10.30pm he was wounded in the head. The wound was very severe.

I handed my rifle to another of my party Pte Brett to hold till I came back from trying to carry Campbell into our lines but was unlucky and fell into the hands of the Turks.

Campbell was then dying quickly. When I was separated from him. There is not the slightest doubt that he died that night.

Signature:—No. 482 [sic] Cpl. William Cliffe[24]

Campbell was probably hit by an unaimed gunshot, randomly fired in the direction of the ANZAC lines. Campbell's fate wasn't officially confirmed until 13 May 1919, more than five years after that fateful first trench raid. A final Court of Enquiry was convened at AIF Headquarters in London, beginning on 27 January 1919 for 'the purpose of Enquiry into and recording an opinion regarding the fate of 558. Pte. CAMPBELL. A. 4th Battalion. A.I.F.'[25] An initial Court of Enquiry, held on 16 July 1915, stated that it was 'reasonable to suppose this man dead'. Unofficial word from a number of sources, including the Red Cross, came through that Campbell, along with Cliffe, were prisoners of war, being held at Afron Kara Hissar in Turkey. Cliffe's wife received three letters from him dated 4, 18 and 27 July 1915, which she took to the local military authorities in early November 1915. The letters reassured her that her husband was faring well in captivity. While he wrote that he was with six other Australians and the crews of an English and an Australian submarine, 'he mentions no names of other prisoners'.[26] Significantly, Campbell's family received no correspondence from their son.

On 24 February 1919 the court's findings were handed down:

The court having considered the Evidence, are of the opinion that:—
(1) No. 558.Pte.CAMPBELL.A. 4th Battalion. Was incorrectly reported as a Prisoner of War at Kara Hissa. TURKEY.
(2) That he was severely wounded in the head on the night of 8/9th May 1915 and was captured by the Turks.
(3) That he died in Turkish hands on the GALLIPOLI PENINSULA on the 9th May, 1915.

On 13 May 1919 final confirmation by mail of Campbell's death, from AIF Headquarters in London, was received in Australia. His death certificate was issued on the same day.[27] After the end of hostilities one family, the Cliffes, welcomed home their son; the other, the Campbells, were left to mourn their loss after years of speculation and uncertainty.

~

On 10 May the long-awaited arrival of Chaplain McKenzie occurred. 'Fighting Mac' spent a frustrating two and a half weeks on board ship off Anzac witnessing the sounds and sights of battle from afar. The following is his account of 25 April from the relative safety of the *Lake Michigan*:

> It is remarkable to relate that when I saw the shells dropping all around us and the rifles speaking and guns going I just felt in a most gleeful happy mood. All fear vanished and I revelled in it and longed to get at them. I can never forget the sight and I am glad to have been in it.[28]

Finally, 'Fighting Mac' reached the shore and his charges in the 4th Battalion. His diary entry for 9 May recorded the moment:

> Sunday May 9th Had a fine service on board and then got ready to disembark which I did on Monday May 10th. After landing the Beach became a 'hot shop' with shrapnel shells and all sought shelter—over a dozen were fired. I had a very narrow squeak. I got covered with earth when I threw myself on the road for safety. A number of shells fell near us. However I got safely up the Hill tho' both shrapnel and bullets were flying overhead. The men's welcome to me was very warm and hearty. They were most grateful to greet me once more.[29]

The battalion's war diary didn't record his arrival on 10 May. There was no reference to McKenzie on 11 May, the day after his arrival, when the body of Lieutenant-Colonel Onslow Thompson was retrieved and buried.[30]

In a series of letters written to Commissioner Hay of the Salvation Army in Sydney, which were published as a single account in *The Sydney Morning Herald*, McKenzie bared his soul and described being at war:

> The Australians are making a wonderful name for themselves for desperate fighting. But it is awful country, and the cover and obstacles are heavy against our forces. They have done marvellous work as it is. You will read the list of casualties long ere you get this note. The sights I see among those are beyond me to describe. Their groans and moaning are fearful in some cases. My heart has been wrung with anguish as I talked to the dear fellows. Australia is paying a heavy toll, and it has only begun. Few of us expect to come out of it with whole skins. Our brigadier [Colonel H.N. MacLaurin, KIA 27/4/1915] and brigade major [Major F.D. Irvine KIA, 27/4/1915—ten minutes before MacLaurin and in the same spot at

Steele's Post] are both gone, with many other brave officers and men. We are holding on like grim death. Our battalion went into the trenches on Sunday, April 25th; they have been out of them for only two and a half hours since then, and in the very front fighting trenches all the time, having won golden opinions for their dash and daring . . .

I am now stationed right up in the firing line with the First Brigade, and burying the dead around here; that is, reading the burial service over them; and, alas, I am kept much too busy in this line. I have had three narrow squeaks—one bullet grazed the top of my head, another my right ear, and once I got smothered with earth from a big shell that fell four feet from me. I, of course, threw myself down and missed the bullets and bolts and scrap-iron. We were close to two bombs dropped by a Taube Aeroplane, and have been near any amount of big gun shells, and the bullets whistle around us by the tens of thousands, while the field guns drop the shells each day by the thousands. It is very remarkable how one gets used to it, and can even sleep through the roar and rattle of these projectiles. I am safely ensconced in a 'dug-out' at night, and even slept on while lying in a big pool of water when it rained on Wednesday night. It is cold, hard and uncomfortable, but one gets quite used to the rough conditions, though I had no sleep for the first night. Some of the bodies of those killed a fortnight ago are now being found and brought in for burial. It was very gratifying to find our Colonel's body [Onslow Thompson]. We buried it at 9 o'clock, after dark, as it lay in an exposed position. I had to kneel down and keep my head and body in a crouching position while reading the burial service. Hundreds of bullets swept over us while this was going on. I don't know what Australian papers say about the brave boys, but I want to tell you that they accomplished a well-nigh impossible task, and have shown themselves to be amongst the best fighters in the world. We are still at it, and have a great task before us; the price will be heavy. My heart is full of one big sob for the loss of so many brave young men, hundreds of whom I know so well. When I think of the soul anguish the mothers of these boys will pass through I can only pray for them. May God comfort them. For myself I have not the slightest fear, and am more than glad to be here with the men, and they in turn have welcomed me like a father. War is Hellish! No one, even with the most vivid imagination, can really grasp its full details until they have seen it and been in it.[31]

The 4th Battalion participated in two more major actions at Gallipoli: the huge Turkish attack of 19 May, and the ANZAC attack at Lone Pine in early August.

In the first, in which the 4th Battalion played a defensive role repelling the Turkish attack, their casualties were only small, with 15 men killed and two men who died of wounds.[32] This was despite the Turkish assault being partially directed at their lines on MacLaurin's Hill and on the Jolly. In the other major engagement at Lone Pine, from 6 to 9 August, the battalion operated offensively and suffered accordingly. Despite gaining ground, unlike the Turks in May, the 4th's losses were horrendous, with 244 officers and enlisted men dying as a result; another hundred or more were wounded.[33]

~

What was the fate of the remaining members of No. 12 Section? How did the war play out for them?

Three of the section—Jack Collyer, Tom Thomson and Alf Robins—died as a result of the fight in Death Trap Valley.

Remarkably, however, the five known No. 12 Section survivors of Death Trap Valley also survived the war. Three of them—Bill Bound, Snowy Robson and Les Lott—were later wounded at Gallipoli, invalided home and discharged medically unfit. The other two—Clyde Bock and Charles Macquarie—finished as sergeants after spending years fighting on the Western Front. In 1918 they were given 'Special 1914' leave as the war wound down. They, too, returned to Australia.

Corporal Charles Macquarie, Jack's mate and section leader, did not get hit during the intense fighting in the valley. Charles wrote to George Collyer from No. 2 Stationary Hospital on Mudros on 3 July, where he was sidelined for about two months due to a gastritis infection. He was discharged to his unit on 4 August. It is not known whether he experienced the carnage at Lone Pine, beginning on 6 August. After the evacuation, Macquarie joined the 4th's sister battalion, the 56th, on 16 February 1916 in Egypt. He rose to the rank of 'temporary company sergeant major' and finished the war as a sergeant in that unit. Almost unbelievably Macquarie fought through Gallipoli, France and Flanders without being wounded. He had occasional stints in hospital for complaints such as trench feet and for dental treatment, but before war's end he returned to Australia as one of the few 'Special 1914' Anzacs for six months' leave; men who enlisted in 1914 and 1915 were granted the option of extended leave in England or Australia.[34]

By the time hostilities ceased, Private Clyde Bock, D Company, 4th Battalion, evolved into Company Sergeant Major Bock of A Company, 56th Battalion. Like Macquarie, he survived the war and doesn't seem to have been wounded, despite fighting on the Western Front for a considerable time. No doubt he and Macquarie had their share of close shaves and minor wounds that did not require medical attention and were not, therefore, recorded. Somewhat embarrassingly for the veteran NCO, Clyde contracted venereal disease during a period of leave in September 1916. He spent a few weeks being treated, after being hospitalised on 12 October 1916. Clyde also had a bout of trench feet in April 1917. He was Mentioned In Despatches in early 1917:

> I have the honour to submit the name of the under-mentioned non-commissioned officer serving under my command whose distinguished and gallant services, and devotion to duty I consider of special mention—No. 230, Company Sergeant-Major CLYDE ERNEST BOCK.

Clyde Bock also received 'Special 1914' leave. He left for Australia on 12 December 1918 aboard HT *Leicestershire*, having well and truly done his bit for King and Country.[35]

Private Bill Bound was wounded on 2 May as a result of the fighting in Death Trap Valley. The nature and severity of his wound are unknown, but he didn't appear to have left Anzac for any further treatment. A telegram sent to his mother on 15 June read in part 'wounded not reported seriously'. Captain Tebbutt probably dealt with it at his regimental aid post near the head of Bridges' Road after the fighting died down. Bill's real suffering came at Lone Pine on 7 August, on the second day of the 4th Battalion's involvement in the battle. He was severely wounded in both hands. As later medical reports described: 'The causation of the disability was explosion of a bomb on active service.' While fighting in the disputed trenches, Bill probably grabbed a Turkish bomb and in endeavouring to throw it back at the enemy was badly wounded when it exploded. Another possible scenario was the premature detonation of one of his own bombs as he attempted to throw it. Either way, Bill was evacuated to Malta where he underwent 55 days' treatment, beginning on 12 August. On 6 September Bill's mother, Rose, wrote to the relevant military authorities seeking more information about his wound. Bill's father had passed away in 1914. Mrs Bound's plaintive request was repeated countless times during the war:

> It is needless for me to say, how disappointed I am, in not receiving any further news, in regard to my Son, Private W.A. Bound. I thought in reply to the Cable sent, I should have received full particulars of injuries received.
>
> It does not seem right that a parent should be kept in suspense so long. No one knows but those who have given up their boys, what a Mother feels, + I am depending on my two sons for support.

Bill, aged 20, and his brother David, aged 22, joined the 4th Battalion on 1 September, 1914. David transferred to the 1st ANZAC Battalion, Imperial Camel Brigade, on 1 January 1916 during the 4th Battalion's training in Egypt. Unfortunately, David was killed in action in Palestine during the advance on Gaza on 19 April 1917.[36]

At the end of his stay in hospital in Valletta, Bill was invalided home on HS *Kanowna* and discharged from the AIF on 9 August 1916 on a pension of 30 shillings per fortnight, starting from 31 August. The fourth and fifth fingers on his left hand were permanently paralysed. Bill's capacity to earn a living was adjudged to be reduced by 75 per cent, hence the pension.[37]

Corporal Snowy Robson was wounded in Loutit's Post on 2 May during the battle for Death Trap Valley by what he claimed to be an explosive bullet. Snowy wrote to his sister:

> . . . when an explosive bullet struck the trench and I got the contents of it in my back. Nothing serious, but I had to stay a week, and when I came back I was informed that I was recommended for the Distinguished Service [sic] medal and full corporal.[38]

Snowy, like his platoon commander Fred Fanning, was another who missed Lone Pine. Robson, who was wounded in the right forearm on 6 June, later recalled:

> The best twenty-four hours I spent while away was lying in a nice, soft bed at No. 1 General Hospital, Cairo with a couple of mails after seven weeks at Gallipoli.[39]

Snowy was invalided home in July 1915 after his wounded arm failed to recover sufficiently for him to be sent back to Gallipoli. He enlisted again on 21 May 1917 as a reinforcement in the Camel Corps. This time he didn't make it out of Australia—he injured himself in camp at Menangle in January 1918. A report stated: 'While skylarking in Camp he fell and bumped his neck on tent peg. He was subsequently admitted to hospital with septic cellulitis of neck.' After an operation, Snowy recovered physically, but was deemed medically unfit and discharged with the rank of sergeant on 27 May 1918. His discharge papers stated 'Discharged Medically Unfit Not Due To Misconduct'; no mention of skylarking for our hero.[40]

Private Les Lott, whose diary was such a marvellous record of the Landing and subsequent events, was another to survive the horror of Death Trap Valley, only to be wounded in August at Lone Pine. Despite surviving three days in the charnel house that the battle became from 6 to 9 August, Les was wounded on

13 August. He had returned to the blood-soaked tunnels and trenches of Lone Pine after less than 24 hours' rest on 10 August. In his own words:

> August 13th 1915. The Turks have retired, and evidently given it up for a bad job. We are due for another spell today, and are busy with our kits.
>
> 2pm the 4th Battn are relieved by the 2nd Battn, 4 of us were left behind to hand over. An Officer, myself on the phone and a sergent and orderly.
>
> The Turks have been shelling us heavy all the morning, and have just started again. 2.30 having handed over to the relieving Bttn, with our kits we are just preparing to rejoin the Bttn when Bang, a shell lands right in among us. The Serj and Orderly (killed) the Officer and myself stop a bit each, and had to be carried away out of action. So my lengthy career on Gallipoli Pen. came to a sudden (end).
>
> Taken to the dressing station. was then despatched to the clearing station on the Beach, where an operation was performed and a finger was amputated, then taken to the pier ready for hospital ship . . . taken on Hospital ship and given supper, which I shall never forget after Bully and biscuits for seventeen weeks. it was a feast for the Gods, and to have a mattress to sleep on was A1.[41]

On 17 August Les, like Bill Bound, ended up at Malta, where he was treated for two months. At the end of this period Les was shipped to the 3rd London General Hospital, Wandsworth, for further treatment, but his wound was so debilitating that he was unable to return to active service, and instead found himself on HT *Ascanius* heading home to Australia on 17 March 1916. In Australia Les was discharged after a second medical on 5 August, nearly 12 months after being wounded in action.[42]

The soldier diarist with the most florid name in the 4th Battalion to participate in the Death Trap Valley action was Private Apcar Leslie De Vine. Les, as he was known, saw out the war as a sergeant in the 4th Battalion. His war service was almost as colourful as his name. Les enlisted on 21 August 1914. Next to the question regarding marital status, he inexplicably answered 'widower' with 'one child aged 3 years', even though he was married to Edith in Bedford, England, in 1909 and she was very much alive. Having survived Death Trap Valley, Les was later wounded in action twice in France, initially on 16 January 1917 and then on 11 September 1918.

During his Western Front service Sergeant De Vine was hauled before a field general court martial, held on 4 December 1916 following an unauthorised excursion. Les's version of his two-day escapade is quite entertaining:

> 26/11/16 Sunday . . . Visited Amiens with Sgts Curran & Mills & Cpls Palmer & Goldwater walking all the way, a distance of 13 kilometres arriving there about 12.30 after eluding the picquets that are stationed on the road, as the town is out of bounds. We all succeeded in having a good time. Have no idea what happened after 5 pm. I woke up during the night while an air raid was in progress on the city and found myself with Sgt Curran under arrest in the city guard room, for having dined too well.
>
> 27/1/16 Sgt R Crawford was sent from the Bn to be our escort to bring us back . . . he arrived at 12.30. We spent the rest of the day together in Amiens, having a good time, caught the 7.30 bus at the station arriving at the Bn about 9 pm where we reported & were placed under close arrest by the RSM Stewart.[43]

Sergeant Bob Crawford was less than diligent in the execution of his orders, no doubt appreciating a day in Amiens with his fellow NCOs. Despite being demoted to corporal and fined a day's pay as punishment, Les and his mates thought that 'we got out of it lightly'.

Les returned to Australia in 1919.[44]

Private Mick Quigley, the 4th Battalion's raconteur, also survived Death Trap Valley with his sense of humour intact. Quig was possibly wounded during his time in the valley. Unfortunately his service record didn't record when he sustained his shoulder wound, mainly because he didn't seek treatment for it immediately. In a letter received by Mr J.H. Ritter of Dubbo on about 20 July, Quig gave an amusing account of his wounds:

> Injuries—Got gently tapped by shrapnel on the shoulder blade. Wasn't much of a hit (as shrapnel hits generally go), but a swelling as big as one's fist ensued, and my right arm became very stiff. After a few days was sent to beach for attention, and was given a job guarding ammunition. Now strange to say, that beach is a veritable deathtrap, far, far worse than the trenches up on the hills. Enemy's shrapnel bursts there ceaselessly and snipers pot away unmercifully and successfully. One tore a hole through my sleeve, but doing no injury. Shortly after, lying there peacefully, shrapnel burst overhead. I thought I was safely ensconsed under the cliff, but, alas, into my chest and ankle two wretched pellets manoeuvred their way. The one in the chest didn't need a bandage, and a slight scar is the only momento now. Had ankle bandaged, and lay there cursing impotently. It wasn't painful, and was told to be ready to embark next day. Began to clean rifle

> shortly after, before handing it in. Suddenly up above shrapnel burst again. Frantically ducking backwards on one foot, I floundered, and the rifle went off with a roar. 'Yer hurt, mate?' inquired the Corporal. 'Only blew me foot orf,' I answered tragically. I thought so at the time. Examination revealed that the instep of the unlucky foot was only grazed, but bleeding slightly. The Corporal roared at me for 'carelessness' and the shock I gave him. Later, I had the doubtful satisfaction of hearing that, one night in the trench, he killed one of our own men, who was scouting out in front. Ten days ago the foot was opened up and the pellet removed. Had ether at 2.30 pm and a hearty tea at 4.30 pm, so the operation wasn't a glaring failure. Walk now with just the suspicion of a limp. Am sick of hospitals, and very keen on getting back to my old comrades. If I am here much longer I will have to go with the Reinforcements—strangers all—and as I have made a couple of true friends in the old lot (the three of us always fought side by side ready in case of one another's disablement), you can imagine my anxiety on this point.[45]

Quig did indeed return to the 4th Battalion on 3 September, another blessed to have missed the horror of Lone Pine. About a month later, on 2 October, Quig once again left Anzac, this time disabled by enteric fever; he was treated on Mudros. Eventually he was invalided to Australia, leaving England on 8 May 1916; his casualty form showed Quig was suffering from 'shell shock'. He was discharged from the Australian Imperial Force on 16 August 1916 as medically unfit. Quig was granted a pension of 3 pounds per fortnight from 17 August 1916. For Michael Quigley the fighting was over; however, he now had to face up to the rest of his life, trying to cope with his memories and physical and mental wounds.[46]

~

Fred Fanning was the officer in charge of Jack's platoon, No. 15, D Company, during training in Egypt and the invasion of Turkey at Gallipoli. Fred came from a family with a strong military background. His father was a retired lieutenant-colonel and Fanning was a second cousin of Lieutenant-General Birdwood. Fanning's family owned Coomeragee, a substantial grazing holding in the Casino district of New South Wales. Fred attended Riverview College in Sydney as a boarder from the age of 12, in 1903. He thrived in this environment and excelled in athletics, rowing, rugby and cadets. He was also prominent in debating at school.[47] According to his personnel dossier Fanning spent nine years as a cadet in the Great Public Schools Battalion of Sydney, the last two as an officer.[48]

Fanning enlisted on 14 September 1914, aged 23, and gave his occupation as an overseer. He was immediately given the rank of second lieutenant and was appointed to H Company as a platoon commander under Captain Coltman. Jack was put in H Company when he enlisted in the battalion at the end of September 1914. There were three references to Fred Fanning in Jack's first diary. All were in regard to the establishment of the camp at Mena. On consecutive days the references were indirect—no name(s)—and disparaging; however, a later one was more positive. The first reference was on Sunday, 6 December:

> We were fallen in to line up kits etc, + mark out positions for the tents when they come, which job took 4 hours, (only) 3 officers + 5 sergeants being in charge. Talk about muddling: they know nothing about the job, + Color-serg. Coxhead, I'll wager, would supervise the lot, + have it finished in half an hour. It was quite dark when we finished.

The supervisors Jack referred to were Captain Coltman, Lieutenant Seldon, Lieutenant Fanning and sergeants Nicholls, Dooling, Rice, Wright and Pitt.

The next day a further attempt was equally frustrating:

> We formed a fatigue, straightening the lines again, or at least, trying to, + when we finished that job, I could see no improvement on yesterday's work.

However, on Thursday, 12 December, Jack praised the efforts of Subalterns Fanning and Seldon to right what Jack saw as a rip-off in regard to the supply and cost of rations at Mena:

> We are told by our officers, that instead of receiving full rations, as laid down by British Army regulations, we are to receive 6d a day, in addition to the present ration of meat, bread, potatoes, tea + sugar. They stipulate also, that the sixpence Must be spent at Dickesons (who have a large marquee on the ground), we not being allowed to handle the money, nor, by what I see, examine the receipts . . . why should we be compelled to spend with him, + why can we not buy what we wish? . . . We must, however, give two of our officers, Lieutenants Fanning + Seldon, their due, for they are doing all in their power to make matters better.

When the eight-company organisation of each AIF battalion was replaced by a four-company structure on 1 January 1915,[49] Fanning was put in charge of No. 15 Platoon in Major James Heane's D Company. Heane was promoted to major on 1 January 1915.[50] Heane was Fanning's immediate superior and, as such, exerted enormous influence over the young officer's development. Fanning was of the same ilk as Heane. Both men were hard and gruff, but fair. After the reorganisation in Egypt, Fanning spent about six months under Heane's scrutiny, tutelage and direction during 1915, before Fanning was incapacitated by illness. A considerable part of their time together was spent in action at Anzac.

Fanning was promoted to lieutenant on the day of the Landing at Gallipoli. After proving to be a calculating, determined operator, he was destined for higher honours. He was Mentioned In Despatches for his pivotal leadership of his platoon in Death Trap Valley and had the honour of leading the first official AIF trench raid on 8 May. Fanning missed Lone Pine because of a disabling bout of dysentery, and soon after was appointed aide-de-camp to the commander of the 2nd Australian Division, Major-General Legge. He returned to the 4th Battalion on 10 October 1915. His mentor, Major Heane, was now absent from the battalion due to the wounds he suffered at Lone Pine on 6 August. The two men were briefly reunited in Egypt in 1916, after Heane had recovered from his wounds, before both left the 4th Battalion.

After the evacuation of Anzac, the AIF returned to Egypt to rest, reorganise and continue training in the desert, even though it soon became clear the Anzacs were now headed for France. Fanning was appointed as A Company commander in the newly formed 56th Battalion, to which he transferred on 16 February 1916.[51] The 56th Battalion was a sister battalion to the 4th Battalion, which was split to give the new formation a hard core of veterans. Fifteen officers, including the new commanding officer of the 56th, Major Humphrey Scott, and 450 NCOs and other ranks transferred to the new battalion from the 4th.[52] Fanning was promoted to captain on 12 March 1916 at Tel-el-Kebir, after being appointed temporary captain earlier.

Fanning was immortalised for his actions in this battalion in H.R. Williams's book, *The Gallant Company*. Williams's reminiscences, while covering a later period of Fanning's military career, gave a clear image of his methods, character and appearance. The then Private Williams described his and A Company's first encounter with their new commanding officer in Eygpt:

> We marched out a little way into the desert, formed line, and stood at the slope, while the captain walked slowly along the line and seemed to peer into each face. In a slow drawl he gave us the command 'Order Arms,'

and then stood us at ease . . . Already the personality of this captain impressed us. He stood about 5 feet 10 inches in height, and was of very active build; his tunic of the best cloth, buff riding-breeches, puttees rolled in the cross, hair as black as midnight, clean shaven, white teeth, head with the poise of a game cock, large blue eyes and heavy black eye-brows. He wore his hat turned down and set at a rakish angle that somehow indicated the character of the wearer. Such is my memory of Captain Fred Fanning on the first day I saw him at Tel-el-Kebir. When the war has become almost forgotten in the mist of passing years the memory will still be with me of this striking personality and great leader of men . . . None of us ever forgot the education he imparted to us and the manner of it. He had a picturesque vocabulary; he knew the sort of training the 4th Battalion had gone through when the 1st Division was being made ready for Gallipoli; and he meant his company in the 56th Battalion to learn in the same style with the same thoroughness[53] . . . His personality gripped us. He made us jump to his commands as nobody had done before. We feared him[54] . . . He himself would flay us unmercifully with his tongue in criticism, overlooking nothing that bore the slightest semblance to slackness. But he was our champion against all the rest of the world, and heaven help the person who tried to take from his company what Fanning considered its right.[55]

Presumably Fanning's demeanour was the same during his time in charge of No. 15 Platoon in the 4th Battalion. The report by James Heane and Major Storey that led to his first Mention In Despatches commended his calm, astute approach in controlling his men in the cauldron of Death Trap Valley. He displayed the same qualities in leading the first trench raid at Anzac, deciding in that case against the unnecessary sacrifice of the men in favour of the intelligence already gathered.

An example of his forthrightness and his consideration for his men came during one of the 56th Battalion's first actions on the Somme on 21 October 1916. His company was nearing the firing line beyond Flers with Bapaume in the distance,[56] and had entered a trench known as Turk Lane. Fanning was nearby in a support trench, preparing his men to relieve part of the Manchester Regiment. Conditions were abysmal: the firing line and its environs was a sea of mud and German shelling was particularly heavy. Again, Williams captured the scene as the company moved into position to begin the relief:

We came to a trench known as Turk Lane, narrow, deep and heavy with mud. We struggled along it, sometimes knee deep in the stinking slime.

> Turk Lane had until recently been German and bodies of dead men were lying on parapet and parados throughout its length. Presently we halted. A boyish-looking Tommy with white face, staring eyes, and blood-stained tunic came along. He asked me to light his cigarette, and if we were going to relieve the front line. I replied in the affirmative, and he added, 'My God you are going into hell up there.' I quite believed him. During the whole afternoon the shelling from both sides was very heavy. But as darkness fell the Germans put over a barrage which lashed the sector into an inferno of bursting and whistling shells. The din was so great that we had to roar at the top of our voices to carry on a conversation. Lieutenant Dykes came into the support trench just as the strafe commenced, and told Captain Fanning that the company was in Turk Lane waiting to move in. While the shelling was at its height a Tommy officer came hurrying along the trench. Upon seeing our little group he called out to Fanning—'Colonel's compliments, sir, and will you relieve the front line at once?'
>
> 'My compliments to your colonel,' replied Fanning, 'I will relieve the front line when it is dark.'
>
> In a few minutes the Tommy officer was back again. 'Colonel So and So's orders that you are to relieve at once.'
>
> 'You tell your colonel from me to go to Hell! I will not take my men over the top to relieve in this barrage while it is still light.' His men didn't move until dark. As they were entrenching, Captain Fanning walked along the company front and to each group said, 'Dig like hell to-night boys. The deeper you are tomorrow the safer you will be.'[57]

Not everyone was a devotee of Fanning. Private Walter Wright, a third reinforcement in the 4th Battalion, arrived on the Gallipoli peninsula on 6 May as part of a 55-strong reinforcing party. Walter was a bit of a larrikin who wrote poetry, won a Military Medal in France and finished the war as a lance corporal; however, on the day his promotion was announced, 7 August 1916, his second field punishment began. At Anzac he was allocated to D Company and probably ended up in No. 15 Platoon, given his testy relationship with Lieutenant Fanning. On 17 January 1916 Walter was awarded ten days' Field Punishment No. 2 for being drunk and for being in possession of firearms at Cairo on 14 January 1916, presumably by Captain Fanning.[58] Field Punishment No. 2 entailed the offender carrying out all their normal military duties, with extra fatigues commensurate with serving a prison sentence involving hard labour. As well, the offender could be restrained by the use of fetters, handcuffs, straps or ropes. On 16 February 1916, Fanning left the 4th Battalion for its sister battalion, the 56th Battalion.

Wright was well pleased: 'Captain Fanning my pet has been transferred and is making himself popular I don't think.'[59]

In fact, Fanning wasn't seeking popularity; instead he was determined his men would be superbly fit, trained and disciplined for the rigours of war, especially battle. As it happened, most of his men respected him, and appreciated the knowledge and the skills he imparted to them. Prior to departing for France in June 1916, Captain Fanning addressed A Company in his usual blunt manner:

> Men, we are leaving for France and hell. Make no mistake as to what that means—death, privation, wounds and suffering. Many of us will leave our bones in France.[60]

Unfortunately, Fred Fanning was one of those to leave his bones in France. He died from severe wounds to his left arm and right leg on 1 November 1916.[61] Red Cross enquiries into the circumstances of his passing left a trove of accounts; many of them not only detailed what happened to Fanning, but also offered tributes to him. The one that resonated the most was the accolade from a soldier who knew Fanning longer than anyone else in the AIF. Clyde Bock was a private, with Fanning as the officer in both H Company and No. 12 Section, No. 15 Platoon, D Company, in the 4th Battalion. Later Bock, like Fanning, joined the 56th Battalion during the reorganisation of the AIF in Egypt in early 1916. This was his response to the Red Cross enquiry:

> Capt. Fanning was killed at Flers on this Battalion's first entry into the Somme Battlefield.
>
> The cause of his death was a large high explosive shell which struck our trench, Lieut Dykes who was with him at the time was killed instantly. He did not appear to suffer pain and was cheerful until the end. When the stretcher bearers were putting him into the ambulance one of them passed the remark 'We must put the worst case on the bottom' Capt. Fanning then said 'I think you can put me there boys. I think I am that chap.' He died on his way to hospital and was buried at the Military graveyard at Fricourt. He was a great loss to our Cause and was the idol of the boys of his Company. Often now I hear the men say 'If our old Boss was here such and such a thing would never have happened.' I was with Capt. Fanning when he left Australia and landed at Gallipoli with him on the memorable 25th April 1915. We landed in the same open boat from the ship [*Lake Michigan*]. After the evacuation we were both transferred to this Battalion and after training in Egypt, sailed for France on 23rd

June 1916. We were both mentioned in Sir Douglas Haig's despatches together in France. He will always live in my memory as the Bravest Gentleman and the finest Soldier ever it was my good fortune to meet. Hoping these few lines will help you in your noble work.

Cert. by letter from Sgt. Major Bock C.
D. Company.
56th Battn. A.I.F.
France
11.3.17.[62]

Notably, Private Bock of 1914 had evolved into Company Sergeant Major Bock of 1917, a vastly experienced NCO.

Fred Fanning was Mentioned In Despatches three times—twice at Gallipoli and once in France. He was the archetypal ANZAC officer.

~

Unlike Fred Fanning, James Heane survived the war as a much-decorated brigadier-general. When news of his DSO came through to Dubbo, his home town, one of the local newspapers reported on 4 June:

MAJOR HEANE HONORED
For Distinguished Service
When soldier James Heane enlisted for service in Sydney, he was appointed to the rank of captain. Being familiar with his capabilities, however, no one in Dubbo expected him to remain in this position, and his early promotion to the rank of major did not come as a surprise. As a gentleman who had just returned from a trip to England remarked in the local Mechanic's Institute one night, Captain Heane is a true stamp of Imperial officer. Major Heane's stern and resolute disposition in military affairs is the outcome of a life in military training.[63]

Major Heane exhibited these qualities when he earned his nickname 'Cast Iron Jimmy', though he was hit a number of times at Anzac, proving he wasn't impervious to Turkish bullets. During the Battle of Lone Pine, Heane was wounded repeatedly as he and his men of D company charged towards their objective early in the evening of 6 August. After initially sustaining a minor wound to the neck as he negotiated No Man's Land, Heane was shot in the left hip after passing the first line of Turkish trenches. He was left foundering, unable to move, and received further shell splinter wounds to his hand, knee and right shoulder by the time he was removed from the battlefield at 8 p.m. that night.[64] Heane was evacuated, initially to Egypt and then to England for further treatment and rehabilitation. He did not rejoin the 4th Battalion until 4 January 1916 at Tel-el-Kebir. When he returned to the fold he was:

> accorded a great reception, which, in his quiet way, he received with some embarrassment. He was never one to like a fuss, and had never sought popularity; but in the stirring times at Anzac his men had become endeared to him to an extent he hardly imagined. They knew that he looked right through his officers at them, and woe betide the company commander or subaltern who neglected or imposed upon them.[65]

Heane was well known for his uncompromising attitude about the wellbeing of his men. During his recuperation in England he wrote a letter to his mother in which he revealed his deep regard for the men of the original enlistment in the 4th Battalion:

> But I guess they will be just like the first lot—buckle to anything without growling. But my love will always be for the first lot. There are very few left, and all were so fine, and we trained them ourselves. It is very sad work for me writing to the relatives of those who are killed.[66]

However, his reunion with the 4th was short-lived. Major Heane transferred to the 1st Battalion as its new commanding officer on 10 January. He was promoted to Lieutenant-Colonel on 1 February 1916. One of its major battles was the successful but costly capture of Pozières between 23 and 27 July. As part of the Australian 1st Division, the battalion helped to wrest the village from the Germans on 23 July. A horrific enemy bombardment followed over the next few days, incurring huge casualties among the Australians. The survivors left in the 1st Division were physically and psychologically gutted. The 1st Battalion was withdrawn in the early hours of 26 July. According to the 1st Battalion's war diary, by noon on 26 July the battalion's casualties were 11 officers, nine of whom died, and some 524 other ranks who were wounded, killed or missing.[67] Heane was upset but proud of his men, the victory tainted by the considerable losses the battalion sustained. Apparently:

> The heavy losses at Pozières distressed him greatly, and nearly broke his heart. Those who were closest to him in those ghastly days testified that

> it needed all his courage and pride to overcome the shock at the loss of so many of his beloved men.[68]

It was also reported that a couple of days after the battle, he addressed a parade of the remnants of the battalion at Tara Hill above Albert, saying:

> As you know, I am a hard man to please. But I feel proud to have held command of men such as you. This Battalion had a wonderful name on Gallipoli, but during this engagement you have done work equal to, if not better, than anything that was done on the Peninsula.[69]

Another account of that speech had tears glistening in Heane's eyes as he spoke.[70]

Thereafter, Heane's military career was a succession of promotions and acknowledgments of his bravery and skill as a leader of men. He finished the war as a colonel operating as a temporary brigadier-general in charge of the 2nd Brigade, which he led from December 1916 to the end of the war, apart from a short period, soon after he took command, when he was wounded in the head by an enemy sniper as he was inspecting the firing line. Under Heane's leadership, the 2nd Brigade participated in many battles, such as Bullecourt and Passchendaele, throughout 1917 and 1918. By war's end Heane was a much-decorated veteran—and still known as 'Cast Iron Jimmy'. He was Mentioned In Despatches seven times, was awarded the Distinguished Service Order and the Belgian Croix de Guerre, and was made a Companion of the Order of the Bath and the Order of St Michael and St George.[71]

~

The 3rd Battalion returned to the firing line on the night of 1 May, taking over the Marine positions of the Portsmouth Battalion on the Jolly adjacent to the 4th Battalion. Their trenches extended to and slightly past Owen's Gully. They remained in these positions until Lone Pine. During the 19 May Turkish onslaught, the 3rd Battalion's line around the head of Owen's Gully was threatened, but the danger soon passed and the Turkish attack was repulsed with heavy losses to the ranks of the Mehmetciks.

Lieutenants Meager and McLeod both died in the chaos of Lone Pine. Tallisker 'Tully' McLeod's death in action on Sunday, 8 August, was described in an article in *The Cootamundra Liberal* on 21 September 1915:

> Poor old 'Mac' was killed in action on the evening of the 8th. He had taken a party one way, and Capt. Price had gone another and the meeting

> point was arranged. Each had got to their respective destinations under very heavy fire, the signal to be a raised bush, but Mac stood up exposing himself above the trenches and sang out to Capt. Price. Capt. Price on looking over saw MacLeod standing there and before he could order him down, a bullet struck him in the head and killed him instantly.

Another version of Tully's death at Lone Pine involved McLeod supervising the construction of a sap from Sasse's Sap to Wood's Post about midday on 8 August. He was shot in the head and killed as he reconnoitred the line the sap was to follow.[72]

The 3rd Battalion suffered huge casualties at Lone Pine, with 21 officers and 490 other ranks being killed or wounded in action.[73]

The Marines of the Portsmouth Battalion were relieved by the 3rd Battalion during the night of 1 May, the relief not being completed until dawn on 2 May. After a short rest in Shrapnel Valley, the Portsmouth Battalion participated in Colonel John Monash's attempt to capture Baby 700. They entered the fray at 3.30 a.m. on 3 May. Unfortunately, the attack failed and the Marines, including the Portsmouth Battalion, suffered heavy casualties. Lieutenant-Colonel Frank Luard was one of these, being wounded in the right knee as he led his men in a charge. Luard's service record claimed he was wounded about 9 May.[74] The remnants of the battalion, along with the Chatham Battalion and the 4th Australian Brigade, were then ordered to hold the all-important trenches at the head of Monash Valley until 12 May. This included Pope's Hill, Quinn's Post and Courtney's Post. The Portsmouth Battalion's eventful Anzac experience ended with their relief by the Light Horse on 12 May.[75] By then, Walter Parker, the most famous Portsmouth Marine of all, was hospitalised and received treatment for his wounds. The battalion was then sent to Cape Helles; Lieutenant-Colonel Frank Luard joined them once his wound had healed. Luard was killed in action while leading his men in an abortive advance at Cape Helles on 13 July, during an offensive. His headstone in Skew Bridge Cemetery near Sedd el Bahr reads '13 July 1915, age 50' yet his service record gives 14 July as the date he died.[76]

Alan Alcock survived the war, ending it as a lieutenant. Alcock was wounded at Anzac on or about 7 May, during the battalion's occupation of the trenches at the head of Monash Valley.[77]

The Mehmetciks who survived their third counterattack were called on once more to die for their country at the hands of the Anzacs. On 19 May, waves of thousands of Turks hurled themselves at the enemy firing line across Second Ridge from 3.20 a.m. in a futile sacrifice.[78] The defensive advantages of properly sited machine guns and well constructed trenches in the ANZAC positions resulted in thousands of Turkish casualties. After three counterattacks, the daily attrition from local attacks, snipers, shrapnel and high explosive artillery and naval shells, and the slaughter of 19 May, very few members of the Turkish regiments present on 25 April were alive or not wounded by 24 May, the day of the Armistice. After one week the Anzacs were complaining about the stench of the dead; after one month it must have been overwhelming. The threat of disease would have been great.

The charismatic Mustafa Kemal not only survived the war but became, as Ataturk, the founding father of modern secular Turkey, where he is still revered today. In 1934 he showed his statesmanship and largesse in the following tribute to his former enemies:

> Those heroes that shed their blood and lost their lives . . . You are now lying in the soil of a friendly country. Therefore rest in peace. There is no difference between the Johnnies and Mehmets to us where they lie side by side now here in this country of ours . . . You, the mothers, who sent their sons from faraway countries wipe away your tears; your sons are now lying in our bosom and are in peace. After having lost their lives on this land they have become our sons as well.[79]

11 A question or two of history

And if the historian cannot write that drama in its full truth, with the interplay of good and ill, wisdom and folly, of all the parties working to its complex conclusion, then so much the less historian he.

Charles Bean in an address to the Royal Historical Society on 22 February 1938[1]

This chapter is not simply a matter of Bean bashing. I am but a boil on the esteemed Bean's bottom. However, boils need to be lanced and unpleasant truths exposed. Charles Bean and his staff deliberately altered the historical record regarding the events in Death Trap Valley on 1 and 2 May, despite a reputation second to none for detail and accuracy.

Charles Edwin Woodrow Bean, or C.E.W. Bean as I knew him in my childhood, is one of my heroes. Everyone in the ANZAC legend was armed and dangerous, apart from stretcher-bearers, chaplains, nurses, journalists and Bean, who let his pen, pencil and typewriter—*his* weapons of war—weave his incredible tales. Bean was an extremely brave and enduring advocate for the Anzacs of World War I. That he took the same risks and endured the same atrocious conditions as the men in the front line for four years, and survived, seems slightly barmy and almost incomprehensible. An unnamed AIF officer wrote to Arthur Bazley after the war:

> Officers and men go into battle more or less compelled to assume a certain courage, even if it be not there—example so compels. Bean had no man to set an example to and no superior who would condemn or applaud. And yet he probably risked dangers just as great as any man of the A.I.F. and that purely from a sense of duty and a desire to chronicle all important doings of the A.I.F.[2]

An example of Bean's remarkable devotion to his task came when he was wounded on the beach at North Anzac while covering the ANZAC August 1915 offensive in that sector. Struck by a stray Turkish bullet on the night of 7/8 August, Bean chose to stay at the front rather than miss the Anzacs' feats. One of Bean's diaries detailed the moment he was hit and his ensuing course of action:

> I was moving on again when something gave me a whack (like a stone thrown hard) in the upper part of the right leg. I could feel it whack the right side of the leg and bruise the inner part of the left side. I was pretty sure I had been hit by a stray which had gone in on the right and not come out, but I couldn't feel any blood, and so thought it might not have penetrated at all. Some of the stones from shell bursts had hit me quite as hard earlier this day—but presently I felt my hand greasy (with blood) in my pants—so I knew I (was wounded and) must go back. I could limp along pretty well . . . I looked in to see Godley and he was very kind and gave me a whiskey and sent me to dressing station. They looked after me well. I walked slowly home along the sap.[3]

Awakened later that morning by his 'Man Friday', Arthur Bazley, Bean, still in pain, refused the advice of the senior medical officer, Colonel Howse, to be evacuated for further treatment. Instead, he stayed in his dugout for the next few days, slowly recuperating under the ministrations of the ever-attendant Bazley and receiving updates from his fellow correspondent, Peter Schuler, about the fighting. Rather fortuitously for Bean, Schuler was at Anzac at the time, having been granted permission by General Sir Ian Hamilton to report from there from 20 July to 20 August.[4] Over 50 years later, on 30 August 1968, Bean died in Concord Repatriation Hospital, Sydney, after battling a long illness, the bullet still lodged in his leg.[5]

Bean's attachment to the men of the first AIF and his overwhelming desire to see their stories told, as well as their contribution to the war and the fledgling Australian nation acknowledged, drove him for decades. At the end of the sixth and last volume of the *Official History* written by Bean and published in 1942, the final three paragraphs provide a moving epitaph, encapsulating his abiding appreciation of the men and their place in our history:

> Twenty-three years ago the arms were handed in. The rifles were locked in the rack. The horses were sold. The guns were sheeted and parked in storage for other gunners. The familiar faded-green uniform disappeared from the streets.
>
> But the Australian Imperial Force is not dead. That famous army of generous men marches still down the long lane of its country's history,

with bands playing and rifles slung, with packs on shoulders, white dust on boots, and bayonet scabbards and entrenching tools flapping on countless thighs—as the French countryfolk and the fellaheen of Egypt knew it.

What these men did nothing can alter now. The good and the bad, the greatness and smallness of their story will stand. Whatever of glory it contains nothing now can lessen. It rises, as it will always rise, above the mists of ages, a monument to great-hearted men; and, for their nation, a possession for ever.[6]

Bean's lifelong commitment to these veterans is evident in the many books he wrote about them, his enormous contribution to the establishment of the Australian War Memorial and his many selfless acts to promote their welfare and the welfare of the nation he so served so well.

~

My first introduction to C.E.W. Bean was via *The Anzac Book* in the late 1960s, courtesy of my aunts Mabel, Alice, Wilga and Connie Musgrave. Their 19-year-old first cousin, Charlie Davis, landed on 25 April 1915 at Anzac as a signaller in the 2nd Battalion. Like many other signallers, he didn't last long, being killed in action on 2 May, a week after the Landing.[7] He sent his adolescent Wollongong cousins postcards from Egypt and the Musgraves, like many families with loved ones fighting and dying at Gallipoli, bought a copy of *The Anzac Book* on its publication in 1916. Over 50 years later, as an 11-year-old, I treasured its contents, marvelling at the Anzacs' cartoons, humorous stories, verse and general irreverence. Who or what was 'Annafarta' and 'Beachy Bill'? David Barker's caricatures captured my attention. Was this what the veterans of the Landing really looked like or were Cyril Leyshon-White's drawings a more accurate representation? The enemy, 'Abdul', seemed almost friendly in Ted Colles's caricature.[8] One of Bean's own contributions, a poetic depiction of the same enemy, 'Abdul', ends with respect for the Anzacs' adversary:

We will judge you, Mr. Abdul,
By the test by which *we* can—
That with all your breath, in life, in death,
You've played the gentleman.[9]

Above all, a sense of incongruity pervaded its pages. On the one hand, the writers and artists seemed to treat their topic frivolously yet, on the other, they were fighting in a war and death was ever present. The opening story, 'The Landing', was akin to a *Boy's Own Annual* account of war. George Johnston, the famous Australian author and child of a Great War veteran, believed *The Anzac Book* 'made the whole campaign seem like a quixotic romp'. Johnson came to this conclusion after first reading the book as a child some 40 years before I did.[10]

Why did *The Anzac Book* appear to celebrate a defeat? Indeed, Gallipoli was a failure, a defeat that left 11,410 sons of the Antipodes resting in the sea and on the shore.[11] The casualties didn't feature at all. The word 'invasion' wasn't used in the text. Australia invaded Turkey, threatening its sovereignty. The Gallipoli Peninsula wasn't a remote part of the Ottoman Empire—it was part of Turkey, the motherland of its empire in much the same way as Britain was at the heart of the British Empire. The Turks responded accordingly, fighting and dying in great numbers to defend their homeland and drive the infidel invader from their territory. Estimates of Turkish casualties during their heroic defence of the peninsula throughout the Allied campaign in 1915 and early 1916 range from 66,000 to 86,000 men killed.[12] Where, in *The Anzac Book*, was Tolstoy's 'blood, suffering and death'? What really happened at Gallipoli?

Thus began a lifelong interest in Gallipoli and C.E.W. Bean, driven initially by my need to seek answers.

Of course, what I didn't realise then was that the book was intended as a light-hearted memoir, an attempt to insulate the public from the horrors of war and to maintain morale at home and in the AIF. By the time the book was published in 1916, the remarkable evacuation of Gallipoli had occurred—a gut-wrenching admission of defeat for the men who fought there. *The Anzac Book* put a positive spin on the Gallipoli experience. As well, Bean wanted to project a certain image of the Anzacs, to emphasise their physical superiority, laconic disregard of enemy fire, ready and irreverent humour, fighting prowess and their ability to cope with whatever conditions they encountered.

Importantly, even as the editor of *The Anzac Book*, Bean was operating under constraints, both official and self-imposed, regarding its content. As Official War Correspondent, he was very mindful of the instructions he'd received from the Defence Department in Australia regarding the nature of his copy. He wasn't allowed to denigrate the Mediterranean Expeditionary Force—the Anzacs being a part of that body—or upset the men's families in his despatches. Had Bean transgressed, he would have been sent back to Australia. Both the British military authorities and the British government had been badly scarred by William Russell's reports from the front during the Crimean War 60 years earlier. Russell, writing for *The Times* newspaper for two years, was scathing about the abject performance of British commanders and the supply shortages the troops endured.[13] Ultimately, criticism in the domestic press of the British war effort in the Crimea helped to bring down the government of the day in early 1855.[14] This time the British War Office and the British government were much more circumspect about what the correspondents could report without censure.

Ellis Ashmead-Bartlett, the controversial British war correspondent, was sent home from Gallipoli by General Sir Ian Hamilton in early October 1915 for having circumvented the official censors. Using Keith Murdoch as his mule, Ashmead-Bartlett attempted to inform the British prime minister, Herbert Asquith, of the debacle occurring at Gallipoli. However, his letter was intercepted at Marseilles by British military intelligence. Hamilton immediately withdrew Ashmead-Bartlett's official authorisation, and the latter returned to London to continue a campaign to evacuate the peninsula.[15] Ironically, it was a letter written by Keith Murdoch to the Australian prime minister, Andrew Fisher, that eventually found its way to Number 10 Downing Street. It concerned Asquith so much that he, in turn, circulated it among the upper echelons of British power, such as the Dardanelles Committee and the Cabinet. As a result, Hamilton was removed as the commanding officer of the Mediterranean Expeditionary Force, and Field Marshal Lord Kitchener was sent to Gallipoli to observe firsthand and report back post haste. Ultimately, a decision to evacuate all three Allied morasses—Suvla, Anzac and Helles—was made. In spite of censorship and threats of accreditation being revoked, the eyewitness accounts from Ashmead-Bartlett and Murdoch in particular heavily influenced the men in the corridors of power and the decisions they made—in this case to abandon the whole enterprise.[16]

The other constraint on Bean was a personal one. When he was appointed Official War Correspondent in September 1914, the Minister for Defence, Senator George Pearce, told Bean that he hoped that on his return from the war Bean would write the history of the Australian part in it.[17] Having survived months under fire with the men at Gallipoli, Bean was determined to tell their story; he wouldn't have done anything to jeopardise that goal. Hence the notice he distributed at Anzac for contributions to *The Anzac Book* near the end of 1915 stated that the 'volume will contain short poems and stories, pictures, jokes, topical advertisements, skits, limericks, cartoons and the Anzac alphabet'.[18]

Some contributions that portrayed the darker side of the fighting at Anzac were rejected for publication but kept by Bean, and after the war they formed part of the archive at the Australian War Memorial in Canberra. Bean's censorship also extended to items that were accepted and published. Private Perry's opening tale, for example, was sanitised by Bean for domestic consumption.[19]

At war's end Senator Pearce was still the Minister for Defence, by which time Bean and his staff were well advanced in their plans for *The Official History*; it had taken on a life of its own. Also, at the age of 40, Bean had accumulated the major influences and experiences that would guide and shape the writing of the book.

~

Bean, although born in Australia, had been educated in England at such august establishments as Clifton College and Oxford University.[20] There he became imbued with a deep love of England and its culture, especially its rich lode of literature, and the Empire. By the time he returned to Australia in 1904, he had graduated from Oxford with two degrees, in the classics and law. After initially working as a lawyer and teacher, Charles Bean found his pre-war place as a journalist for *The Sydney Morning Herald* from June 1908.[21] He worked in various roles at the paper, with some of his articles from these assignments turning into books. His writings during this period reflected his growing awareness of the issues that were close to the emerging psyche of Australian society. These included the maintenance of the White Australia policy, the need for a strong local military establishment headed by its own navy, and the prowess of the bushmen and the unforgiving land they inhabited as examples of the new world at its best. Even though Bean emphasised the differences between Mother England and its pioneering progeny, above all he understood and enhanced the relationship between Australia and Great Britain.

In September 1914 Bean was the winner of a vote held by the Australian Journalists' Association to select an official correspondent to accompany the troops overseas to wherever and whatever eventuated.[22] The greatest influences on Bean's adult life were the unending burdens of duty, fighting and sacrifice the AIF shouldered during World War I—seen, shared and experienced firsthand in his role as the Official War Correspondent. His mission to record those tumultuous and tragic years seemed preordained. Where others died around him in battle, he survived, all the while accumulating a vast, intimate knowledge and understanding of the men and their leaders over the course of the war.

Charles Bean was the most prolific and influential writer of Australian military history. His style gave voice to the trials, tribulations, tragedies and triumphs of the ordinary soldier in volume after volume of the *Official History*. The level of detail is extraordinary. Military historians, certainly those in Australia, have used his writing methods as a blueprint for their own stories. On 22 February 1938 Bean explained his modus operandi in an address to the Royal Australian Historical Society, emphasising the freedom the government gave him to present his views. Unlike the wartime restrictions he so assiduously observed, there would be no censorship, apart from the omission of technical naval details that might benefit regional rivals. Bean resolved that his account would focus on questions relating to the Australian national character and the nation's contribution to World War I, Australia's first test on the international stage. He determined that only a detailed examination would suffice. He wanted to present the micro and macro faces of war, from the troops in the firing line to the commanders in their headquarters. Bean believed:

> that their subject should be viewed from the front line as well as from the rear, and that, as far as possible, the responsibility for the events described should be attributed to the men actually responsible—at least sufficiently to prove that the responsibility for important decisions, which the official reports tend to lay unduly on commanders, was in fact constantly taken also by subordinates.[23]

In order to better understand the ebb and flow of battle, Bean enthused:

> . . . we Australian historians had the chance of discovering by *finding out and questioning the men who were actually there*; occasionally by watching the incident or even being there ourselves. To give the reader such information meant undoubtedly to furnish more detail than has been put into a war history, at least in modern times. 'One may doubt,' says Mr John North, 'if history was ever writ so large.' But it seemed to me vital, and the field of our subject was not too great to allow us often to describe action in such terms. *Add to this the conviction that many instances of self-sacrifice, of devoted endurance and bravery must never be heard of unless we record them, and you have the clue to our decision to tell the story in detail* [emphasis added].[24]

In order for the project to enjoy international credibility, Bean wanted this level of historical scrutiny: '. . . it therefore has to carry within its covers not merely our bare conclusions of fact, but also *the evident proof of them*, a result to be attained only by writing in detail.'[25] Bean was emphatic in his address to the society about the validity of the evidence gleaned from veterans who participated in a particular action:

> In dealing with the accounts of separate eyewitnesses it has been a perpetual marvel to me how exactly their narratives dovetail . . . My experience . . . has been that, if several soldiers have seen the same occurrence, at any rate in

> battle, and are interrogated about it, whether at the time or many years afterwards, their accounts will in the great majority of cases agree even in matters of detail.[26]

This was very true in regard to the three main chroniclers of No. 15 Platoon's experiences in Death Trap Valley on 1 May. All three accounts—Les Lott, Snowy Robson and Charles Macquarie—were written in the weeks and months after the battle. All three produced narratives that dovetailed on important points.

Bean adhered to the legal principle of not using hearsay evidence and was quite dismissive of second- or thirdhand reports or accounts from wounded or overstrained men:

> . . . the facts had to be *sought from the actual eye-witnesses or actors, interviewed as soon as possible after the event,* generally over a cup of tea in a dugout or mess-hut; and when one found it, whether it related to an action that won a Victoria Cross, or to less spectacular incidents, it was often surprisingly different from what the most careful and conscientious commander, working in the intense pressure of a campaign, had reported.[27]

Above all else, Bean wanted the participants to tell the story through the historian, so the reader could attempt to come to some understanding of battle, the war and Australia's place in it.

Charles Bean reiterated this dictum in the preface to the first volume of the *Official History, The Story of Anzac*:

> In his search for rigid accuracy the writer was guided by one deliberate and settled principle. The more he saw and knew of the men and officers of the Australian Imperial Force the more fully did the writer become convinced that the only memorial which could be worthy of them was the bare and uncoloured story of their part in the war. From the moment when, early in the war, he realised this, his duty became strangely simple—*to record the plain and absolute truth so far as it was within his limited power to compass it.*[28]

Record it Bean and his staff did—on a vast scale. He wrote six volumes of the history and edited the other six. In an article in *The Bulletin* in 1942, he recounted that the 12 volumes of the *Official History* consisted of:

> roughly 10,000 pages, four million words, 2250 maps and sketches, 1500 illustrations; the actions and names of probably 8000 men and women,

> perhaps more, cited, and footnoted with particulars of practically every one of these persons.[29]

An exhaustive proofreading process for each chapter followed. Some, like the early Gallipoli ones, were checked more than 20 times. However, Bean knew that:

> To write in detail means to multiply the risk of error . . . it is due solely to the endless care exercised by the staff that the number of even slight errors that have been brought to our knowledge is almost negligible. As far as possible they have been corrected in subsequent editions . . .[30]

In *The Bulletin* article, Bean praised his faceless staff for their efforts and attention to detail:

> It is impossible, of course, to attain complete accuracy in such a task; but I say the staff mainly responsible—John Balfour, Arthur Bazley and the draughtsmen, W.S. Perry, Peter Wightman and Alan S. Murray (with J.L. Treloar, T.H.E. Heyes and A.J. Withers largely supplying the records)—have achieved the nearest thing humanly attainable to it . . . However, there it stands. Time may knock off a corner or dint a feature here or there; but at least, in the main, it and what it delineates can now not be lost.[31]

Bean's first volume, *Official History of Australia in the War of 1914–1918, Volume 1, The Story of Anzac,* published in 1921, was revised for its second edition, published in 1933. Bean was reluctant to alter his original narrative too much, so he put the amendments in the preface, arguing that 'there are no grounds for any important alteration of the general narrative'.[32] In the preface to the first edition of *Volume 1*, Bean set out the difficulties he faced in writing the story of Anzac and the methods he used to obviate this problem:

> But the official narratives of Gallipoli and even of Pozières and Bullecourt are meagre in the extreme. Of the Landing and other fighting in Gallipoli there exists no such record from which even the shortest history of those events could be written. For the volumes dealing with that campaign the writer has had to rely almost entirely upon his private diaries and upon notes of his conversations with officers and men at the time and afterwards.[33]

Fortunately, Bean's numerous diaries and notebooks became an unparalleled resource for researchers and historians in this country and overseas. Their preservation and ready availability online and at the Australian War Memorial are a boon for researchers, whether your interest is familial or historical. Somewhat alarmingly, according to Denis Winter, who has researched and written extensively on Australia and World War I using the records from the War Memorial:

> At the end of the 1950s he [Bean] went through every single sheet of paper in his own records, cutting extracts out of his diaries and workbooks, writing warnings in margins and withholding large quantities of material, particularly letters written during the writing of the official history. We thus know today what Bean intended us to know.[34]

One wonders what gems Bean destroyed.

Of course, C.E.W. Bean placed a rider on each of his diaries and notebooks. As an experienced journalist, historian and writer, he was well aware of the pitfalls of subjectivity creeping into a narrative at the expense of objectivity and, therefore, historical accuracy. He jotted the entries in the notebooks and diaries at all hours and under all sorts of conditions so he had reservations about the authenticity of what he recorded:

> The use of these diaries and notes is subject to conditions laid down in the terms of gift to the Australian War Memorial. But, apart from those terms, I wish the following circumstances and considerations to be brought to the notice of every reader and writer who may use them.
>
> These writings represent only what at the moment of making them I believed to be true. The diaries were jotted down almost daily with the object of recording what was then in the writer's mind. Often he wrote them when very tired and half asleep; also, not infrequently, what he believed to be true was not so—but it does not follow that he always discovered this, or remembered to correct the mistakes when discovered. Indeed, he could not always remember that he had written them.
>
> These records should, therefore, be used with great caution, as relating only what their author, at the time of writing, believed. Further, he cannot, of course, vouch for the accuracy of statements made to him by others and here recorded. But he did try to ensure such accuracy by consulting, as far as possible, those who had seen or otherwise taken part in the events. The constant falsity of second-hand evidence (on which a large proportion of war stories are founded) was impressed upon him by the second or

third day of the Gallipoli campaign, notwithstanding that those who passed on such stories usually themselves believed them to be true. All second-hand evidence herein should be read with this in mind.[35]

No such stipulation was attached to the volumes of his official histories or his other publications pertaining to the war. Nor were there any other constraints imposed, apart from Bean's obsession with presenting the Anzacs and their feats as accurately as possible. When writing, Bean was, for the most part, clear in his mind as to the course of events and the roles played by various individuals. Researchers and historians refer to Bean's works, using them not only as a starting point but also as the definitive account of Australia's involvement in World War I. Many writers accept his version as gospel.

Inevitably, mistakes and omissions were made. The sheer scale of his project meant that corrections would need to be made. Bean admitted as much in the preface to the revised edition of *Volume 1* published in 1933 that, 'Since the publication of the first edition of this volume in 1921, additional data have become accessible both in documentary form and in published works', necessitating additions and revisions to his narrative.[36]

In researching and writing *Jack's Journey* I came across mistakes and omissions that Bean and other writers have made in regard to those events in Death Trap Valley on 1 and 2 May 1915, nearly 100 years ago. Those in Charles Bean's works have affected subsequent accounts, effectively altering history. What most startled me was the realisation that Bean's errors and omissions were deliberate. He indulged in a form of historiographical skulduggery by choosing to change the historical record.

What did Bean do that was so reprehensible?

Charles Bean omitted any reference to the 4th Battalion in Death Trap Valley on 1 and 2 May, and misrepresented what happened in the revised *Official History* and in a subsequent publication, *Gallipoli Mission*, despite knowing only too well what really transpired. The main focus of Bean's subterfuge was omitting Jack and his 4th Battalion mates and their crucial role in saving the Royal Marines in the outposts during the third Turkish counterattack and, instead, giving all the credit to the 3rd Battalion.

~

When I began researching Jack's story in 2005, I had a copy of his personnel dossier and his three diaries. Jack's third diary, the Gallipoli diary, ended somewhat dramatically as No. 12 Section, No. 15 Platoon, with Jack leading them, went into action in the evening of 25 April 'towards the right wing of the firing line'.

I knew he was wounded on 1 May and subsequently died of his wound on 4 May. The Collyer family consensus was that Jack was wounded while helping someone.

The big questions were: where was he and what was he doing when he was wounded?

Naturally enough I turned to Bean, hoping for enlightenment, but drew a blank. The 4th Battalion war diary was equally frustrating, although it revealed they had hurriedly returned to the firing line to reinforce the Marines. In *The Fighting Fourth*, published in 2007, Ron Austin offered some insights, but didn't mention Jack or No. 15 Platoon in the body of the narrative in regard to Death Trap Valley on 1 May 1915. He did reveal that Major James Heane received the DSO for leading D Company, 4th Battalion, while they rescued some Marines who had become isolated on 1 May.[37] Jack was in D Company and he'd been hit on 1 May—I wondered, perhaps he was involved?

After making contact with Jack's nephew, Ray Warry, in 2008 we did a swap. I sent copies of Jack's three diaries his way; in return Ray sent me a copy of Corporal Macquarie's letter to George Collyer, which detailed the circumstances of Jack being wounded. Macquarie's letter was a revelation, but it still left some unanswered points. Above all else, where were Jack and No. 15 Platoon on 1 May? From the letter it was clear they were reinforcing Marines in the firing line and, therefore, they were part of James Heane's rescue party. Now, at least, I knew what Jack was doing. He *was* helping someone when he was wounded.

I even found the letter and memorandum from the Royal Marine's hierarchy, complimenting Heane and his men for their gallant work, in the 1st Brigade archive online at the AWM site. However, it was the repeated reference to Les Lott's diary in Kit Denton's *Gallipoli: One Long Grave* that led me to the Australian War Memorial, seeking its annotated copy of Lott's diary. Finding that diary in 2009 was the big breakthrough—a Eureka moment! Phil Tardiff had transcribed the diary, replete with valuable annotations and illustrations. In it was an extraordinary account by Lott, detailing many crucial aspects of Heane's party and their heroics in Death Trap Valley on 1 and 2 May, saving the Marines. I was gobsmacked! Unfortunately, I was in the Reading Room at the War Memorial where overt displays of euphoria are *verboten*, and I had to settle for some silent fist clenching. Thanks to Les Lott, Phil Tardiff and Kit Denton, I now knew the truth about Death Trap Valley and the 4th's involvement. Lott told me where Jack was on 1 May—Death Trap Valley.

Another Eureka moment occurred in the National Library in 2011, when I found Snowy Robson's letter to his sister in *The Tamworth Daily Observer*, detailing his amazing achievements. I can't begin to imagine the Eureka moments Charles Bean must have had writing the official histories.

Thus armed, I went back to Bean's revised first volume to re-examine it. Surely there was a reference that I'd missed or misinterpreted. After all, two men in the 4th had been awarded medals specifically for their leadership and bravery rescuing the Marines on 1 May, and more than 30 men had died doing it. There was also their involvement on Sunday, 2 May; the remnants of No. 3 Platoon, A Company, 4th Battalion, were in the valley holding their own against the Turkish onslaught, and what was left of Fred Fanning's platoon were in Loutit's Post, pouring rifle fire into the assaulting waves of Turkish troops.

The reference to the outposts and the Marines in the body of Bean's volume was reasonably vague, but additional information appeared in the preface. It began with the heading: 'The Marines on MacLaurin's Hill. Further light has been thrown upon the position of the Marines in Wire Gully and their rescue by Sergeants Meager and McLeod.'[38] The account went on to detail the increasingly tenuous occupation of the outposts by Empson and Alcock and their men and how, during a major Turkish incursion in the early hours of 2 May, the cavalry, in the form of two newly promoted lieutenants, Meager and McLeod, from the 3rd Battalion and their platoons, arrived and saved the Marines.[39] Bean's version omitted any reference or acknowledgment of the role and heroism of the 4th Battalion. Sure, the two platoons from the 3rd Battalion played a role on 2 May, but where were Major Heane, Lieutenant Fanning and No. 15 Platoon and No. 3 Platoon from the 4th Battalion in Bean's version of events? What about Snowy Robson's extraordinary feats? Hadn't the 4th Battalion been singled out by the Marines' commanding officers as the saviours of the Marines in the valley on 1 May? Despite these obvious questions, Bean's account described Meager and McLeod's platoons as the rescuers of the Marines.

Tellingly, what I did notice in Bean's narrative were extracts from Lieutenant-Colonel Frank Luard's letter, which eulogised only Heane and his men from D Company, 4th Battalion, for their actions. The first small extract was harmless enough: 'without means of reinforcement, replenishment or retreat'.[40] This was Bean's description of the awful plight of the outpost's Marine garrison, although it did start to ring some bells. The next extract was in the form of a footnote and exposed Bean's misrepresentation of history. Having detailed the brave work of Meager, McLeod and their men, Bean finished the story:

> For the time being the useless earthwork lay unoccupied by either side. Street's Trench was garrisoned; but on May 5th, when Meager and McLeod were withdrawn, Loutit's old position was abandoned. [Footnote 32]

I then scanned down the page to the footnote at the bottom of the page:

> 32. With reference to the incident above related, Lieut.-Colonel F.W. Luard, commanding the Portsmouth Battalion, wrote: 'The officers and men of the Portsmouth Battalion, R.M.L.I., have been greatly moved by this splendid act of Imperial comradeship.'[41]

The implication was that Luard was praising the men of the 3rd Battalion. In fact, before and after this comment were direct references to the 4th Battalion; one was even in the same sentence!

The relevant section of the letter of commendation stated:

> 1. On the 1st instant [1 May] a platoon of the Portsmouth Battalion was forced to be in an isolated trench, without means of reinforcements, replenishment, or of retreat . . .
> 2. From this dangerous position the platoon was rescued by a most gallant effort made at heavy sacrifice by the adjacent unit 'D' Coy. 4th Bn. Australian Infantry. (MAJOR HEANE)
> 3. The officers and men of the Portsmouth Bn. R.M.L.I. have been greatly moved by this splendid act of Imperial Comradeship and desire that an expression of their deep gratitude may be conveyed to the 4th Bn. Australian Infantry through the Brig'r Genl. Commdg. R.M.Bde.[42]

There was no mention of either the 3rd Battalion or No. 3 Platoon, A Company, 4th Battalion, who were also involved, in the document. The accompanying letter from the general commanding the RMLI, Brigadier-General Charles Trotman, added his personal gratitude and admiration for 'the conduct of Major Heane and the NCOs and the men of his Company who acted so nobly'. Again, there was no reference to the 3rd Battalion. The only unit mentioned in either document was D Company, 4th Battalion, under the leadership of Major Heane. Significantly, the 3rd Battalion was still in its dangerous digs on the beach at Anzac for most of 1 May. According to their war diary, they didn't make a move towards the firing line until 5 p.m. on Saturday. They didn't begin their relief of the Marines until 9 p.m. that night. They didn't enter Death Trap Valley until the early hours of 2 May, the relief not being completed until daybreak.

This self-imposed censorship of the 4th's involvement continued in Bean's 1948 book, *Gallipoli Mission*, based on his 1919 pilgrimage to Anzac. One of the aims of the mission was to 'locate sites and to answer puzzles about the Anzac fighting'.[43] In Chapter 12, 'Other Riddles of the Landing', Bean ventured into

Wire Gully, located the outposts and the detritus of the occupants—sun helmets of the Marines and jam tins and other rubbish deposited there from the firing line above it. Some skeletons that Bean identified as Turkish were found. In the course of briefly describing the history of the outposts, Bean once again focused exclusively on the 3rd Battalion:

> The Marines in their turn were heroically relieved by Sergeants H.R.W. Meagher and T.D. McLeod of the 3rd Battalion.
>
> Eventually having proved a death-trap (though the scene of a series of fine actions, including that which brought the first Victoria Cross to be won at Anzac), these outposts were all given up—the last of them on May 5th.[44]

Again, Bean refused to divulge the 4th's heroics, although he did acknowledge that other brave deeds occurred. This was his chance to right the historical record and at least mention Heane, Fanning, Robson and the other men from the 4th Battalion, including those, like Jack, who died simply doing their duty. In the foreword to *Gallipoli Mission*, Bill Gammage commented that Bean 'wanted to pay homage to the Anzac dead, and to use their faith and fire to inspire his fellow Australians to national greatness'.[45] He certainly did not pay homage to the dead of the 4th Battalion who fell in Death Trap Valley in early May 1915, saving the Marines, nor did he acknowledge the crucial role played by the survivors from the 4th Battalion.

Bean seemed to rely on Lieutenant-Colonel Robert Owen, commanding officer of the 3rd Battalion, in the aftermath of the battle for some of his information in regard to the course of events in the valley, and as to who deserved recognition for saving the Marines. Owen, it must be remembered, was not present in Death Trap Valley when the 3rd Battalion relieved the Marines. Bean may well have talked to Meager and McLeod in the wake of the action. His emphasis on the 3rd Battalion continued in *Gallipoli Mission* when Bean, again in a footnote, this time concerning Walter Parker's Victoria Cross, wrote:

> Others were deserved, as the reader will see at *Vol. 1, pp. 540–2*, and *Preface to 2nd Edition, pp. xix–xxii*; but that battle left the inexperienced staffs far too busy, with the task of rebuilding their units and carrying on, to attend to recommendations for awards; also witnesses were dead or in hospital, and records almost non-existent.[46]

There was little doubt he was referring to the 3rd Battalion. The first reference in the *Official History*, '*Vol. 1, pp. 540–2*', was his initial attempt to portray Meager and McLeod's men as the saviours of the Marines. The second reference, '*Preface to 2nd Edition, pp. xix–xxii*', was his one-sided revised version—'The Marines on MacLaurin's Hill', which only praised the 3rd Battalion. There was no mention of the 4th Battalion in either account. For a writer who prided himself on accuracy and the minutiae of his subject, Bean's deliberate omission of any reference to the 4th Battalion's role in saving the Marines in *Gallipoli Mission* or the *Official History* was historiographically flawed.

This intentional and calculated approach to expunge the 4th Battalion from this action was made worse when other evidence from Bean's personal writings surfaced. Even allowing for his rider cautioning against the veracity of the entries in both his notebooks and diaries, the entries proved Bean had knowledge of the involvement of the 3rd and 4th battalions. On page 26 of one of his notebooks, dated April–June 1915, Bean gave an abridged version of the action in Death Trap Valley and the involvement of the 3rd and 4th battalions:

> A Co 3Bn occupied 'RMLI Bn Trench' as it is now known. They were 100 yds down Wire Gully in 3 tiers, with no communication. This is the trench (filled in now with dead) in wh RMLI were on Thursday + wh they left afterwards.
>
> The RMLI when they ran left some wounded in the trench. A platoon of 3 bn. knowing the trench, Sergt Macleod + Sergt Meagher (since officers), went out + stopped until the 4bn cut down to them. They got some Turks cut off + as they tried to get back thro a whole night they were shooting them until abt 200 shot. Heane of 4 Bn was in (nearest Coy) of 4th Bn + as the RMLI authorities dealt with him they—to his gt surprise—recommended him for a DSO for this work—wh he got.[47]

This short account implied that the 4th Battalion helped the relieving troops of the 3rd Battalion out of a sticky situation, 'until the 4th cut down to them', and assisted in driving the Turks out of the position, which in fact they did. The reference to Heane was not very complimentary, but it still placed him in the vicinity of the action. These two references should have piqued his professional interest, as should the awarding of the DSO to James Heane, specifically for his orchestration of the Marines' rescue on 1 May.

Bean's diary entry for 15 May 1915 was also damning. Regardless of when it was actually written, once again it referred to both AIF battalions—the 3rd and the 4th:

> I don't quite know what date—but 2 platoons of marines made themselves one of their shallow trenches near Maclagans HQ.—in front of our present line—+ tried to connect up with their left by a trench across the gully (w the were, now/ the gap) + got cut off. Two platoons of the 3rd Bn. (some say 4th*)* went to their rescue + stayed w them 48 hours until the 4th Bn cut a sap thro' to them. In another portion of trench 3 men of the 3rd stayed w them 48 hours rather than leave some wounded men. The 4th Bn was thanked for this by the Gen. commdg the Marine Bde (Gen Trottman). There were Turks in the same trench as tt in wh these wounded men were—only further along it. (acc. to Col. Owen)[48]

The first reference to the 4th Battalion—'some say 4th'—may have been regarded as hearsay, but when added to a raft of other evidence that was available during the war, and post-war in Bean's own archives, it should have sparked the normally fastidious official historian to investigate further. Bean admitted in his address to the Royal Australian Historical Society in 1938 that, although hearsay was not admissible as evidence, it was suitable 'as a general guide to the direction in which the truth might be found'. In this case, Bean didn't follow it up or, if he did, he chose to ignore what he discovered. The other relevant reference in the diary entry was the thanks the 4th received from General Trotman, the commanding officer of the Royal Marine Light Infantry Brigade. Significantly, in his diary Bean acknowledged that the general's thanks were directed to the 4th Battalion yet, when he wrote his *Official History*, he redirected Trotman's sentiments to the 3rd Battalion.

Bean's cautionary rider on the content of his diaries and notebooks worked two ways in relation to his interpretation of the events in Death Trap Valley on 1 and 2 May. Firstly, he seemed to regard the crucial actions of Heane and his men as lacking credibility; indeed, what the 4th Battalion did on 1 May has been downplayed by Bean in his notes and ignored in his published work. However, his diary clearly shows he was aware they played a role. Secondly, Bean's obsession with accuracy and not relying on second- or thirdhand accounts should have pricked his professional interest enough to ensure he interviewed Heane and some of his men, notably Snowy Robson, both of whom were present at Anzac after the action. These two veterans were available to be interviewed post-war yet Bean appeared not to have availed himself of their recollections of 1 May in particular, or of 2 May.

The fact that Snowy Robson was one of the first Australian recipients of the Distinguished Conduct Medal in World War I, for his heroics in this action, demanded Bean's time and attention. Snowy was a perfect fit for Bean's Anzac legend—an unassuming hero who listed his occupation as a bushman hailing from Uralla. Undoubtedly, Bean knew of Snowy's exploits via the Gallipoli grapevine. He admitted that hearsay was a prompt for further investigation. The wording on Lieutenant-Colonel Bennett's recommendation for Snowy's medal was not hearsay. Bennett wrote: 'All sources agree that this soldier's conduct largely saved the situation.'[49] Obviously, the 4th's commanding officer received reports from Major Heane and Lieutenant Fred Fanning, who both witnessed what Snowy did. The heroics of Heane and his men was common knowledge in the 4th Battalion. Howard McKern's diary entry for 9 May, noting the Marines' 'thanks and appreciation' for the actions of D and A companies on 1 May,[50] and Jack Massie's reference in a letter to his mother on 10 May that 'one of our boys called Robson has been recommended for the D.C.M.', also showed this.[51] References to the medals awarded to Heane and Robson in the battalion war diary in May and June in Routine Battalion Orders, authorised by Lieutenant-Colonel Bennett, also showed official acknowledgment and not just hearsay, if Bean had bothered to investigate.

Clearly, Bean knew soon after the action of 1 and 2 May that the 4th Battalion played a significant role in saving the Marines. Surely the 4th's heroics were a godsend for his view of the Anzacs—distinguishing themselves in the field, saving their British brothers, despite horrific casualties in the face of a rampant enemy raining hell on them. Bean's rival and fellow Gallipoli correspondent, Charles Smith, certainly thought it was worth writing about. His article lauding Heane and his men was written months after the battle, Smith only learning of their heroics when he arrived at Anzac in July 1915. He described their remarkable story as one of the 'gems' among the debris of war.

The detailed checking processes used in the writing of the *Official History* would have been used on the revised second edition of Volume 1 of the *Official History*'s version of the events in the outposts on 1 and 2 May. This raises the question of complicity between Bean and his staff to omit the 4th Battalion and, instead, promote the 3rd Battalion as the saviours of the Marines in Death Trap Valley—in effect, a conspiracy. There seems little doubt that at least some of Bean's staff were privy to the deception, given the thorough checking process Bean and his staff employed. Bean's staff were dedicated, incredibly knowledgeable and very well organised. Men such as Arthur Bazley and John Balfour began their association with Bean and the collection and classifying of records during World War I. Both these men served at Gallipoli and the Western Front in various roles, often, though not always, related to Bean's service. After the war they devoted decades of selfless service to the writing process of the *Official History* volumes.

Arthur Bazley's relationship with Charles Bean began before his enlistment. He joined the AIF specifically to work for Bean. According to an article in *Stand-To* in 1959, Arthur Bazley joined Bean before enlisting on 5 October 1914, having been introduced by a mutual friend, Archie White, a fellow journalist, on a Friday night in early October. White had arranged the meeting, believing it would be beneficial to both parties. Bazley recalled their initial meeting, his excitement quite palpable:

> Bean, who was wearing gold-rimmed pince-nez and a straw hat—but I forget now whether the hat-band or his tie were the colours of his old school, Clifton College, Bristol—thereupon asked me quietly whether I would like to go away with him. Would I? I had been trying without success for the past two months to join the A.I.F., but the age for enlistment was 19, and my father thought I should wait until I reached that age.
>
> By the following afternoon I had got into the A.I.F.—by the old simple expedient, followed by numbers of others in those days, of overstating my age . . . While waiting in the corridor—I heard Plant (the attestation officer at Victoria Barracks, later Major-General E.C.P. Plant) say: 'Well, Bean, if he is 18 when he comes in here we can't take him.' He need not have worried on that score—the only one who showed any sign of worry was C.E.W. Bean who, being the man he was, realised he was condoning something that he know [sic] was not altogether right . . . Officially I was posted as 'batman' to Mr. Bean, who was 'graded' (for precedence in mess, billeting, etc.) as a captain. I must confess that I did not know then what was meant by the word 'batman'—I soon learnt; but my duties, far from being those of an officer's servant, were largely those of a clerk and typist.
>
> So began for me a close and active association lasting for over thirty years, with one of the finest men I have ever known, and of whom no less a figure than the late General Sir Brudenall White, in a letter he wrote to me in October, 1939, said that he could only describe Bean as 'Australia's greatest son.'[52]

In 1939, Bean wrote this wonderful appraisal of Arthur Bazley:

> . . . has been responsible from the first for the war records side of my work. He probably knows more about the war records of Australia . . . than any other man; certainly more than I do. He is accustomed to making quick researches and setting them forth in clear style, & is extraordinarily

> thorough. In addition he has the ability to write and edit, as his work for Reveille, & the editing of many regimental histories show . . . As you know he is tireless, and the work he has done out of office hours is probably nearly as valuable as that which he has done in them. He is completely loyal, and an unselfish companion to work with . . .[53]

Bill Gammage described Bazley's knowledge of the first AIF as 'inexhaustible'.[54]

In the *Stand-To* article, Bazley described his role 'as librarian and 'deviller'. According to Janda Gooding in *Gallipoli Revisited*, this meant Bazley:

> paid attention to the smallest details, kept all the papers in order and maintained an index of the documents so that they could quickly locate a reference to a person, place or event. He also solved problems, typed up material, ran errands and generally supported Bean in his work. Other staff came and went over the years, but Bazley and Balfour remained vital to the efficient organisation of the team.[55]

Bazley's devotion to Bean and his almost unparalleled knowledge of the AIF and documents deemed to be relevant to each part of the *Official History* are to be applauded. However, these attributes place him squarely in the frame as Bean and Balfour's co-conspirator.

What was John Balfour's role in the Bean team? According to Arthur Bazley:

> Balfour, the senior member of the staff, was given the very responsible task of checking the facts in the manuscripts of all the volumes—a job well suited to his acute and mathematical mind; he was the 'back-stop' not only for C.E.W. Bean, but also for the writers of the other volumes in the series . . . In addition to that work, he also compiled the biographical footnotes of the people mentioned in the volumes and the indexes to those volumes.[56]

Balfour was a crucial member of the staff, whose input was vital to the integrity and accuracy of the writing of the *Official History*.

At the end of the preface in the sixth and final volume of the *Official History* Bean wrote he thanked various organisations and individuals, but he reserved his warmest regards for John Balfour and Arthur Bazley:

> . . . but foremost, to Mr J. Balfour, responsible for checking and indexing the work, Mr A.W. Bazley in charge of the historian's records and

> correspondence [Bean also mentioned Miss Ida McAulay, Mr W.S. Perry and Mr P.R. Wightman] . . . who together have formed the backbone of the small staff that has carried through this long task with devotion and thoroughness.[57]

As senior Bean staffers, Bazley and Balfour must have seen the letters from General Trotman and Lieutenant-Colonel Luard, praising Major Heane and his men of the 4th Battalion for rescuing the Marines on 1 May. The 1st Brigade archive for May 1915 that holds these documents was one Bean used to write the *Official History*. The documents appeared consecutively in the file. At the very least Bazley, in his role as keeper and finder of war records, would have known of their existence. He obviously accessed these documents in order for Bean to misuse the extract from Luard's letter. John Balfour, in his role of checking the accuracy of Bean's works, would have checked the original documents against Bean's draft. He would also have seen the Marines' documents. Both Bazley and Balfour would have noticed there was no reference to the 3rd Battalion in either document. In spite of this they colluded with Bean to champion the role of the 3rd Battalion at the expense of the 4th Battalion.

There was also a discrepancy between the date the Marines' documents used—1 May—for the rescue of the Marines and the date that can be discerned from Bean's version of events in the *Official History*. In order to make the events fit his time frame, Bean never mentioned the date 2 May; instead he described the action as occurring 'During the night of 1 May'. Bean does mention things hotting up at 2.30;[58] however, surprisingly, or not, he doesn't use 'a.m.' after 2.30. To have done either of these things would have clearly placed Meager and McLeod's 3rd Battalion relief party, correctly, on 2 May, at odds with the date of 1 May, which Luard and Trotman recorded for the rescue of the Marines by Major James Heane and his men of the 4th Battalion. Having said that, Bean's deceitful footnote did not show the date of 'this splendid act of Imperial comradeship' performed by Meager and McLeod's men. It couldn't, because the subterfuge would have been exposed sooner.

Apart from the documents written by the Marine commanders, there were other records, including official ones, detailing the presence, heroics and sacrifice of the 4th Battalion in Death Trap Valley that Bean's staff, certainly Bazley and Balfour, would have seen. These included medal citations and recommendations for Heane and Robson, casualty figures for the 4th Battalion for May, Red Cross Records for missing and wounded men from the 4th Battalion, entries in one of Bean's diaries for May 1915 and in one of his notebooks for April–June 1915, the 4th Battalion war diary entries after 1 and 2 May, and documents in the 1st

Australian Division Summary of Operations for May 1915 archive. There seems little doubt that Bazley and Balfour conspired with Bean to alter the historical record through misrepresentation and omission of the 4th Battalion's involvement in saving the Royal Marines.

When writing about battles that occurred in France, there was one unofficial record that Bean perused and used in the *Official History* which gave a detailed account of No. 3 Platoon, A Company's travails in Death Trap Valley—Les De Vine's precious diary. Apparently, Bean met De Vine post-war when De Vine was rewiring Bean's Victoria Barracks' office. Bean heard about the diary and subsequently referred to it extensively in his Pozières narrative.[59] We can only assume Bean read the diary entries that clearly outlined the events of 1 and 2 May.

In his portrayal of the people and events in Death Trap Valley on 1 and 2 May 1915, Bean ignored the tenets underpinning his approach to writing the *Official History*. He did not 'record the plain and absolute truth', nor did he attempt to 'by finding out and questioning the men who were actually there', and he distorted 'the evident proof', thereby, unfortunately, fulfilling his belief that 'many instances of self-sacrifice, of devoted endurance and bravery must never be heard of (unless we record them)'.

Why did Bean and senior members of his staff erase the 4th's role and misrepresent what happened?

I believe he was upset by the 3rd Battalion's lack of medals for their heroism during the relief on 2 May and over the next 48 hours—perhaps not without justification. And yet, without the Herculean efforts of No. 15 Platoon and No. 3 Platoon from the 4th Battalion on 1 May, there wouldn't have been any Marines in the outposts to be relieved on 2 May—the valley would have been under Turkish control and the main firing line on MacLaurin's Hill and the northern part of Johnston's Jolly would have been threatened. The evidence shows that the parties from the 4th Battalion saved the Marines in the valley on consecutive days—initially, on their own on 1 May, and in conjunction with the 3rd Battalion on 2 May. They also played an important role in thwarting the Turk's third counterattack in the Central Sector of the ANZAC and Marine firing line, especially on Saturday, 1 May.

Lieutenants Meager and McLeod and their men—particularly Privates Ward, Beal and Hatton—definitely performed above and beyond the call of duty during the relief. Bean knew these men were worthy candidates for medals. In the light of Lieutenant-Colonel Owen's repeated calls for bravery awards for these men, Bean may well have felt aggrieved and frustrated; after all, he had an interest in the 3rd Battalion. His brother, Jack, to whom Charles was close, was the 3rd Battalion's medical officer. Jack Bean wasn't at Anzac on 1 or 2 May. He suffered a gunshot wound to his buttocks on 25 April while performing his duty soon after the Landing and was evacuated to Egypt for further treatment. Jack Bean didn't rejoin his battalion until early July 1915.[60] Regardless, to change the historical record by omission and historiographical sleight of hand cannot be justified.

Bean's betrayal went beyond what he wrote. Whether the boys in the 4th Battalion died or survived, Charles Bean denied their families any public acknowledgment of their courage and sacrifice. He denied them their place in history. In Bean's own words:

> And if the historian cannot write that drama in its full truth, with the interplay of good and ill, wisdom and folly, of all the parties working to its complex conclusion, then so much the less historian he.[61]

British historians' accounts of the Royal Marines at Anzac from 28 April to 13 May were concerned with presenting the Marines in the best possible light in the face of some Australian criticism of their performance, particularly during their occupation of the firing line during the third Turkish counterattack. Naturally enough, these sources concentrated on Walter Parker's Victoria Cross in regard to Death Trap Valley and the Marines' occupation of the outposts. Empson and his men were portrayed as gallant in their defence of the isolated trench. Parker was eulogised but no Australians were praised or recognised as being involved. The Marines were finally compelled to withdraw from the outposts, taking their wounded with them. No reasons for the evacuation were given in these accounts, apart from a shortage of ammunition. There were certainly no references to the Marines retreating, having had their line broken. The 4th Battalion's feats on 1 and 2 May 1915 have been expunged from British military history as effectively as they were omitted from Bean's *Official History* and *Gallipoli Mission*.

~

In this book I have tried to give a balanced account of the events in Death Trap Valley on 1 and 2 May 1915 and the roles played by the participants, attempting to redress the historical imbalance propagated by Charles Bean and English versions of the Marines' occupation of the isolated trench. These events occurred 100 years ago, on a peninsula in a remote Turkish valley in a place called Gallipoli that is geographically a world away yet occupies a special place in the hearts of Australians.

I hope I have paid homage to the men from Australia, Great Britain, New Zealand, the Indian subcontinent, Germany and the Ottoman Empire who valiantly fought and died during the Landing at Anzac so long ago. Jack Collyer was just one of those young men who gave his life for his country. His journey epitomises those of so many on both sides who naively went to war in 1914.

Appendix 1: Casualties in 4th Battalion, 1 and 2 May 1915[1]

To follow are lists of men from the 4th Battalion who were killed in action on 1 and 2 May. The majority of the men from A and D companies were killed in Death Trap Valley.

A Company

Lance Corporal William Smith (861), KIA, 1 May
Private Frederick Richards (1318), KIA, 1 May
Private Frederick Waine (1337), KIA, 1 May
Private Percy Tuck (1520), KIA, 1 May
Private William Andersen (846), KIA, 1 May
Private Thomas Bann (678), KIA, 1 May
Private Guthrie Craig (637), KIA, 1 May
Private Lawrence Edwards (864), KIA, 1 May
Private Matthew Stackpool (610), KIA, 1 May
Private Jack Stewart (63), KIA, 1 May
Private John Clancy (327), KIA, 1 May
Private Frank Cooke (649), KIA, 1 May
Private Eric Cusack (513), KIA, 1 May
Private Ernest Edmondson (655), KIA, 1 May
Private Edward Ward (1201), KIA, 1 May
Private Stanley Beer (673), KIA, 1 May
Private Henry Preece (952), KIA, 1 May
Private Henry Murr (1042), KIA, 2 May
Total: 18 KIA (17 on 1 May; 1 on 2 May)

B Company

Private William O'Connor (1082), KIA, 1 May

Private Herbert Hardwick (342), KIA, 2 May
Private Joseph Higginbottom (336), KIA, 2 May
Total: 3 KIA (1 on 1 May; 2 on 2 May)

C Company

Private William Carey (1249), KIA, 1 May
Private John Riddell (444), KIA, 1 May
Private William Robertson (1046), KIA, 1 May
Private George Newhouse (1415), KIA, 2 May
Second Lieutenant Sydney Bewicke, KIA, 2 May
Total: 5 KIA (3 on 1 May; 2 on 2 May)

D Company

Corporal Donald Usher (1335), KIA, 1 May
Private Kenneth Gillies (1265), KIA, 1 May
Private John Farnsworth (562), KIA, 1 May
Private Tom McKay (298), KIA, 1 May
Private Newton Brand (592), KIA, 1 May
Private Keith Chambers (239), KIA, 1 May
Private William Hall/Holder (1086), KIA, 1 May
Private Robert Heaslip (353), KIA, 1 May
Private Thomas Holland (593), KIA, 1 May
Private William Wilkinson (421), KIA, 1 May
Private Leslie Munro (969), KIA, 1 May
Private Arthur Flintoff (1261), KIA, 1 May
Lance Sergeant Lafayette Sherburne (312), KIA, 1 May
Private Thomas Davis (1488), KIA, 2 May
Private Alfred Robins (1426), KIA, 2 May
Total: 15 KIA (13 on 1 May; 2 on 2 May)

To follow are lists of men from the 4th Battalion who were wounded in action on 1 and 2 May. Some of these men died of their wounds. Again, most of the men wounded in action in A and D companies were hit in Death Trap Valley.

A Company

Lieutenant John Christie, WIA, 1 May
Sergeant Walter Oakes (651), WIA, 1 May
Private John Cuthbertson (616), WIA, 1 May
Private William Dudley (40), WIA, 1 May

Private Harry Richards (1067), WIA, 1 May
Private Thomas James (1279), WIA, 1 May
Private Joseph Wilson (742), WIA, 1 May
Private Charles Peat (99), WIA, 1 May
Private Thomas Ryan (100), WIA, 1 May
Private William Blair (1076), WIA, 1 May
Private William Montgomery (1293), WIA, 1 May
Private Carl Leyon (1285/1139), WIA, 1 May; DOW, 2 May
Private Alexander Yates (1169), WIA, 1 May; DOW, 2 May
Private Cecil Haache (804), WIA, 1 May; DOW, 9 May
Private Richard Sherrin (1627/1511), WIA, c. 1 May
Private Ernest Turner (522), WIA, 2 May
Private John Downie (1346), WIA, 2 May; DOW, 3 May
Total: 17 WIA (4 DOW)

B Company

Private Albert Ball (658), WIA, c. 1 May
Private Stanley Dennis (273), WIA, c. 1 May
Private Harold Williams (543), WIA, c. 1 May
Private Waterford Phillips (816), WIA, 2 May
Private Leo Atkinson (282), WIA, 2 May
Private James Davidson (982), WIA, 2 May
Private Allan Turnbull (763), WIA, 2 May
Private Hugh McKiernan (1150), WIA, 2 May
Total: 8 WIA

C Company

Lance Sergeant Jack Steber (382), WIA, 1 May
Private James Broderick (827), WIA, 1 May; DOW, 4 May
Private Reginald Kain (1388), WIA, prior to 30 April; DOW, 1 May
Private Stanley Randall (694), WIA, 2 May
Total: 4 WIA (2 DOW; 1 DOW was WIA before 1 May)

D Company

Corporal Charles Lawler (225), WIA, 1 May
Lance Corporal William Harkin (1019), WIA, 1 May
Lance Corporal Arthur Chamberlain (1114), WIA, 1 May
Private Sidney Clarkson (631), WIA, 1 May
Private Victor Mercer (209), WIA, 1 May

Private Ernest Miller (985), WIA, 1 May
Private Ernest Robson (574), WIA, 1 May
Private William Wallen (1117), WIA, 1 May
Private James Watt (1083), WIA, 1 May
Private Benjamin Bathurst (844), WIA, 1 May
Private Alfred Fuller (940), WIA, 1 May
Private Jonathon Hodgson (488), WIA, 1 May
Private Giles Sykes (579), WIA, 1 May
Private John 'Jack' Collyer (1241), WIA, 1 May; DOW, 4 May
Private John McGennan (134), WIA, c. 1/2 May; DOW, 4 May
Private Thomas Thomson (1115), WIA, c. 1/2 May; DOW, 11 May
Lieutenant William French, WIA, 1/2 May
Captain Charles Coltman, WIA, 2 May
Private Ernest 'Snowy' Robson (1088), WIA, 2 May
Private John Collins (194), WIA, 2 May
Private William Bound (1090), WIA, 2 May
Private Charles Maurer (115), WIA, 2 May
Corporal Bertie Knowles (1024), WIA, c. 2 May
Sergeant Edmund Guthrie (549), WIA, prior to 30 April; DOW, Egypt, 1 May
Total: 24 WIA (4 DOW; 1 DOW was WIA before 1 May)

Machine Gun Section

Sergeant George Thomas (790), WIA, c. 1 May; DOW, 6 May
Total: 1 DOW

Company unknown

Private George Hayward (489), WIA, 1 May
Private Cyril Humphries (683), WIA, 1 May
Private Henry Wilkinson (1071), WIA, 1 May
Private Arthur Dinnes (1344), WIA, 1 May
Private William Graham (1363), WIA, 1 May
Private David Bound (1079), WIA, c. 1 May
Private James Honan (351), WIA, 2 May
Private Harold Keech (206), WIA, 2 May
Private Archibald Willis (102), WIA, 2 May
Private Stanley Adamson (112), WIA, 2 May
Total: 10 WIA

Approximate number of 4th Battalion casualties in A and D companies, 1 and 2 May 1915

	Killed in action	*Wounded in action*
1 May	30	32
2 May	3	8
Total	**33**	**40**

Notes: Total number of soldiers wounded in A and D companies: approximately 40. This figure is derived from 40 wounded in action (WIA) minus 7 died of wounds (DOW), plus 7 of the 11 men whose company could not be ascertained from their records. Total number of deaths in A and D companies: 40. This figure is derived from 33 killed in action (KIA) plus 7 DOW.

There were approximately 80 casualties in A and D companies on 1 and 2 May, but readers should bear in mind that B and C companies might have also lost men in the valley. Equally, not all the casualties in A and D companies were incurred in the valley. There were other men, about 20, whose casualty forms do not give the date on which they were wounded; however, there is a possibility that they were wounded on or about 1 or 2 May, owing to their admission to a ship for treatment or for transport to a hospital for further treatment on or near these dates.

Approximate 4th Battalion casualties for 1 and 2 May

Deaths: 52 (including 2 men who died of wounds incurred before 1 May)
Wounded: 53 (originally there were 62 men wounded in action, but 9 later died of their wounds)
Total casualties (approximately): 105

Appendix 2: Heane's probable Death Trap Valley party

These men belonged to 4th Battalion, D Company and were probably in No. 15 Platoon—Nos 9, 10, 11 and 12 sections.

Major James Heane—D Company Commanding Officer
Captain Charles Coltman—D Company 2IC, WIA, 2 May
Lieutenant Fred Fanning—No. 15 Platoon Commanding Officer
Sergeant Willie Wright (418)—No. 15 Platoon Sergeant
Corporal Charles Macquarie (495)—No. 12 Section NCO
Corporal Charles Lawler (1337)
Corporal Donald Usher (1335), KIA, 1 May
Lance Corporal William Harkin (1019), WIA, 1 May
Lance Corporal Arthur Chamberlain (1114), WIA, 1 May
Private Clyde Bock (230), No. 12 Section
Private Bill Bound (1090), No. 12 Section, WIA, 2 May
Private John 'Jack' Collyer (1241), No. 12 Section, WIA, 1 May; DOW, 4 May
Private Les Lott (1397), No. 12 Section
Private Alf Robins (1426), No. 12 Section, KIA, 2 May
Private Ern 'Snowy' Robson (1086), No. 12 Section, WIA, 2 May
Private Tom Thomson (1115), No. 12 Section, WIA, 1/2 May; DOW, 11 May
Private Sid Bartle (1204)
Private Esmond Brunker (1323)
Private Ben Marshall (588)
Private Ben Bathurst (844), WIA, 1 May
Private Kenneth Gillies (1265), KIA, 1 May
Private John Farnsworth (562), KIA, 1 May
Private Tom McKay (298), KIA, 1 May
Private Newton Brand (592), KIA, 1 May

Private Keith Chambers (239), KIA, 1 May
Private William Hall/Holder (1086), KIA, 1 May
Private Robert Heaslip (353), KIA, 1 May
Private Thomas Holland (593), KIA, 1 May
Private William Wilkinson (421), KIA, 1 May
Private Leslie Munro (969), KIA, 1 May
Private Arthur Flintoff (1261), KIA, 1 May
Private Thomas Davis (1488), KIA, 2 May
Private Sidney Clarkson (631), WIA, 1 May
Private Victor Mercer (209), WIA, 1 May
Private Ernest Miller (985), WIA, 1 May
Private Ernest Robson (574), WIA, 1 May*
Private William Wallen (1117), WIA, 1 May
Private James Watt (1083), WIA, 1 May
Private Alfred Fuller (940), WIA, 1 May
Private Jonathon Hodgson (488), WIA, 1 May
Private Giles Sykes (579), WIA, 1 May
Private John McGennan (134), WIA, c. 1/2 May; DOW, 4 May
Private John Collins (194), WIA, 2 May
Private Charles Maurer (115) WIA, 2 May

* Remarkably, there were two Ern Robsons in D Company. They enlisted within a few days of one another in early September 1914. Snowy (1088) was in Jack's section.

Appendix 3: Likely party from No. 3 Platoon

These men belonged to 4th Battalion, A Company and were probably in No. 3 Platoon—Nos 9, 10, 11 and 12 sections.

Lieutenant John Christie, WIA, 1 May
Sergeant Walter Oakes (651), WIA, 1 May
Corporal Thomas McEnery (1302)
Lance Corporal William Smith (861), KIA, 1 May
Private Les De Vine (330)
Private Michael Quigley (740)
Private John Cuthbertson (616), WIA, 1 May
Private William Dudley (40), WIA, 1 May
Private Harry Richards (1067), WIA, 1 May
Private Thomas James (1279), WIA, 1 May
Private Joseph Wilson (742), WIA, 1 May
Private Charles Peat (99), WIA, 1 May
Private Thomas Ryan (100), WIA, 1 May
Private William Blair (1076), WIA, 1 May
Private William Montgomery (1293), WIA, 1 May
Private Carl Leyon (1285/1139), WIA, 1 May; DOW, 2 May
Private Alexander Yates (1169), WIA, 1 May; DOW, 2 May
Private Cecil Haache (804), WIA, 1 May; DOW, 9 May
Private Richard Sherrin (1627/1511), WIA, c. 1 May
Private Ernest Turner (522), WIA, 2 May
Private John Downie (1346), WIA, 2 May; DOW, 3 May
Private Frederick Richards (1318), KIA, 1 May
Private Frederick Waine (1337), KIA, 1 May
Private Percy Tuck (1520), KIA, 1 May

Private William Andersen (846), KIA, 1 May
Private Thomas Bann (678), KIA, 1 May
Private Guthrie Craig (637), KIA, 1 May
Private Lawrence Edwards (864), KIA, 1 May
Private Matthew Stackpool (610), KIA, 1 May
Private Jack Stewart (63), KIA, 1 May
Private John Clancy (327), KIA, 1 May
Private Frank Cooke (649), KIA, 1 May
Private Eric Cusack (513), KIA, 1 May
Private Ernest Edmondson (655), KIA, 1 May
Private Edward Ward (1201), KIA, 1 May
Private Stanley Beer (673), KIA, 1 May
Private Henry Preece (952), KIA, 1 May
Private Henry Murr (1042), KIA, 2 May

The following 10 members of the 4th Battalion were wounded that weekend, but their company and platoon could not be ascertained from their service records. Statistically most of these casualties would have happened in Death Trap Valley, therefore some, if not most, of these men were in one of the two 4th Battalion parties sent into the valley on 1 and 2 May.

Private Stanley Adamson (112), WIA, 2 May
Private David Bound (1079), WIA, c. 1 May
Private Arthur Dinnes (1344), WIA, 1 May
Private William Graham (1363), WIA, 1 May
Private George Hayward (489), WIA, 1 May
Private James Honan (351), WIA, 2 May
Private Cyril Humphries (683), WIA, 1 May
Private Harold Keech (206), WIA, 2 May
Private Henry Wilkinson (1071), WIA, 1 May
Private Archibald Willis (102), WIA, 2 May

Notes

Author's note

1 Figes, O., *Crimea: The Last Crusade,* Penguin Books, London, 2011, page 298.

Introduction

1 Bean, C.E.W., *Official History of Australia in the War of 1914–18. Vol I: The Story of Anzac—From the Outbreak of the War to the End of the First Phase of the Gallipoli Campaign, May 4, 1915,* 13th Edn, Angus & Robertson, Sydney, 1942, page 29.

2 Andrews, E.M., *The Anzac Illusion: Anglo-Australian Relations during World War I,* Cambridge University Press, Cambridge, 1993, page 7.

3 National Archives of Australia, First Australian Imperial Force Personnel Dossiers, 1914–20, Series B2455, Collyer, J., 3273151.

4 Ibid.

5 Bean, C.E.W., *Official History, Vol. I*, page 52.

6 National Archives of Australia, First Australian Imperial Force Personnel Dossiers, 1914–20, Series B2455, Thompson, A.J. Onslow, 1832217.

7 Bean, C.E.W., *Official History*, *Vol. I*, page 52.

8 Ibid., page 53.

9 4th Battalion Personnel dossiers survey, in author's possession.

10 Bean, C.E.W., *Official History*, *Vol. I*, page 60.

11 4th Battalion Personnel dossiers survey, in author's possession.

12 National Archives of Australia, First Australian Imperial Force Personnel Dossiers, 1914–20, Series B2455, Arnold, R., 3036090.

13 4th Battalion Personnel dossiers survey, in author's possession.

14 Ibid.

15 Bean, C.E.W., *Official History*, *Vol. I*, page 59.

16 4th Battalion Personnel dossiers survey, in author's possession.
17 Bean, C.E.W., *Official History, Vol. I*, page 60.
18 Austin, R., *The Fighting Fourth: A History of Sydney's 4th Battalion 1914–19*, Slouch Hat Publications, Victoria, 2007, page 15.
19 Ibid.
20 Ibid., page 19.
21 Scarborough Maritime Heritage Centre, 'The Colonials—Gallipoli 1915', extract from *Neath a Foreign* Sky by Paul Allen: www.scarboroughsmaritimeheritage.org.uk/greatwar/f14-colonials-gallipoli.php
22 Kennedy Hickman, World War I/II: Lee Enfield Rifle: militaryhistory.about.com/od/smallarms/p/leeenfield.htm
23 Haythornthwaite, P.J., *The World War One Source Book*, Arms and Armour Press, London, 1998, page 63.
24 Collyer, J., Voyage Diary, 6 December 1914, private collection, in the author's possession.
25 Smith, H., Diary, 20 October 1914, AWM 2DRL/0318.

1 The voyage

1 *The Sydney Morning Herald,* 7 October 1914.
2 AWM8 23/21/1, 4th Infantry Battalion Embarkation Roll, October 1914.
3 Quote from McKernan, M., *Padre: Australian Chaplains in Gallipoli and France,* Allen & Unwin, Sydney, 1986, page 4.
4 Paterson, B., *Happy Dispatches: Journalistic Pieces from Banjo Paterson's Days as a War Correspondent*, Lansdowne Press, Sydney, 1980, page 91.
5 Semmler, C., *The Banjo of the Bush: The Work, Life and Times of A. B. Paterson*, Lansdowne Press, Melbourne, 1966, pages 170–1.
6 Quote from Austin, R., *The Fighting Fourth: A History of Sydney's 4th Battalion 1914–19*, Slouch Hat Publications, Victoria, 2007, page 24.
7 Leslie, G.H., Memoir, 1915, AWM PR88/067.
8 Wilson, G., *Bully Beef and Balderdash: Some Myths of the AIF Examined and Debunked*, Big Sky Publishing, Australia, 2012, page 318.
9 Quote from McKernan, M., *Padre*, page 4.
10 Ibid., page 3.
11 Wikipedia, Great White Fleet: en.wikipedia.org/wiki/Great_White_Fleet
12 Quote from McKernan, M., *Padre*, page 6.
13 Bean, C.E.W., *Official History of Australia in the War of 1914–18. Vol I: The Story of Anzac—From the Outbreak of the War to the End of the First Phase of the Gallipoli Campaign, May 4, 1915,* 13th Edn, Angus & Robertson, Sydney, 1942, page 98.

14 Bruce, G., *Harbottles Dictionary of Battles*, Van Nostrand Reinhold Company, New York, 1981, pages 249–50.
15 Smith, H., Diary, 8 November 1914, AWM 2 DRL/0318.
16 Quote from McKernan, M., *Padre*, page 6.
17 Coates, J., *An Atlas of Australia's Wars*, Oxford University Press, Melbourne, 2006, page 34.
18 Schuler, P., *Australia in Arms*, Unwin, Melbourne, 1916, page 46.
19 Paterson, *Happy Dispatches*, pages 95–7.
20 Report by anonymous German naval officer, *Emden*, AWM 3DRL 606/267/1.
21 Australian Dictionary of Biography, William Chidley by Sally McInerney: adb.anu.edu.au/biography/chidley-william-james-5579
22 Ibid.
23 *The Sydney Morning Herald,* 12 May 1911.
24 Australian Dictionary of Biography, William Chidley by Sally McInerney: adb.anu.edu.au/biography/chidley-william-james-5579
25 *The Sydney Morning Herald*, 12 May 1911.
26 McKern, H., Diary, 13 November 1914, AWM 2DRL/0507.
27 Smith, H., Diary, 25 November 1914, AWM 2DRL/0318.
28 Giddings, O., Diary, 25 November 1914, AWM PRO2028.
29 Bean, C.E.W., *Official History, Vol. I*, page 112.
30 *New Encyclopaedia Britannica*, Encyclopaedia Britannica, Chicago, 1988, page 353.
31 *Casino and Kyogle Courier,* 1 May 1915.

2 Egypt

1 Heane, J., Letter to brother, *The Dubbo Liberal and Macquarie Advocate*, 10 September 1915.
2 *The Mildura Cultivator*, 20 January 1915.
3 Anzac History, Smythe, V., Letter to family, 29 November 1914: www.smythe.id.au/lestweforget/ch3.htm
4 Anzac History, Smythe, B., Letter to family, 3 December 1914: www.smythe.id.au/lestweforget/ch3.htm
5 Roberts, R., Diary, 3 December 1914, AWM PRO0395.
6 Giddings, O., Diary, 3 December 1914, AWM PRO2028.
7 McDonald, W., Diary, 2 December 1914, AWM PRO1798.
8 Barr, T., Diary, 3 December 1914, AWM PR91/051.
9 McKern, H., Diary, 3 December 1914, AWM 2DRL/0507.
10 Ward, O., Letter to family, 11 February 1915, *Windsor and Richmond Gazette,* 26 March 1915.

11 National Archives of Australia, First Australian Imperial Force Personnel Dossiers, 1914–20, Series B2455, Bean, J., 3061116.

12 Wren, E., *Randwick to Hargicourt: History of the 3rd Battalion, AIF,* Ronald G. McDonald, Sydney, 1935, page 26.

13 Brugger, S., *Australians and Egypt 1914–19,* Melbourne University Press, Carlton, 1980, page 37.

14 National Archives of Australia, First Australian Imperial Force Personnel Dossiers, 1914–20, Series B2455, Parker, P., 8008238.

15 *Casino and Kyogle Courier*, 1 May 1915.

16 Bean, C.E.W., *Official History of Australia in the War of 1914–18. Vol I: The Story of Anzac—From the Outbreak of the War to the End of the First Phase of the Gallipoli Campaign, May 4, 1915,* 13th Edn, Angus & Robertson, Sydney, 1942, page 153.

17 Ibid., page 116.

18 Ibid.

19 Baines, J., & Malek, J., *Atlas of Ancient Egypt*, Equinox, Oxford, 1987, pages 140 and 156.

20 Ibid., page 33.

21 Ibid., page 140.

22 Howell-Price, O., Letter to family, 12 December 1914, AWM 1DRL362.

23 Meggy, A., Letter to sister Dolly, 19 January 1915, AWM 2DRL492.

24 National Archives of Australia, First Australian Imperial Force Personnel Dossiers, 1914–20, Series B2455, Cox, E., 3435921, and Cox, M., 3436988.

25 Ward, O., Letter to family, 11 February 1915, *Windsor and Richmond Gazette,* 26 March 1915.

26 Cox, E., Personnel Dossier 3435921, and Cox, M., Personnel Dossier 3436988.

27 Gammage, B., *The Broken Years: Australian Soldiers in the Great War*, Penguin Books, Australia, 1975, pages 43–4.

28 *Anzac Memorial,* Returned Soldiers Association, Sydney, 1916, page 69.

29 McKern, H., Diary, 31 December 1914, AWM 2DRL/0507.

30 Giddings, O., Diary, 31 December 1914, AWM PRO2028.

31 *The Sydney Morning Herald,* 12 March 1915.

32 Australian Dictionary of Biography, Walter Dexter: adb.anu.edu.au/biography/dexter-walter-ernest-5972

33 McKernan, M., *Padre: Australian Chaplains in Gallipoli and France,* Allen & Unwin, Sydney, 1986, page 29.

34 Ibid., page 32.

35 Heane, J., Letter to Captain Ley, 17 and 19 March 1915, *The Dubbo Liberal and Macquarie Advocate*, 23 April 1915.

36 Bean Letter, *The Argus*, 1 March 1915.

37 4th Battalion Personnel dossiers survey, in author's possession.

38 National Archives of Australia, First Australian Imperial Force Personnel Dossiers, 1914–20, Series B2455, Robertson, J., 8033642.

39 National Archives of Australia, First Australian Imperial Force Personnel Dossiers, 1914–20, Series B2455, Murray, R., 7983954.

40 National Archives of Australia, First Australian Imperial Force Personnel Dossiers, 1914–20, Series B2455, Lawrence, W., 7377787.

41 Austin, R., *The Fighting Fourth: A History of Sydney's 4th Battalion 1914–19*, Slouch Hat Publications, Victoria, 2007, page 29.

42 Bean, C.E.W., *Official History, Vol. I*, page 136.

43 *The Dubbo Liberal and Macquarie Advocate*, 15 September 1914.

44 Ibid.

45 Williams, H.R., *The Gallant Company: An Australian Soldier's Story*, Angus & Robertson, Sydney, 1933, page 16.

46 National Archives of Australia, First Australian Imperial Force Personnel Dossiers, 1914–20, Series B2455, Wright, W., 3451151.

47 Bean, C., *What to Know in Egypt: A Guide for Australian Soldiers*, Société Orientale De Publicité, Cairo, 1915, pages 14–15.

48 Ibid., page 16.

49 Ibid., page 13.

50 Ibid., pages 28–9.

51 Gammage, B., *The Broken Years*, page 43.

52 Brugger, S., *Australians and Egypt 1914–19*, page 152.

53 Hagan, J., Diary, 12 December 1914, AWM PR 84/188.

54 Heane, J., Diary excerpts, *The Dubbo Liberal and Macquarie Advocate*, 28 May 1915.

55 Barrett, P., & Collinson, K., *The Happy Warrior: An Anthology of Australian and New Zealand Military Poetry*, Sid Harta Publishers, Victoria, 2001, page 45.

56 NSW State Records, Bann, T., Letter to aunt, 22 January 1915: www.records.nsw.gov.au/state-archives/research-topics/war-and-australia/anzacs/images-1/thomasbann_letter2_71770_sc2928.jpg/view

57 McKernan, M., *Gallipoli: A Short History*, Allen & Unwin, Sydney, 2010, page 25.

58 Quote from McKernan, M., *Padre*, page 24.

59 Bond, Lt. Col., *The Army That Went with the Boys: A Record of Salvation Army Work with the Australian Imperial Force,* Salvation Army, Melbourne, 1919, page 104.

60 Quote from McKernan, M., *Padre*, pages 24, 25.

61 Quote from ibid., page 29.

62 Meggy, A., Letter to family, 19 January 1915, AWM 2DRL492.

63 Austin, R., *The Fighting Fourth*, page 17.

64 AWM4 23/21/1, First World War Diaries, 4th Infantry Battalion, January 1915.

65 NSW State Records, Bann, T., Letter to aunt, 22 January 1915: www.records.nsw.gov.au/state-archives/research-topics/war-and-australia/anzacs/images-1/thomasbann_letter2_71770_sc2928.jpg/view

66 De Vine, L., Diary, covering dates from 11 January 1915 to 5 March 1915, AWM 1DRL0240/2.

67 Ward, O., Letter to family, dated 11 February 1915, *Windsor and Richmond Gazette,* 26 March 1915.

68 De Vine, L., Diary, covering dates from 11 January 1915 to 5 March 1915, AWM 1DRL0240/2.

69 Sacred Destinations, The Citadel, Cairo: www.sacred-destinations.com/egypt/cairo-citadel

70 Digital Library, Dictionary of Islamic Architecture: archnet.org/library/dictionary/entry.jsp?entry_id=DIA0061&mode=full.

71 Bean, C.E.W., *Official History, Vol. I*, page 165.

72 Heane, J., Letter to Captain Ley, dated 17 and 19 March 1915, *The Dubbo Liberal and Macquarie Advocate*, 23 April 1915.

73 McLeod, T., Letter to family, 1 April 1915, AWM 2DRL/0145.

74 Project Gutenberg EBook, Hamilton, I., Diary, 29 March 1915: www.gutenberg.org/files/19317/19317.txt

3 'Gollipoli Peninsular', 25 April 1915

1 De Vine, L., Diary, 3 April 1915, AWM 1DRL0240/2.

2 Wilson, G., *Bully Beef and Balderdash: Some Myths of the AIF Examined and Debunked*, Big Sky Publishing, Australia, 2012, pages 283–6.

3 Lott, L., Diary, 3 April 1915, AWM MSS1122.

4 Austin, R., *The Fighting Fourth: A History of Sydney's 4th Battalion 1914–19*, Slouch Hat Publications, Victoria, 2007, page 31.

5 De Vine, L., Diary, 5 April 1915, AWM 1DRL0240/2.

6 Sloan, J., Letter, 22 May 1915, AWM PR00035.

7 AWM4 1/4/1, First World War Diaries, General Staff, General Headquarters, Mediterranean Expeditionary Force, Part 2, March–April 1915.

8 Bean, C.E.W., *Official History of Australia in the War of 1914–18. Vol I: The Story of Anzac—From the Outbreak of the War to the End of the First Phase of*

the Gallipoli Campaign, May 4, 1915, 13th Edn, Angus & Robertson, Sydney, 1942, page 185.

9 Ibid., page 209.

10 AWM4 1/42/2, 1/42/3, First World War Diaries, Headquarters, 1st Australian Division, March 1915, Part 1, April 1915; Part 2, April 1915.

11 Bean, C.E.W., *Official History, Vol. I*, page 209.

12 Moorehead, A., *Gallipoli*, Macmillan, Melbourne, 1973, page 125.

13 Hutchison, W., Diary, 7 April 1915, AWM 1DRL/0372.

14 *Dubbo Dispatch,* 25 June 1915.

15 *The Dubbo Liberal and Macquarie Advocate,* 10 June 1915.

16 Lott, L., Diary, 7–11 April 1915, AWM MSS1122.

17 Quote from McKernan, M., *Padre: Australian Chaplains in Gallipoli and France,* Allen & Unwin, Sydney, 1986, page 42.

18 Hutchison, W., Diary, 14 April 1915, AWM 1DRL/0372.

19 De Vine, L., Diary, 14 April 1915, AWM 1DRL0240/2.

20 McKern, H., Diary, AWM 2DRL/0507.

21 Lott, L., Diary, 7–11 April 1915, AWM MSS1122.

22 Barr, T., Diary, AWM PR91/051.

23 Edwards, R., Diary, 15 April 1915, AWM PR91/192.

24 Quote from Williams, P., *The Battle of Anzac Ridge: An Anzac Victory, 25 April 1915*, Australian Military History Publications, Loftus, 2007, pages 38–9.

25 Ibid.

26 Navy and Army Despatches, Dardanelles and Gallipoli, 17 September 1915: www.naval-history.net/WW1Battle1503Dardanelles2.htm

27 Quote from Williams, P., *The Battle of Anzac Ridge*, page 41.

28 AWM4 1/25/1, First World War Diaries, Headquarters, Australian and New Zealand Army Corps, General Staff, Part 7, April 1915.

29 AWM4 1/4/1, First World War Diaries, General Staff, General Headquarters, Mediterranean Expeditionary Force, Part 2, March–April 1915.

30 De Vine, L., Diary, 22 April 1915, AWM 1DRL0240/2.

31 Bruce, G., *Harbottles Dictionary of Battles,* Van Nostrand Reinhold Company, New York, 1981, pages 136–7.

32 AWM4 23/1/3, First World War Diaries, 1st Infantry Brigade, Part 3, April 1915 Appendices.

33 AWM4 1/4/1, First World War Diaries, General Staff, General Headquarters, Mediterranean Expeditionary Force, Part 2, March–April 1915.

34 Project Gutenberg EBook, Hamilton, I., Diary, 22 April 1915: www.gutenberg.org/files/19317/19317.txt

35 AWM4 23/1/3, First World War Diaries, 1st Infantry Brigade.

36 De Vine, L., Diary, 23 April 1915, AWM 1DRL0240/2.

37 AWM4 23/21/2, First World War Diaries, 4th Infantry Battalion, 24 April 1915.

38 Tebbutt, A., *Medical Report on Landing at Gallipoli*, AWM25 367/144.

39 McKern, H., Diary, 24 April 1915, AWM 2DRL/0507.

40 AWM4 6/4/1, First World War Diaries, Senior Chaplain, Other Protestant Denominations, Headquarters AIF, London August 1914–October 1917, Part 1.

41 Quote from McKernan, M., *Gallipoli: A Short History*, Allen & Unwin, Sydney, 2010, page 96.

42 Quote from McKernan, M., *Padre,* page 50.

43 Ibid., page 42.

44 Bosward, C., Diary, 23 April 1915, AWM 3DRL4104.

45 De Vine, L., Diary, 24 April 1915, AWM 1DRL0240/2.

46 Sloan, J., Letter, 22 May 1915, AWM PR00035.

47 Macquarie, C., Letter to George Collyer, dated 3 July 1915, private collection, in author's possession.

48 National Archives of Australia, First Australian Imperial Force Personnel Dossiers, 1914–20, Series B2455, Macquarie, C., 1967586.

49 National Archives of Australia, First Australian Imperial Force Personnel Dossiers, 1914–20, Series B2455, Bock, C., 3095139.

50 National Archives of Australia, First Australian Imperial Force Personnel Dossiers, 1914–20, Series B2455, Bound, W., 3100611.

51 National Archives of Australia, First Australian Imperial Force Personnel Dossiers, 1914–20, Series B2455, Robson, E., 8037170.

52 National Archives of Australia, First Australian Imperial Force Personnel Dossiers, 1914–20, Series B2455, Robins, A., 8033821.

53 National Archives of Australia, First Australian Imperial Force Personnel Dossiers, 1914–20, Series B2455, Lott, L., 8205200.

54 National Archives of Australia, First Australian Imperial Force Personnel Dossiers, 1914–20, Series B2455, Thomson, T., 1838680.

55 AWM4 23/1/3, First World War Diaries, 1st Infantry Brigade, Part 3, April 1915.

56 AWM4 23/21/2, First World War Diaries, 4th Infantry Battalion, 25 April 1915.

57 AWM 1DRL/0428, Australian Red Cross Society, Wounded and Missing Enquiry Bureau Files, 1914–18 War.

58 De Vine, L., Diary, 25 April 1915, AWM 1DRL0240/2.

59 Wilson, G., 'Brigadier-General James Heane', Celebrities of the AIF, *Reveille*, Vol. 10, March 1937.

60 National Archives of Australia, First Australian Imperial Force Personnel Dossiers, 1914–20, Series B2455, Reynolds, F., 8031250.

61 Tebbutt, A., Medical Report on Landing at Gallipoli, AWM25 367/144.

62 Sloan, J., Letter, 22 May 1915, AWM PR00035.

63 De Vine, L., Diary, 25 April 1915, AWM 1DRL0240/2.

64 Lott, L., Diary, 25 April 1915, MSS1122.

65 McKern, H., Diary, 25 April 1915, AWM 2DRL/0507.

66 Royal Marines Museum Archive, B/1/84, Chater, A.R., War Diary, Chatham Battalion, RMLI, 28 April–27 July 1915.

67 Cameron, D., *25 April 1915: The Day the Anzac Legend was Born*, Allen & Unwin, Sydney, 2007, page 45.

68 *Field Service Regulations Part 1: Operations 1909*, Harrison & Sons, London, 1912, page 17.

69 Williams, P., *The Battle of Anzac Ridge,* page 104.

70 Lott, L., Diary, 25 April 1915, AWM MSS1122.

71 *Anzac Memorial,* Returned Soldiers Association, Sydney, 1916, page 69.

72 Austin, R., *The Fighting Fourth,* page 39.

73 *The Dubbo Liberal and Macquarie Advocate,* 25 June 1915.

74 Ibid., 23 July 1915.

75 Ibid., 25 June 1915.

76 Ibid., 23 July 1915.

77 Bean, C.E.W., *Official History, Vol. I*, page 400.

78 McCay, J., Interview with Bean, C., 1920, AWM38 3DRL606/28A/1.

79 Tebbutt, A., Medical Report on Landing at Gallipoli, AWM25 367/144.

80 McCay, J., Interview with Bean, C., 1920, AWM38 3DRL606/28A/1.

81 AWM4 23/21/2, First World War Diaries, 4th Infantry Battalion, 25 April 1915.

82 *Anzac Memorial*, Returned Soldiers Association, Sydney, 1916, page 69.

83 Bean, C., *Gallipoli Mission*, Australian Broadcasting Corporation, Sydney, 1990, page 376.

84 Williams, P., *The Battle of Anzac Ridge*, page 47.

85 Dolan, H., *36 Days*, page 337.

86 Williams, P., *The Battle of Anzac Ridge*, page 87.

87 Figes, O., *Crimea: The Last Crusade,* Penguin Books, London, 2011.

88 Erickson, E., *Ottoman Army Effectiveness in World War I: A Comparative Study*, Routledge, Abingdon, 2007, page 24.

89 Aker, S., *The Dardanelles: The Ari Burnu Battles and the 27th Regiment 1935,* AWM MSS1886.

90 Haythornthwaite, P., *The World War One Source Book,* Arms and Armour Press, London, 1998, page 68.

91 AWM4 1/27/2, First World War Diaries, Intelligence, ANZAC Headquarters, April 1915.

92 Erickson, E., *Ottoman Army Effectiveness,* page 24.

93 Ibid.

94 AWM 23/25/3, First World War Diaries, 8th Infantry Battalion, 25 April 1915.

95 AWM4 23/21/2, First World War Diaries, 4th Infantry Battalion, 25 April 1915.

96 Lott, L., Diary, 25 April 1915, AWM MSS1122.

97 Quote from Maitland, G., *Battle History of the Royal New South Wales Regiment, Vol. I: 1885–1918*, Kangaroo Press, Sydney, 2001, page 40.

98 *The Dubbo Liberal and Macquarie Advocate*, 25 June 1915.

99 Hutchison, W., Diary, 25 April 1915, AWM 1DRL/0372.

100 Edwards, R., Diary, 25 April 1915, AWM PR91/192.

101 Bean, C., *Official History, Vol. I*, page 459.

102 Lott, L., Diary, 25 April 1915, AWM MSS1122.

103 Erkal, S., Turkish General Staff Ankara, *A Brief History of the Canakkale Campaign in the First World War (June 1914–January, 1916)*, The Turkish General Staff Printing House, Ankara, 2004, pages 75–6.

104 Uyar, Mesut, *Brothers in Arms: Turkish Officers in the Canakkale Campaign*, 18 Mart University, Turkey, 2006, page 23.

105 Oakes, W., Unit History, 8th Infantry Battalion, 1914–1918, MSS0954.

106 Williams, P., *The Battle of Anzac Ridge*, page 131.

107 Bean, C., *Official History, Vol. I*, page 543.

108 AWM4 23/21/2, First World War Diaries, 4th Infantry Battalion, 26 April 1915.

109 Lott, L., Diary, 26 April 1915, AWM MSS1122.

110 Bean, C., *Official History, Vol. I,* pages 460–1.

111 Quote from Maitland, G., *Battle History of the Royal New South Wales Regiment,* page 40.

112 Roberts, C., *The Landing at Anzac 1915*, Army History Unit, Big Sky Publishing, Sydney, 2013, pages 147–8.

113 AWM4 23/21/2, First World War Diaries, 4th Infantry Battalion, 26 April 1915.

114 Bean, C., *Official History, Vol. I*, page 490.

115 Ibid.

116 Lott, L., Diary, 26 April 1915, AWM MSS1122.

117 AWM4 1/42/4, First World War Diaries, General Staff Headquarters, 1st Australian Division, Part 3, May 1915.

118 Tebbutt, A., Medical Report on Landing at Gallipoli, AWM25 367/144.

119 Aker, S., *The Dardanelles*, AWM MSS1886.

120 Wilson, G., 'Brigadier-General James Heane', Celebrities of the AIF, *Reveille*, Vol. 10, March 1937.

121 Bean, C., *Official History, Vol. I*, page xviii.

122 Massie, R., Letter to mother, 4 May 1915, AWM 3DRL/3701.

123 Bean, C., *Official History, Vol. I,* page 493.

124 Austin, R., *The Fighting Fourth,* page 62.

125 AWM4 23/21/2, First World War Diaries, 4th Infantry Battalion, 26 April 1915.

126 Aker, S., *The Dardanelles*, AWM MSS1886, page 80.

127 *The Dubbo Liberal and Macquarie Advocate*, 25 June 1915.

128 Tebbutt, A., Medical Report on Landing at Gallipoli, AWM25 367/144.

129 Austin, R., *The Fighting Fourth*, page 44.

130 Lott, L., Diary, 26 April 1915, AWM MSS1122.

131 *The Tamworth Daily Observer,* 10 July 1915.

132 Hutchison, W., Diary, 26 April 1915, AWM 1DRL/0372.

133 4th Battalion Personnel dossiers survey, in author's possession.

134 Aker, S., *The Dardanelles*, AWM MSS1886, page 81.

135 AWM4 23/21/2, First World War Diaries, 4th Infantry Battalion, April 1915.

136 Bean, C., *Official History, Vol. I,* page 521.

137 Erickson, E., *Gallipoli and the Middle East 1914–1918,* Amber Books, London, 2008, page 83.

138 4th Battalion Personnel dossiers survey, in author's possession.

139 Bean, C., *Official History, Vol. I,* page 522.

140 *The Tamworth Daily Observer,* 10 July 1915.

141 *Dubbo Dispatch,* 23 July 1915.

142 *The Dubbo Liberal and Macquarie Advocate,* 25 June 1915.

143 Ibid.

144 AWM4 23/21/2, First World War Diaries, 4th Infantry Battalion, 28 April 1915.

145 Lott, L., Diary, 28 April 1915, AWM MSS1122.

146 AWM4 1/27/2, First World War Diaries, Intelligence, ANZAC Headquarters, April 1915.

147 AWM4 23/21/2, First World War Diaries, 4th Infantry Battalion, 29 April 1915.

148 Lott, L., Diary, 29 April 1915, AWM MSS1122.

149 De Vine, L., Diary, 29 April 1915, AWM 1DRL0240/2.

150 Edwards, R., Diary, 29 April 1915, AWM PR91/192.

151 AWM4 23/21/2, First World War Diaries, 4th Infantry Battalion, 30 April 1915.

152 Lott, L., Diary, 30 April 1915, AWM MSS1122.

153 Edwards, R., Diary, 30 April 1915, AWM PR91/192.

154 Bosward, C., Diary, 30 April 1915, AWM 3DRL4104.

155 De Vine, L., Diary, 30 April 1915, AWM 1DRL0240/2.

156 Tebbutt, A., Medical Report on Landing at Gallipoli, AWM25 367/144.

157 Macquarie, C., Letter to George Collyer, 3 July 1915.

158 AWM4 1/42/2, First World War Diaries, 4th Infantry Battalion, May 1915; AWM4 1/42/4, Part 4, May 1915.

159 Royal Marines Museum Archive, B/1/84, Chater, A.R., War Diary, Chatham Battalion, RMLI, 28 April–27 July 1915.

160 Bean, C., *Official History, Vol. I,* page 536.

161 AWM4 23/27/2, First World War Diaries, 10th Infantry Battalion, 29 April 1915.

162 Bean, C., *Gallipoli Mission*, Australian Broadcasting Corporation, Sydney, 1990, page 51.

163 AWM4 23/21/2, First World War Diaries, 4th Infantry Battalion, 30 April 1915.

164 Erickson, E., *Ottoman Army Effectiveness*, page 39.

165 Bosward, C., Diary, 1 May 1915, AWM 3DRL4104.

166 4th Battalion Personnel dossiers survey, in author's possession.

167 Bosward, C., Diary, 1 May 1915, AWM 3DRL4104.

4 Death Trap Valley

1 Wren, E., *Randwick to Hargicourt: History of the 3rd Battalion, AIF,* Ronald G. McDonald, Sydney, Australia, 1935, page 58.

2 Bean, C., *Gallipoli Mission*, Australian Broadcasting Corporation, Sydney, 1990, page 144.

3 Ibid., page 51.

4 Ibid., page 376.

5 De Vine, L., Diary, 30 May 1915, AWM 1DRL0240/2.

6 Bean, C.E.W., *Official History of Australia in the War of 1914–18. Vol II: The Story of Anzac—From 4 May 1915 to the Evacuation,* University of Queensland Press, St Lucia, 1980, page 47.

7 Bean, C., *Official History, Vol. I,* page 450.

8 Hart, P., *Gallipoli,* Profile Books, Great Britain, 2011, page 91.

9 Bean, C., *Gallipoli Mission,* page 255.

10 Ibid., page 254.

11 Roberts, C., *The Landing at Anzac 1915*, Army History Unit, Big Sky Publishing, Sydney, 2013, page 123.
12 Bean, C., *Gallipoli Mission,* page 352.
13 Ibid., page 375.
14 Ibid., page 145.
15 James, R., *Gallipoli*, Batsford, London, 1965, page 173.
16 Bean, C., *Gallipoli Mission,* page 145.
17 Anzac History, Smythe, B., Letter to family, 9 May 1915: www.smythe.id.au/letters/15_16.htm
18 Bean, C., *Official History, Vol. I,* page 530.
19 Wren, E., *Randwick To Hargicourt,* page 58.
20 *Field Service Regulations Part 1: Operations 1909*, Harrison & Sons, London, 1912, page 99.
21 Bean, C., *Official History, Vol. II,* page 179.
22 Pugsley, C., *Gallipoli: The New Zealand Story,* Penguin, New Zealand, 2008, page 179.
23 Ibid., page 214.
24 Bean, C., *Official History, Vol. I,* page 349.
25 Roberts, C., *The Landing At Anzac 1915,* page 111.
26 AWM 23/20/2, First World War Diaries, 3rd Infantry Battalion, 25 April 1915.
27 Wright, L., Diary, 25 April 1915, AWM PR86/208.
28 Wren, E., *Randwick to Hargicourt,* page 48.
29 Bean, C., *Official History, Vol. I,* pages 430–3.
30 Bean, C., *Gallipoli Mission,* page 90.
31 Wren, E., *Randwick to Hargicourt,* pages 57–8.
32 Ibid., pages 58–9.
33 Bean, C., *Official History, Vol. I,* pages 528–9.
34 Quote from Hart, P., *Gallipoli,* pages 116–17.
35 Anzac History, Smythe, B., Letter to family, 9 May 1915: www.smythe.id.au/letters/15_16.htm
36 Ibid.
37 Bean, C., *Official History, Vol. I,* page 530.
38 Anzac History, Smythe, B., Letter to family, 9 May 1915: www.smythe.id.au/letters/15_16.htm
39 AWM28, Recommendation files for honours and awards, AIF, 1914–18 War.
40 Ibid.
41 Blumberg, H., *Britain's Sea Soldiers: A Record of the Royal Marines During the War 1914–1919,* Devonport, 1927, pages 135–6.

42 Field, C., *Britain's Sea-Soldiers: A History of the Royal Marines and Their Predecessors and Their Services in Action, Ashore and Afloat*, *Vol. II,* Lyceum Press, Liverpool, 1924, page 302.
43 De Vine, L., Diary, 28 April 1915, AWM 1DRL0240/2.
44 Bosward, C., Diary, 28 April 1915, AWM 3DRL4104.
45 4th Battalion Personnel dossiers survey, in author's possession.
46 Hart, P., *Gallipoli,* pages 28–9.
47 Blumberg, H., *Britain's Sea Soldiers*, page 130.
48 AWM 23/20/2, First World War Diaries, 3rd Infantry Battalion, 28 April 1915.
49 Howell-Price, O., Letter, 9 May 1915, AWM 1DRL362.
50 Anzac History, Smythe, B., Letter to family, 9 May 1915, www.smythe.id.au/letters/15_16.htm
51 AWM4 23/20/2, First World War Diaries, 3rd Infantry Battalion, 29 April 1915.
52 Anzac History, Smythe, B., Letter to family, May 1915: www.smythe.id.au/letters/15_16.htm
53 Bean, C., *Official History, Vol. I,* page 535.
54 Ibid.
55 Hart, P., *Gallipoli,* page 117.
56 Owen, R., Personal Records of Lieutenant-Colonel R. Owen, AWM 2DRL/0130, Report dated 14 May 1915.
57 Ibid.
58 Blumberg, H., *Britain's Sea Soldiers*, page 134.
59 Bean, C., *Official History, Vol. I,* page 532.
60 Blumberg, H., *Britain's Sea Soldiers*, page 135.
61 Bean, C., *Official History, Vol. I,* page 533.
62 Baker, T.H., 'Account of the operations, Chatham Battalion, Royal Marine Light Infantry', *Royal Naval Division Magazine,* Issue No. 3, December 1997.
63 Bean, C., *Official History, Vol. I,* page 537.
64 Royal Marines Museum Archive, B/1/84, Chater, A.R., War Diary, Chatham Battalion, RMLI, 28 April–27 July 1915.
65 Bean, C., *Official History, Vol. I,* page 541.
66 The National Archives (London), ADM 1/8453/77, Parker, W., VC File.
67 Baker, T.H., 'Account of the operations, Chatham Battalion, Royal Marine Light Infantry', *Royal Naval Division Magazine,* Issue No. 3, December 1997.
68 The National Archives (London), ADM/196/64, Royal Navy Officers Service Records, Empson, R.
69 The National Archives (London), ADM/196/64, Royal Navy Officers Service Records, Alcock, A.

70 Imperial War Museum (London), 3077, 95/16/1, Empson, R., Papers.

71 Baker, T.H., 'Account of the operations, Chatham Battalion, Royal Marine Light Infantry', *Royal Naval Division Magazine,* Issue No. 3, December 1997.

72 Keegan, J., *The Face of Battle*, Jonathan Cape, Great Britain, 1976, page 273.

73 The National Archives (London), ADM/196/64, Royal Navy Officers Service Records, Alcock, A.

74 Bean, C., *Official History, Vol. I,* page xx.

75 The National Archives (London), ADM/196/64, Royal Navy Officers Service Records, Empson, R.

76 *The London Gazette*, No. 9094, 13 September 1915.

77 Blumberg, H., *Britain's Sea Soldiers*, page 138.

5 The Battle of Death Trap Valley, 1 May 1915

1 Lott, L., Diary, 1 May 1915, AWM MSS112.

2 Erickson, E., *Gallipoli and the Middle East 1914–1918,* Amber Books, London, 2008, page 83.

3 Erkal, S., Turkish General Staff Ankara, *A Brief History of the Canakkale Campaign in the First World War (June 1914–January, 1916*), The Turkish General Staff Printing House, Ankara, 2004, page 83.

4 Ibid., page 82.

5 Erickson, E., *Gallipoli and the Middle East,* page 83.

6 Bean, C.E.W., *Official History of Australia in the War of 1914–18. Vol I: The Story of Anzac—From the Outbreak of the War to the End of the First Phase of the Gallipoli Campaign, May 4, 1915,* 13th Edn, Angus & Robertson, Sydney, 1942, page 539.

7 Hart, P., *Gallipoli,* Profile Books, Great Britain, 2011, page 183.

8 AWM4 1/27/3, First World War Diaries, Intelligence, ANZAC Headquarters, Part 1, May 1915.

9 Ibid.

10 Ibid.

11 Baker, T.H., 'Account of the operations, Chatham Battalion, Royal Marine Light Infantry', *Royal Naval Division Magazine,* Issue No. 3, December 1997.

12 *Mansfield and North Notts Advertiser*, 22 June 1917.

13 The National Archives (London), ADM 1/8453/77, Parker, W., VC File.

14 AWM4 23/21/2, First World War Diaries, 4th Infantry Battalion, 30 April 1915; AWM4 23/21/3, First World War Diaries, 4th Infantry Battalion, 1–2 May 1915.

15 Macquarie, C., Letter to George Collyer, 3 July 1915, private collection, in author's possession.

16 Bean, C., Notebook April–June 1915, AWM38 3DRL 606/25/1.

17 US Naval Observatory Records for 30 April 1915: aa.usno.navy.mil/data/docs/RS_OneDay.php

18 AWM4 23/21/2, First World War Diaries, 4th Infantry Battalion, 30 April 1915.

19 Lott, L., Diary, 1 May 1915, MSS1122.

20 *The Sun* interview reported in *The Uralla Times,* 4 September 1915.

21 Macquarie, C., Letter to George Collyer, 3 July 1915.

22 The National Archives (London), ADM/159/14, Royal Navy Officers Service Records, Minter, M.

23 The National Archives (London), ADM/159/203, Royal Navy Service Records, Parker, W.

24 *Mansfield and North Notts Advertiser,* 22 June 1917.

25 The National Archives (London), ADM 1/8453/77, Parker, W., VC File.

26 Ibid.

27 Ibid.

28 Ibid.

29 Snelling, S., *VCs of the First World War: Gallipoli*, Allan Smith Publishing, United Kingdom, 1995, page 90.

30 *Mansfield and North Notts Advertiser,* 22 June 1917.

31 The National Archives (London), ADM 1/8453/77, Parker, W., VC File.

32 World War I Casualty Lists of Royal Navy and Dominion Navies, 1–31 May 1915: www.naval-history.net/xDKCas1915-05May.htm

33 The National Archives (London), ADM 1/8453/77, Parker, W., VC File.

34 Ibid.

35 Erickson, E., *Gallipoli and the Middle East,* page 83.

36 Royal Marines Museum Archive, B/1/84, Chater, A.R., War Diary, Chatham Battalion, RMLI, 28 April–27 July 1915.

37 Quote from Hart, P., *Gallipoli,* page 182.

38 AWM4 23/31/8, First World War Diaries, 14th Infantry Battalion, 1 May 1915.

39 Bean, C., *Official History, Vol. I*, pages 541–2.

40 AWM4 23/21/3, First World War Diaries, 4th Infantry Battalion, 1 May 1915.

41 AWM4 1/42/4, First World War Diaries, General Staff Headquarters, 1st Australian Division, Part 4, May 1915.

42 Bean, C., *Official History, Vol. I,* page 542.

43 Quote from Maitland, G., *Battle History of the Royal New South Wales Regiment, Vol. I: 1885–1918*, Kangaroo Press, Sydney, 2001, page 48.

44 Bean, C.E.W., *Official History of Australia in the War of 1914–18. Vol II: The Story of Anzac—From 4 May 1915 to the Evacuation,* University of Queensland Press, St Lucia, 1980, page 95.

45 Pugsley, C., *Gallipoli: The New Zealand Story,* Penguin, New Zealand, 2008, page 217.

46 *The London Gazette*, No. 9094, 13 September 1915.

47 AWM4 23/1/5, First World War Diaries, 1st Infantry Brigade, Part 3, May 1915 Appendices.

48 Lott, L., Diary, 1 May 1915, AWM MSS1122.

49 *The Tamworth Daily Observer*, 10 July 1915.

50 Macquarie, C., Letter to George Collyer, 3 July 1915.

51 Lott, L., Diary, 1 May 1915, AWM MSS1122.

52 *The Tamworth Daily Observer,* 10 July 1915.

53 *The Sun* reported in *The Uralla Times,* 4 September 1915.

54 Macquarie, C., Letter to George Collyer, 3 July 1915.

55 *The Tamworth Daily Observer,* 10 July 1915.

56 *The Uralla Times,* 4 September 1915.

57 Lott, L., Diary, 1 May 1915, AWM MSS1122.

58 Macquarie, C., Letter to George Collyer, 3 July 1915.

59 De Vine, L., Diary, 1 May 1915, AWM 1DRL0240/2.

60 AWM28, Recommendation files for honours and awards, AIF, 1914–18 War.

61 National Archives of Australia, First Australian Imperial Force Personnel Dossiers 1914–20, Series B2455, Christie, J., 3247676.

62 De Vine, L., Diary, 1 May 1915, AWM 1DRL0240/2.

63 Royal Marines Museum Archive, B/1/84, Chater, A.R., War Diary, Chatham Battalion, RMLI, 28 April–27 July 1915.

64 Bean, C., *Official History, Vol. I*, page 542.

65 Baker, T.H., 'Account of the operations, Chatham Battalion, Royal Marine Light Infantry', *Royal Naval Division Magazine,* Issue No. 3, December 1997.

66 AWM28, Recommendation files for honours and awards, AIF, 1914–18 War.

67 *The Tamworth Daily Observer*, 10 July 1915.

68 Erkal, S., Turkish General Staff Ankara, *A Brief History of the Canakkale Campaign in the First World War (June 1914–January, 1916)*, The Turkish General Staff Printing House, Ankara, 2004, page 84.

69 De Vine, L., Diary, 1 May 1915, AWM 1DRL0240/2.

70 Owen, R., Report, 14 May 1915, AWM 2DRL/0130.

71 AWM 23/20/2, First World War Diaries, 3rd Infantry Battalion, 1 May 1915.

72 Owen, R., Report, 14 May 1915, AWM 2DRL/0130.

73 Ibid.

74 National Archives of Australia, First Australian Imperial Force Personnel Dossiers, 1914–20, Series B2455, McLeod, T., 1954911.

75 National Archives of Australia, First Australian Imperial Force Personnel Dossiers, 1914–20, Series B2455, Meager, H., 8039782.

76 National Archives of Australia, First Australian Imperial Force Personnel Dossiers, 1914–20, Series B2455, Fanning, F., 3547736.

77 Owen, R., Report, 14 May 1915, AWM 2DRL/0130.

78 US Naval Observatory Records for 1 May 1915: aa.usno.navy.mil/data/docs/RS_OneDay.php

6 The Battle of Death Trap Valley, 2 to 5 May 1915

1 Lott, L., Diary, 2 May 1915, AWM MSS1122.

2 Owen, R., Report, 14 May 1915, AWM 2DRL/0130.

3 Bean, C.E.W., *Official History of Australia in the War of 1914–18. Vol I: The Story of Anzac—From the Outbreak of the War to the End of the First Phase of the Gallipoli Campaign, May 4, 1915,* 13th Edn, Angus & Robertson, Sydney, 1942, page 541.

4 Ibid., page xxi.

5 Lott, L., Diary, 2 May 1915, AWM MSS1122.

6 McLeod, T., Letter to family, 15 May 1915, AWM 2DRL/0145.

7 Ibid.

8 McGuirk, A., Letter to father, 30 July 1915, AWM PR89/156.

9 Bean, C., *Official History, Vol. I*, page xxi.

10 Owen, R., Report, 14 May 1915, AWM 2DRL/0130.

11 De Vine, L., Diary, 2 May 1915, AWM 1DRL0240/2.

12 The National Archives (London), ADM 1/8453/77, Parker, W., VC File.

13 Maitland, G., *Battle History of the Royal New South Wales Regiment, Vol. I: 1885–1918*, Kangaroo Press, Sydney, 2001, page 48.

14 Bean, C., Notebook, April–June 1915, AWM38 3DRL606/25/1.

15 Lott, L., Diary, 2 May 1915, AWM MSS1122.

16 AWM28, Recommendation files for honours and awards, AIF, 1914–18 War.

17 Baker, T.H., 'Account of the operations, Chatham Battalion, Royal Marine Light Infantry', *Royal Naval Division Magazine,* Issue No. 3, December 1997.

18 Jerrod, D., *The Royal Naval Division*, Hutchinson & Co., London, 1923, page 118.

19 Wren, E., *Randwick to Hargicourt: History of the 3rd Battalion, AIF,* Ronald G. McDonald, Sydney, Australia, 1935, page 72.

20 AWM4 23/1/5, First World War Diaries, 1st Infantry Brigade.

21 Ibid.

22 AWM4 1/42/3, First World War Diaries, General Staff Headquarters, 1st Australian Division, Part 2, April 1915.
23 The National Archives (London), ADM/159/203, Parker, W., Service Record.
24 The National Archives (London), ADM 1/8453/77, Parker, W., VC File.
25 Wren, E., *Randwick to Hargicourt,* pages 71–3.
26 Snelling, S., *VCs of the First World War: Gallipoli*, Allan Smith Publishing, United Kingdom, page 91.
27 De Vine, L., Diary, 2 May 1915, AWM 1DRL0240/2.
28 AWM4 23/21/3, First World War Diaries, 4th Infantry Battalion, 2 May 1915.
29 AWM4 1/42/4, First World War Diaries, General Staff Headquarters, 1st Australian Division, Part 4, May 1915.
30 De Vine, L., Diary, 2 May 1915, AWM 1DRL0240/2.
31 Wakeford, M., Letter to family, *Illawarra Mercury*, 25 June 1915.
32 De Vine, L., Diary, 2 May 1915, AWM 1DRL0240/2.
33 Ibid., 3 May 1915.
34 Owen, R., Report, 14 May 1915, AWM 2DRL/0130.
35 Bean, C., Notebook, April–June 1915, AWM38 3DRL 606/25/1.
36 Bean, C., *Official History, Vol. I,* page 542.
37 Ibid., page xxi.
38 Bean, C.E.W., *Official History of Australia in the War of 1914–18. Vol II: The Story of Anzac—From 4 May 1915 to the Evacuation,* University of Queensland Press, St Lucia, 1980, page 55.
39 Bean, C., *Gallipoli Mission*, Australian Broadcasting Corporation, Sydney, 1990, page 144.
40 Erkal, S., Turkish General Staff Ankara, *A Brief History of the Canakkale Campaign in the First World War (June 1914–January, 1916)*, The Turkish General Staff Printing House, Ankara, 2004, page 85.
41 Bean, C., *Gallipoli Mission,* page 353.
42 Quote from Erkal, S., *A Brief History of the Canakkale Campaign*, page 85.

7 Jack's fate

1 Macquarie, C., Letter to George Collyer, 3 July 1915, private collection, in author's possession.
2 Ibid.
3 Quote from Curran, T., *Across the Bar: The Story of Simpson. The Man with the Donkey: Australia and Tyneside's Great Military Hero,* Ogmios Publications, Brisbane, 1994, page 297.
4 Tebbutt, A., Medical Report on Landing at Gallipoli, AWM25 367/144.

5 Tyquin, M., *The Medical War: The Australian Army Medical Services in the Dardanelles Campaign of 1915*, NSW University Press, Australia, 1993, page 16.
6 Curran, T., *Across The Bar,* page 135.
7 AWM 1DRL/0428, Australian Red Cross Society, Wounded and Missing Enquiry Bureau Files, 1914–18 War.
8 Wilson, G., *Donkeys, Dust and Delusions: The Myth of Simpson and His Donkey Exposed,* Big Sky Publishing, Newport, 2012, page 117.
9 AWM 1DRL/0428, Australian Red Cross Society, Wounded and Missing Enquiry Bureau Files, 1914–18 War.
10 Wright, L., Diary, 25 April 1915, AWM PR 86/208.
11 Curran, T., *Across The Bar,* page 276.
12 Hugo, E., The Diaries of Lt-Col Edward V. Hugo, 2 May 1915, The Archives of the Royal College of Surgeons of England, RCSEng MS0057/1.
13 Butler, A., *Official History of the Australian Army Medical Services 1914–1918, Vol. I,* Australian War Memorial, Sydney, 1938, page 166.
14 Tyquin, M., *The Medical War*, page 95.
15 Harris, K., *More Than Bombs and Bandages: Australian Army Nurses at World War One,* Big Sky Publishing, Australia, 2011, page 81.
16 Hugo, E., Diaries, 3 May 1915, RCSEng MS0057/1.
17 Wakeford, M., Letter to family, *The Illawarra Mercury,* 25 June 1915.
18 AWM4 26/62/4, First World War Diaries, No. 1 Australian Casualty Clearing Station, 25 April to 4 May; Part 1 May 1915.
19 Butler, A., *Official History of the Australian Army Medical Services 1914–1918, Vol. I,* page 147.
20 Corbin, J., Diary, 27 April 1915, AWM PR00176.
21 Tyquin, M., *The Medical War*, page 16.
22 Quote from Curran, T., *Across The Bar*, page 279.
23 Tyquin, M., *The Medical War,* page 16.
24 AWM4 26/44/3, First World War Diaries, 1st Field Ambulance, 3 May 1915.
25 Corbin, J., Diary, Notes on Evacuation of Wounded, AWM PR00176.
26 Butler, A., *Official History, Vol. I,* page 144.
27 Corbin, J., Diary, 3 May 1915, AWM PR0176.
28 Ibid.
29 Ibid.
30 Hugo, E., Identity Statement, RCSEng MS0057/1.
31 Syme, G., *Medical Journal of Australia*, April 1916, AWM PR87/226.
32 Butler, A., *Official History of the Australian Army Medical Services 1914–1918, Vol. I*, page 181.
33 Tyquin, M., *The Medical War*, page 209.

34 Ryan, C., Narrative recorded by A. Butler, 14 March 1919, AWM 1DRL/0560.

35 National Archives of Australia, First Australian Imperial Force Personnel Dossiers, 1914–20, Series B2455, Tucker, E., 11613029; Marshall, C., 8213793; Gibson, E., 5029663; Wakeford, M., 8399000; Peters, E., 8015447; and Durham, S., 352959.

36 Wakeford, M., Letter to family, *The Illawarra Mercury*, 25 June 1915.

37 Gibson, E., Diary, 26 April 1915, AWM PR01269.

38 Young, M. (ed.), *We Are Here Too: The Diaries and Letters of Sister Olive L.C. Haynes, November 1914 to February 1918*, Australian Down Syndrome Association Incorporated, Adelaide, 1991, page 9.

39 Rowden, G., Letter, 25 April 1915, AWM PR03269.

40 Tucker, E., Diary, 25 April 1915, AWM41 MS1053.

41 Syme, G., *Medical Journal of Australia*, April 1916, AWM PR87/226.

42 Hugo, E., Diary, 6 May 1915, RCSEng MS0057/1.

43 Ibid., 26 April 1915.

44 Ibid., 2 May 1915.

45 Ryan, C., Narrative recorded by A. Butler, 14 March 1919, AWM 1DRL/560.

46 46 Butler, A., *Official History of the Australian Army Medical Services 1914–1918, Vol. I*, page 164.

47 Ibid., page 165.

48 Carberry, A., *The New Zealand Medical Service in The Great War 1914–1918,* Whitcombe and Tombs, Auckland, 1924, pages 37–8.

49 Tucker, E., Diary, 28 April 1915, AWM41 MS1053.

50 Wakeford, M., Letter to family, *The Illawarra Mercury*, 25 June 1915.

51 Tyquin, M., *The Medical War*, page 71.

52 Rees, P., *The Other ANZACS: Nurses at War 1914–1918*, Allen & Unwin, Sydney, 2008, page 166.

53 Harris, K., *More Than Bombs and Bandages*, page 187.

54 Rees, P., *The Other ANZACS*, page 16.

55 Tyquin, M., *The Medical War,* page 60.

56 Gibson, E., Diary, 9 April 1915, AWM PR01269.

57 Hugo, E., Diary, 4 May 1915, RCSEng MS0057/1.

58 Wakeford, M., Letter to family, *The Illawarra Mercury*, 25 June 1915.

59 Tucker, E., Diary, 2 May 1915, AWM41 MS1053.

60 Syme, G., *Medical Journal of Australia*, AWM PR87/226.

61 Hugo, E., Diary, 3 May 1915, RCSEng MS0057/1.

62 Ibid., 5 May 1915.

63 Macquarie, C., Letter to George Collyer, 3 July 1915.

64 Wakeford, M., Letter to family, *The Illawarra Mercury*, 25 June 1915.

65 Hague Peace Conference, 1899: en.wikipedia.org/wiki/Hague_Conventions_of_1899_and_1907

66 *The Uralla Times,* 4 September 1915.

67 Anzac History, Smythe, B., Letter to family, 9 May 1915: www.smythe.id.au/letters/15_16.htm

68 *The Argus,* 8 June 1915.

69 Shadbolt, M., *Voices of Gallipoli*, Hodder & Stoughton, Auckland, 1988, page 56.

70 Hugo, E., Diary, 5 May 1915, RCSEng MS0057/1.

71 Butler, A., *Official History of the Australian Army Medical Services 1914–1918, Vol. I,* page 181.

72 Gibson, E., Diary, Appendix, AWM PR01269.

73 National Archives of Australia, First Australian Imperial Force Personnel Dossiers, 1914–20, Series B2455, Collyer, J., 3273151.

74 Syme, G., Undated letter, AWM PR87/226.

75 Collyer, J., Personnel Dossier, 3273151.

76 Macquarie, C., Letter to George Collyer, 3 July 1915.

77 Macquarie, C., Personnel Dossier, 1967586.

78 Macquarie, C., Letter to George Collyer, 3 July 1915.

79 Collyer, J., Personnel Dossier, 3273151.

80 Ibid.

81 Ibid.

82 Ibid.

83 Ibid.

84 Ibid.

8 Casualties

1 AWM4 1/42/4, First World War Diaries, General Staff Headquarters, 1st Australian Division, Part 4, May 1915.

2 4th Battalion Personnel dossiers survey, in author's possession.

3 Ibid.

4 Lott, L., Diary, 2 May 1915, AWM MSS1122.

5 AWM4 1/42/4, First World War Diaries, General Staff Headquarters, 1st Australian Division, Part 4, May 1915.

6 4th Battalion Personnel dossiers survey, in author's possession.

7 Ibid.

8 Ibid.

9 AWM 1DRL/0428, Australian Red Cross Society, Wounded and Missing Enquiry Bureau Files, 1914–18 War.

10 Ibid.

11 Ibid.
12 Ibid.
13 Ibid.
14 National Archives of Australia, First Australian Imperial Force, 1914–1920, Personnel Dossiers, Series B2455, Ponting, F., 8020126.
15 4th Battalion Personnel dossiers survey, in author's possession.
16 AWM28, Recommendation files for honours and awards, AIF, 1914–18 War.
17 4th Battalion Personnel dossiers survey, in author's possession.
18 Ibid.
19 Leslie, G.H., Memoir, 1915, AWM PR88/067.
20 Wren, E., *Randwick to Hargicourt: History of the 3rd Battalion, AIF,* Ronald G. McDonald, Sydney, Australia, 1935, page 71.
21 De Vine, L., Diary, 2 May 1915, AWM 1DRL0240/2.
22 National Archives of Australia, First Australian Imperial Force, 1914–1920, Personnel Dossiers, Series B2455, Cooke, F., 3401607.
23 AWM Search The Roll of Honour, 3rd Battalion, 1 and 2 May 1915.
24 National Archives of Australia, First Australian Imperial Force, 1914–1920, Personnel Dossiers, Series B2455, Hammond, L., 4256134.
25 National Archives of Australia, First Australian Imperial Force, 1914–1920, Personnel Dossiers, Series B2455, Heylen, W., 4736218.
26 National Archives of Australia, First Australian Imperial Force, 1914–1920, Personnel Dossiers, Series B2455, Bass, C., 3055387.
27 Wren, E., *Randwick To Hargicourt,* page 71.
28 McGuirk, A., Letter to father, dated 30 July, 1915, AWM PR89/156.
29 National Archives of Australia, First Australian Imperial Force, 1914–1920, Personnel Dossiers, Series B2455, Pritchard, C., 8018857.
30 The figure for the 4th Battalion (see page 312) is based on the author's own research. AWM Search The Roll of Honour, 1st–16th Battalions, 1 May 1915.
31 The National Archives (London), ADM 1/8453/77, Parker, W., VC File.
32 Owen, R., Report, 14 May 1915, AWM 2DRL/0130.
33 World War I Casualty Lists of Royal Navy and Dominion Navies, 1–30 April 1915: www.naval-history.net/xDKCas1915-04Apr.htm
34 World War I Casualty Lists of Royal Navy and Dominion Navies, 1–31 May 1915: www.naval-history.net/xDKCas1915-05May.htm
35 Ibid.
36 Ibid.
37 The National Archives (London), ADM 1/8453/77, Parker, W., VC File.
38 Jerrold, D., *The Royal Naval Division,* Hutchinson & Co., London, 1923, page 118.

39 Blumberg, H., *Britain's Sea Soldiers: A Record of the Royal Marines During the War 1914–1919,* Devonport, 1927, page 138.

40 World War I Casualty Lists of Royal Navy and Dominion Navies, 1–31 May 1915: www.naval-history.net/xDKCas1915-05May.htm

41 The National Archives (London), ADM/159/14, Minter, M.

42 The National Archives (London), ADM/159/203, Parker, W.

43 World War I Casualty Lists of Royal Navy and Dominion Navies, 1–30 April 1915: www.naval-history.net/xDKCas1915-04Apr.htm; World War I Casualty Lists of Royal Navy and Dominion Navies, 1–31 May 1915: www.naval-history.net/xDKCas1915-05May.htm

44 The National Archives (London), ADM/196/64, Alcock, A.

45 Blumberg, H., *Britain's Sea Soldiers*, page 170.

46 Erickson, E., *Gallipoli and the Middle East 1914–1918,* Amber Books, London, 2008, page 84.

47 Uyar, Mesut, *Brothers in Arms: Turkish Officers in the Canakkale Campaign*, 18 Mart University, Turkey, 2006, page 14.

48 Erkal, S., Turkish General Staff Ankara, *A Brief History of the Canakkale Campaign in the First World War (June 1914–January, 1916)*, The Turkish General Staff Printing House, Ankara, 2004, page 85.

49 Erickson, E., *Ottoman Army Effectiveness in World War I: A Comparative Study,* Routledge, Abingdon, 2007, page 40.

50 Aker, S., *The Dardanelles: The Ari Burnu Battles and the 27th Regiment 1935*, AWM MSS1886.

51 Bean, C., Notebook, April–June 1915, AWM38 3DRL606/25/1.

52 Wakeford, M., Letter to family, *The Illawarra Mercury*, 25 June 1915.

9 Recognition

1 Heane, J., Letter to brother, 28 July 1915, *The Dubbo Liberal and Macquarie Advocate*, 10 September 1915.

2 Street, L., Letter to mother, 5 May 1915, AWM 1DRL578.

3 Bean, C., AWM38 3DRL6673/644.

4 Bazley, A., 'Australia's Official History of World War I', *Stand-To,* Vol. 6, No. 5, February–August 1959.

5 Wilson, G., *Donkeys, Dust and Delusions: The Myth of Simpson and His Donkey Exposed,* Big Sky Publishing, Newport, 2012, page 330.

6 *The Telegraph*, 8 August 2012.

7 The National Archives (London), ADM 1/8453/77, Parker, W., VC File.

8 Ibid.

9 Ibid.

10 Snelling, S., *VCs of the First World War: Gallipoli*, Allan Smith Publishing, United Kingdom, 1995, page 92.

11 Bean, C.E.W., *Official History of Australia in the War of 1914–18. Vol I: The Story of Anzac—From the Outbreak of the War to the End of the First Phase of the Gallipoli Campaign, May 4, 1915,* 13th Edn, Angus & Robertson, Sydney, 1942, page xx.

12 Bean, C., *Gallipoli Mission*, Australian Broadcasting Corporation, Sydney, 1990, page 144.

13 The National Archives (London), ADM/159/203, Royal Navy Officers Service Records, Parker, W.

14 The National Archives (London), ADM 1/8453/77, Parker, W., VC File.

15 Baker, T.H., 'Account of the operations, Chatham Battalion, Royal Marine Light Infantry', *Royal Naval Division Magazine,* Issue No. 3, December 1997.

16 The National Archives (London), ADM 1/8453/77, Parker, W., VC File.

17 Ibid.

18 Ibid.

19 Wren, E., *Randwick to Hargicourt: History of the 3rd Battalion, AIF,* Ronald G. McDonald, Sydney, Australia, 1935, page 72.

20 Blumberg, H., *Britain's Sea Soldiers: A Record of the Royal Marines During the War 1914–1919,* Devonport, 1927, page 174.

21 AWM28, Recommendation files for honours and awards, AIF, 1914–18 War.

22 Bean, C., Notebook, April–June 1915, AWM38 3DRL 606/25/1.

23 Heane, J., Letter to brother, *The Dubbo Liberal and Macquarie Advocate,* 10 September 1915.

24 AWM4 1/42/4, Part 4, First World War Diaries, General Staff Headquarters, 1st Australian Division, May 1915.

25 *Dubbo Dispatch*, 4 June 1915.

26 National Archives of Australia, First Australian Imperial Force Personnel Dossiers, 1914–20, Series B2455, Robson, E., 8037170.

27 AWM28, Recommendation files for honours and awards, AIF, 1914–18 War.

28 *Anzac Memorial,* Returned Soldiers Association, Sydney, 1916, page 69.

29 *The Sun* reported in *The Uralla Times*, 4 September 1915.

30 *The Tamworth Daily Observer*, 7 September 1915.

31 Ibid.

32 Ibid.

33 Owen, R., Report, 14 May 1915, AWM 2DRL/0130.

34 National Archives of Australia, First Australian Imperial Force, 1914–1920, Personnel Dossiers, Series B2455, Owen, R., 7998000.

35 *The Illawarra Mercury*, 7 December 1915.
36 Wilson, G., *Dust, Donkeys and Delusions*, pages 359–62.
37 *The London Gazette,* 1 June 1915.
38 National Archives of Australia, First Australian Imperial Force, 1914–1920, Personnel Dossiers, Series B2455, Humberstone, R., 7031910.
39 AWM28, Recommendation files for honours and awards, AIF, 1914–18 War.
40 National Archives of Australia, First Australian Imperial Force, 1914–1920, Personnel Dossiers, Series B2455, Fanning, F., 3547736.
41 Ibid.
42 AWM28, Recommendation files for honours and awards, AIF, 1914–18 War.
43 Ibid. Lieutenants Meager and McLeod, Special Mentions.
44 Owen, R., Report, 14 May 1915, AWM 2DRL/0130.
45 Travers, T., 'The Ottoman Crisis of May 1915 at Gallipoli', *War in History*, January, 2001, pages 72–3.

10 Combatants

1 Massie, R., Letter to mother, 4 May 1915, AWM 3DRL/3701.
2 Edwards, R., Diary, 1 May 1915, AWM PR91/192.
3 4th Battalion Personnel dossiers survey, in author's possession.
4 Austin, R., *The Fighting Fourth: A History of Sydney's 4th Battalion 1914–19*, Slouch Hat Publications, Victoria, 2007, page 52.
5 Lott, L., Diary, 2 May 1915, AWM MSS1122.
6 Massie, R., Letter to mother, 4 May 1915, AWM 3DRL/3701.
7 Ibid., 5 May 1915.
8 Bosward, C., Diary, 9 May 1915, AWM 3DRL4104.
9 De Vine, L., Diary, 5 May 1915, AWM 1DRL0240/2.
10 Ibid., 8 May 1915.
11 Street, L., Letter to mother, 16 May 1915, AWM 1DRL578.
12 Ibid.
13 De Vine, L., Diary, 30 April 1915, AWM 1DRL0240/2.
14 *The Dubbo Liberal and Macquarie Advocate,* 7 July 1915.
15 McKern, H., Diary, 9 May 1915, AWM 2DRL/0507.
16 AWM4 23/21/3, First World War Diaries, 4th Infantry Battalion, 9 May 1915.
17 Massie, R., Letter to mother, dated 10 May 1915, AWM 3DRL/3701.
18 AWM4 1/42/4, Part 4, First World War Diaries, General Staff Headquarters, 1st Australian Division, May 1915.
19 AWM4 23/21/4, First World War Diaries, 4th Infantry Battalion, June 1915.
20 AWM4 1/42/4, Part 4, First World War Diaries, 4th Infantry Battalion, May 1915.

21 Lott, L., Diary, 8 May 1915, AWM MSS1122.

22 National Archives of Australia, First Australian Imperial Force, 1914–1920, Personnel Dossiers, Series B2455, Cliffe, W., 3256757.

23 AWM28, Recommendation files for honours and awards, AIF, 1914–18 War.

24 National Archives of Australia, First Australian Imperial Force, 1914–20, Personnel Dossiers, Series B2455, Campbell, A., 1851423.

25 Ibid.

26 National Archives of Australia, First Australian Imperial Force, 1914–1920, Personnel Dossiers, Series B2455, Cliffe, W., 3256757.

27 National Archives of Australia, First Australian Imperial Force, 1914–20, Personnel Dossiers, Series B2455, Campbell, A., 1851423.

28 Quote from McKernan, M., *Padre: Australian Chaplains in Gallipoli and France,* Allen & Unwin, Sydney, 1986, page 61.

29 Ibid., pages 76–7.

30 AWM 23/21/3, First World War Diaries, 4th Infantry Battalion, 11 May 1915.

31 *The Sydney Morning Herald*, 5 July 1915.

32 Austin, R., *The Fighting Fourth*, page 55.

33 Ibid., page 81.

34 National Archives of Australia, First Australian Imperial Force, 1914–1920, Personnel Dossiers, Series B2455, Macquarie, C., 1967586.

35 National Archives of Australia, First Australian Imperial Force, 1914–1920, Personnel Dossiers, Series B2455, Bock, C., 3095139.

36 National Archives of Australia, First Australian Imperial Force, 1914–1920, Personnel Dossiers, Series B2455, Bound, D., 3100604, and Bound, W., 3100611.

37 National Archives of Australia, First Australian Imperial Force, 1914–1920, Personnel Dossiers, Series B2455, Bound, W., Personnel Dossier, 3100611.

38 *The Tamworth Daily Observer,* 7 October 1915.

39 *Anzac Memorial*, Returned Soldiers Association, Sydney, 1916, page 69.

40 National Archives of Australia, First Australian Imperial Force, 1914–1920, Personnel Dossiers, Series B2455, Robson, E., 8037170.

41 Lott, L., Diary, 6–13 August 1915, AWM MSS1122.

42 National Archives of Australia, First Australian Imperial Force, 1914–1920, Personnel Dossiers, Series B2455, Lott, L., 8205200.

43 De Vine, L., Diary, 26 and 27 November, 7 December 1915, AWM 1DRL0240/2.

44 National Archives of Australia, First Australian Imperial Force, 1914–1920, Personnel Dossiers, Series B2455, De Vine, L., 3503131.

45 *Dubbo Dispatch*, 23 July 1915.

46 National Archives of Australia, First Australian Imperial Force, 1914–1920, Personnel Dossiers, Series B2455, Quigley, M., 1851423.

47 Rodgers, J., *To Give and Not to Count the Cost: Riverview and the Great War*, St Ignatius' College, Riverview, Lane Cove, 2009, page 113.

48 National Archives of Australia, First Australian Imperial Force, 1914–1920, Personnel Dossiers, Series B2455, Fanning, F., 3547736.

49 Bean, C.E.W., *Official History of Australia in the War of 1914–18. Vol I: The Story of Anzac—From the Outbreak of the War to the End of the First Phase of the Gallipoli Campaign, May 4, 1915,* 13th Edn, Angus & Robertson, Sydney, 1942, page 136.

50 National Archives of Australia, First Australian Imperial Force, 1914–1920, Personnel Dossiers, Series B2455, Heane, J., 4749612.

51 Fanning, F., Personnel Dossier, 3547736.

52 Austin, R., *The Fighting Fourth*, page 94.

53 Williams, H.R., *The Gallant Company: An Australian Soldier's Story*, Angus & Robertson, Sydney, 1933, page 16.

54 Ibid., page 17.

55 Ibid., page 78.

56 Ibid., page 89.

57 Ibid., pages 85–8.

58 National Archives of Australia, First Australian Imperial Force, 1914–1920, Personnel Dossiers, Series B2455, Wright, W., 3450562.

59 Austin, R., *The Fighting Fourth*, page 94.

60 Adam-Smith, P., *The Anzacs*, Nelson Publishers, Melbourne, 1978, page 205.

61 Williams, H.R., *The Gallant Company,* page 96.

62 AWM 1DRL/0428, Australian Red Cross Society, Wounded and Missing Enquiry Bureau Files, 1914–18 War.

63 *Dubbo Dispatch,* 4 June 1915.

64 AWM People Profiles, James Heane: www.awm.gov.au/units/people_18338.asp/

65 Wilson, G., 'Brigadier-General James Heane', Celebrities of the AIF, *Reveille,* Vol. 10, March 1937.

66 *The Dubbo Liberal and Macquarie Advocate*, 10 December 1915.

67 AWM4 23/18/9, First World War Diaries, 1st Infantry Battalion, July 1916.

68 Wilson, G., 'Brigadier-General James Heane', Celebrities of the AIF, *Reveille,* Vol. 10, March 1937.

69 Stacey, V., Kindon, F., & Chedgey, H., *The History of the First Battalion AIF 1914–1919,* James Lee, Sydney, 1931, page 59.

70 Blair, D., *Dinkum Diggers: An Australian Battalion At War,* Melbourne University Press, Australia, 2001, page 118.

71 National Archives of Australia, First Australian Imperial Force, 1914–1920, Personnel Dossiers, Series B2455, Heane, J., 4749612.

72 Cameron, D., *The Battle for Lone Pine: Four Days of Hell at the Heart of Gallipoli,* Penguin, Australia, 2012, page 263.

73 Bean, C., *Official History, Vol. II,* page 566.

74 World War I Casualty Lists of Royal Navy and Dominion Navies, 1–31 May 1915, Luard, F.: www.naval-history.net/xDKCas1915-05May.htm

75 Blumberg, H., *Britain's Sea Soldiers: A Record of the Royal Marines During the War 1914–1919,* Devonport, 1927.

76 Luard, F.: www.cwgc.org/find-war-dead.aspx?cpage=11&sort=name&order=asc

77 The National Archives (London), ADM/196/64, Royal Navy Officers Service Records, Alcock, A.

78 Carlyon, L., *Gallipoli*, Macmillan Australia, Sydney, 2001, page 280.

79 AWM People Profiles, Kemal Attaturk: www.awm.gov.au/encyclopedia/attaturk/

11 A question or two of history

1 Bean, C., 'The writing of the Australian Official History of the Great War—Sources, methods and some conclusions', *Journal of the Royal Australian Historical Society,* Vol. xxiv, 1938, Part 2, page 112.

2 Bazley, A., 'Australia's Official History of World War I', *Stand-To,* Volume 6, No. 5, February–August, 1959, page 25.

3 Bean, C., *Gallipoli Correspondent: The Frontline Diary of C.E.W. Bean,* Allen & Unwin, Sydney, 1983, pages 146–7.

4 Ibid., page 147.

5 AWM People Profiles, Charles Bean: www.awm.gov.au/about/charles-bean/

6 Bean, C., *Official History of Australia in the War of 1914–18. Vol. VI: The Australian Imperial Force in France during the Allied Offensive 1918,* 1st Edn, Angus & Robertson, Sydney, 1942, page 1096.

7 National Archives of Australia, First Australian Imperial Force, 1914–1920, Personnel Dossiers, Series B2455, Davis, C., 1858027.

8 Bean, C. (ed.), *The Anzac Book*, Cassell & Company, London, 1916.

9 Ibid., page 59.

10 Gerster, R., *Big-Noting: The Heroic Theme in Australian War Writing*, Melbourne University Press, Melbourne, 1987, page 30.

11 Carlyon, L., *Gallipoli*, Macmillan Australia, Sydney, 2001, page 531.

12 Erickson, E., *Ordered to Die: A History of the Ottoman Army in the First World War*, Greenwood Press, London, 2001, page 94.

13 Figes, O., *Crimea: The Last Crusade,* Penguin Books, London, 2011, page 310.

14 Ibid., page 311.

15 McKernan, M., *The Gallipoli Letter*, Allen & Unwin, Sydney, 2010, page 28.

16 Ibid., page 30.

17 Bean, C., 'The Writing of the Official History', *Journal of the Royal Australian Historical Society*, Vol. xxiv, 1938, Part 2, page 85.

18 Winter, D., *Making the Legend: The War Writings of C.E.W. Bean*, University of Queensland Press, St Lucia, 1992, page 60.

19 Gerster, R., *Big-Noting: The Heroic Theme in Australian War Writing*, Melbourne University Press, Melbourne, 1987, page 31.

20 Inglis, K., *Anzac Remembered: Selected Writings*, Melbourne University Press, Melbourne, 1998, pages 67–8.

21 Ibid., page 71.

22 Ibid., page 76.

23 Bean, C., 'The Writing of the Official History', *Journal of the Royal Australian Historical Society*, Vol. xxiv, 1938, Part 2, page 92.

24 Ibid.

25 Ibid., page 93.

26 Ibid., page 109.

27 Ibid., pages 110–11.

28 Bean, C.E.W., *Official History of Australia in the War of 1914–18. Vol I: The Story of Anzac—From the Outbreak of the War to the End of the First Phase of the Gallipoli Campaign, May 4, 1915,* 13th Edn, Angus & Robertson, Sydney, 1942, page xxx.

29 *The Bulletin*, 27 May 1942, page 2.

30 Bean, C., 'The Writing of the Official History', *Journal of the Royal Australian Historical Society*, Vol. xxiv, 1938, Part 2, pages 108–9.

31 *The Bulletin,* 27 May 1942, page 2.

32 Bean, C., *Official History, Vol. I,* page v.

33 Ibid, page xxv.

34 Winter, D., 'The Anzac Book: A re-appraisal', *Journal of the Australian War Memorial,* April 1990, No. 16.

35 Bean documents caveat, 16 September 1946: https://www.awm.gov.au/collection/records/awm38/3drl606/description.asp

36 Bean, C., *Official History, Vol. I,* page v.

37 Austin, R., *The Fighting Fourth: A History of Sydney's 4th Battalion 1914–19*, Slouch Hat Publications, Victoria, 2007, page 37.

38 Bean, C., *Official History, Vol. I,* page xix.

39 Ibid., page xxi.

40 Ibid., page xx.

41 Ibid., page xxi.

42 AWM 23/1/15, First World War Diaries, 1st Infantry Brigade, Part 3, May 1915 Appendices.

43 Bean, C., *Gallipoli Mission*, Australian Broadcasting Corporation, Sydney, 1990, page v.

44 Ibid., page 144.

45 Ibid., page vi.

46 Ibid., page 144.

47 Bean C., Notebook, April–June 1915, AWM38 3DRL606/25/1.

48 Bean, C., Diary, May 1915, AWM38 3DRL606/7/1.

49 AWM28, Recommendation files for honours and awards, AIF, 1914–18 War.

50 McKern, H., Diary, 9 May 1915, AWM 2DRL/0507.

51 Massie, R., Letter to mother, 10 May 1915, AWM 3DRL/3701.

52 Bazley, A., 'Australia's Official History of World War 1', *Stand-To*, February–August 1959, Vol. 6, No. 7.

53 Stanley, P., speech on the occasion of the 60th anniversary of the Australian War Memorial: www.awm.gov.au/events/talks/60th/

54 AWM People Profiles, Arthur Bazley: www.awm.gov.au/people/1439.asp

55 Gooding, J., *Gallipoli Revisited: In the Footsteps of Charles Bean and the Australian Historical Mission*, Hardie Grant Books, Melbourne, 2008, page 193.

56 Bazley, A., 'Australia's Official History of World War 1', *Stand-To*, February–August 1959, Vol. 6, No. 7.

57 Bean, C., *Official History of Australia in the War of 1914–18. Vol. VI: The Australian Imperial Force in France during the Allied Offensive 1918,* 1st Edn, Angus & Robertson, Sydney, 1942, page vii.

58 Bean, C., *Official History, Vol. I*, page xx.

59 Bennett, S., *Pozières: The ANZAC Story*, Scribe, Melbourne, 2012, page 319.

60 National Archives of Australia, First Australian Imperial Force, 1914–1920, Personnel Dossiers, Series B2455, Bean, J., 3061116.

61 Bean, C., 'The Writing of the Official History', *Journal of the Royal Australian Historical Society*, Vol. xxiv, 1938, Part 2, page 112.

Appendix 1: Casualties in 4th Battalion, 1 and 2 May 1915

1 The source of all three appendices is the author's research: 1377 personnel dossiers survey of the original 4th Battalion intake and the first three reinforcements.

Bibliography

Books

Adam-Smith, P., *The Anzacs*, Nelson Publishers, Melbourne, 1978.

Andrews, E.M., *The Anzac Illusion: Anglo-Australian Relations During World War I,* Cambridge University Press, Cambridge, 1993.

Anzac Memorial, Returned Soldiers Association, Sydney, 1916.

Aspinall-Oglander, C.F., *Military Operations: Gallipol,* two volumes plus appendices and maps, Heinemann, London, 1929 and 1932.

Austin, R., *Gallipoli: An Australian Encyclopedia of the 1915 Dardanelles Campaign,* Slouch Hat Publications, Victoria, 2005.

——, *The Fighting Fourth: A History of Sydney's 4th Battalion 1914–19*, Slouch Hat Publications, Victoria, 2007.

Baines, J., & Malek, J., *Atlas of Ancient Egypt*, Equinox, Oxford, 1987.

Barrett, P., & Collinson, K., *The Happy Warrior: An Anthology of Australian and New Zealand Military Poetry*, Sid Harta Publishers, Victoria, 2001.

Bean, C. (ed.), *The Anzac Book*, Cassell & Company, London, 1916.

——, *ANZAC to Amiens*, Australian War Memorial, Canberra, 1946.

——, *Gallipoli Correspondent: The Frontline Diary of C.E.W. Bean,* Allen & Unwin, Sydney, 1983.

——, *Gallipoli Mission*, Australian Broadcasting Corporation, Sydney, 1990.

——, *Official History of Australia in the War of 1914–18. Vol. VI: The Australian Imperial Force in France during the Allied Offensive 1918,* First Edition, Angus & Robertson, Sydney, 1942.

——, *What to Know in Egypt: A Guide For Australian Soldiers*, Société Orientale De Publicité, Cairo, 1915.

Bean, C.E.W., *Official History of Australia in the War of 1914–18. Vol. I: The Story of Anzac—From the Outbreak of the War to the End of the First Phase of the Gallipoli Campaign, May 4, 1915,* Thirteenth Edition, Angus & Robertson, Sydney, 1942.

——, *Official History of Australia in the War of 1914–18. Vol. II: The Story of Anzac—From 4 May 1915 to the Evacuation,* University of Queensland Press, St Lucia, 1980.

Bennett, S., *Pozières: The ANZAC Story*, Scribe, Victoria, 2012.

Blair, D., *Dinkum Diggers: An Australian Battalion at War,* Melbourne University Press, Australia, 2001.

Blumberg, H., *Britain's Sea Soldiers: A Record of The Royal Marines During the War 1914–1919,* Devonport, 1927.

Bond, Lt. Col., *The Army That Went with the Boys: A Record of Salvation Army Work with the Australian Imperial Force,* Salvation Army, Melbourne, 1919.

Broadbent, H., *Gallipoli: The Fatal Shore*, Penguin, Australia, 2005.

Bruce, G., *Harbottles Dictionary of Battles*, Van Nostrand Reinhold Company, New York, 1981.

Brugger, S., *Australians and Egypt 1914–19,* Melbourne University Press, Carlton, 1980.

Butler, A., *Official History of the Australian Army Medical Services 1914–1918, Vol. I,* Australian War Memorial, Sydney, 1938.

Cameron, D., *25 April 1915: The Day the Anzac Legend Was Born*, Allen & Unwin, Sydney, 2007.

——, *The Battle for Lone Pine: Four Days of Hell at the Heart of Gallipoli,* Penguin, Australia, 2012.

Carbery, A., *The New Zealand Medical Service in the Great War 1914–1918,* Whitcombe and Tombs, Auckland, 1924.

Carlyon, L., *Gallipoli*, Macmillan Australia, Sydney, 2001.

Caulfield, M., *Voices of War: Stories from the Australians at War Film Archive,* Hodder, Australia, 2006.

Chambers, S., *Gallipoli-Anzac: The Landing,* Pen & Sword Books, Great Britain, 2008.

Chasseaud, P., & Doyle, P., *Grasping Gallipoli: Terrain, Maps and Failure at the Dardanelles, 1915,* Spellmount Limited, United Kingdom, 2005.

Coates, J., *An Atlas of Australia's Wars*, Oxford University Press, Melbourne, 2006.

Coulthard-Clark, C., *Where Australians Fought: The Encyclopaedia of Australia's Battles,* Allen & Unwin, Sydney, 1998.

Curran, T., *Across the Bar: The Story of Simpson, the Man with the Donkey: Australia and Tyneside's Great Military Hero,* Ogmios Publications, Brisbane, 1994.

De Vries, S., *Australian Heroines of World War One*, Pirigos Press, Brisbane, 2013.

Denton, K., *Gallipoli Illustrated*, Rigby, South Australia, 1981.

——, *Gallipoli: One Long Grave,* Time-Life Books, Sydney, 1986.

Dolan, H., *36 Days: The Untold Story Behind the Gallipoli Landings,* Pan Macmillan, Sydney, 2010.

East, R. (ed.), *The Gallipoli Diary of Sergeant Lawrence of The Australian Engineers — 1st AIF 1915*, Melbourne University Press, Melbourne, 1983.

Erickson, E., *Gallipoli and The Middle East 1914–1918,* Amber Books, London, 2008.

——, *Ordered to Die: A History of the Ottoman Army in the First World War*, Greenwood Press, London, 2001.

——, *Ottoman Army Effectiveness in World War I: A Comparative Study,* Routledge, Abingdon, 2007.

Erkal, S., Turkish General Staff Ankara, *A Brief History of the Canakkale Campaign in the First World War (June 1914–January, 1916)*, The Turkish General Staff Printing House, Ankara, 2004.

Fasih, M., *Gallipoli, 1915: Bloody Ridge Diary*, Denizler, Kitabevi, Istanbul, Turkey, 2003.

Fewster, K., & Basarin, H. and V., *A Turkish View of Gallipoli,* Hodja, Richmond, 1985.

——, *Gallipoli: The Turkish Story*, Allen & Unwin, 2003.

Field Service Regulations Part 1: Operations 1909, Harrison & Sons, London, 1912.

Field, C., *Britain's Sea-Soldiers: A History of the Royal Marines and Their Predecessors and Their Services in Action, Ashore and Afloat, Vol. II,* Lyceum Press, Liverpool, 1924.

Figes, O., *Crimea: The Last Crusade,* Penguin Books, London, 2011.

Gammage, B., *The Broken Years: Australian Soldiers in the Great War*, Penguin Books, Australia, 1975.

Gerster, R., *Big-Noting: The Heroic Theme in Australian War Writing*, Melbourne University Press, Melbourne, 1987.

Glen, F., *Bowler of Gallipoli: Witness to the Anzac Legend,* Australian Military History Publications, Canberra, 2004.

Gooding, J., *Gallipoli Revisited: In the Footsteps of Charles Bean and the Australian Historical Mission,* Hardie Grant Books, Melbourne, 2008.

Hamilton, I., *Gallipoli Diary, Vol. 1*, Unwin, England, 1920.

Harris, K., *More Than Bombs and Bandages: Australian Army Nurses at World War One,* Big Sky Publishing, Australia, 2011.

Hart, P., *Gallipoli,* Profile Books, Great Britain, 2011.

Haynes, J., *Cobbers: Stories of Gallipoli*, ABC Books, Sydney, 2005.

Haythornthwaite, P. J., *The World War One Source Book*, Arms and Armour Press, London, 1998.

Herbert, A., *Mons, Anzac and Kut*, Arnold, London, 1919.

Inglis, K., *Anzac Remembered: Selected Writings*, Melbourne University Press, Melbourne, 1998.

James, R., *Gallipoli*, Batsford, London, 1965.

Jerrold, D., *The Royal Naval Division*, Hutchinson & Co., London, 1923.

Keegan, J., *The Face of Battle*, Jonathan Cape, Great Britain, 1976.

Kent, D., *From Trench and Troopship: The Experience of the Australian Imperial Force 1914–1919,* Hale & Iremonger, NSW, 1999.

King, J., *Gallipoli Diaries: The Anzacs' Own Story Day by Day*, Kangaroo Press, Rosevillle, 2003.

King, J., & Bowers, M., *Gallipoli: Untold Stories*, Doubleday, Australia and New Zealand, 2005.

Larson, M., *Shattered Anzacs: Living with the Scars of War*, University of New South Wales Press, Sydney, 2009.

Liddle, P., *Gallipoli 1915: Pens, Pencils and Cameras at War*, Brassey's Defence Publishers, London, 1985.

——, *Men of Gallipoli: The Dardanelles and Gallipoli Experience, August 1914 to January, 1916*, David & Charles Publishers, New York, 1988.

Lindsay, P., *The Spirit of Gallipoli: The Birth of the ANZAC Legend*, Hardie Grant Books, Victoria, 2006.

Little, M., *The Royal Marines and the Victoria Cross,* Royal Marines Museum, Southsea, 2002.

Loch, S., *To Hell and Back*, HarperCollins, Australia, 2007.

Macleod, J., *Reconsidering Gallipoli*, Manchester University Press, United Kingdom, 2004.

McCarthy, D., *Gallipoli to the Somme: The Story of C.E.W. Bean,* Leo Cooper, Great Britain, 1983.

McKernan, M., *Gallipoli: A Short History*, Allen & Unwin, Sydney, 2010.

——, *Padre: Australian Chaplains in Gallipoli and France,* Allen & Unwin, Sydney, 1986.

——, *The Gallipoli Letter*, Allen & Unwin, Sydney, 2010.

Maitland, G., *Battle History of the Royal New South Wales Regiment, Vol. I: 1885–1918*, Kangaroo Press, 2001.

Matthews, T., *Crosses: Australian Soldiers in the Great War 1914–18,* Boolarong Publications, Brisbane, 1987.

Moorehead, A., *Gallipoli*, Macmillan, Melbourne, Australia, 1973.

Morice, J., *Six-Bob-A-Day-Tourist*, Penguin Books, Melbourne, 1985.

Murray, J., *Gallipoli as I Saw It*, William Kimber, London, 1965.

Neave, D., & Smith, C., *Aussie Soldier: Up Close and Personal*, Big Sky Publishing, Queensland, 2008.

New Encyclopaedia Britannica, Encyclopaedia Britannica, Chicago, 1988.
North, J., *Gallipoli: The Fading Vision*, Faber & Faber, London, 1966.
Odgers, G., *Diggers: The Australian Army, Navy and Air Force in Eleven Wars from 1860 to June 1944,* Lansdowne Publishing, Sydney, 2000.
Paterson, B., *Happy Dispatches: Journalistic Pieces from Banjo Paterson's Days as a War Correspondent*, Lansdowne Press, Sydney, 1980.
Prior, R., *Gallipoli: The End of the Myth*, University of New South Wales Press, Sydney, 2009.
Pugsley, C., *Gallipoli: The New Zealand Story,* Penguin, New Zealand, 2008.
Rae, R., *Scarlet Poppies: The Army Experience of Australian Nurses during World War One,* College of Nursing, 2005.
Rees, P., *The Other ANZACS: Nurses at War 1914–1918*, Allen & Unwin, Sydney, 2008.
Roberts, C., *The Landing at Anzac 1915*, Army History Unit, Big Sky Publishing, Sydney, 2013.
Robertson, J., *Anzac and Empire: The Tragedy and Glory of Gallipoli*, Hamlyn, Australia, 1990.
Robson, L., *The First A.I.F.: A Study of Its Recruitment 1914–1918,* Melbourne University Press, Carlton, 1970.
Rogers, J., *To Give and Not to Count the Cost: Riverview and the Great War*, Lane Cove, 2009.
Ross, J., *The Myth of the Digger: The Australian Soldier in Two World Wars*, Hale & Iremonger, Sydney, 1985.
Scates, B., *Return to Gallipoli: Walking the Battlefields of the Great War,* Cambridge University Press, Cambridge, 2006.
Schuler, P., *Australia in Arms*, Unwin, Melbourne, 1916.
Semmler, C., *The Banjo of the Bush: The Work, Life and Times of A. B. Paterson*, Lansdowne Press, Melbourne, 1966.
Shadbolt, M., *Voices of Gallipoli*, Hodder & Stoughton, Auckland, 1988.
Snelling, S., *VCs of the First World War: Gallipoli*, Allan Smith Publishing, United Kingdom, 1995.
Stacey, V., Kindon, F., & Chedgey, H., *The History of the First Battalion AIF 1914–1919,* James Lee, Sydney, 1931.
Stanley, P., *Bad Characters: Sex, Crime, Mutiny, Murder and the Australian Imperial Force*, Murdoch Books, Australia, 2010.
Steel, N., & Hart, P., *Defeat at Gallipoli*, Macmillan, London, 1995.
Swifte, T., *Gallipoli: The Incredible Campaign*, Macquarie Publications, Dubbo, 1985.
Travers, T., 'The Ottoman Crisis of May 1915 at Gallipoli', *War in History*, January 2001.

Travers, T., *Gallipoli 1915*, Tempus Publishing, United Kingdom, 2002.

Tyquin, M., *The Medical War: The Australian Army Medical Services in the Dardanelles Campaign of 1915*, NSW University Press, Australia, 1993.

Uyar, Mesut, *Brothers in Arms: Turkish Officers in the Canakkale Campaign*, 18 Mart University, 2006.

Williams, H.R., *The Gallant Company: An Australian Soldier's Story*, Angus & Robertson, Sydney, 1933.

Williams, P., *The Battle of Anzac Ridge: An Anzac Victory, 25 April 1915*, Australian Military History Publications, Loftus, Australia, 2007.

Wilson, G., *Bully Beef and Balderdash: Some Myths of the AIF Examined and Debunked*, Big Sky Publishing, Australia, 2012.

——, *Donkeys, Dust and Delusions: The Myth of Simpson and his Donkey Exposed,* Big Sky Publishing, Newport, 2012.

Winter, D., *Making the Legend: The War Writings of C.E.W. Bean*, University of Queensland Press, St Lucia, 1992.

Wren, E., *Randwick to Hargicourt: History of the 3rd Battalion, AIF,* Ronald G. McDonald, Sydney, Australia, 1935.

Young, M., *We Are Here Too: The Diaries and Letters of Sister Olive L.C. Haynes, November 1914 to February 1918*, Australian Down Syndrome Association Incorporated, Adelaide, 1991.

Australian War Memorial

AWM38 Rider on Bean's document collection, 16 September 1946.

AWM, Roll of Honour database, April–May, 1915:

www.awm.gov.au/research/people/roll_of_honour/introduction/

AWM 1DRL/0428, Australian Red Cross Society Wounded and Missing Enquiry Bureau Files, 1914–18 War.

AWM 3DRL6673, Item 64, Bean, C.

AWM8 4th Infantry Battalion Embarkation Rolls, 23/21/1, 23/21/2.

AWM MSS1886, Aker, S., *The Dardanelles: The Ari Burnu Battles and the 27th Regiment 1935.*

AWM PR91/051, Barr, T., Diary.

AWM 3DRL4104, Bosward, C., Diary.

AWM PR00176, Corbin, J., Notes.

AWM 1DRL0240/2, De Vine, L., Diary.

AWM PR91/192, Edwards, R., Diary.

AWM PR01269, Gibson, E., Diary.

AWM PRO2028, Giddings, O., Diary.

AWM PR 84/188, Hagan, J., Diary.

AWM 1DRL362, Howell-Price, O., Letter.
AWM 1DRL/0372, Hutchison, W., Diary.
AWM PR88/67, Leslie, G., Memoir.
AWM MSS1122, Lott, L., Diary.
AWM 3DRL/3701, Massie, R., Letters.
AWM38 3DRL606/28A/1, McCay, J., Interview.
AWM PRO1798, McDonald, W., Diary.
AWM PR89/156, McGuirk, A., Letter.
AWM 2DRL/0507, McKern, H., Diary.
AWM 2DRL/0145, McLeod, T., Letters.
AWM 2DRL492, Meggy, T., Diary.
AWM MSS0954, Oakes, W., Unit History 8th Infantry Battalion 1914–1918.
AWM 2DRL130, Owen, R., Personal Records.
AWM PRO0395, Roberts, R., Diary.
AWM PR03269, Rowden, G., Letter.
AWM 1DRL/0560, Ryan, C., Narrative.
AWM PR00035, Sloan, J., Letter.
AWM 2DRL/0318, Smith, H., Diary.
AWM 1DRL578, Street, L., Letters.
AWM PR87/226, Syme, G., Letters.
AWM25 367/144, Tebbutt, A., Report.
AWM41 MS1053, Tucker, E., Diary.
AWM 1DRL0240/2, Vine, L., Diary.
AWM PR 86/208, Wright, L., Diary.
AWM 3DRL606/267/1, Report by anonymous German naval officer, *Emden*.
AWM4 1/4, First World War Diaries, General Staff, General Headquarters, Mediterranean Expeditionary Force.
AWM4 1/27, First World War Diaries, Intelligence, ANZAC Headquarters.
AWM4 1/42 First World War Diaries General Staff, Headquarters, 1st Australian Division.
AWM4 6/4 First World War Diaries, Senior Chaplain, Other Protestant Denominations, Headquarters AIF.
AWM4 23/1, First World War Diaries, 1st Infantry Brigade.
AWM4 23/18, First World War Diaries, 1st Infantry Battalion.
AWM4 23/20, First World War Diaries, 3rd Infantry Battalion.
AWM4 23/21, First World War Diaries, 4th Infantry Battalion.
AWM4 23/25, First World War Diaries, 8th Infantry Battalion.
AWM4 23/27, First World War Diaries, 10th Infantry Battalion.
AWM4 23/31, First World War Diaries, 14th Infantry Battalion.

AWM4 1/25/1, First World War Diaries, Headquarters, Australian and New Zealand Army Corps, General Staff, Part 7, April 1915.

AWM4 26/62 First World War Diaries, No. 1 Australian Casualty Clearing Station

AWM8 23/21/1, 4th Infantry Battalion Embarkation Roll, October 1914.

AWM28 Recommendation files for honours and awards, AIF, 1914–18 War.

AWM38 3DRL606/7/1, Bean, C., Diary, May 1915.

AWM38 3DRL06/25/1, Bean, C., Notebook, April–June 1915.

National Archives of Australia

Author's research: 1377 personnel dossiers survey of original 4th Battalion intake and the first three reinforcements.

National Archives of Australia, First Imperial Force Personnel Dossiers, 1914–20, Series B2455:

Bass, C., 3055387.
Bean, J., 3061116.
Bock, C., 3095139.
Bound, D., 3100604.
Bound, W., 3100611.
Campbell, A., 1851423.
Christie, J., 3247676.
Cliffe, W., 3256757.
Collyer, J., 3273151.
Cooke, F., 3401607.
Cox, E., and Cox, M., 3435921 and 3436988.
Davis, C., 1858027.
De Vine, L., 3503131.
Durham, S., 352959.
Fanning, F., 3547736.
Gibson, E., 5029663.
Hammond, L., 4256134.
Heane, J., 4749612.
Heylen, W., 4736218.
Humberstone, R., 7031910.
Lawrence, W., 7377787.
Lott, L., 8205200.
Macquarie, C., 1967586.
Marshall, C., 8213793.
McLeod, T., 1954911.
Meager, H., 8039782.

Murray, R., 7983954.
Owen, R., 7998000.
Parker, P., 8008238.
Peters, E., 8015447.
Ponting, F., 8020126.
Pritchard, C., 8018857.
Quigley, M., 1851423.
Reynolds, F., 8031250.
Robertson, J., 8033642.
Robins, A., 8033821.
Robson, E., 8037170.
Thompson, A.J. Onslow, 1832217.
Thomson, T., 1838680.
Tucker, E., 11613029.
Wakeford, M., 8399000.
Wright, W., 3451151.
Wright, W., 3450562.

Newspapers

The Argus
The Bulletin
Casino and Kyogle Courier
The Cootamundra Liberal
Dubbo Dispatch
The Dubbo Liberal and Macquarie Advocate
The Illawarra Mercury
The London Gazette
Mansfield and North Notts Advertiser
The Mildura Cultivator
The Mudgee Guardian & North-Western Representative
The Sydney Morning Herald
Tamworth Daily Observer
The Telegraph (London)
The Uralla Times
Windsor and Richmond Gazette

Journal articles

Baker, T., 'Account of the operations, Chatham Battalion, Royal Marine Light Infantry', *Royal Naval Division Magazine,* Issue No. 3, December 1997.

Barrett, J., 'Historical Reconsiderations VII: No straw man: C.E.W. Bean and some critics', *Australian Historical Studies*, Vol. 23, No. 89, April 1988.

Bazley, A., 'Australia's Official History of World War I', *Stand-To,* Vol. 6, No. 5, February–August 1959.

Bean, C., 'Our war history', *The Bulletin*, 27 May 1942.

——, 'The technique of a contemporary war historian', *Historical Studies*, Vol. 2, No. 6, November 1942.

——, 'Writing the War History', *Reveille,* Vol. 6, No. 10, June 1933.

——, 'The writing of the Australian Official History of the Great War—Sources, methods and some conclusions', *Journal of the Royal Australian Historical Society,* Vol. XXIV, 1938, Part 2.

Donnellan, G., 'Fighting Mac', Celebrities of the AIF, *Reveille,* Vol. 6, March 1933.

Wilson, G., 'Brigadier-General James Heane', Celebrities of the AIF, *Reveille,* Vol. 10, March 1937.

Winter, D., 'The Anzac Book: A re-appraisal', *Journal of the Australian War Memorial*, April 1990, No. 16.

Websites

AWM People Profiles, Arthur Bazley: www.awm.gov.au/people/1439.asp

AWM People Profiles, Charles Bean: www.awm.gov.au/about/charles-bean/

AWM People Profiles, James Heane: www.awm.gov.au/units/people_18338.asp/

AWM People Profiles, Kemal Attaturk: www.awm.gov.au/encyclopedia/attaturk/

AWM Stanley, P., Speech on the occasion of the 60th anniversary of the Australian War Memorial: www.awm.gov.au/events/talks/60th/

Anzac History, Smythe, B., Letters to family, 3 December 1914 and 9 May 1915: www.smythe.id.au/lestweforget/ch1.htm

Anzac History, Smythe, V., Letter to family, 29 November 1914: www.smythe.id.au/lestweforget/ch1.htm

Australian Dictionary of Biography, William Chidley: adb.anu.edu.au/biography/chidley-william-james-5579

Australian Dictionary of Biography, Walter Dexter: adbb.anu.edu.au/biography/dexter-walter-ernest-5792

Digital Library, Dictionary of Islamic Architecture: archnet.org/library/dictionary/entry.jsp?entry id=DIA0061&mode=full

Great White Fleet: en.wikipedia.org/wiki/Great White Fleet.

Hamilton, I., *Gallipoli Diary*, Vol. 1: www.gutenberg.org/files/19317/19317-h/19317-h.htm

Kennedy Hickman, World War 1/11: Lee Enfield Rifle: militaryhistory.about.com/od/smallarms/p/leeenfield.htm

Navy and Army Despatches, Dardanelles and Gallipoli: www.naval-history.net/WW1Battle1503Dardanelles2.htm

NSW State Records, Bann, T., Letter to aunt, 22 January 1915: http://www.records.nsw.gov.au/state-archives/research-topics/war-and-australia/anzacs/images-1/thomasbann_letter2_71770_sc2928.jpg/view

Scarborough Maritime Heritage Centre, 'The Colonials—Gallipoli 1915', extract from *Neath a Foreign Sky* by Paul Allen: www.scarboroughsmaritimeheritage.org.uk/greatwar/f14-colonials-gallipoi.php

US Naval Observatory Records: aa.usno.navy.mil/data/docs/RS OneDay.php

Wikipedia, Hague Peace Conference, 1899: http://en.wikipedia.org/wiki/Hague_Conventions_of_1899_and_1907

World War 1 Casualty Lists of Royal Navy and Dominion Navies, 1–30 April 1915: www.naval-history.net/xDKCas1915-04Apr.htm

World War 1 Casualty Lists of Royal Navy and Dominion Navies, 1–31 May 1915: www.naval-history.net/xDKCas1915-05May.htm

Other

The Archives of the Royal College of Surgeons of England, RCSEng MS0057/1, The Diaries of Lt-Col Edward V. Hugo.

Imperial War Museum (London), IWM Docs: 3077, 95/16/1, The Papers of Lieutenant R. Empson.

The National Archives (London), ADM/196/64, Royal Navy Officers Service Records.

The National Archives (London) Minter, M., Service Record, ADM/159/14.

The National Archives (London) Parker, W., Service Record, ADM/159/203.

The National Archives (London) Parker W., VC File, ADM 1/8453/77.

Royal Marines Museum Archive, B/1/84, Chater, A. R., War Diary, Chatham Battalion, RMLI 28 April–27 July 1915.

Acknowledgments

There is a chain linking the researching, writing and publication of *Jack's Journey*. Each link has played a part in the production of this story. The first one is my mate David McClymont, who let me borrow Jack's diaries in 2005 to see what I could do with them. Little did we realise what would transpire. I do remember speculating with Mac about where my journey would go—I don't think we mentioned getting Jack's story published. If we did, it was fanciful thinking.

Jack's nephew, Ray Warry, has been a constant support. We have been in regular contact over the years, and he is one of the few people I can speak to who has a complete understanding of the story. We have spent many hours chatting about some aspect or other. Ray has been to Gallipoli twice and paid tribute to his uncle at the Lone Pine Memorial. He sent me a copy of Charles Macquarie's letter to George Collyer—an absolute gem!

My research steered me to the Australian War Memorial, where I passed many happy hours, frenetically copying diaries and letters in pencil. The staff were professional and very helpful—particularly Eric Carpenter, Guy Olding and David McGill, who went out of their way to assist me on a number of occasions. David found a copy of the map showing Marine Trench in Death Trap Valley—a Eureka moment! The staff at the National Library were also happy to help me, particularly with my ongoing inability to master microfilm readers, while the staff at Wollongong University Library were equally generous with their time and understanding as once again I battled the dreaded microfilm readers.

Two ladies from opposite ends of the earth played significant roles in the research. Dianne Strang, who was working for Bob O'Hara's research company in London, found Walter Parker's VC file and, on impulse, copied it. What a trove of information! In Mudgee, Sandy Sheridan, trawling *The Mudgee Guardian* for her own research, found many references to Jack that she happily shared with me. Again, they were invaluable and I thank both ladies for their diligence and support.

I'd like to thank Jen Roberts, who was an articulate sounding board and friend, regularly offering criticisms and encouragement, including important endnote and bibliography advice. Another wonderful woman I want to warmly acknowledge is Ngaire Meunier, who created computer files of maps, photographs and books that I used extensively. She also took an avid interest in my research over the years.

My mates, Phil Holmes and David McClure, read the manuscript and told me what they thought of it, which was, fortunately, very constructive. Peter Waples did invaluable research at the Royal College of Surgeons in London, where he uncovered the wonderful diary of Edward Hugo, the surgeon on the *Gascon* in 1915. Peter also read the manuscript and was quite forthright in his advice, which I appreciated. Thanks, boys.

The next two links were vital—Brett Martin and Warren Brown. Marto, an old mate from university, was very interested in the story and introduced me to Warren over a beer or two. Warren was suitably impressed and orchestrated the contact with Allen & Unwin. Brett and Warren have been very supportive, helping me to achieve a dream. Thanks, fellas.

My first meeting with my publisher, Jane Palfreyman, was memorable. I was nervous when I approached her and gave a garbled spiel about what I'd found. Something must have attracted her attention because she readily accepted my manuscript. My second meeting with Jane was even more memorable because Allen & Unwin wanted to publish my story and we discussed the book. Almost immediately the machinery of publication swung into action, and I met Sarah Baker, my project editor. Sarah and her offsider, Susin Chow, turned my manuscript into a book over the next five months. I can't thank Sarah enough for her remarkable industry, efficiency and friendship. It was a pleasure to work with her. To the rest of the team at Allen & Unwin who played a part, a heartfelt thanks.

I am indebted to Charles Bean. I stand in awe of him as a historian and as a person. His dedication to the men of the 1st AIF was inexhaustible. That he was flawed merely changes his status from god to demigod. Bean's diaries and notebooks are a largely untapped lode. His numerous published works are a wonderful record of one of the most significant episodes in our nation's history. Both these sources were fundamental to the writing of *Jack's Journey*.

For the last link in the chain, I would like to acknowledge the support and interest of my extended family. To Olena, my long-suffering wife, who mastered the intricacies of the story, a big thanks. She enjoyed reading the book, and her computer and editing skills were wonderful, often compensating for my neolithic electronic inadequacies.

Index

Page numbers in italic refer to maps or illustration